WILEY

The Open
University

CHILDREN'S
CULTURAL WORLDS

edited by Mary Jane Kehily
and Joan Swann

First published 2003 by John Wiley & Sons Ltd in association with The Open University

The Open University
Walton Hall
Milton Keynes
MK7 6AA
United Kingdom
www.open.ac.uk

John Wiley & Sons Ltd
The Atrium
Southern Gate
Chichester
PO19 8SQ
www.wileyeurope.com or www.wiley.com

Other Wiley editorial offices: John Wiley & Sons Inc., 605 Third Avenue, New York, NY 10158–0012, USA; Jossey-Bass, 989 Market Street, San Francisco, CA 94103–1741, USA; Wiley-VCH Verlag GmbH, Pappelallee 3, D-69469 Weinheim, Germany; John Wiley & Sons Australia Ltd, 33 Park Road, Milton, Queensland 4064, Australia; John Wiley & Sons (Asia) Pte Ltd, 2 Clementi Loop #02–01, Jin Xing Distripark, Singapore 129809; John Wiley & Sons Canada Ltd, 22 Worcester Road, Etobicoke, Ontario, Canada M9W 1L1.

Library of Congress Cataloging-in-Publication Data

Children's cultural worlds / edited by Mary Jane Kehily.
    p. cm.
    Includes bibliographical references and index.
   ISBN 0–470–84694–1 (pbk. : alk. paper)
   1. Children. I. Kehily, Mary Jane.
  HQ781 .C545 2003 305.23—dc21
                  2002152556

British Library Cataloguing in Publication Data

A catalogue record for this book is available from the British Library.

ISBN 0 470 84694 1

Edited, designed and typeset by The Open University.

Printed in the United Kingdom by Scotprint, Haddington.

Contents

Contributors

Peter Barnes is a senior lecturer in the Centre for Childhood, Development and Learning at the Open University. As a psychologist he has contributed to the production and presentation of courses on child development and education, particularly in the areas of children's personal and social development. His main research interests include play, collaborative learning and the socialization of children. He was the editor of *Personal, Social and Emotional Development of Children* (Oxford, Blackwell Publishers/The Open University, 1995).

David Buckingham is Professor of Education at the Institute of Education, University of London, where he directs the Centre for the Study of Children, Youth and Media. He has directed several major research projects on young people's relationships with the media and on media education, and has lectured on these topics in more than twenty countries worldwide. He is the author of numerous books, including *Children Talking Television* (Routledge, 1993), *Moving Images* (Manchester University Press, 1996), *The Making of Citizens* (Routledge, 2000), *After the Death of Childhood* (Polity Press, 2000) and *Media Education: Literacy, Learning and Popular Culture* (Polity Press, 2003).

Christine Hall is a former English teacher who now works as a senior lecturer in the School of Education at the University of Nottingham. She is course leader for the Master of Arts in Children's Literature and director of initial teacher training. She researches and writes about children's literature and literacy, and teacher education. She has extensive experience in editing children's books and some experience of writing books for children. Recent academic publications include *Children's Reading Choices* (Routledge, 1999) a study of children's out-of-school reading habits.

Mary Jane Kehily is a lecturer in Childhood Studies at The Open University. Her background is in cultural studies and education and her research interests are in gender and sexuality, narrative and identity, and popular culture. She has published widely on these themes. Recent publications include *Sexuality, Gender and Schooling: shifting agendas in social learning* (Routledge, 2002); 'Sexing the subject: teachers, pedagogies and sex education', *Sex Education*, 2002, **3**(3); and 'Learning to laugh? A study of schoolboy humour in the English secondary school' in *What About the Boys? Issues of masculinities in schools* (edited by Martino and Meyenn, Open University Press, 2001, with Nayak). She is also director of a research project exploring the cultural meanings of drugs and drug use in young people's lives.

Janet Maybin is a senior lecturer in the Centre for Language and Communications at The Open University. She has contributed to courses on children and young people's language and learning, particularly from a cross-cultural perspective, and has edited a number of books on research and practice in this area. Her research interests include children's informal peer-group talk and children's and adults' uses of literacy to manage relationships with other people and to construct identity. Recent publications include 'Children's voices: talk, knowledge and identity' in *The Sociolinguistics Reader*, vol. 2, (edited by Cheshire and Trudgill, Edward Arnold, 1998), ' "What's the hottest part of the Sun? Page 3!" Children's exploration of adolescent gender identities through informal talk' in *Gender Identity and Discourse Analysis* (edited by Litosseliti and Sunderland, Benjamins, 2002).

Joan Swann is a senior lecturer in the Centre for Language and Communications at The Open University. She worked initially as a secondary school teacher before joining The Open University. She has contributed to several Open University courses, particularly in the areas of language and education, English language and linguistics. As a sociolinguist, her main research interests are in language and gender, children's language and classroom language, and she has researched and published widely in these areas. Recent publications include *Introducing Sociolinguistics* (Edinburgh University Press, 2000, with Mesthrie, Deumert and Leap); 'Yes, but is it gender?' in *Gender Identity and Discourse Analysis* (edited by Litosseliti and Sunderland, Benjamins, 2002); and 'Schooled language: language and gender in educational settings' in *The Handbook of Language and Gender* (Holmes and Meyerhoff, Blackwell Publishers, 2003).

Introduction

This book is about children and young people's everyday cultural activity: the practices, beliefs and values, and cultural artefacts with which children routinely engage. These can take many forms, including children playing or chatting with friends, sending each other text messages, experimenting with clothes, hairstyles and music, reading books and playing computer games. The everyday familiarity of these and many other cultural activities is the starting point for the chapters in this book. But the chapters also address a number of key issues in childhood and youth studies. Why do children play, for instance? What is the significance of friendship in children's lives? How do children use language to create and sustain relationships with others? What kinds of cultural resources do adults need to make available to children? Is it important for children to read 'good' literature? Do newer media have a negative influence on children, or can they bring cognitive and social benefits? How do children engage with media and other cultural resources – as viewers and listeners, and as consumers with increasing amounts of spending power? Are children the victims of powerful market forces, or can they be regarded as creative consumers?

Seeing children's activities as 'cultural' raises questions about the meaning of *culture* itself. *Culture* is used with a range of meanings in both academic and everyday discourse. It can refer to the traditions of a particular society or community, but it is often used more narrowly to refer to artistic forms and practices (in the sense of 'high culture'). Here we extend the notion of culture to include more commonplace routines and practices that characterize and bind together a particular community or group. Culture, in this sense, can be observed and studied in day-to-day engagements with the social world. Taking up a perspective developed by the writer and cultural critic Raymond Williams (1961, 1989), we seek to point out that culture is *ordinary*. Williams referred to the everydayness of culture as a *way of life* that makes sense to individuals involved in a particular community. This perspective also sees culture as a form of action: it is not just something that people have, it is also what people do. The anthropologist Brian Street (1993) argued that 'culture is a verb', meaning that it is better seen as a dynamic process than as a fixed entity. Culture is something that people actively reproduce in their day-to-day activity and frequently challenge or subvert.

How can this understanding of culture be applied to children and childhood? This book explores the many ways in which children make sense of the world around them and take their place in that world through everyday cultural practices. Collectively the chapters suggest that children are active 'meaning-makers' in their lives. Through negotiations with the social world and the exercise of agency, children give shape to their own lives and actively ascribe meanings to events. In this way children can be seen as developing their own cultures.

In order to explore children's cultural activity, the chapters draw on insights from a range of academic areas, including anthropology, folklore, sociology, cultural studies, developmental psychology, linguistics, psychoanalysis, and literary studies. The authors also look at the issue of how adults carry out research on or with children. Is it possible for adults to gain access to children's worlds and to understand the meaning of children's activities? Many of the researchers whose work is discussed draw on an ethnographic approach, in which the researcher attempts to become an insider within a community, both observing and taking part in activities, checking out intuitions with research participants and trying to understand things from participants' own perspectives. In researching life in a US nursery school William Corsaro became 'big Bill', an outsized contributor to three to five-year-old children's daily activities; and Mary Jane Kehily became an 'honorary member' of a group of nine to ten-year-old girls who met at school to discuss friends, boyfriends and puberty (both studies are referred to in Chapter 2).

The work we discuss is also informed by different sources of evidence: direct observation of children's activities; asking children themselves for information (e.g. via interviews or focus groups); looking at children's recordings of events (e.g. in diaries and other forms of writing, or in pictures); adults' recollections of their own childhoods; published autobiography; literary accounts. All of these provide useful insights into children's cultural worlds, but they are also, necessarily, partial. This is partly because children's worlds themselves are multifaceted, but also because any form of evidence is best seen as representation: children present certain aspects, or 'sides' of themselves in interviews; adults recollect or emphasize certain events and not others. The chapters that follow acknowledge the strengths and limitations of different research methodologies, but also concede that researchers can only ever hope to gain access to particular versions of children and childhood.

Any examination of children's cultural worlds raises the question of how separate these are. To what extent do children inhabit worlds that are distinct from those of adults? One tradition of child research takes this view as its starting point. Allison James characterizes this longstanding approach as being about 'the tribal child':

> This acknowledges children's different social status in a celebration of the relative autonomy of the cultural world of children ... [the] project was akin to the anthropologist endeavouring to describe another people's worldview. [Researchers] wanted to make visible the existence of a separate children's culture with belief systems and social practices foreign to an adult's eye.

> (James, 1999, pp. 237–8)

Some of the chapters build on this research tradition, focusing particularly on activities carried out between children themselves: children's negotiation of friendships, for instance, children hanging out with others, children's creation of their own personal spaces, the notion of 'youth cultures' and young people's participation in subcultural activity. But, as earlier books in this series have pointed out, distinctions between 'children' and 'adults' are in part at least socially constructed, according to particular patterns of relationship and power between generations (see also Alanen and Mayall, 2001). It is also important to recognize that what counts as 'children's culture' is highly variable historically, geographically, socially and contextually. Furthermore, children are not just children: they are also girls or boys, preschoolers or teenagers, they belong to particular social or ethnic groups, they live in urban or rural settings, and they differ in many other ways. Children's cultural worlds are, therefore, characterized by diversity; they reflect broader social structures and values; in interacting with one another children may reproduce these, or sometimes actively resist them.

While the chapters examine children's own activities, they also look at adult interventions in children's cultural worlds. In many societies, what children do when they are on their own and especially when they are with peers is a perennial source of adult anxiety. Adults often try to manage children's activities: for instance, parents and teachers may encourage 'suitable' forms of play, or 'suitable' friendships. Children's literature is usually written and distributed by adults and is often selected by adults (librarians, parents, teachers) on behalf of children. More generally, there is a vast array of products – TV programmes, videos, computer games, toys, clothing – produced by adults but designed to appeal specifically to children. The book looks at some of these products (particularly children's books and media) in their own terms – for instance, at the cultural messages made available in literature designed for children. But the chapters also look at how children themselves engage with such products, bringing to bear their own interpretations, adapting and shaping them to their own ends.

Chapter 1 'Play and the cultures of childhood' introduces the book and sets out themes and issues that will emerge through subsequent chapters. These include a consideration of the distinctiveness of children's cultural worlds; children as active 'meaning-makers'; the significance of play, games and toys; historical and cultural diversity amongst children; children and the broader social/cultural world; and adult interventions in children's cultural worlds. The chapter offers a way into these themes via the work of the Opies and further discussion of more recent research on children's lore. The chapter considers different (adult) conceptions of play (play as educational, as a means of relating to others, as related to personal and social development, etc.) as well as children's own accounts of what they are doing as they play. Illustrations are drawn from children of different ages, from different cultural groups and across different cultural/geographical contexts.

Chapter 2 'Children's friendships' examines the nature of friendship and the significance of friends in children's lives. The chapter describes the changing nature of friendships during the childhood years and the effects of social context on the development of such relationships. Examples of children's talk with and about friends offer an insight into children's perspectives on friendship. The chapter recognizes that children's friendships provide a site for companionship and support, but that they can also be fraught with difficulty. Negative experiences of children's friendship are discussed. The latter part of the chapter identifies some of the issues involved in establishing the longer-term consequences of children's friendships.

Chapter 3 'Language, relationships and identities' builds upon the discussion of relationships and identities in the previous two chapters by focusing upon children's written and spoken language. This chapter explores the many ways in which children use language and the ways that language mediates and structures children's lives and experiences. Language can be understood as a cultural resource that may be creatively adapted and managed by children. The chapter considers how children use language to explore their social and material world, pursue relationships with others and develop and try out their own sense of identity. Through a diverse range of practices such as telephone talk, diary writing, text messaging on mobile phones and the use of internet chat rooms, the chapter provides an insight into the changing nature of children's language use and the considerable ingenuity of children and young people in this domain.

Chapter 4 'Children's literature' considers a wide range of literature produced for children that has come to constitute part of children's symbolic culture. The chapter develops an analysis of how children's literature represents particular sets of beliefs and values about children and childhood. Looking at forms of literature available to children, including fairy tales, folk tales and 'classics', the chapter explores some of the purposes ascribed to literature for children and the cultural messages these convey at different historical periods. The latter part of the chapter considers ideological debates on children's books and the effects of these. Finally the chapter considers the role of children as readers of literature by providing some examples of children's interactions with literary texts.

Chapter 5 'Multimedia childhoods' describes the relationship between childhood and the multimedia world children inhabit. Issues such as whether the media have a negative influence on children and the exaggerated optimism of the 'electronic age' are discussed in relation to the ways in which children use media forms and make sense of them. The chapter considers the challenges posed by the proliferation of new technologies and the growing polarization between media-rich and media-poor parts of the world. The chapter also indicates that children can no longer be excluded or protected from the adult world of violence, commercialism and politics and that new strategies may be needed in order to protect their rights as citizens and consumers.

Chapter 6 'Youth cultures' focuses on the distinctiveness of children's cultural worlds through the concept of youth culture. The chapter traces the development of 'youth' as a social category that shapes and defines children's lives between the ages of thirteen to eighteen. This approach emphasizes the experiences and activities of young people, particularly those who participate in subcultures. Examples of youth culture are drawn from different social and historical contexts, including skinheads, ducktails, rastas and punks. Gender differences in youth subcultures are considered through an analysis of some key studies. The chapter also discusses how youth cultures have changed and developed. The final section of the chapter invites an evaluation of some of the strengths and limitations of seeing youth as a separate and discrete social category.

Chapter 7 'Consumption and creativity', the final chapter in the volume, considers the everyday experiences of children and young people in relation to issues of consumerism and patterns of consumption. Ways in which children are positioned as consumers are discussed and placed within the context of children's relationship to the world of consumption and the active and sometimes unpredictable ways they make sense of it. Different expressions of consumption and creativity are focussed upon, including popular music, comics and magazines and new technology. The chapter points to the diverse do-it-yourself culture of children and young people to suggest that creativity and agency remain key features of children's cultural worlds.

Across these chapters we have tried to represent something of the diversity of children's cultural worlds, drawing on material from a range of historical, geographical and social contexts. Such diversity is represented differently in different chapters, however. Chapters 1 and 2 on children's play and friendship discuss psychological research that has often been dominated by studies carried out in North America and Europe, but also refer to other traditions such as anthropology that provide a broader range of evidence. Chapter 3 on children's language is able to draw on a wealth of research carried out in monolingual, bilingual and multilingual communities in several parts of the world. Chapter 4, on children's literature, restricts itself to English language texts and begins with an in-depth historical account before broadening out to other contexts. Chapters 5, 6 and 7, on media, youth cultures and children as consumers, discuss phenomena that are often associated with childhoods in the North but also consider the extent to which these may cross national boundaries and may sometimes be considered global. There are problems of terminology in discussing different parts of the world. Often we refer to specific geographical locations. In common with other books in this series, on those (few) occasions where we need to make broader comparisons we use the terms 'North' to refer to the richer, more industrialized countries, and 'South' to denote the poorer, less industrialized ones. We restrict the terms 'West' and 'Western' to refer to the cultural beliefs and practices associated with highly industrialized societies.

Preparation of this book (and others in the series) has been linked to the production of audio-visual case studies of childhoods in three locations: Cape Town (South Africa), Chittagong (Bangladesh), and Oakland (California, USA). The books and audio-visual material together make up the Open University course U212 *Childhood*. Many of the themes of the book were explored with children, parents and other community members in these three locations, and quotations are included in some of the chapters.

We would like to thank those who contributed to the development of this book by commenting on draft material, particularly Dr Allison James (University of Hull) and Professor Peter Hunt (Cardiff University).

Mary Jane Kehily and Joan Swann
The Open University, 2003

References

ALANEN, L. and MAYALL, B. (eds) (2001) *Conceptualizing Child–Adult Relations*, London and New York, Routledge/Falmer.

JAMES, A. (1999) 'Researching children's social competence: methods and models' in WOODHEAD, M., FAULKNER, D. and LITTLETON, K. (eds) *Making Sense of Social Development*, London and New York, Routledge in association with The Open University.

STREET, B. (1993) 'Culture is a verb: anthropological aspects of language and cultural process' in GRADDOL, D., THOMPSON, L. and BRYAM, M. (eds) *Language and Culture: British studies in applied linguistics 7*, Clevedon, Multilingual Matters.

WILLIAMS, R. (1961) *The Long Revolution*, London and New York, Columbia University Press.

WILLIAMS, R. (1989) *Resources of Hope: culture, democracy, socialism*, edited by ROBIN GALE, London, New York, Verso.

Chapter 1
Play and the cultures of childhood

Peter Barnes and Mary Jane Kehily

CONTENTS

LEARNING OUTCOMES

When you have studied this chapter, you should be able to:

1   Give an account of the place of play in the study of childhood and the perspectives that may be employed in the study of children's play.

2   Reflect on some of the ways in which children's worlds have a distinct character in terms of traditions, lore and games.

3   Discuss some of the features of children's play and the ways in which these may be significant.

4   Describe the changing nature of play over the course of time and the effects of social context on children's playtime activities.

5   Identify the place of toys in childhood and some of the historical changes affecting children's toys and playthings.

1 PERSPECTIVES ON CHILDREN'S PLAY

Leah is on the phone

Three-year-old Leah is fascinated by the telephone and always wants to talk on it. It's her fourth birthday soon, and her mum has talked about having a party. Leah is playing in her bedroom and picks up her toy phone, announcing: 'Yes the party is ready, we're waiting for you to come. I know we're taking so long because the baby's trying to get dressed and we're trying to decorate the house. Bye! Bye!' She turns to her mother, 'She said she's waiting for us. I said "I'm sorry we're taking so long". She said, "It doesn't matter, it doesn't matter".' (Based on material from *All Our Children*, BBC)

Box-out

Gary and Shane are fourteen years old and go to a south London secondary school. One of their favourite games is 'box out'. This is:

> ... the practice of boxing (striking) any item out of another player's hand. The boxer could then claim possession either of the object boxed or of an equivalent value in cash. Such a 'box out' could happen at any time during the school day and anywhere within the school. A boy could be writing in class when suddenly his pen might be boxed out of his hand. The boxer would then call 'box-out!', thus making a formal claim to the nature of the event – it was not an accident; it was not merely to be annoying; it was an act within the game.
>
> (Hewitt, 1997, pp. 32–3)

Stenana

A game played in an open square by boys and girls of various ages in the townships of Cape Town, South Africa. Any number of children can be on both teams. They roll up a pair of socks to make a ball. They build a pile of stones in the middle. The children of one team get hold of the sock and throw it at the other team. If they hit them they are out and have to stand outside the circle. The other team try to knock over the pile of stones in the middle. If they succeed everyone on their team is back in again (The Open University, 2003a).

Baya Horo ibira (the ogre is coming)

This is a traditional game of Huli children in Papua New Guinea.

One player decides to dress up as an ogre. He/she ties a piece of string around the nose, tongue and chin, and places a bent stick into each nostril. Two boar's tusks protrude from the mouth, and the head or body is dressed with ferns and feathers. The intention is to frighten children who are crying in the expectation that they will forget the temporary absence of their parents.

(Goldman, 1998, p. 89)

When children engage in games such as the ones described above are they just playing or is something more serious going on? Play is often regarded as one of the most distinctive features of childhood – something that all children have in common, and which makes their world strikingly different from that of an adult. Indeed, for many people it is children's capacity for play, their enthusiasm for play and the importance attached to being allowed to play that defines what childhood is about. Children differ in the games they play of course, not least according to their age and gender, but all children play. Although adults can join in children's play they may not always be welcome.

In this introduction we will outline some major theories about the functions of play in childhood. The rest of the chapter then concentrates on attempts to describe and understand children's play as a distinctive culture of childhood.

Children's enthusiasm for play defines what childhood is about.

1.1 Play in childhood – an historical perspective

One of the first and most influential attempts to explain the importance of children's play came with the publication of *Emile*, by Jean Jacques Rousseau in 1762. Rousseau describes the ideal education for a young man, with a strong emphasis on encouraging free expression and natural playfulness: 'Is it nothing to jump, play, and run all day? He will never be so busy in his life.' (Rousseau, 1979 [1762], p. 107).

Rousseau's view of play has come to represent a particular ideological position about the nature and status of childhood itself. His views are frequently described as an expression of a Romantic discourse on childhood, which is in opposition to equally powerful discourses that did not regard the freedom to play as consistent with a healthy childhood, nor as contributing to a civilized society. On the contrary, according to this more Puritan discourse of childhood, allowing children to give free vent to playful pleasures was seen as a risk to the 'civilizing process', which can only be achieved through strict training and sound teaching. The Puritan view was that children's play is linked to the animal origins of humankind, and can involve the expression of base instincts. The challenge for adults is to channel children's play into creative forms of work that will bring children to moral and intellectual enlightenment. Romantics saw these strategies designed to 'civilize' children as producing unnecessary forms of repression, and insisted that children's capacity for spontaneity and playfulness is itself naturally creative – a fundamental aspect of being human with which adults lose touch as they become mature.

Allow about 10 minutes

ACTIVITY 1   What is play?

We have contrasted two widely differing views on play as a feature of childhood. These views have been influential and are underpinned by their ideological stance on childhood itself.

Think about a range of situations where children of different ages are playing, including the examples at the beginning of the chapter. Do you see these as healthy expressions of playful curiosity, or as potentially worrying and dangerous?

Suggest some reasons for your response and make a note of some of the feelings that this debate about play may have generated for you.

COMMENT

The example of three-year-old Leah talking to an imaginary friend on a toy phone seems innocent enough, but your reaction to the 'box-out' game may have been different. Some kinds of play can involve children excluding other children from the game, as well as teasing and even bullying in some cases. Play is not always benign and positive. Play produces power relations and social hierarchies among children, placing some in a subordinate position to others.

Despite the ambivalence that may surround certain types of play, there is little argument that playing has become one of the defining features of

Play is the child's work.

childhood in contemporary Western societies, alongside schooling. Moreover, the emergence of modern constructions of the playful child was closely linked to industrialization, and the campaigns to remove children from the labour force in nineteenth-century Europe (see Cunningham, 2003).

The power of this emergent image of childhood as a time for play is illustrated by the account offered by the nineteenth-century social commentator Henry Mayhew of his meeting with a young girl selling watercress on the streets of London. After speaking with her and learning of her hardships, Mayhew suggests that the Watercress Girl has been deprived of her childhood because her responsibilities did not allow her time for play (see Kehily and Montgomery, 2003).

Educationists were quick to adopt the idea that play is the natural way for children to learn. In nineteenth-century Germany, Friedrich Froebel founded the first kindergarten in 1837. He was deeply opposed to approaches based on obedience and training: 'The plays of childhood are the germinal leaves of all later life, for the whole man is shown and developed in these … play is not trivial, it is highly serious and of deep significance' (Froebel, 1889, cited in Blackstone, 1971, p. 13). Susan Isaacs, one of the pioneers of nursery education in England, put it even more bluntly when she famously coined the expression: 'Play is … the child's work' (Isaacs, 1929).

Play-based learning has since become one of the basic principles of so-called progressive or child-centred education, in opposition to curricula and teaching methods based around formal skills (see Miller, Soler and Woodhead, 2003).

1.2 Play and learning

Educationists weren't the only ones to recognize the significance of play. Charles Darwin's evolutionary theories prompted biologists and developmental psychologists to ask about its place within the long period of immaturity that is a feature of human childhood. The Dutch biologist Karl Groos challenged conventional wisdom. In a paper published in 1898 he turned on its head the idea that children play because they are young and frolicsome, arguing instead that human immaturity is important in order that children have time to play, and learn the complex skills required to reach adult maturity (Groos, 1898). Following Groos, researchers wanted to find out more about the characteristics of play, especially its importance for children learning how to think, communicate and co-operate with others.

Major child development theorists differ in the significance they attach to play. Jean Piaget (1896–1980) saw play mainly as an opportunity for children to practise and consolidate newly emerging skills, where failures wouldn't have serious consequences as, for example, when a young child practises piling bricks one on top of another. For the Russian psychologist Lev Vygotsky (1896–1934), play has a more crucial role in children's development, as one of the tools through which they extend their skills. He saw play contexts as liberating children from situational constraints, enabling them to explore ways of talking, thinking, feeling and behaving that wouldn't otherwise be possible. A good example of Vygotsky's view on the importance of play is when children engage in a game of make-believe or pretend in order to try out adult roles, talk and interaction.

One of Piaget's main contributions has been his attempt to link types of play to the main stages within his wider theory of development (see Table 1).

Table I Piaget's play stages.

Types of play	Example	Stage of development
Solitary play involving repetition of newly learned skills	Practising piling bricks one on top of another	Sensorimotor (approx. one to two years old)
Beginning to use objects and actions symbolically, e.g. where stones can represent apples, or a stick can be used to 'shoot' with	A make-believe game where a child behaves as if they were a parent, a nurse, Superman, etc.	Pre-operational (approx. three to six years old)
Fully collaborative play with others, ability to understand different players' points of view	Elaborate role playing, games with rules, eventually including renegotiating rules	Concrete operational (approx. seven years and older)

1.3 Play and emotion

While the theorists mentioned so far mainly emphasized children's intellectual development, others have been much more interested in the significance of children's play for their emotional development and psychological adjustment. Building on his psychoanalytical work with adult patients, Sigmund Freud explored the possibility that the inner world of a child's psyche could be revealed through their play. Freud believed that children enact difficult and troubling situations during play in order to control them. In one of his writings, Freud (1920) describes his observations of his eighteen-month-old grandson whose play repeated the same action of throwing an object out of view, accompanied by a long drawn out sound that Freud interpreted as an attempt to say the German word 'fort', meaning 'gone'. Later he watched his grandson repeating the same game, throwing a cotton reel on a string out of his cot until he had lost sight of it (and saying 'gone'). Freud suggested that the game represented the boy's attempt to come to terms with loss and particularly with the absence of his mother.

Other psychoanalysts elaborated on this view of children's play as a vehicle for expressing feelings, and as potentially therapeutic. During the 1920s, Melanie Klein began to use miniature dolls in her work with children, as resources for children to enact their inner feelings and anxieties.

During the Second World War, Anna Freud set up a nursery for children in London. She recognized the potential of observing children's play as a method of diagnosis, as well as its potential therapeutic value for children who had experienced emotional trauma, such as the loss of a parent. These insights into the emotional significance of play and its potential within therapeutic work have since been greatly elaborated within play therapy, as summed-up by another leading advocate:

> … the child is given the opportunity to play out his accumulated feelings of tension, frustration, insecurity, aggression, fear, bewilderment, confusion.
>
> By playing out these feelings he brings them to the surface, gets them out in the open, faces them, learns to control them, or abandons them.
>
> (Axline, 1947, p. 16)

1.4 Play, self and social understanding

A third major area for research concentrates especially on role play in pretend and make-believe situations. These kinds of play are seen as crucial for children's personal development, as a form of rehearsal for future roles in adult life. Researchers have also pointed to the importance of role play to a child's developing sense of identity. G. H. Mead (1934), in what has become a classic text, explored the development of language, play and games in children. Mead's analysis indicates that when children engage in role-play activities such as 'cowboys and Indians', 'mothers and fathers', 'doctors and nurses', they imagine themselves in different social roles in ways that enable them to develop a sense of themselves as individuals with a distinct character. Most important within Mead's theory is the idea that it is only by playing other roles that children develop a mature, reflective sense of who they are, and how they are seen by others.

Children's role play is not just about developing a mature sense of self. The acting out of imaginary roles and social contexts can also be seen as a way of making sense of the here and now. The following activity aims to help you explore this idea further.

Allow about 10 minutes

A C T I V I T Y 2   Playing at anthropologists

The anthropologist William Bascom (1969) recorded the following example of children's role play while he was making a study of the Yoruba people of southwest Nigeria. Bascom describes how he had been carrying out an interview with a father, while his three children had been watching.

Read the extract and consider the significance of the children's new game.

> During my work with their father these three children invented a new game, playing anthropologist. One sat in my chair on my cushion, with paper and pencil in hand. The second sat in their father's chair, acting as 'interpreter,' while the third sat on a bench as the informant customarily did. The second child turned to the first and said, 'You are my master,' and then to the third child, saying in Yoruba, 'The white man wants you to tell about Odua.' The third child replied in Yoruba and the second turned to the first and 'interpreted,' making a series of meaningless sounds which were supposed to sound like English. The first child scribbled on the paper, and replied with more nonsense

syllables and the second child turned to the third with a new question in Yoruba.

(Bascom, 1969, p. 58)

COMMENT

There are many ways of making sense of the children's new game. The game is rooted in the present and in roles that would be very unfamiliar to the children. So, playing these roles cannot be seen in simple terms as preparation for adulthood. In the enactment of this fieldwork encounter, the children are engaged in making sense of the world around them. The seemingly alien experience of seeing their father being interviewed by a researcher who is talking in a strange language, through an interpreter, is played out in touching and closely observed detail. The children's role play demonstrates their remarkable social understanding, in terms of recognizing the multiple perspectives of those involved. They playfully replicate the power relations of the adult encounter, the communication through two languages and the mediating role of the interpreter. The new game demonstrates the children's knowledge of the adult world and at the same time can be seen as an attempt to own the experience by acting it out. Playing anthropologist may be a way of incorporating an adult experience into the children's personal repertoire. In this respect role play serves to make sense of adult experience by making it accessible through play. Finally, it is worth noting that the role play of the Yoruba children involves very skilful levels of imitation. The children impersonate the three adults, their gestures and ways of speaking. The questions mimic the role of anthropologist and the children's attempts to use English mimic the sound of the English language. The use of mimicry demonstrates children's ability to observe, incorporate and make fun of the adult world around them.

In a recent study of nine to eleven-year-old children in the UK, Kehily encountered imitative play similar to that described by Bascom (Kehily *et al.*, 2002). The research aimed to explore how children understand emotional, caring and family relationships and involved extensive interviews with children in school. During the fieldwork, children quickly incorporated the tape recorder into their games and discussions, often parodying the research interview structure and process. In moments when they were not being tape recorded they would produce an imaginary tape recorder, ask each other questions and nod in response to answers, presumably mimicking my interview style.

A child's drawing of the interview process, collected by Mary Jane Kehily.

1.5 Play and children's cultures

In this brief review we have outlined some major theories about the importance of children's play and the functions it serves in their learning, emotional development and social understanding. One feature shared by all these views on play is that it is seen as purposeful. It is not just about having fun, but about the serious business of growing up. It is seen as a means to an end, of becoming a more mature, competent, socially integrated person. These approaches to play are important, especially within educational and clinical work, but they aren't the only possibilities for thinking about children's play. In the rest of the chapter, we will be concentrating on attempts to understand play in its own right, as a distinctive feature of children's cultural worlds. We will be asking about the variety of ways of playing, about historical continuities in the ways children play, as well as about the evidence of change. The chapter focuses upon particular forms of children's play culture, expressed within role play, imaginative play, and traditional games and rhymes. We will be asking how far children's culture is a distinct world set apart from adult society, and how far it is accessible to the inquisitive eye of the adult researcher.

SUMMARY OF SECTION I

- Children's play can be interpreted from different perspectives using different research methods and traditions.

- Debates about the purpose and significance of children's play reflect ideological struggles about the nature and status of childhood itself.

- Developmental psychologists and educators have emphasized play as a learning experience through which children prepare for adult life.

- Psychoanalytical approaches to play suggest that children enact difficult and troubling experiences in order to control them.

- Theories about children's pretend and role play emphasize the potential for rehearsing identities and developing social understanding.

2 A CHILD'S WORLD?

We begin with the work of Peter and Iona Opie, who pioneered the idea that children's play culture exists and can be studied on its own terms, not just because of its importance for children's learning and development. As folklorists, the Opies suggest that the cultural worlds of children are sustained by the games and activities that they engage in and that these offer adults a glimpse into the world of the child.

2.1 Trick or treat?

Earlier this evening, the front door bell rang. I opened the door to be confronted by a boy, aged about fourteen, with a green face, bright red lips and what appeared to be a grossly deformed hand. You may think that this is an unusual sight in Buckinghamshire, but you may understand better once you know that that the date is 31 October – Hallowe'en. The apparition was only the first of three equally gruesome callers, the others somewhat younger, all offering me a choice: 'trick or treat?'.

Allow about 15 minutes

A C T I V I T Y 3   Examining cultural heritage

This turn of events is becoming increasingly familiar to many across the UK. Nor is it peculiar to the UK, as the following personal account by Julie Wheelwright of her Canadian experience makes plain. Read it and note down any points of difference and agreement with your own contemporary experience of Hallowe'en as an adult – whether as a parent, a householder, a teacher – and your recollections of this particular time of year as a child.

If Hallowe'en and the practices that now accompany it are not part of your personal experience then read the following account for information, identify an equivalent practice involving children from within your own cultural heritage, and reflect upon it in a similar way.

> Given that Hallowe'en came over with those 19th-century Irish immigrants fleeing the potato famines, it seems ironic that it is now understood as a North American tradition, fast gaining popularity in the UK. But my memories of bitter nights – harbinger of long, hard winters – is exactly what the ancient Celts were celebrating in Ireland. The modern ritual has its origins in the ancient Celtic fire festival and New Year, the night when fairies would traipse through the land. At this bewitching time, people would imitate fairies, going from house to house begging treats and, if they were not given, playing practical jokes upon the owner. Throughout my childhood [in western Canada in the 1960s], Hallowe'en was a huge event, the run-up a fever-pitch of excitement second only to Christmas. There were weeks during recess [school break time] when we'd grill each other with, 'So, what are you going as?' and then further time spent convincing a parent to stoop· over a sewing machine or make a trip uptown to the department stores. Ghosts, cowboys, goblins, skeletons, fairies and monsters were popular.

Hallowe'en was full of forbidden pleasures. Going out after dark with a bunch of other kids, getting a sackful of treats and having permission to pull a few 'tricks' like wrapping trees in toilet paper or setting off firecrackers. But this misrule was balanced by churches and schools turning us all into UN volunteers. Every year, I took a Unicef collection box on Hallowe'en which we would shake at our neighbours who kept a stack of pennies ready on a tray next to the candy. While we gorged, we remembered the children of Biafra.

There was a darker side to Hallowe'en, too. It flourished in 'real life' ghost stories, and urban legends about children who died eating apples that had razor blades embedded in their flesh or who went mad from drugged candy bars. Yet these were apocryphal tales not linked to anyone we ever knew, and no neighbours refused us entry except the Jehovah's Witnesses who lived down the road. Parents would maintain a respectful distance as children charged up garden paths.

Now that I live in England with my two young daughters, I am conscious that Hallowe'en has an entirely different meaning. The biggest single influence over my daughter's excitement about Hallowe'en is her general infatuation with witches and wizardry, inspired by J. K Rowling's Harry Potter series. Hallowe'en themes are with us all year through television programmes such as Sabrina and Buffy the Vampire Slayer. When we gave a Hallowe'en party last year, all 10 girls came dressed as witches, and 'playing Harry Potter' is a favourite after-school game.

The idea of trick or treat, however, seems alien here. The children who call at my south London home on Hallowe'en are rare and, even in those neighbourhoods where children fill up loot bags, the process is orchestrated by parents. Other friends report that Hallowe'en on the street runs a definite second to private fancy-dress parties and certainly to Guy Fawkes night.

But when I watch my daughter getting dressed for her party, donning false fingernails and taking up her home-made wand, I realise there is an eternal magic to Hallowe'en that transcends cultural boundaries. For one night at least, the children, like ancient Celtic fairies, are in control.

(Wheelwright, 2000)

COMMENT

Wheelwright's account highlights a number of features, some of which will be elaborated in the following pages.

1 This description points to some of the 'darker' elements of childhood experience – the 'forbidden pleasures', the 'misrule', the 'frightening stories'.

2 These nefarious activities are, to a degree, 'balanced' by adult-inspired efforts to turn them to a socially acceptable and safe purpose, i.e. collecting money for 'good causes'.

3 International comparisons – here between Canada and England – prompt comments about differences, both in the significance of the

event and the form that it takes. Nevertheless, for this parent at least, there is 'an eternal magic' that 'transcends cultural boundaries'.

4   The activities that children engage in around Hallowe'en have a long history in ancient ritual and religious observance and their spread can be traced through significant population movements – in this instance the nineteenth-century emigration of families from Ireland to North America.

5   The form and meaning of the activity is significantly influenced by other elements of children's cultural worlds, in particular the high levels of interest in and excitement about witches and wizards engendered by J. K. Rowling's books about Harry Potter, which achieved cult status among a large number of children at the turn of the twenty-first century. In ways like these, children play an active part in shaping longstanding traditions to incorporate particular themes and priorities of the moment. Traditions are not static.

2.2 Celebrating Hallowe'en

When the Opies carried out a large-scale survey of the pursuits and traditions of British schoolchildren in the 1950s they noted that where Hallowe'en celebrations were concerned 'Britain has the appearance of a land inhabited by two nations with completely different cultural backgrounds' (Opie and Opie, 1959, p. 268 of the 1967 paperback edition). Those living to the north and west of a line from the mouth of the Humber to Knighton, then south along the English-Welsh border and on through Dorset reported enthusiastic celebrations; those on the other side of the line did not (see Figure 1). For a child in Forfar it was 'one of the most enjoyable days in the year' and for a contemporary in Longton, Stoke on Trent, it was 'the most special day I like best' (p. 268). The celebrations took a variety of forms, with a turnip or swede lantern being an essential component, and it was common for children to dress up in an effort to disguise themselves.

Figure 1
Map of the UK: 'a land inhabited by two nations'.

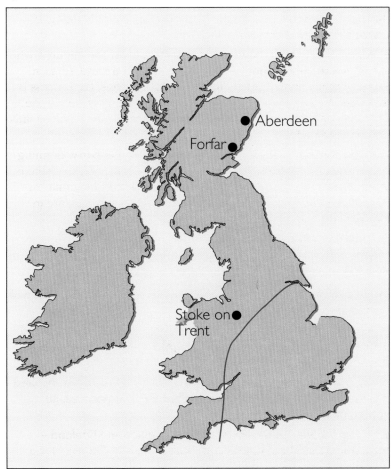

> On Hallowe'en … young boys and girls dress up in old clothes and put
> on masks or blacken their faces with soot. They then go round the doors
> guising which means they dance and sing and recite poetry. They also
> carry turnips which are hollowed out, with holes for nose and eyes. A
> candle is placed inside which lights up the eyes and nose and makes it
> look ghostly.
>
> (fourteen-year-old boy from Forfar, quoted in Opie and Opie, 1959,
> p. 269)

Where Hallowe'en was celebrated there were often parties that included
traditional games such as 'Duck Apple'.

> A large bowl or tub is filled with cold water (sometimes soapy water)
> and a number of apples floated in it. One or two players at a time get
> down on their knees and, with their hands behind their backs (not
> infrequently with their hands tied behind their backs), try to get hold of
> one of the apples with their teeth. 'When they have done this they must
> lift the apple out of the basin. If they do this they may eat it.'
>
> (Opie and Opie, 1959, p. 272)

As the night before All Souls' day, Hallowe'en is the time above all others
when supernatural forces are said to prevail and when divinations are most
likely to succeed. As such it can be regarded as an opportunity to test age-
old experiments.

> At midnight … all the girls line up in front of a mirror. One by one each
> girl brushes her hair three times. While she is doing this the man who is
> to be her husband is supposed to look over her shoulder. If this
> happens the girl will be married within a year.
>
> (fourteen-year-old girl from Aberdeen, quoted in Opie and Opie, 1959,
> p. 274)

Prone to mischief

Hard on the heels of Hallowe'en, and with some features in common, comes
Mischief Night – 4 November – which, in the 1950s, affected most of
Yorkshire, and parts of Lancashire, Cheshire, Derbyshire, Nottinghamshire
and Lincolnshire. It is a time when 'children are half under the impression
that lawlessness is permissible' and 'youngsters bent on mischief roam the
streets in happy warfare with the adult world' (Opie and Opie, 1959, p. 276).
The following report in *The Guardian* (6 November 1985) shows how this
'tradition' manifested itself in the 1980s.

> Yorkshire was counting the cost yesterday of another Mischief Night –
> the traditional pranks on bonfire night eve which have degenerated into
> vandalism.
>
> West Yorkshire fire service reported a record 298 calls in a day. It said
> 223 of the calls were made between 6pm and midnight, and about 87
> were about bonfires lit maliciously.

One premature bonfire set light to a house at Crigglestone, near Wakefield. Other fires were started by fireworks dropped through letterboxes and rubbish lit in plastic litter bins.

A Leeds woman, aged 65, got glass splinters in an eye when a brick was thrown through a bus window. Bricks smashed four other bus windows and six bus shelter windows, and eggs and paint were thrown at buses. Gangs roamed the streets, breaking windows and throwing stones at houses.

It was experiences like these that prompted the poet Philip Larkin (himself a Yorkshire resident) to propose an adult response to Mischief Night. He nominated Herod's Eve 'on which bands of adults might roam the streets and bash the hell out of anyone under sixteen found out of doors' (Larkin, 1983, p. 114). Such a suggestion, whether intended facetiously or not, serves as a prompt to reflect on the boundaries between childhood and adulthood. How is it that reckless and antisocial behaviour may be condoned, by some at least, when it is carried out by children, whereas the equivalent behaviour by adults would be swiftly condemned and could result in legal action? What are the factors that influence whether childish pranks come to be regarded as vandalism or constitute a personal threat? What significance is attributed to the age of the child, is it an individual or group action, and how significant and costly is any damage that's caused? As we start to explore children's worlds in greater depth it is important to ask how far these are particular to children and childhood and whether they have counterparts in adult experience.

2.3 A thing of the past?

What are we to make of the accounts above of a feature of British childhoods dating from the 1950s? Are they representative of children's experiences in time and place? Popular celebrations in other cultural contexts may include occasions that have points of similarity with Hallowe'en. In Thailand and Cambodia for example, Songkran, the Buddhist new year, is celebrated by a raucous and disorganized street party where adults and children throw flour and water over each other. As it is so uninhibited, it is considered a less appropriate thing for older people to do and therefore it is mostly the young who participate.

In the case of Hallowe'en, is there a danger of creating an overly romantic and sentimental adult view of childhood, which bears only a passing resemblance to the lived experience of most children? Fifty years and more on, have the worlds of children changed to such an extent that experiences of this sort have faded into insignificance or been transformed out of all recognition?

Allow between 30
minutes and I hour

A C T I V I T Y 4   **Childhood experiences**

Now make a list of events and experiences of this sort that you can recall
from your own childhood, and write some notes on them for your own
use. You might consider, for example:

1   Whether these were widely shared occasions or ones that were
    particular to the area in which you were growing up or which took a
    distinctive form there.

2   Their origins, so far as you are aware of them. Were they religious (like
    Hallowe'en or Songkran), or did they commemorate an historical event
    (e.g. the Gunpowder Plot of 1605) or mark a date on the calendar with
    particular connotations (e.g. May Day)?

3   In what respects these were occasions when children were allowed or
    encouraged to take part, but generally under adult supervision, and in
    what respects they were initiated and run by children themselves.

If possible, when you have made your list, invite a friend to make their
own. Compare your experiences and note both the common ground and
the points of difference. Can you identify explanations for any differences
– your respective ages, gender, regional location, family background,
cultural heritage, and so on?

If you have the opportunity, ask some children about their present-day
experiences of these sorts of activity. What form do they take? What part do
they play in them? To what extent are they initiated and overseen by adults
such as parents and teachers?

Look out for reports in the press – both national and local – that relate to
these questions. What picture do they paint?

Children's Song

We live in our world,
A world that is too small
For you to stoop and enter
Even on hands and knees,
The adult subterfuge.
And though you probe and pry
With analytic eye,
And eavesdrop all our talk
With an amused look,
You cannot find the centre
Where we dance, where we play,
Where life is still asleep
Under the closed flower,
Under the smooth shell
Of eggs in the cupped nest
That mock the faded blue
Of your remoter heaven.

(Thomas, 1955)

Our day-to-day knowledge of children's cultures comes from a variety of sources. In many significant respects it is the stuff of personal observation, conversation, recollection and what we see and hear in the media. We witness children going about their lives and take incidental note of what they do. Parents see themselves as having responsibilities for their children's well-being and an interest in their developing lives. Teachers want to understand children's worlds better in order to relate to them more effectively. And perhaps for most of us there is an underlying curiosity to compare what we observe children doing today with what we recall of our own childhood. In making these observations, however, we need to acknowledge that just as there were significant elements of our own lives as children that were inaccessible to those around us – often by design – so what we can see and be aware of about children today may be only a partial picture. The poem *Children's Song* by R. S. Thomas may conjure up a sentimental view of childhood that is alien to many, but its underlying message, that it is hard for adults to enter the world of childhood, is one worthy of reflection.

SUMMARY OF SECTION 2

- Children's engagement with customs and practices such as Hallowe'en illustrates both regional and national variations and changes of form over time.
- Experiences of some customs raise questions about how far they are the preserve of children themselves and how much they are affected by adult interventions.

3 THE FOLKLORE TRADITION

3.1 The study of folklore

Although it would be unwise to dismiss casual adult observations as a merely anecdotal and partial source of insight into the world of childhood, greater weight is likely to be placed on data that are gathered in more systematic ways that meet at least some of the criteria characteristic of research.

That said, children's cultural worlds have not been the object of much research activity, nor is it a subject that attracts the funding enjoyed by more mainstream topics for enquiry. This may be because those who study folklore or childlore are dealing with what one of their number has called 'the non-serious things of life' (Sutton-Smith, 1970) as distinct from those issues of child development and socialization that have more distinct implications for survival and for the adult that the child will subsequently become. Nevertheless, this 'expressive culture' forms a significant part of children's experience of childhood and as such should be taken seriously and not dismissed as trivial.

The term 'folklore' was coined in the mid nineteenth century by William Thoms to refer to cultural products such as customs, observances and superstitions, together with genres such as ballads and proverbs. The Folklore Society was formed in the UK in 1878. One of its founders was Lady Alice Bertha Gomme, who carried out a survey that became a classic in the field. Her book, *The Traditional Games of England, Scotland and Ireland* (1894–98), contains detailed descriptions of around 800 children's games, with a particular emphasis on singing games. These descriptions were mostly based on the recollections of 76 middle-class, adult correspondents, and as a consequence not only were the games already part of history at the time they were reported and recorded, they were also drawn from just one segment of society and what was recorded was subject to the fallibility and distortions of human memory. However, the book does report some observations of and evidence from children themselves, including working-class children, and a particular feature of Gomme's work was her interest in girls' games.

Gomme's research was prompted by her concern that the games she was recording were on the verge of extinction. This desire to document games before they disappear for ever has been the continuing motivation for much subsequent research; whether the concern is justified will be discussed in due course. Regardless of motive, however, the pioneering work of Gomme inspired the studies of folklore that followed in the twentieth century.

3.2 Peter and Iona Opie – folklorists

By far the largest and most frequently cited of these more recent studies into the worlds of children in the UK is that undertaken by the folklorists Peter and Iona Opie. As you read the following brief account of the background to their life's work, its intended purpose and the ways in which information was gathered, reflect on the significance of these for the interpretations and understanding that have been derived from it.

In the early 1950s Peter and Iona Opie set out to identify and chart the traditions and pursuits of British schoolchildren. Their motives were straightforward: in the light of public concern that such lore was in decline, they wanted to find out how much of it still existed and to record it. In so doing they also wanted to construct an account of how children amused themselves in their own free time at a certain point in history.

They used the correspondence columns of *The Sunday Times* newspaper to recruit 151 school teachers across the UK who agreed to report on the lives of the seven to eleven-year-old children in their schools. The teachers asked the children to write about the games they played out of school, the rhymes they used, and the rules and conventions that governed the things they did.

The children's accounts of Hallowe'en traditions reproduced in Section 2.2 exemplify the sort of information that was provided. The full wealth of the findings of this extensive investigation has been published in four books over a period of nearly forty years, 1959 to 1997, covering children's lore, their games in the street and playground and their singing games.

Iona and Peter Opie actively researching children's games, 1962.

READING

Now study Reading A by Iona Opie. As well as relying on reports from their correspondents, Iona Opie engaged in a programme of observations at first hand. For several years from 1960 to the early 1980s she regularly visited the playground of the junior school (for children aged seven to ten) in the Hampshire village where she lived. There she watched and talked to the children when they came out to play, and kept extensive field notes.

She was engaging in a form of observational research and one of its significant features is the desire to understand the world as it is lived in by the subjects of her enquiry:

Iona Opie observing 'the people in the playground'.

> I wanted to experience the life of the playground at its own pace so, when I was not writing down the games and jokes the children brought to me, I wandered round as inconspicuously as I could, looking and listening. My role was passive. I did not dart about asking specific questions and trying to jog the children's memories. [...] Nevertheless I was not able to become invisible, and I must have upset the natural balance of the playground by letting it be known that I enjoyed riddling and story-telling sessions.
>
> (Opie, 1993, p. 1)

The notes for some of these visits, covering the period January 1978 to July 1980, were subsequently published as a book – *The People in the Playground* – and the extract in Reading A, typical in tone of the rest, is her account of one day, 4 June 1979.

Note the variety of the games being played and the mix between those that might be thought of as traditional and those which have incorporated contemporary themes. Note, too, the divisions in the activities between boys and girls.

3.3 'Children don't play games any more'

In the account of activities around Hallowe'en the question was raised as to whether these were features of a childhood now passed. Similar sentiments are regularly expressed about children's games more widely. When Iona Opie first visited her local school in 1960 the deputy head teacher assured her that the children did not play games any more, and similar views have been widely reported by other researchers who have observed children in school playgrounds (e.g. Blatchford, 1989).

Allow about 10 minutes

ACTIVITY 5   Picturing children's games

The painting reproduced here is *Children's Games* by the Dutch artist Pieter Brueghel the Elder. It was painted in 1560 and now hangs in the Kunsthistorisches Museum in Vienna.

1   Study it and try to identify ten of the games (there are said to be eighty or so represented overall). Make a list of these.

2   Which of them are familiar to you as games that you played as a child?

3   Which of them do you know or think are still to be seen in your community today?

Children's Games by Pieter Brueghel the Elder (1560).

In passing, you may like to note that many of the children depicted look more like adults than children (this is more apparent in the enlarged detail).

Detail from
Children's Games –
spinning tops, bowling
hoops and leapfrog.

Leapfrog in the 1950s
had changed little
from Brueghel's day.

Doubtless you will recognize some of these games as being similar, in one form or another, to ones you have played yourself as a child, regardless of where you spent your childhood. Marbles, leapfrog and blind man's buff are among the more widespread games. If you are less sure about whether they are still played today you should note the comments of June Factor, a contemporary Australian researcher of folklore, who has observed that the games identifiable in Brueghel's picture 'are still paralleled in thousands of contemporary school playgrounds, in dusty streets, on sandhills and in mountain villages' (Factor, 2001, p. 30). She notes that the only one that cannot be observed in present-day Australia is whipping tops.

Concerns about the decline in children's games predate Opie's deputy head teacher's by a long way. Samuel Pepys recorded similar sentiments in his diary on 25 July 1664, and writers to newspapers and other social commentators have been doing so ever since. Indeed, the regularity of these claims led the Opies to comment that the belief that traditional games are dying out is itself traditional. Over the years many reasons has been identified for this supposed decline: in the nineteenth century the new National Schools and the coming of the railways were among the culprits; in the earlier part of the twentieth century it was cinema, radio and the gramophone; in the 1950s, television; and most recently pop music and computer games have been held responsible (Opie and Opie, 1997). (These issues are addressed in more detail in Chapters 5 and 7.) It is possible to view these concerns as an expression of perennial adult anxieties that childhood is not what it used to be. A further and more recent development has been a growing concern for children's safety in the playground and the schools' accountability in the event of an accident. One survey found that some schools were banning traditional games like conkers and British Bulldog from the playground on the grounds that they were dangerous and that parents might seek compensation if their child were injured (Lowe, 2000).

A game of conkers in full swing.

The 'climate of increased public and professional anxiety' about the safety of children remains a feature of many Western societies (Scott *et al.*, 1998). The idea that children are at risk and that parents and professionals are responsible for their safety has an impact on the everyday lives of children. Some children are no longer allowed to play outside the home, use public transport or walk to school. Awareness of risk and the more pervasive surveillance of children's

In British Bulldog a group of players rush at an individual – the 'bulldog' – who tries to capture one of them for his side by lifting them off the ground.

activities may suggest that children in the West no longer have the time and space to play. However, a contrasting and more positive view is presented by many of those who research children's play and folklore in detail. In a recent collection of such studies 'the picture of children's free play activities which emerges is … one of vibrancy, creativity, continuity and variety, not one of decline' (Bishop and Curtis, 2001, p. 2).

3.4 Continuity and change

Among the playground observations in Reading A, Opie notes how the game of miming incorporated characters from television programmes and popular songs. This is an illustration of the way in which the culture of lore, games and songs that children engage in is not static but is constantly changing and evolving. This is undoubtedly one explanation for the expressions of concern about the demise of children's play – that what is being looked for is a replica of past practice rather than evidence for a dynamic incorporation of contemporary images and experiences into historically embedded practices.

Illustrations of continuity and change come from the work of Georgina Boyes (Boyes, 1995). A Derbyshire girl who was asked for a skipping rhyme in 1994 offered 'High, low, dolly, pepper', the self-same rhyme to be found in Alice Gomme's collection a hundred years earlier. When asked for her favourite 'dip' (a method for deciding who should start a game) a girl from Sheffield provided:

Ickle ockle
Chocolate bottle
Ickle ockle out
If you want a chocolate bottle
Please walk out.

Boyes notes that this formula is one 'which, the Opies report, has been delighting children with its "spell-like jingle" for over a hundred years – sound, rather than sense, underlies its constant form across large areas of northern England and Scotland' (Boyes, 1995, p. 143).

As evidence of how children can be active agents in creating new varieties of games and rhymes that reflect wider social changes in the culture of which they are a part, consider the following dipping rhyme, collected in the 1950s:

> I went to a Chinese laundry
> To buy a loaf of bread;
> They wrapped it up in a tablecloth
> And this is what they said:
> Eeenie, meenie, macca, racca, …
>
> (Opie and Opie, 1969, p. 41)

Now contrast it with the following rhyme collected in the 1980s:

> I went to a Chinese restaurant,
> To buy a loaf of bread, bread, bread,
> They wrapped it up in a five pound note
> And this is what they said, said, said:
>
> My – name – is –
> Alli, alli,
> Chickerlye, chickerlye,
> Om pom poodle,
> Walla, walla whiskers,
> Chinese chopsticks,
> Indian chief says 'How!'
>
> (Opie and Opie, 1985, p. 465)

The words had changed to reflect a context in which Chinese restaurants had replaced Chinese laundries. In 1994, Boyes recorded the following variant as a clapping rhyme in Sheffield:

> My Nannan sent me shopping
> To buy a loaf of bread, bread, bread
> She wrapped it up in a five pound note
> And this is what she said, said, said
> My name is Elvis Presley
> Girls are sexy
> Sitting in the back room
> Drinking Pepsi
> Having a baby
> In the Royal Navy
> Do us a favour –
> Get lost.
>
> (Boyes, 1995, pp. 142–3)

Although the references to Elvis Presley and Pepsi pre-date the mid 1990s, this example of a continuing adaptation is evidence of how traditions are kept alive by children themselves, albeit in a changing format. But is there a wider function that these games, songs and related practices serve which adds weight to why they might command our interest?

3.5 Oral culture as a means of empowerment

When five-year-old Jessica Grugeon started school in Bedfordshire, England, in the late 1970s, her mother observed her initiation into the world of playground songs and rhymes (Grugeon, 1988). Jessica soon had a repertoire of ten songs, each with their own patterns of dancing or clapping. She had known none of them when she started school and had quickly picked them up in play with older girls. All the songs, such as 'I went to a Chinese restaurant', 'My boyfriend's name is Tony' and 'When Susie was a baby' were to be found in other parts of the UK (Opie and Opie, 1985) and some, indeed, world wide (Arleo, 2001).

> When Susie was a baby
> She went a ga ga ga
> When Susie was a toddler
> She went scribble, scribble
> When Susie was a schoolgirl
> She went miss, miss, I don't know
> where my pencil is
> When Susie was a teenager, she went
> oh ah I lost my bra
> I left my knickers in my boyfriend's car
> When Suzie was a mummy
> She went, go and shut that door
> When Suzie was a granny,
> She went knit, knit you silly old twit
> When Suzie was a skellington
> She went click clack, click, clack, click
> When Suzie was an angel
> She went go and start again.
>
> (Grugeon, 1988, pp. 165–6)

The transmission of these playground songs and games from one generation to the next is initiated and mediated by the children themselves, without adult intervention. When Grugeon returned to the school playground eight years later, she collected many of the same songs that her young daughter had learned, albeit in slightly different versions. From her analysis of these songs and games she argued that far from being just a quaint relic of childhood's past they are 'powerful agents for socialization, enculturation and resistance' (Grugeon, 1988, p. 167). For example, normative femininity is powerfully encoded in songs such as 'When Susie was a baby' in ways that enable girls to learn and comment upon gender roles. For the girls between the ages of five and nine years who are the almost exclusive practitioners and participants, the games both transmit the social order and cultural information and provide the means to challenge it. They might be regarded as subversive acts of resistance while still predicting a future of marriage, domesticity and childrearing.

Grugeon's more recent observations in school playgrounds have detected 'a new stereotype of femaleness' (Grugeon, 2001, p. 101), which she attributes to manifestations of 'girl power' in the media, as typified by girl bands like the Spice Girls, and to a greater concern for equal opportunities in schools. This change was identifiable in the ways in which girls playing these games utilized the space in the playground: in the 1980s they tended to be marginalized on the edges as the boys played football in the central space, whereas in the 1990s

> there was a confident and noisy exuberance about their games [...]
> Kicking legs in a chorus-line style, the girls with linked arms surged towards each other in two opposing lines, chanting the challenge 'Coming to get you', pulling the nominated victim from one team to the other in a show of controlled aggression or what almost seemed like female solidarity. Boys on the periphery looked on.

(Grugeon, 2001, p. 113)

Examples such as this serve to illustrate how elements of children's playground culture and experience may have wider implications for their engagement with society.

SUMMARY OF SECTION 3

- One feature of children's cultural worlds is a wide variety of lore that appears to be peculiar to this stage of life.
- Children's lore has long historical traditions but is a living and evolving entity and children themselves are active agents in creating this change.
- The lore and games of childhood are not necessarily conspicuous and are sometimes part of an intended private world. Nevertheless, folklore researchers have clear evidence of their continuing existence.
- The games that children play and the rituals they engage in can be seen to play a part in their induction into wider cultural worlds.

4 THE SOCIAL DYNAMICS OF PLAY

Sections 2 and 3 have concentrated mainly on children's games and lore, studied within a folklore tradition. This section shifts attention to one of the most distinctive features of children's play – play as a social process. Play usually involves children playing with other children, and it frequently involves children enacting social roles and relationships, such as pretending to be someone else. The social and imaginative dimensions of children's play have invited the interest of anthropologists and sociologists, as well as cultural psychologists. One question asked by anthropologists has been how far children's play draws upon and reflects aspects of the cultural worlds that children inhabit. Thomas Gregor's (1977) anthropological study of the Mehinaku in Brazil observed several features of children's games that appeared to mirror the structure and values of the adult society. He commented that, like Mehinaku social life itself, children's games were non-competitive, did not involve hierarchies and did not identify winners and losers. Gregor observed that although most aspects of Mehinaku social life were open and public, children's games were played on the outskirts of the village in areas hidden from public view and particularly from adults. Consider the description of Mehinaku children at play:

> What is to me the most stirring of the games of role playing is 'Women's Sons' (*teneju itai*). Held at a good distance from the village where the children cannot be seen either by their parents or their other siblings, 'Women's Sons,' quite unlike most plaza games, is played by boys and girls together. The age of the players runs from about five to twelve years.
>
> The game begins as the children pair off as married couples. The husband and wife sculpt a child from a clump of earth, carving arms, legs, features, and even genitals. They cradle the baby in their arms and talk to it. The mother holds the child on her hip and dances with it as she has seen her own mother do with younger siblings. After the parents have played with the child for a while, it sickens and dies. The parents weep and dig a grave for the infant and bury it. All the mothers then form a circle on their knees in traditional fashion and, with their heads down and their arms over each other's shoulders, they keen and wail for the lost offspring.
>
> On the occasions that I have seen *teneju itai* played, the children were enormously amused by the entire enactment. When the time came to bury the 'babies,' the boys smashed them into pieces and the girls interrupted their ritual crying with bursts of giggling and shrieks of laughter. Nevertheless, Women's Sons provides a tragic commentary on Mehinaku life – death in infancy and early childhood is all too common in the village. The game helps the children prepare for the time when they may lose a sibling and, later on, an offspring of their own. It also teaches them how to express and cope with grief through the medium of ritual crying. A poignant amalgam of tragedy and burlesque, *teneju itai* will help the young villagers to face the bitter fact of death in future years.
>
> (Gregor, 1977, pp. 112–13)

This description vividly illustrates the way in which children's role-play relates to and is an integral part of the broader culture. The cultural specificity of Women's Sons reflects a feature of Mehinaku life that can be enacted to the point of parody.

In contrast to the game played by the Mehinaku children, consider the following example of two six-year-old girls at play in the UK in 2001.

LAURA:	We're the two lost babies, yeah
AALLIYAH:	Yeah we're the two lost babies …
LAURA:	Pretend we saw a boat
AALLIYAH:	No this is the boat, yeah. (*moving onto a low stool*) Now get behind.
	(*Both shuffle the 'boat' around the 'water' amid some argument about which way it should go*)
LAURA:	Pretend we were in a fight.
	(*playfighting in boat*)
LAURA:	Then something terrible happens.
AALLIYAH:	What?
LAURA:	Happens to the water and then I couldn't swim … (*both children fall out of the 'boat'. Laura moves Aalliyah face down on the 'water'*) Pretend you couldn't swim. Here's your help. (*throws a jumper over Aalliyah*)
AALLIYAH:	Get it off of me.
LAURA:	Pretend I'm the horrible one, yeah, and she's the good one … No you're still stuck in the water (*begins to cover Aalliyah with newspaper*)
AALLIYAH:	No more paper on me, your mom's gonna …
LAURA:	One more. Then you came out. You messed up all the papers.

(The Open University, 2003b)

Laura and Aalliyah's pretend play of 'lost babies' works with an imaginary script rather than with the rituals and practices of the adult world. It is unlikely that the two girls would have experience of the kind of risk and adventure they are enacting. In this example play allows the children to act out difficult scenes and emotions such as rivalry, conflict and death by drowning. In a cultural context where children are generally protected from knowledge of death and where conflict between children is frequently met with adult intervention, pretend play may offer children a way of exploring themes and issues that are not part of their daily life.

Laura and Aalliyah in their pretend boat.

When Joshua was in Egypt land.

4.1 Play in imaginary worlds

Much of the play in which children engage at all ages involves other children. It is a social activity frequently centring around roles, relationships, social practices and rituals. At the same time, some play is essentially solitary. Children can temporarily withdraw from the realities of the physical world around them and can create a fantasy world in which a cardboard box becomes a boat or the space under a table becomes a cave that is home to monsters. Such play is often still about social themes but these are constructed through children's imagination, as with the child phoning a friend that began the chapter. Joshua, an eight-year-old boy living in Cape Town, South Africa, uses books to create an imaginary world for himself.

My favourite place is the library 'cos there's lots of books there to read and I can broaden my imagination and learn more things. It's like you go into a completely different world … When I read the *Odyssey* I am Odysseus. When I read books on Egyptian mythology I'm Pharoah Tutankhamun … I read mostly fantasy books and then it's like you're in another world.

(The Open University, 2003c)

Although children's imaginative activity is commonplace, the fantasies and imaginings involved are mostly short-lived and serve the purposes of the moment. For a smaller number of children, however, the imaginary worlds that they create take on a character of their own that becomes more elaborate and is sustained for months if not years on end. These imaginary worlds are sometimes referred to as 'paracosms' (Silvey and MacKeith, 1988).

In the 1970s Robert Silvey wrote an article about the fantasy world that he constructed during his childhood. The New Hentian States, as he named this world, was a federal republic occupying a large island in the South Atlantic inhabited by a race of peaceful Indians. The Government Handbook that the young Silvey wrote described its social, economic and political institutions. His interest in this world lasted until he was at least fifteen years old and although it was in many respects private it was not secret since it was known to his family and some friends. As an adult, Silvey reflected that the satisfaction he derived from this fantasy world stemmed from the feeling that he was creating order out of chaos and making something that hadn't existed before.

Silvey invited readers with personal experience of similar worlds to contact him and fifty-seven people did so. Together with a psychiatrist, Stephen MacKeith, he analysed those responses that met the criteria that the fantasy world must have existed for months or years and that, as a child, the originator was proud of it and consistent about it. The worlds that were revealed, most of which belonged to people born before 1950, assumed a multitude of forms, for example Teddyland, elaborate railway systems and African republics.

Mohawk Country

Beryl created her first private world when she was about five, though her interest reached its peak between the ages of nine and sixteen. The island she created had no structure, government or history and its location was vague. Her interests lay in its geography and natural features and, as an adult, she was still able to describe in detail the features of its coastline, the sealife, the wide plains and the Mohawk country where there were Indians and herds of wild horses. Beryl herself lived in a log hut accompanied by a wild dog and she rode around the imaginary island on an Arab mare. She invented all sorts of adventures and stories, including the Olympic Games, but they all had to be logical and natural. Another contrast with Silvey's paracosm was that Beryl went to great lengths to keep hers totally secret. As for explaining her absorption in this world, she did not regard it as an escape from difficult relationships. She did, however, feel that it was only in solitary imaginative play that she could fully express herself. Some of the themes and characters may well have been stimulated by her own wide reading and her particular interest in myths and legends. She thought other children's imaginations were very limited: 'My secret world was different, and far, far better' (see Cohen and MacKeith, 1991).

4.2 Rituals of inclusion and exclusion

So far we have concentrated on the way social and cultural themes are incorporated into children's play and fantasy worlds. But play is a social process in another sense. When a group of children begin to play they have many decisions to make. Studies of children's play have pointed to the social dynamics between children at play – especially the ways children are included and excluded. Engagement in play may involve them in negotiations concerning who can play and who can't play and on what basis. These decisions are not necessarily benign as they may produce power relations and social hierarchies among children. Sometimes these negotiations take place outside the play. Sometimes they are ritualized within the play itself.

The following rhymes, which are ways of counting people out of playground games, were documented in the Opie's study.

> Iky Moses King of the Jews
> Sold his wife for a pair of shoes
> When the shoes began to wear
> Iky Moses began to swear
> When the swearing began to stop
> Iky Moses bought a shop
> When the shop began to sell
> Iky Moses went to H-E-L-L
>
> Ching Chong Chinaman
> Born in a jar
> Christened in a teapot
> Ha Ha Ha!
>
> (cited in Cohen, 1997)

The sociologist Phil Cohen (1997) points out that the tendency on the part of folklorists to celebrate children's culture overlooks the less harmonious aspects of children's play. Children may devise many ways to exclude others and in doing so may draw upon forms of sexism and racism embedded in cultural stereotypes and popular prejudices of the day. Thirty years after the Opies collected these skipping rhymes Cohen noted that similar jingles were being recited in inner city playgrounds in the UK, directed at ethnic minority groups from the Asian subcontinent.

Ethnography is a 'method of fieldwork research, largely derived from anthropology, where the researcher attempts to enter into the culture of a particular group and provide an account of meanings and activities "from the inside" ' (O'Sullivan et al., 1994, p. 109).

The American sociologist Barrie Thorne (1993) used ethnographic methods to study the social worlds of boys and girls (aged nine to ten) in a public elementary school. While Iona Opie was a passive observer, ethnographers seek to become active participants in the lives of those whom they are researching. Thorne's study captures the energetic and highly charged nature of children's cultural worlds in which play involves multiple engagements with imaginative forms of physicality, talk and action. The rapid movements of children at play initially appeared haphazard and chaotic. However, after several months of research Thorne began to make sense of their play from the perspective of the children themselves. Her analysis suggests that children's play has a structure and an internal logic that makes sense to those involved. Through patterns of friendship and rituals children create meanings for themselves and others. An example of this can be found in playground chasing games. In one such game Thorne describes and comments on the widespread invocation of 'cooties' or rituals of pollution in which individuals or groups are treated as carriers of contagious 'germs'. She documented the experiences of some unfortunate children whose social undesirability was captured by labelling them 'cootie queen' or 'cootie king'. In the main it was girls who were seen as a source of contamination. In one school they were referred to by boys as 'girl stain'. This involved boys treating girls and objects associated with girls as polluting, while the reverse did not occur. Thorne's analysis of these games points to the relationship between children's cultural worlds and the broader context of power relations in which they exist:

> When pollution rituals appear, even in play, they … enact larger patterns of inequality, by gender, by social class and race, and by bodily characteristics like weight and motor co-ordination … In contemporary US culture even young girls are treated as symbolically contaminating in a way that boys … are not. This may be because in our culture even at a young age, girls are sexualised more than boys, and female sexuality, especially when 'out of place' or actively associated with children, connotes danger and endangerment.

(Thorne, 1993, pp. 75–6)

Thorne points to the further significance of gender in children's cultural worlds through her conceptualization of 'borderwork' – a term used to characterize the ways in which children tend to form single-sex friendship groups that serve to create and strengthen gender boundaries. She suggests that children's play creates a spatial separation between boys and girls that they work to maintain through games and social interactions more generally. Drawing up boundaries, however, also creates opportunities for transgression, crossing the line to disrupt gender-appropriate behaviour or 'border crossing' as Thorne terms it. While most children adhered to gender-defined boundaries, Thorne did notice that border crossing appeared to be acceptable among girls or boys who had achieved a position of high status within their peer group.

In a study that takes up some of the themes of Thorne's work, Epstein (1997) observed children's school-based cultures in the UK. She discusses the ways in which heterosexuality underpins understandings of gender among children themselves and among teachers and other adults in school. Epstein suggests that the playground culture of skipping rhymes and games such as kiss chase (and a local variant – 'kiss, cuddle, torture') engage children in constructions of themselves as heterosexual and gendered. For girls this may involve developing a sense of themselves as feminine with investments in the practices of heterosexual romance such as dating, marriage and motherhood. For boys, however, this is more likely to involve a construction of themselves as tough and distanced from femininity by choosing torture over kissing. Samantha and Louise (age nine to ten) explain:

> SAMANTHA: And we play this game called 'kiss, cuddle and torture', but we don't really do any of it, but 'cos, like, we catch [the boys], put them like in jail and then, then, when we've got all of them, we'll ask them and they'll go 'torture' …
>
> LOUISE: We never say torture, we [the girls] always say, give us a cuddle.

(Epstein, 1997, p. 44)

4.3 Play and the construction of masculinities

The gendered nature of children's play identified by Thorne and Epstein is also evident in a wide range of play and leisure activities enjoyed by both adults and children. Rule-governed games such as football, baseball and basketball, while played by girls and women, are commonly seen as boys' games. The popular and highly lucrative world of organized football most notably remains a predominantly male domain, spawning hundreds and thousands of games in which boys around the world aspire to be heroes of 'the beautiful game'.

Studies of boys and young men in Western societies point to the significance of game-playing and 'play fighting' as a salient feature in interactions between male peer groups. Many of these interactions involve boys using language and physicality in competitive ways whereby the 'game' becomes an arena for competing masculinities. Ellen Jordan's (1995) study of seven-year-old boys in Australian schools suggests that a 'warrior' discourse informs the fantasy play of most boys. In games drawing upon, for example, the adventures of King Arthur, Superman, the Lone Ranger and the Ninja Turtles, boys position themselves as heroes of their own text and position others as cowards and 'baddies'. Jordan suggests that boys who are not capable of positioning themselves within these narratives risk being excluded from peer play. In studies that focus upon older boys, the fantasy element may be less evident but the notion of the omnipotent masculine hero remains. The play of adolescent boys commonly involves play fighting and competitive duelling that can be verbal and physical. Researchers working with adolescent boys have identified the following forms of play:

- 'Back slap and chase' – hitting a boy hard on the back and running before the slap is returned (Back, 1990).

- 'Sounding' – the verbal trading of ritualistic insults among African-American boys in the US. The insults are usually directed against a boy's mother (Labov, 1972).

- 'Blowing competitions' – a UK equivalent of the above (Kehily and Nayak, 1997).

- 'Dozens' – the ritual exchange of insults among male fraternities in the USA, usually involving sexist jokes (Lyman, 1987).

- 'Punch-'n'-run' – an intra-male contest to see who can deliver the most blows, usually to the upper arm (Kehily and Nayak, 1997).

Back's (1990) study of young people in a youth club setting in the UK commented on these forms of play.

> Duelling play is a process whereby young people test out the boundaries of interpersonal relationships (i.e. how far play can be extended and pushed). These exchanges have greater significance than just play for play's sake. They not only mark the boundaries of tolerance within friendships but they also mark those who are included in the peer group – those who are 'alright' – and those who are excluded – 'wallies'.
>
> (Back, 1990, p. 10)

READING

Now read Reading B by Roger Hewitt, which takes up many of the themes discussed above. It is based upon research with fourteen-year-old boys in a secondary school in London, UK and describes a play activity known as 'boxing-out'. As you read the extract make a note of the ways in which boxing-out can be used by boys to construct a particular masculine identity.

COMMENT

Hewitt notes that the game is played by about half the boys in the school year group. Among these boys the game offers scope for group activity and co-operation that is premised upon an unbridled form of competitive individualism. Boys who are successful at the game demonstrate a vigilance and opportunism that is entirely motivated by self-interest. But why? What is the point of a game that involves constant hassle and the risk of financial penalties? Hewitt suggests that the game has parallels with trickster figures in different societies. The male figure of the rogue, living on his wits and doing 'what a man's gotta do' informs the rule-making and rule-breaking of box-out and taxing.

SUMMARY OF SECTION 4

- Play is culturally specific, reflecting the structure and values of adult society.
- Ethnography can be used to study children's cultures.
- Play can be a social activity and a solitary pastime in which children create their own meanings and develop a sense of identity.
- Play produces power relations and social hierarchies among children.
- Play activities may draw upon larger patterns of inequality such as gender difference, social class and ethnicity.

5 THE PLACE OF TOYS IN CHILDREN'S PLAY

When we discuss play and childhood, toys probably come quickly to mind. This final section of the chapter will briefly consider the place of toys in the culture of childhood and how they relate to wider questions about the nature of play. As has been clear in the discussion so far, the primary component in children's play is other children rather than objects or artefacts. This was certainly the case historically, but it is also true of the contemporary scene, despite the penetration of the commercial toy industry into the culture of childhood in many areas of the world. As John and Elizabeth Newson put it: 'Play comes first; toys merely follow. We do not play as a *result* of having toys; toys are no more than pegs on which to hang our play.' (Newson and Newson, 1979, p.12). Iona Opie's observations of children in the school playground (Reading A) also highlight the relative significance of engagement with other children rather than with play objects.

When playful activity does incorporate 'things' they are not necessarily toys in the sense of the commercially produced objects that are bought from shops. Throughout history children have made use of the objects in their immediate environment and such improvisation remains the only option for large numbers of children throughout the world for whom gifts of commercially manufactured toys are an unattainable luxury.

Any artefact may well be called a toy in the sense that 'anything is a toy if I choose to describe what I am doing with it as play', in the words of a toy designer quoted by Newson and Newson, 1979, p. 13. It is as well to keep in mind, however, the distinction between this use of the term and the one reserved for the commercial product.

The intricate structure of a wire truck from Zimbabwe.

5.1 The growth of commercial playthings

Well into the nineteenth century, play for the large majority of British children did not involve manufactured objects. There were hoops, tops, hobby horses, balls, rag dolls and knuckle bones, but these were either converted from objects that had started life with another purpose or they were crafted by parents or relatives – or by the children themselves – out of materials that were readily available. The street games, singing games, board and card games that were part of the Victorian child's culture were forms of play that required little in the way of props; they were traditions of play that were transmitted socially. Any manufactured toys were the property of the wealthy and privileged minority. Indeed, objects such as ceramic dolls, mechanical soldiers and toy theatres were often designed for adults and were only played with by children by chance or under sufferance. Museums housing collections of toys provide a valuable and interesting record

A Zimbabwean boy steering his home-made truck constructed from discarded bicycle spokes and other wire.

of the artefacts that have been an integral part of children's play through time and space. However, it is important to be aware that the toys that find their way into such exhibits are not necessarily representative of their era and place. The home made 'folk' toys and the cheap toys that might have been part of children's everyday lives are less likely both to have survived or to have ended up in a museum.

This picture changed dramatically during the course of the twentieth century with the expansion in the market for factory made toys. At the start of the century one half of the toys sold in the USA were imported, mostly from German craft producers. By 1920 it is estimated that 90 per cent of the toys sold in the USA were produced within the country, mostly in factories (Kline, 1993).

Factory production meant lower costs and wider distribution and as a consequence certain lines of toys and games became integrated into people's purchasing habits and were established as popular features of both home and school. A further development was seen in the second half of the twentieth century with the growth of mass marketing and television promotion of toys, first in the US and then more widely. This phenomenon is discussed more fully in Chapter 7. Between 1955 and 1985 toy sales in the US increased tenfold (Kline, 1993). Western childhoods are now synonymous with commercially produced toys, as Kline observes:

Victorian girl with a hoop.

'Shoe doll' from the Edinburgh Museum of Childhood.

The sweeping invisible hand of mass-merchandising strategies … transformed toy stores into citadels for playthings, making Christmas seem like a festival of toys. Toys have become the supreme emblems of the young child's dearest pleasures, a parent's way of saying how special and precious the child is. Meanwhile our conception of play has narrowed its scope: the very word 'play' now conjures first and foremost the activities that revolve around the relationship between child and toy. The twin dynamics of mass production and mass marketing has penetrated deeply into all aspects of children's culture: few people can look at children's play and not see there a 'timeless' source of energy and creativity that can never be subdued by toys.

(Kline, 1993, p. 147)

Allow about 10 minutes

A C T I V I T Y 6 **Toys in play**

Recall the toys that you played with as a child and make a list of the ones that you remember as being significant for you in some way.

1 Were they objects that you constructed yourself or were made for you?

2 Were they mass-produced specifically for a child market?

3 What part did they have in your play?

4 Did they form part of your solitary play?

5 Did they encourage or require social play?

6 What was their particular significance for you so that you remember them now?

C O M M E N T

As a boy growing up in the suburbs of a south-coast English town in the 1950s, Peter Barnes had a large collection of Dinky Toys made from dye-cast metal and very hard wearing. He writes:

When I was about ten years old I subscribed to the *Meccano Magazine*, produced by the Hornby company, which manufactured Dinky Toys. Each month's issue announced the appearance of at least two new models and some of my pocket money was directed at increasing my collection. These model vehicles featured routinely in my play with friends at home, forming part of imaginative scenarios, and as many of them were of a size to slip into a pocket they were taken to school, where they were incorporated into similar activities in the playground. The same toys featured in my solitary play as the imaginary situations served just as well when there was no one else.

I looked after my Dinky Toys with great care and was concerned about any scratches or chipped paint. I remember that when I sold a number of them to the mother of a younger boy it was as if I were saying goodbye to part of my childhood.

By contrast I also recall, at the age of about twelve or thirteen, a friend and I constructed a 'go-cart' out of pieces of wood that we found in the garage and a set of pram wheels obtained from a long forgotten source. We spent many happy and mildly terrifying hours on a nearby hill racing down the uneven slope and hauling the contraption back to the top for a further descent until the wheels finally buckled. I sensed then that the whole activity didn't entirely meet with my parents' approval and this added further to its excitement.

A go-cart constructed out of pieces of wood and a set of pram wheels.

In response to Peter Barnes, Mary Jane Kehily writes:

> As a girl growing up in a small town in Warwickshire, England in the 1960s I didn't collect anything. To this day I haven't got a matching set of china or glasses. It's not that I wasn't interested or that I think collecting is a masculine preserve. It's more that growing up in a working-class family as the eldest of six children there was no space for personal collections of any sort. I do recall finding the odd hiding place and attempting to secrete my treasures there but the little ones (our family term for the two youngest siblings) always found them and the collection would be ransacked and dispersed about the house. Peter's collection of Dinky Toys, carefully garaged, speak to me of a middle-class childhood far removed from my own. If we had been neighbours during our childhood years, I would be one of the kids Peter wasn't allowed to play with.

This somewhat speculative thought serves to remind us, as adults, that childhood is a class-cultural experience reflected in play, toys and engagements with the social world more generally.

SUMMARY OF SECTION 5

- Toys are not a necessary part of play. For many children, past and present, toys have been crafted and improvised from natural objects and discarded household goods.
- Nevertheless, the more recent mass production and marketing of toys has permeated deeply into all aspects of children's culture.

6 CONCLUSION

This chapter has explored aspects of lore, games and play that are a significant feature of the worlds of children. The early part of the chapter considered some of the ways in which children's play can be interpreted from different perspectives, using different research methods and traditions. A common approach to play is to regard it as a learning experience in which children prepare for adulthood. Questions have been raised about how far and by what means it is possible for adults to gain access to the cultural worlds of children, either through personal reminiscence or active research, and also about the continuity and change in those worlds over time. Folklore and ethnography are discussed as two approaches to the research and study of children's play. Studies at different times and in different geographical locations indicate that play is culturally specific, reflecting the structure and values of adult society. Through play children create meaning and develop a sense of identity. The effects of play, however, are not always positive. Play produces power relations and social hierarchies among children themselves, placing some children in a subordinate position. The topics treated here particularly in relation to meaning-making, creativity and identities are part of a larger whole that will be explored in more detail as you progress through this book.

REFERENCES

ARLEO, A. (2001) 'The saga of Susie: the dynamics of an international handclapping game' in BISHOP, J.C. and CURTIS, M. (eds) *Play Today in the Primary School Playground*, Buckingham, Open University Press.

AXLINE, V. M. (1947) *Play Therapy*, New York, Ballantine.

BACK, L. (1990*) Racist Name-calling and Developing Anti-racist Initiatives in Youth Work*, Research Paper in Ethnic Relations, no. 14, Coventry, University of Warwick.

BASCOM, W. (1969) *The Yoruba of Southwest Nigeria*, New York, Holt, Rinehart and Winston.

BISHOP, J. C. and CURTIS, M. (2001) *Play Today in the Primary School Playground: life, learning and creativity*, Buckingham, Open University Press.

BLACKSTONE, T. (1971) *A Fair Start: the provision of pre-school education*, London, Allen Lane.

BLATCHFORD, P. (1989) *Playtime in the Primary School: problems and improvements*, Windsor, NFER-Nelson.

BOYES, G. (1995) 'The legacy of the work of Iona and Peter Opie' in BEARD, R. (ed.) *Rhyme, Reading and Writing*, London, Hodder and Stoughton.

COHEN, D. and MACKEITH, S. A. (1991*) The Development of Imagination: the private worlds of childhood*, London, Routledge.

COHEN, P. (1997) *Forbidden Games: race, gender and class conflicts in playground culture*, Barking, University of East London Dagenham Centre for New Ethnicities Research.

CUNNINGHAM, H. (2003) 'Children's changing lives from 1800 to 2000' in MAYBIN, J. and WOODHEAD, M. (eds) *Childhoods in Context*, Chichester, John Wiley and Sons Ltd/The Open University (Book 2 of the Open University course U212 *Childhood*).

EPSTEIN, D. (1997) 'Cultures of schooling/cultures of sexuality', *International Journal of Inclusive Education*, **1**(1), pp. 37–53.

FACTOR, J. (2001) 'Three myths about children's folklore' in BISHOP, J. C. and CURTIS, M. (eds) *Play Today in the Primary School Playground*, Buckingham, Open University Press.

FREUD, S. (1995 [1920]) 'Beyond the pleasure principle' in STRACHEY, J. (ed.) *The Standard Edition of the Complete Psychological Works of Sigmund Freud*, Vol. XVII, London, The Hogarth Press.

GOLDMAN, L. R. (1998) *Child's Play: myth, mimesis and make-believe*, Oxford, Berg.

GREGOR, T. (1977) *Mehinaku: the drama of daily life in a Brazilian Indian village*, Chicago, University of Chicago Press.

GROOS, K. (1898) *The Play of Animals*, New York, Appleton.

GRUGEON, E. (1988) 'Children's oral culture: a transitional experience' in MACLURE, M., PHILLIPS, T. and WILKINSON, A. (eds) *Oracy Matters*, Milton Keynes, Open University Press.

GRUGEON, E. (2001) 'Girls' traditional games on two playgrounds' in BISHOP, J. C. and CURTIS, M. (eds) *Play Today in the Primary School Playground*, Buckingham, Open University Press.

HEWITT, R. (1997) ' "Box-out" and "taxing" ' in JOHNSON, S. and MEINHOF, U. H. (eds) *Language and Masculinity*, Oxford, Blackwell.

ISAACS, S. (1929) *The Nursery Years*, London, Routledge and Kegan Paul.

JORDON, E. (1995) 'Fighting boys and fantasy play: the construction of masculinity in the early years of school', *Gender and Education*, **7** (1), pp. 69–86.

KEHILY, M. J., MAC AN GHAILL, M., EPSTEIN, D. and REDMAN, P. (2002) 'Private girls and public worlds: producing femininities in the primary school', *Discourse*, **23**(2), pp. 166–77.

KEHILY, M. J. and MONTGOMERY, H. K. (2003) 'Innocence and Experience' in WOODHEAD, M and MONTGOMERY, H. K. (eds) (2003) *Understanding Childhood: an interdisciplinary approach*, Chichester, John Wiley and Sons Ltd/The Open University (Book 1 of the Open University course U212 *Childhood*).

KEHILY, M. J. and NAYAK, A. (1997) 'Lads and Laughter: humour and the production of heterosexual hierarchies', *Gender and Education*, **9** (1) pp. 69–87.

KLINE, S. (1993) *Out of the Garden*, London, Verso.

LABOV, W. (1972) *Language in the Inner City: studies in the black English vernacular*, Pennsylvania (PA), University of Pennsylvania Press.

LARKIN, P. (1983) *Required Writing: miscellaneous pieces 1955–1982*, London, Faber and Faber.

LOWE, C. (2000) 'Play's the thing', *Times Educational Supplement*, 22 December.

LYMAN, P. (1987) 'The fraternal bond as a joking relationship: a case study of the role of sexist jokes in male group bonding' in KIMMELL, M. (ed.) *Changing Men*, London, Sage.

MEAD, G.H. (1934) *Mind, Self and Society*, Chicago, University of Chicago Press.

MILLER, L. K., SOLER, J. and WOODHEAD, M. (2003) 'Shaping early childhood education' in MAYBIN, J. and WOODHEAD, M. (eds) (2003) *Childhoods in Context*, Chichester, John Wiley and Sons Ltd/The Open University (Book 2 of the Open University course U212 *Childhood*).

NEWSON, J. and NEWSON, E. (1979) *Toys and Playthings*, Harmondsworth, Penguin Books.

OPIE, I. (1993) *The People in the Playground*, Oxford, Oxford University Press.

OPIE, P. and OPIE, I. (1959) *The Lore and Language of Schoolchildren*, Oxford, Oxford University Press.

OPIE, P. and OPIE, I. (1969) *Children's Games in Street and Playground*, Oxford, Oxford University Press.

OPIE, I. and OPIE, P. (1985) *The Singing Game*, Oxford, Oxford University Press.

OPIE, I. and OPIE, P. (1997) *Children's Games with Things*, Oxford, Oxford University Press.

O'SULLIVAN, T., HARLEY, J., SAUNDERS, D., MONTGOMERY, A. and FISKE, J. (1994) *Key Concepts in Communication and Cultural Studies*, London and New York, Routledge.

ROUSSEAU, J.-J. (1979) *Émile, or On Education*, translated by Allan Bloom, New York, Basic Books (first published 1762).

SCOTT, S., JACKSON, S. and BACKETT-MILBURN, K. (1998) 'Swings and roundabouts: risk anxiety and the everyday worlds of children', *Sociology*, **32**(4), pp. 689–705.

SILVEY, R. and MACKEITH, S. (1988) 'The paracosm: a special form of fantasy' in MORRISON, D. C. (ed.) *Organizing Early Experience*, New York, Baywood Publishing.

SUTTON-SMITH, B. (1970) 'Psychology of childlore: the triviality barrier', *Western Folklore*, **29**, pp. 1–8.

THE OPEN UNIVERSITY (2003a) U212 *Childhood*, Video 3, Band 2, 'Street and playground games', Milton Keynes, The Open University.

THE OPEN UNIVERSITY (2003b) U212 *Childhood*, Video 3, Band 3, 'Pretend play', Milton Keynes, The Open University.

THE OPEN UNIVERSITY (2003c) U212 *Childhood*, Video 3, Band 1, 'My space', Milton Keynes, The Open University.

THOMAS, R. S. (1955) 'Children's song' in *Children in Art*, London, MQ Publications Ltd and the National Gallery Company Ltd.

THORNE, B. (1993) *Gender Play: girls and boys in school*, Buckingham, Open University Press.

WHEELWRIGHT, J. (2000) 'Ghosts of a childhood past', *The Guardian*, 25 October.

READING A

The people in the playground

Iona Opie

Monday 4 June 1979

A boy ran out and took cover behind a corner of the school wall. Another zoomed out making a noise that was certainly not human. Another walked jauntily by eating an apple with a bottle top; as he scooped small portions into his mouth he assured his friend, 'I *like* eating it like this. I'm using it as Chinese food.' Children seem born with one lobe of their brain steeped in fantasy, which dries out as they grow up.

The crowd along the marbles fence was bigger than ever. Boys were showing each other the stakes they had brought to school. One was examining the contents of a brown plastic pochette and considering whether it was worth playing for. I looked into the pochette too. The marbles were scratched and chipped. The owner said defensively, 'I've got 143 at home. I've got a big blue see-through, but I keep that at home safe.' The other boys chimed in like small-town business men boasting to their wives: 'I've got an orange see-through,' 'I've got 179 marbles,' 'I've got 257.' They always know exactly how many marbles they own.

Somebody's marble had shot through the fence and could not be retrieved. The boys were making fanciful suggestions about how to get it back, and trying to throw stones so that they would hit the marble from behind and drive it towards the fence again. They shouted that they needed a stick, or a spoon, and pushed against the fence so that it began to sag. 'You could get out of this school,' said an 8-year-old in an awestruck voice. 'Look, we've made a big gap.'

The sweet hackneyed strains of the 'London Bridge' tune told me that Cross the Bible was being skipped; and near the skippers two little girls were clapping hands and chanting:

> Under the bram bushes,
> Under the sea,
> Johnny broke a bottle
> And he blamed it on to me.
> I told my Momma,
> I told my Poppa,
> And johnny got a whacking on his –
> Ooh ah, cha cha cha.

'Come on,' said the intelligent girl from last week, who has a new friend. 'Come and see what we're playing. It's rather a silly game, but Cheryl likes it. We play it with crisps. One of us holds out a crisp and the other one has to run past and grab it as they run.' They showed me. It was fun. I would have liked to have tried it myself. Mrs _____ came up, sipping coffee. 'Do you ever find any new games?' she asked. 'Yes, I've just found one,' I answered.

They are still enjoying the nameless, casual lifting game I have noticed over the past ten years and have thought of as too unimportant to be worth describing. Today it had a name, which must raise its status. 'It's called

Run, Pick Up and Throw. You put your hands together in a hand-grip, and the other person does the same, and you run and sort of hook on to her, and put your weight on her, and she lifts you round.'

Hand-clapping was more noticeable than usual. Instead of being used as a time-filler while waiting for the teacher, it was being played all through playtime. Several times I heard little chants arising from corners: 'Who stole the bread from the baker's shop? Number One stole the bread from the baker's shop' and so on. And skipping was not being ignored; there were at least three long ropes in motion.

The most polished entertainment was a game called Miming, played with great earnestness by three 9-year-old girls. 'One person is on it, and you can have TV programmes or pop songs or books or theatre, and you've got to mime it. If it's TV you draw a square in the air. If it's radio you do a smaller square. If it's a book you put your hands together and open and shut them. And if it's a theatre you draw some curtains. Then you say how many words it is and you mime each word – well, you mime each bit of a word, because if it's Starsky and Hutch you mime Star and then Sky. Then the others have to guess.' This is the modern form of Charades, played by all ages at social gatherings and often simply called 'The Game'.

The girls in the 8-year-olds' queue were sorrowing over a multiple murder. 'Some baby chicks have just been squashed. We'll show you.' The chicks were probably blackbirds, not long out of the egg and now extremely flat. 'It was a girl called Caroline. She trod on them.' 'Stamped on them, did she?' I said idly. 'Not really stamped. She just trod on them, deliberately.' They demonstrated how Caroline had lowered her shoe on to the fledgelings, calmly and – for all I know – with the most merciful intentions.

The boys in the queue were grumbling. 'We're getting bored with marbles, and we can't play football because someone broke that window, look. Not last Friday but the Friday before. William Johnson did it. I could kill 'im.'

Perhaps it was only because the value of marbles had gone down that the naughtiest of the naughty boys suddenly gave me one. He put it in my hand and said, 'Here you are. Stick it in your stamp album. It's a china.' It was an attractive small white china marble. 'You can't buy them like that now,' I said, murmuring my thanks. 'It's a peppermint,' declared his crony, the next in line. 'They come up the drains,' said the next. The queue was moving, and the young teacher bringing up the rear said, 'Ah well!' and I replied, 'As you say.'

Source

OPIE, I. (1993) *The People in the Playground,* Oxford, Oxford University Press, pp. 146-8.

READING B

'Box-out' and 'taxing'

Roger Hewitt

The Game

The game, or perhaps it could be called a system of playful behaviours, that I am going to describe here is one in which (1) individual gain, (2) coordination through sharing a relation to a set of rules, and (3) the boundaries of the system and of coordination, were all evident in clear relief. It was never played by girls in the mixed secondary school where it was recorded. It was made up of two aspects, the 'box-out' and the 'taxing'. 'Boxing-out' was the practice of boxing (striking) any item out of another player's hand. The boxer could then claim possession either of the object boxed or of an equivalent value in cash. Such a 'box-out' could happen at any time during the school day and anywhere within the school. A boy could be writing in class when suddenly his pen might be boxed out of his hand. The boxer would then call 'box-out!', thus making a formal claim to the nature of the event – it was not an accident; it was not merely to be annoying; it was an act within the game …

The ability to play the game well was said to involve a watchfulness, quickness and opportunism that not all could boast. It was played by approximately thirty of the sixty boys in the year group. These were subdivided into smaller groups of about four to eight members each. Membership was constituted by a pact established through a short ritual in which each boy wishing to join would hook the little finger of either hand with the hooked little finger of one member of the existing group of players. This was referred to as 'joining in'. If a boy no longer wished to be a player he would have to 'join out' using the same ritual. Boys would not usually be members of more than one 'box-out' group.

The 'taxing' part of the game came about whenever a debt incurred through a box-out was not met by a stipulated time. It happened only rarely that a boy boxing an item out of a player's hand wanted to have the object. More normally he would strike the object out, calling 'box-out!', and then add, say, '25 pence by tomorrow', or '50 pence by Wednesday'. Most of the groups allowed three days of grace before the debt had to be paid. If the debtor failed to produce the money at the stated time he would then fall foul of a severe interest system, the 'tax' levied on any debt. This could be something like 10 pence per day while the debt was unpaid, or might itself increase on a daily or weekly basis. Never would boys pay on the spot because they would soon seek an opportunity to box-out the person to whom they owed the money, and thereby remove the debt with a counter-debt. They would alternatively seek to box-out another boy and place *him* in debt, hoping to persuade the second boy to pay and thereby offset the original debt. Those who did not manage this would start to fall into debt during the course of a week and then might gradually slip further as the term progressed. Some boys amassed debts of 'several thousands of pounds' which were then wiped off with a settlement of £3.00 or £5.00. Beside such dramatic cases, most boys sought to end each week owing less than they were owed, so that they would enter the following week ahead. Thus the game did not have visible winners and losers. Rather, the box-out and taxing worked as a total system within which small gains and losses were continually made by all players to some degree [...]

Constructing the social

If one were to sketch the different modalities of 'the social' evident in this game, one unavoidable reference point would have to be the ferocious levels of competitive individualism it displays. This aspect is evident in many very obvious ways, starting with the act of boxing-out itself. This last would be true of any non-team competitive game, of course, but many of the other features would not. In looking at much of the talk we find it given over to the following: re-interpreting rules; bending rules; creating/trying to create new rules – all of these being attempts to influence the grounds of play to gain advantage in specific transactions. It also includes: threatening; arguing against the legitimacy of other claims; pestering for payment; and setting tax-rates. These constitute an exploration of achieving the maximum gain for the self that is commensurate with the continued existence of the game, but as the game was also what created the possibility of individual gain there was, at one level at least, one dimension of 'the social' that was generated from individual need. What this schoolboy culture had here created was, therefore, a mechanism in which the simplest basis of social coherence was derived from the collective exploration of individual gain. The game also had an associated imagery that drew on connotations of the adult world of the street hustler. The basis of the box-out itself was the exploitation of the momentary weakness or inattention of others. Furthermore, the severity of the taxing system was based on the principle that the debtor had no choice, although the three-day rule balanced a limited amount of benefit with the heavy penalties. It became a form of sanctioned victimization. The game thus acted out in shadow form the street-level perception of success at the expense of others, the merciless ethic of pawnbroker economics, of victim against victim. Nevertheless, it did hang together and did offer a number of recognizable roles and, in different terms, subject positions for players.

What the discussion above, concerning attempts to infringe the constraints on players, suggests, is that, as well as the subject positions allowed and determined by the game itself, there was a meta-ludic level – negatively evident where individual, naked egos scrabbled for advantage at the edge of the system, and positively evident in such things as the essentially socialized behaviour related to the entry and exit ritual – from which players might speak of what was and was not socially reasonable or acceptable.

If we leave to one side the naked egos for one moment, we have the following levels of the social:

1   The game-transcending social world of bonds which underwrite ritual elements, promises, and the illegitimacy of the threat of actual violence.

2   The social world of the game itself, its rules, practices and permitted subject positions – the player-selves.

This second world is itself broken down into the subject positions of (a) the individual player-selves; and (b) what we might call the *choric* player-selves – that most social of all dimensions within the game where players discussed and adjudicated, witnessed and pronounced on disputes.

Now if we consider the nature of rule-breaking in each of these levels of the social, we find some interesting parallels with a division in the types of trickster figures found in the oral cultures of a number of different societies. On the one hand, there are trickster figures who are particularly involved in various forms of gross and unreasonable behaviour which affront the rules and norms of their society … They are often gluttonous, and sometimes have gargantuan sexual appetites. They violate even the strictest taboos, they sow confusion everywhere they go, and frequently contradict common sense. The other type of trickster – Anansi as found in west Africa and in the Caribbean would be one example, and Robin Hood would be another – is commonly concerned with overcoming those more powerful than himself and with outwitting people. He is generally intelligent and strategic in his thinking, and admired for his ability, as with Anansi the spider-man, to wriggle and limbo dance through the cracks in the system.

Thus one type of trickster is concerned with melting the glue that holds society together, the other with using the system to his own best advantage […]

At the level of the social glue, the 'denial of the coordinative' potential, through the deliberate use of unacceptable utterances – this may include swearing in some social groups, using latinate expressions in others, or strategic switching to certain dialects in yet others – or the use of wilful silences and the withholding of ratifications, seems to correspond to the taboo-breaking trickster who specifically seeks to disrupt people and things. Unlike the tricksters, however, both language users and box-out players do keep at least one foot in the door of the social.

The strategic and intelligent trickster, however, is very much a gamesman, and operates at the second level of the social identified above: working within systems, not seeking to undo them. His intentions are self-centred but he needs the system and therefore plays it. Being nice to people (being emphatically coordinative) is often part of this strategy. (Indeed, these kinds of tricksters, like Ture of the Zande, are often said to be 'engaging rogues', Evans-Pritchard, 1967, p. 30.) But he is first and foremost a declarative, egocentric being and his strategies therefore are always in need of devious interpretation.

The parallel with the taboo-breaking trickster is not made to suggest that certain of the boys who played box-out were deliberately attempting to cause trouble. They were not. But, like this type of trickster, they annunciated a certain asocial naivety, and by their actions caused the social to become explicitly and defensively articulated.

References

Evans-Pritchard, E. (1967) *The Zande Trickster*, Oxford, Clarendon Press.

Source

Hewitt, R. (1997) ' "Box-out" and "taxing" ' in Johnson, S. and Meinhof, U. H. (eds) *Language and Masculinity*, Oxford, Blackwell. pp. 32-33, 40-42.

Chapter 2
Children's friendships

Peter Barnes

CONTENTS

LEARNING OUTCOMES

When you have studied this chapter, you should be able to:

1 Describe the changing nature of friendships during the course of the childhood years.

2 Distinguish different research traditions in the study of friendships, notably developmental versus ethnographic methods and other approaches such as longitudinal studies.

3 Give examples of the effects of social context on how friendships are enacted.

4 Illustrate ways in which children's talk with and about friends provides insights into the nature of their friendships.

5 Illustrate ways in which friendships can provide the site for negative experiences.

6 Identify some of the issues involved in establishing the longer term consequences of childhood friendships.

1 THE SIGNIFICANCE OF FRIENDSHIP

The finger of friendship is the little finger. They link the little fingers of their right hands and shake them up and down, declaring:

Make friends, make friends,
Never, never break friends.

They quarrel, and their friendship is ended with the formula,

Break friends, break friends,
Never, never make friends,

repeated in a like manner, but, in Croydon, with the little fingers moistened, and in Portsmouth with linked thumbs. They make up again, intoning,

We've broken before,
We break now –

and they separate their little fingers,

We'll never break any more,

and they intertwine their little fingers again, squeezing tightly (Weston-Super-Mare).

(Opie and Opie, 1959, pp. 324–5)

These rituals, reported by children and collected by Peter and Iona Opie as part of their study of children's lore which was described in Chapter 1, serve to illustrate the abiding significance for children of making, keeping and losing friends. You may recall similar chants from your own childhood, and they remain in use today – one currently to be heard in Milton Keynes in Buckinghamshire, England, for example, is:

> Make up, make up,
> Never, never break up.

An important feature of many of the games and activities from childhood so comprehensively catalogued by the Opies is that children engage in them with other children, and in many instances these children would describe one another as their 'friends'. Similarly, as adults, we identify some of those we associate with as 'friends', and in so doing distinguish them from other people whom we might refer to as 'neighbours', 'colleagues' or 'acquaintances' or, more specifically, in terms of their particular role or function, for example, the postman, Jane's teacher. 'Friend' has a particular meaning and status – it is not a word that we use lightly – and friends, and the experience of 'friendship', play an important and valued part in our lives at a number of levels. Although the meaning for children of 'friend' and 'friendship' may change over the course of childhood, they are important and valued by children, and, typically, these relationships are recognized and respected by those with responsibility for them.

In this chapter we will look at the place of friends and friendship in childhood and at some of the research which attempts to understand the nature of friendship, its changing character and its impact on children's lived experience. In the context of this book as a whole there are two themes to keep in mind. The first is that children's friendships with their peers provide an arena for many aspects of their cultural worlds. For example, children play with friends, they share experiences of television with friends, they go shopping with friends. The second, and related, theme is that within and through their friendships children have opportunities to explore dimensions of experience which can have both formative and lasting effects. For example, within friendship relationships children may experience affection, intimacy, communication, sharing and co-operation. Paradoxically, friendship is also a site for conflict and the experience of what it is to feel jealous, angry and excluded. By comparing themselves with their friends, children may achieve a developing understanding of who they are and what they aspire to become – and what they aspire not to become. They may further extend their range of emotional experience, both positive and negative. They may find new and different opportunities to be creative and to come to regard themselves as autonomous individuals in their own right. In sum, children's experiences around friendship are closely tied to the development of their personal identity. Such considerations place childhood friendships and peer relationships on a par with the family and the school as highly significant for children's lives.

Allow up to 40 minutes

ACTIVITY 1   Friends reunited

Think of someone you would currently describe as your friend. Write down some of the features of that relationship which are important to you and which distinguish it from those with people you would not refer to as friends – for example, it may be the things you do together and the things you talk about.

Now think back to your childhood and identify two significant friends from different points in time – say, when you were eight or nine years old, and then when you were in your mid teens. The following questions are intended to help you to explore those friendships and what they meant to you. Use them as prompts, recognizing that not all of them may be relevant.

1 How did you become friends?

2 What was special about the nature of these relationships that made them friendships?

3 Where did you spend time with these friends – in the family home, at school, in the playground, on the street? To what extent were the things you did together open and public and to what extent were they carried on out of sight of adults?

4 Were these friends of the same gender as you? To what extent was gender a factor in the style and nature of the friendships that you had?

5 What did your parents think about your friendships? Did they approve of and encourage them, or did they disapprove and try to discourage them? Can you remember why?

6 Were there times when you were in conflict with your friends in a significant way? Did the friendships survive? If so, what was it that kept you together as friends?

7 Looking back as an adult, how would you describe the influence that these friends had on you at the time? Did that influence endure in any identifiable way?

You may find it interesting and illuminating to ask other people how they would answer these questions – particularly if they are of the opposite gender to you or come from a different social or cultural background. Obviously, to do so would take further time; the allowance given here assumes that you carry out the activity just on yourself.

These questions address a number of aspects of friendships which are taken up in various ways during the course of this chapter. As you read about the research and the experiences of others, you should try to relate them to your own personal account, noting the similarities and contrasts and reflecting on their possible implications.

READING

Now read the Reading, which is an the extract from Lorna Sage's autobiography *Bad Blood*.

Lorna Sage was born in 1943 and spent most of her childhood in the village of Hanmer in Flintshire, on the border between England and Wales. Her grandfather was the local vicar and as a young child she lived at the vicarage with her mother while her father was away in the army. After her grandfather's death the family moved into a council house – 4 The Arowry. In this extract Lorna Sage graphically recalls the friendships she, aged eight, struck up with her new neighbours.

As you read, note what these friendships meant to Lorna and how she highlights the negative aspects as well as the positive. How do her memories of friendships at the age of eight and nine compare with your own?

COMMENT

It was important to the lonely eight-year-old Lorna to have friends of any description, and the move to a new house provided two friends who were neighbours.

She recalls these relationships as being the source of experiences of intoxicating intimacy. They could also be the site of quarrels and rejections, possibly assisted by tensions associated with there being three of them. And this experience encompassed both being excluded and, in turn, forming an alliance to shut out another. But the abiding memory is of an extended collaboration over a doll's wedding which, nearly fifty years later, is recalled as a piece of idyllic fantasy at work.

You may feel that accounts like this should be treated with circumspection. Human memory is selective and the further back one goes the greater the likelihood that what is recalled will be partial and coloured by intervening experiences. Our adult memories of childhood have to be interpreted with an awareness of the filters through which they have had to pass on their way to being expressed. Arguably, that process is all the more apparent when there is a wider audience for the memories as in the case of a published autobiography like Lorna Sage's, when the author may be seeking to present themselves and their childhood experience in particular ways and for particular effect. None of this is to deny the value of personal reminiscence and autobiography as evidence, but it serves as a reminder not just to accept it in an unquestioning way.

Selective memory aside, the lasting import of social relationships like the ones you recalled in Activity 1 and that Lorna Sage recounts in this reading suggest that friendship and peer relationships are ways through which children develop a sense of themselves in relation to their society. However, the nature of those relationships is difficult to chart with any precision, as the anthropologist Allison James acknowledges:

> For any particular child, participation in this tangled web of social relationships helps shape the identity and sense of Self which is assumed as s/he moves towards adulthood to become a person in society. But, although in this sense the socialised child may in adult life bear eventual witness to its orbit and effectiveness, the actual process of socialisation can only ever be but haltingly documented.

(James, 1993, p. 203)

The following sections begin to explore what some of those processes might be. Before proceeding, however, it is important to bear in mind that a great deal of the evidence on the forms that friendships take comes from a relatively restricted set of geographical, social and cultural contexts. Much of the published research originates from North America and Europe and while there are undoubtedly common features, worldwide, to the forms that friendships take and the functions they serve, there are also important variations. This chapter will attempt to reflect some of that variation, but it is important to approach the research-based accounts that follow in a critical way which enquires about the generality of the findings.

SUMMARY OF SECTION I

- Making, keeping and losing friends are important features of children's cultural worlds.

- Children's experiences around friendship are closely tied to the development of their personal identity.

- Memories of childhood can be a useful starting point for studying friendships, but they should be handled with care.

- Much of the published research on childhood friendships originates from North America and Europe.

2 THE NATURE OF FRIENDSHIP

2.1 The place of friends in children's lives

> At varying points in development, some children may be more interested in painting or reading or even daydreaming than in interacting with other children. But, for the most part, friendships are among the central ingredients in children's lives from as early as age three – or in some cases, even earlier – through adolescence. Friendships occupy, both in their actual conduct and in the world of thought and fantasy, a large proportion of children's waking hours. They are often the sources of children's greatest pleasures and deepest frustrations.
>
> (Rubin, 1980, pp. 12–13)

Zick Rubin, an American social psychologist, summarizes some key features of friendships during childhood: friends are present in one form or another from an early age; they absorb a considerable amount of children's time either as actual social interaction or in reflecting on what friends have said or done; and they provide children with both positive and negative experiences.

As we shall see, the nature of children's friendships changes with age, but in general terms friends appear to play an increasingly significant part in children's lives as they grow older. Research in the USA indicates that whereas only ten per cent of a two year old's interactions involve other children, by the ages of four or five about three out of four children are involved in a close relationship with another child (Hartup, 1992). Similarly, three quarters of a sample of seven year olds in the English Midlands had an identifiable special friend, and over 80 per cent of these children were said by their mothers to make friends easily (Newson and Newson, 1976). And in another study, about 80 per cent of the American teenagers who were sampled reported having several good friends and at least one best friend, whereas fewer than ten per cent of them had no contact with friends outside school (Crockett *et al.*, 1984).

Further insights are provided by adolescents and adults in a Chicago-based study who carried electronic pagers with them wherever they went during the course of a week. Every two hours they were contacted by the researchers and asked to report what they were doing, and with whom (Larson and Bradney, 1988). On nearly 30 per cent of the occasions that they were paged the teenagers said they were with friends, a proportion considerably higher than for adults in the sample. Each time the teenagers were paged they completed a short questionnaire about how they were feeling. When they were with friends they reported higher levels of enjoyment and excitement than when they were alone or with their family.

Statistics such as these, coupled with what children say about the importance of their friendships, emphasizes their significance. Willard Hartup, an American psychologist who has researched children's friendships extensively, notes that 'becoming friends and maintaining these relationships are regarded by children themselves as among the most significant achievements of childhood and adolescence' (Hartup, 1992, p. 176).

However, without necessarily challenging Hartup's assessment, it is important to pause before arriving at generalizations about the nature and process of friendship on the strength of the sort of evidence cited above. Reflection on your own experience, as prompted by Activity 1, may suggest sources of variation in the opportunities for making and sustaining friendships and the sorts of friendships engaged in and their wider significance. Contrast, for example, the likely experience of children living in remote rural settings and those in a densely populated urban area, or the differences relating to whether the friendships forged at school are the same as those that are enjoyed out of school. Friendships may be specific to the classroom or the street. They are influenced by social and cultural context and, often, by gender. In Sections 3 and 4 we will explore some of these variations and their implications in more detail.

Reflecting on your response to Activity 1, you may also have identified contrasts between the salient features of your friendships when aged eight or nine and those of your teenage years. The form that friendship takes, and the meaning that it takes on, change over the course of the childhood years.

2.2 The changing face of friendship

First encounters

In the extract at the start of this section Rubin indicates that friends start to play a part in children's lives from the age of three years or earlier. Developmental psychologists have suggested that the origins of these relationships may be traced to the ways in which, during the first year of life, infants tend to treat one another as physical objects to be explored and manipulated, in much the same way as their toys are. One of the early forms of play that children engage in has been styled 'parallel play' since it is characterized by children sitting side by side, performing similar actions with the same toy but without directly engaging with one another. When they do touch it is as if they are treating the other as an inanimate object.

Then, typically during the second year of life, children become aware that these other small humans behave differently from inanimate objects such as toys in that they can both initiate and respond to social behaviour. Once this milestone has been passed the social nature of young children's interactions becomes increasingly apparent, so that by the age of two-and-a-half, or thereabouts, they are able to sustain social interactions with one another. They remain attentive to one another over a period of time, they take turns in pursuing an activity, and they respond to one another's actions in an appropriate way. Similar patterns occur in the exchanges between younger children and adults – their parents and other familiar adults in particular – but here the adult is an experienced participant who knows a variety of ways to hold a child's attention and manage an exchange. What makes the equivalent achievements remarkable when children interact in this way with others of the same age is that both parties are likely to be equally inexperienced and far less tolerant than adults; they have to share the responsibility for the exchange.

Psychologists see the sustained attention, turn-taking and mutual responsiveness which characterise these early exchanges in varying degrees of sophistication as being fundamental to social relationships throughout childhood, and into adulthood as well. It is within these early social exchanges that patterns of friendship can be realized. Two US researchers, Judith Rubenstein and Carollee Howes, observed the play of eight pairs of nineteen-month-old toddlers who had been visiting each other's homes two or three times a week over several months (Rubenstein and Howes, 1976). The children spent about half of their time interacting with one another, far more than children of the same age who were not so familiar with one another. Furthermore, when the pairs of children were together they played with their toys in ways which were judged to be more creative than they did when they were alone.

Two factors appear to influence the formation of 'successful' friendships of this kind. The first is frequent contact with one another, especially one-to-one; this helps to reduce the apprehension associated with unfamiliarity. The second is that the children are similar in certain respects, such as temperament and behavioural styles. Young children tend to show clear preferences in their choice of play companions: the physically active choose others who engage in similar activity, the quieter, reflective children likewise.

Children's views on friendship

One of the limitations of studying very young children's friendships is that they aren't able to share their ideas about friends. But older children can. What do they say? In one research study children aged between six and fourteen years were asked to write an essay about what they expected of their best friend that was different from what they expected from people who were not best friends (Bigelow and La Gaipa, 1980). Almost a thousand children took part; half of them living in Scotland and half in Canada. The researchers analysed the content of the essays for similar themes and characteristics and then looked to see whether these were related to the ages of the children.

A shared activity brings children together.

The youngest children distinguished best friends from acquaintances on the grounds that the former lived nearby, gave help, enjoyed the same activities and shared similar expectations. For the nine to ten year olds the emphasis was on sharing with one another, in particular sharing values, norms, rules and sanctions. Admiring and being accepted by the friend was also important. What the older children (eleven to twelve) had in common was the importance they attributed to being understanding, loyal, genuine, having interests in common and being willing to listen to and respect personal secrets. The pattern of results was similar regardless of whether the children lived in Scotland or Canada.

Bigelow and La Gaipa further proposed that the relationship between the clusters based on the analysis of the content of the essays and the age of the children was evidence of a distinct sequence of stages in the development of children's expectations for friendship. They labelled these stages Reward–Cost, Normative and Empathic. The characteristics and stages are summarized in Table 1.

Table 1 Characteristics of best friends identified by Bigelow and La Gaipa (1980)

Age	Features	Stage
7–8 years	Living nearby, common activities, similar expectations	Reward–Cost
9–10 years	Shared values, rules and sanctions	Normative
11–12 years	Understanding, self disclosure, common interests	Empathic

Are there stages?

This interest in the identification of distinctive stages in the development of friendship is characteristic of certain approaches to developmental psychology, most particularly that inspired by Jean Piaget. The work of Piaget is discussed in Woodhead (2003).

Seen from a *developmental* perspective, children's ideas about friendship unfold through a sequence of stages which does not vary; each new stage represents a fundamental reorganization of children's understanding. In this respect, say Bigelow and La Gaipa, 'age-related changes in conceptions of friendship can be understood as a specific instance of more basic changes in the development of social cognitions' (1980, p. 20).

The American psychologist Robert Selman (1980) is another advocate of this view. He put forward the hypothesis that the development of children's conceptions of friendship would relate closely to the more general development of social understanding, in other words the ways in which children construe, interpret and represent other people's points of view. Selman investigated this hypothesis by telling children stories which centred around a dilemma to do with friendship, for example, where a character promises to be with different friends at the same time. Then he asked them a series of probing questions about such things as the nature of the characters' relationships with one another, how old friendships are maintained and new ones begun, what sort of understanding friends ought to have of one another, and how the dilemma in the story might best be resolved.

An example of one of the stories and of a follow-up question is provided in Box 1.

Box 1 An example of Selman's dilemmas

Kathy and Debby have been best friends since they were five. A new girl, Jeanette, moves into their neighbourhood. Kathy doesn't like Jeanette because she thinks she is a show-off. One day Jeanette invites Kathy to go with her to the circus and this places Kathy in a dilemma because she has already promised Debby that she will play with her on that day. What will Kathy do?

This story readily lends itself to questions about the nature of the relationships between Kathy and Debby and between Kathy and Jeanette, about the formation of new friendships and the maintenance of old ones, and about trust and understanding between friends.

From his analysis of interviews with a large number of American children aged between three and fifteen, Selman claimed to find evidence for the four stages in the development of their ideas about friendship outlined below. In support of his initial hypothesis, these corresponded to different levels of skill at social perspective taking.

Momentary physical playmate

According to Selman, the youngest children, typically aged three to five years, define friends in terms of shared activities and geographical associations: they are the children they play with, they live nearby and go to the same school. Even if they have lasting relationships with other children, they tend to refer to them in the here and now and there is no reference to personal characteristics and psychological attributes, nor to a sense of the other child's internal thoughts and feelings.

One-way assistance

For children at the next stage (six to eight years), a friend is someone who helps you or who does things that please you. As a consequence, friends need to become aware of one another's likes and dislikes, but, according to Selman, children at this stage don't as yet acknowledge the *reciprocal* nature of friendship.

Fairweather co-operation

Selman found that reciprocal understanding is a key feature of children at the third stage (nine to twelve years). They understand that just as they evaluate the actions of their friends, so their friends make judgements about them and it is necessary for both parties to be adaptable. But although these children try to take account of their friends' preferences, specific disagreements and conflicts may bring the friendship to an end. Selman calls this 'fairweather co-operation' to indicate that there is little sense of an enduring relationship which can withstand trials and tribulations.

Mutual concern

By the final stage, children – typically, eleven to fifteen years – are able to take the perspective of other people. Friendship is seen as a bond which is built over time and is made strong and stable by expressions of mutual support, concern and understanding. Building this sort of relationship is helped by having friends who share compatible interests and values and who have compatible personalities. Such friendships can withstand minor conflicts, and because a lot of personal time and effort has been invested in them they are often fiercely protected. When children at this stage talk about friendship they refer to *psychological* attributes rather than the physical ones that characterise younger children's accounts.

Selman, then, sees children's ideas about friendship developing in a linear and systematic fashion. At each stage there is a reorganization in their understanding of what it means to be a friend, and this is part of a wider development in their cognitive abilities. Rubin (1980) likens this to climbing a ladder and resting at each rung in order to consolidate the new level of interpersonal awareness that has been achieved.

Allow about 10 minutes

A C T I V I T Y 2   Similarities and differences

Look back at the notes you made in response to Activity 1. In what ways, if at all, do your recollections of the nature of your friendships at age eight or nine and in your mid teens correspond with the classifications and stages put forward by Bigelow and La Gaipa and by Selman?

Can you see any limitations in thinking about the nature of children's friendships in terms of stages?

C O M M E N T

Although descriptions of developmental stages may relate to experience up to a point, it is important to guard against slotting things into seemingly neat compartments. Another limitation of Selman's research is that it is mainly based on asking children to think about hypothetical dilemmas rather than their own personal experiences. Next we turn to a rather different tradition of friendship research which involves directly observing children and listening to their talk.

2.3 Analysing talk about friends

The sociologist William Corsaro spent several months closely observing children, aged between three and five, in a nursery school on the campus of a US university. He made detailed field notes of the children's activities and their social interactions and also video recorded them (Corsaro, 1985). This is an example of an *ethnographic* approach to studying children, characterized by extensive observation of and involvement in their activities over a period of time. One of Corsaro's interests was in how these young children talked with one another about their friendships and the meanings they ascribed to the word 'friend'. He identified six distinct categories of such talk. The first centred around children using reference to friendship in successful attempts to gain access to other children's play.

William Corsaro
with some friends.

In the following extract Martin and Dwight, aged three, are playing in a
climbing box when Denny runs by:

MARTIN TO DENNY: Denny!

DENNY TO MARTIN: Martin!

Denny climbs in box next to Martin.

MARTIN TO DENNY: Dwight is here.

DENNY TO MARTIN: Can I come?

MARTIN TO DENNY: Yeah, you can come.

DENNY TO MARTIN: Yeah, 'cause I'm your friend, right?

MARTIN TO DENNY: 'Cause I'm your friend.

(Corsaro, 1985, pp. 163)

The second category covered instances where children talked about being
friends because they were playing together. These first two categories,
together, accounted for two-thirds of the references to friendship and they fit
closely with the picture that has already been painted of friendships at this
age, namely that they are based on physical proximity – sometimes labelled
propinquity – or bonds that are formed by short-lived activities, such as
playing together.

Corsaro's remaining four categories, though less frequently observed
in the nursery setting, indicate an interesting diversity in the ways that
friendship is talked about, even at this comparatively young age. In the
following extract Peter, Graham, Frank, Lanny and Antoinette are playing
with water in an outdoor sandpit; each has their own hose.

A structure for experiencing and talking about friendship.

LANNY:	Hey, we made the best waterfall, see?
FRANK TO LANNY:	Yeah.
PETER TO LANNY:	That's not a waterfall.
LANNY TO PETER:	Yes it is –
PETER:	Lanny's can't. Lanny's isn't.
LANNY TO FRANK:	I did the – a waterfall, right, Frank?
FRANK TO LANNY:	Yeah
ANTOINETTE:	Frank's is.
FRANK TO LANNY:	Don't Lanny. Lanny!
LANNY TO FRANK:	Yes. Mine is, isn't it Frank?
FRANK TO LANNY:	It's mine
LANNY TO FRANK:	It's both of ours, right?
FRANK TO LANNY:	Right, and we made it ourselves.
LANNY TO FRANK:	Right
PETER TO GRAHAM:	Graham, we're not going to be Frank's and Lanny's friend, right?
GRAHAM TO PETER:	I am.
FRANK TO PETER:	I'm gonna throw water on you if you don't stop it. And tell the teachers.

(Corsaro, 1985, p. 164)

Here, there is competition among the children and Peter ends up trying to use friendship as a way of marking who is on whose side. Shortly afterwards Peter tries to get Graham to come and play next to him:

PETER TO GRAHAM:	Graham – if you play over here where I am, I'll be your friend.
GRAHAM TO PETER:	I wanna play over here.
PETER TO GRAHAM:	Then I'm not gonna be your friend.
GRAHAM TO PETER:	I'm not – I'm not gonna let – I'm gonna tell my mom to not let you –
PETER TO GRAHAM:	All *right*, I'll come over here.

(Corsaro, 1985, p. 165)

In this fourth episode Peter is trying – and failing – to use friendship as a means of social control, attempting to get Graham to play with him in return for being his friend. Corsaro observed that these two boys played together a lot, rather than with other children, and the exchange above illustrates how Peter was keen to protect their joint activities from the intrusions of others.

Corsaro's fifth category covered those occasions when the children referred to friendship in the course of expressing concern for the welfare of their playmates, most frequently when one of them was absent from the nursery. The sixth and last, of which only one example was recorded, extends that expression of concern further. Jenny and Betty, not yet four years old, are climbing in a large wooden box. Betty has just returned to play with Jenny after having played with another child for much of the morning. A third girl, Ellen, approaches and offers them pieces of paper.

ELLEN:	Do you guys want – do you guys – want a ticket?
JENNY TO ELLEN:	No, we don't!

Ellen now moves to the other end of the box.

BETTY TO JENNY:	I do like you, Jenny. I do.
JENNY TO BETTY:	I know it.
BETTY TO JENNY:	Yeah. But I just ran away from you. You know why?
JENNY TO BETTY:	Why?
BETTY TO JENNY:	Because I –
JENNY TO BETTY:	You wanted to play with Linda?
BETTY TO JENNY:	Yeah.
JENNY TO BETTY:	I ranned away with you. Wasn't that funny?
BETTY TO JENNY:	Yes
JENNY TO BETTY:	Cause I wanted to know what happened.
BETTY TO JENNY:	I know you wanted – all the time you wanna know because you're my best friend.
JENNY TO BETTY:	Right.

(Corsaro, 1985, p. 166)

This last example of three year olds making reference to friendship in their talk is noteworthy in that the two girls are discussing friendship at a fairly abstract level. Their notion of being 'best friends' is a measure of how much they care about each other, and they also demonstrate their *mutual concern* for how their actions might affect one another's feelings. Betty feels she needs to explain why she ran away, and, in return, Jenny expresses her need to know what happened to Betty. As we have seen, according to some researchers in the field of children's friendship this mutual concern is a feature of more advanced levels, when children are eleven and older. William Damon, working within a similar stage theory model as Robert Selman, has typified the most advanced level of friendship in the following terms:

> Friends are persons who understand one another, sharing with each other their innermost thoughts, feelings, and other secrets; therefore, friends are in a special position to help each other with psychological problems (loneliness, sadness, loss, fear, and so on) and must, in turn, avoid giving psychological pain or discomfort to each other.

(Damon, 1977, pp. 161–2)

How is it, then, that Jenny and Betty, still only three years old, appear to be operating at that level? Corsaro offers two explanations. First, Damon's association of the level with a particular age is based on research in the same tradition as Selman's, where children were interviewed and asked hypothetical (what if …?) questions, whereas Jenny's and Betty's expression of their friendship is taken from their spontaneous talk while interacting with one another. This is a valuable reminder of the need for caution over judging children's competencies on the basis of 'formal' experimental tasks. Second, Corsaro notes that the two girls had a closer relationship than most of the other children in the nursery school and played together a great deal. The fact that they talked about their friendship in the way that they did suggests that children who develop intensive and long-term relations may, through those relations, acquire abstract conceptions of friendship at an early age.

How do simple hierarchical development models such as those proposed by Bigelow and La Gaipa and by Selman fare in the face of such evidence and arguments? Allison James has pointed out that any individual child might be at different stages of friendship with different people. She argues that it is

> through its discrete performance that children learn about and experience friendship, which means that the social contexts in which children find themselves, not simply their age, play the greater part in shaping children's understanding of the concept.

(James, 1993, p. 216)

Teenagers talking

In his research on children in the nursery school William Corsaro makes inferences about their understanding of the nature of friendship through analysis of the ways they talk to and interact with one another. However, at this age their ability to acknowledge and articulate that understanding is limited. As Allison James has noted from her own study of children in an English nursery school, 'many of the four-year-old children were more concerned about their status as someone who has friends rather than the experience of being friends' (James, 1993, p. 210).

By contrast, talking about friendships and their meaning is less of a problem for older children, and that often reveals the importance of talk *between* friends. The following example comes from an interview with Jack, an American thirteen year old.

INTERVIEWER:	Why is Jimmy your best friend?
JACK:	I don't know, I guess it's because we talk a lot and stuff.
INTERVIEWER:	What do you talk about?
JACK:	Secret stuff, you know, what we think of him or her or whoever. And sports, things we both like to do.
INTERVIEWER:	How did you meet Jimmy?
JACK:	I don't know; hanging around, I guess. We just sort of got friendly after a while.
INTERVIEWER:	When did you get friendly?
JACK:	After we found out we didn't have to worry about the other guy blabbing and spreading stuff around.
INTERVIEWER:	Why would you worry about that?
JACK:	Well, you need someone you can tell anything to, all kinds of things that you don't want to spread around. That's why you're someone's friend.
INTERVIEWER:	Is that why Jimmy is your friend?

JACK: Yes, and we like the same kinds of things. We speak the same language. My mother says we're two peas in a pod.

[...]

INTERVIEWER: What would you say you like best about Jimmy?

JACK: Well, you know, we can say what we want to around each other, you don't have to act cool around him or anything. Some of the older kids are always pretending to be big shots, acting real tough. That kind of stuff, it ... turns me off.

INTERVIEWER: How do you know who to become friends with and who not to?

JACK: Well, you don't really pick your friends, it just grows on you. You find out that you really can talk to someone, you can tell them your problems, when you understand each other.

(Damon, 1977, pp. 163–4)

On the strength of interviews like this, Damon notes that talk between friends is important as the mechanism for 'psychological assistance, secret sharing and the establishment of mutual understanding' (1977, p. 164).

SUMMARY OF SECTION 2

- The nature of children's friendships changes with age.
- Some developmental psychologists have identified distinct stages in children's conceptions of the nature of friendship and relate these age-related changes to more basic changes in social cognition.
- Analysis of the talk between friends provides an alternative route to understanding the differing conceptions of friends and friendship.

3 PUTTING FRIENDS IN THEIR PLACE

3.1 Friends in the locality

Friends at home

As we have seen, friendships among three and four-year-old children often come about because they find themselves in the same place at the same time – propinquity. Playing alongside one another at nursery school is but one example. In many social groups parents and carers also play an important part in shaping children's choice of friends. If the parents' friends have children of a similar age, it is often assumed that the children will establish an equivalent relationship to that of the parents. Nor are these 'accidental' factors in how friendships are formed merely a feature of the earlier years of childhood.

Commenting on the friendships to be found among seven year olds in Nottingham in the 1960s, John and Elizabeth Newson (1976) noted that children who lived at one end of a school's catchment area were unlikely to be allowed to go on their own to visit children living at the other end, thus making friendships formed at school more difficult to sustain out of school hours. Similarly, there was a disjunction when children living near one another attended different schools and so had fewer common interests, given the dominant influences of school on their everyday lives. As a consequence, Newson and Newson suggest, 'some of those friendships will be the products of use, habit and expedience, rather than the marriage of true minds' (1976, p. 178).

For many parents, too, there is a strong desire that their children should have 'suitable' friends who will be a 'good influence' on them. Evidence from the mothers of these same Nottingham children found that just over a third had already actively discouraged a specific friendship by the time their child was seven, and a further third said that they would act to discourage one if the circumstance arose. The words of one of these mothers set out some of the reasons and some of the dilemmas:

> There's one little boy I'm not so keen on as the others, but I shan't say anything directly; but I would do if it was someone I disliked – if the child were a rough, wandering type of child – wild and so on. I should hate Mark to become wild! So I would just – I think I'd stop him; I *might* say 'I don't want you to play with him'; I'm not quite sure as to whether I'd do that, or whether I'd be crafty, and always have him busy when this child called. I'm not sure: I might do that.
>
> (Newson and Newson, 1976, p. 218)

You may find it instructive to refer back to your answer to question 5 in Activity 1 which asked about your parents' approval of your friends. And, if you have children of your own, you might care to reflect on what action you would take and how you would justify it.

Friends in school

The management of children's friendships is also exercised, consciously or otherwise, within schools. Friendships may be encouraged or discouraged through the separation of girls and boys, the allocation of individuals to particular classes or work groups, as well as through seating patterns within the classroom, which sometimes take account of children's preferences but sometimes do not.

The age-banded structure which typifies much school experience also has a strong impact on friendship. At the boys' schools I attended, for example, the single-year-band classes created a context in which the vast majority of our friendships were within that year. In part this was influenced by opportunities to meet – the teaching timetable and age-related sports fixtures, for example – but alongside these, as I recall, was an unwritten code that discouraged fraternizing outside of the year, especially with younger boys.

Even within a year group, the demands and regulation of the school day may place constraints. When studying a group of Canadian teenagers, Amit-Talai was struck by the limited opportunities they had for developing friendships in school (Amit-Talai, 1995). They were subject to monitoring by staff wherever they were and throughout the school day, including during recess, or break time, and lunchtime. This monitoring was described as being edged with an undertone of anticipating suspicion. Once the students had finished eating their lunch in the cafeteria, the teachers were quick to move them on, and the regular washroom gatherings of girls – chatting, doing their hair and putting on make-up – were regularly interrupted by the arrival of a teacher who would usher them out.

The demands of school don't always provide opportunities for the development of friendships.

Amit-Talai also noted the limited opportunities that most of these teenagers had for socializing with their peers outside of school. Few regularly invited their friends into the family home; instead, they would hang around outside the house or walk round the block. Those who were in part-time jobs not only had less spare time to spend with friends but also found that work patterns made it difficult to schedule social encounters. She came to the conclusion that the discontinuity of friendships that was a feature of these teenagers' lives was not a feature of the 'storm and stress' of adolescence, as some had suggested, but was better accounted for in terms of the contexts at home and school within which they led their lives.

Friends in the neighbourhood

Contextual effects of this type are also highlighted in a study which compared the friendship patterns of twelve-year-old children in Monterey and Yuba, two contrasting neighbourhoods in Oakland, California (Berg and Medrich cited in Rubin, 1980). Monterey is an affluent, white neighbourhood with large, widely dispersed houses at some distance from the park and the recreation centre. The children living there reported having only one or two friends, who often lived some considerable distance away from them. They relied on their parents to transport them to see these friends and to take part in social activities which were usually planned in advance. These children said that they chose their friends on the grounds that they had things in common. Yuba, by contrast, is an inner-city neighbourhood populated by low-income, predominantly black families. The twelve year olds here typically had four or five close friends and a yet wider range of friends beyond that. They moved as they chose, mostly in large groups, through the recreation centres, shops and public spaces in the tight-knit neighbourhood.

The researchers noted the similarities between the lives of the children in Monterey and those of their parents; both were relatively formal and scheduled. They also highlighted the ways that the children developed a view of friendship which emphasized selectivity and psychological compatibility. In similar ways, the Yuba children's social lives conformed to the more inclusive and spontaneous social character of their neighbourhood. The two settings appear to offer children different advantages and disadvantages. Although children in Monterey evidently enjoyed many more material benefits, they were prone to complain that there weren't enough children around and that they were reliant on others in order to carry out their social lives. On the other hand, the researchers suggest that they may have formed deeper friendships than those of the more inclusive children of Yuba.

Further contrasts and comparisons of friendships in adjacent but contrasting communities are featured in Box 2.

The research from Monterey and Berlin underlines the apparently universal importance of closeness in friendship, and, at the same time, demonstrates the effects of culture on children's observable behaviour (Schneider, 2000).

Box 2 Either side of the wall

Before the reunification of Germany in 1990, the lives of children in the two sectors of the city of Berlin – East and West – were very different. Features of schooling and family life appeared to affect both the opportunities that children had to make friends with one another and the nature of the friendships that occurred.

In East Berlin, primary school aged children spent most of the day, including the time after school, under adult supervision, either in schools or in day-care centres. The adult supervisors actively encouraged a spirit of co-operation among the children by praising co-operative behaviour when they saw it and criticizing instances of conflict as being immature. The adults also became involved in resolving disagreements between children.

In West Berlin, by contrast, it was the parents who had the primary responsibility for what their children did after school. And although the schools themselves went some way towards promoting mutual helpfulness, the staff neither adhered to a fixed ideology nor monitored children's social behaviour to anything like the extent of their counterparts in the East.

The researchers who were observing and recording the children in these two situations judged that those in East Berlin showed evidence of more mature concepts of friendships than their peers in

West Berlin. Was this, perhaps, attributable to the greater prominence of discussion about responsibilities of children for one another?

Did the apparently more mature concepts of friendships shown by children in East Berlin have implications for their actual friendships? The evidence suggested that on both sides of the Wall friends often disagreed with each other about the quality of their friendships. Furthermore, children in East Berlin reported greater conflict with their friends than did children in West Berlin. The researchers suggested that although the children in the East had a heightened awareness of conflict through having heard it discussed and criticized so extensively, they nevertheless remained unskilled in resolving conflicts for themselves because this was something which adults typically did for them. These same children also reported having less fun with their friends, and this, the researchers suggest, could well be an outcome of the levels of adult supervision which tended to suppress the exuberance that might otherwise be found in children's play and interactions at that age.

Those contrasts apart, however, the researchers found no differences between the two groups of children in these different cultural settings in measures of the closeness of the relationships between friends.

(Sources: Oswald and Krappmann, 1995; Little et al., 1999)

Friendship on the street

Despite the differences in their experiences, the children in Monterey and Berlin were growing up within families and communities which provided them with emotional, social and physical support. For many children, however, circumstances require them to rely to a much greater extent on one another. What forms does friendship take for the large number of children who are growing up on the streets of large cities worldwide? During the research for this book we interviewed Shane, Steven and Wilfred, who were street children in Cape Town, South Africa, all in their early teens. Here they talk about what their three-year-long friendship means and the contexts in which it has particular significance:

WILFRED: We are good friends. We know each other a long time. Sometimes we are bad to each other and sometimes we are good to each other. My friends, if they fight with big boys in Cape Town then I help him. When I saw him, I have a fight and then he help me. And he as well, you see. That's why we're together.

STEVEN: One time I saw Wilfred, he's hungry, then he's by the home. Then I don't know Wilfred, then I stay by his house, next to his house. Then he come to me, then he ask me some bread. Then I give him two slice of bread and that's why we are – he's my friend.

SHANE: I get the money, then I go to the shop, then I buy me sweets and drinks and I take for Steven and for Wilfred with me and I say it for him, go and buy it and I'll stay by the shop. And it's good. He's my friend.

(The Open University, 2003a)

Shane, Steven and Wilfred: Cape Town street children.

The picture the three boys paint is one of mutual support, whether in fights with others or in the sharing of food and drink. When they fight among themselves the rift is relatively short lived and the strength of their friendship prevails. As Wilfred says:

> And then we must fight … And then I'm angry or I'm sad and I go home and sit there in the road, you see. And I sit in the sun and I saw him run up and down and don't worry about him. And the next time they call me and I walk with him. And then when it come, then everything is go down, is go away, like the devil is go away. I wish that Steven come back, you are my friend, OK. And we're all together.

(The Open University, 2003a)

Although these three boys rely on one another's friendship to a significant extent, they are not totally dependent on their street relationships. Shane lives as one of his aunt's large family in a township. Wilfred often stays there, too. Likewise, Steven has a family but is rarely at home. Merle, Shane's aunt, provides her perspective on the interplay between family and friends:

> Wilfred and Steven are Shane's friends. I don't actually know a lot about their background or what's the reason that they're out of the house, you see. But they are Shane's friends and because they are Shane's friends they are also like family to us here, you see. So, that, that is just the way it works here.

(The Open University, 2003b)

Where there is no family of any sort to provide support and regulation, relationships with the peer group take on an even greater significance. A study of street children in Belo Horizonte, the fourth largest city in Brazil, identified how the gang – known there as the *turma* – provided many of them with the sense of support, companionship and protection that might otherwise have been found within the family (Campos *et al.*, 1994). This support came at a cost, however. The *turma* had its own strict code of behaviour, and to gain entry prospective members had to steal and prove their willingness to abide by the norms of the group. If they broke the rules they were punished, often in violent and sadistic ways. These children's experiences contrasted with children who worked on the streets but had a home base. For the latter the peer group was important, but this was balanced by the influence of their parents and wider family networks. These influences appeared to make for distinctions, too. The researchers found that the home-based street children were less likely to engage in drug abuse and illegal economic activities and they were also more likely to combine their work on the streets with attendance at school.

3.2 A wider view

With the exception of the illustrations from South Africa and Brazil, the studies referred to in the preceding section come from North America and Europe, as is the case with much of this chapter so far. As was noted earlier, in part this is because comparatively little research has been published on the concepts and functions of friendship in Asian, African and Latin American cultures. Is the Western experience of friendship as the location for affectionate and intimate relationships between people – both children and adults – universal? One writer on the subject has argued that this particular kind of interpersonal relationship is a 'sociological luxury' which is ill-afforded in many other cultures (Paine cited in James, 1993, p. 205).

Friendship among the !Kung

An illustration that might fit that view comes from the !Kung, a hunter-gatherer society in Southern Africa who have a nomadic life style. !Kung communities are small and membership of the community constantly changes, and in such settings children form friendships with whomever is available. It is not uncommon to find friendships forming between young children and teenagers and there isn't the preference for friends of the same sex which is so often apparent elsewhere. Friendships are inevitably transitory and dependent on external factors. During the winter, when the !Kung are camped at one of the few permanent water holes, communities grow in size and children have a greater chance to form friendships. In the summer, on the other hand, people disperse and sometimes travel only in family groups, which restricts the children's opportunities to make friends. For Nisa, an elderly !Kung woman recalling her childhood friendships, the emphasis appears to be more on group activities and shared experiences than on personal preferences and close relationships. The following extract is taken from an interview with Nisa recorded and translated by the American anthropologist Marjorie Shostak.

> A few months later, we left Chotana and went back to live again at our old water hole. All my friends were there, and when I saw them I was happy again. We played and played and danced and sang, played music and sang and danced, and my heart was happy to be with the children I liked.
>
> We used to make believe about everything. We made believe we cooked food and took it out of the fire. We had trance dances and sang and danced and danced and sang and the boys cured us. They went, 'Xai–I! Kow-a-di-li!' They cured us and we sang and danced and danced, danced all day.
>
> Sometimes we played with the children from another village; sometimes we just played by ourselves. Other times, the other children came and found us playing and went back with us to our little village. They'd greet us just as adults do, 'How are all of you?' And we'd answer, 'Eh, we're just fine'.
>
> (Shostak, 1983, pp. 124–5)

In societies such as the !Kung where life is organized around hunting and gathering, the proximity of physical danger is another reason for children and young people to be in mixed-age groups. This has the added feature of providing a way of transferring culturally and economically important skills from one generation to the next (Konner, 1981).

Individualism versus collectivism

The example of friendships among the !Kung draws attention to the very different bases for friendship in different societies. Critics of Western research frequently make the point that patterns of friendship in countries such as the USA, the UK, Canada and Australia are founded on a belief system that emphasizes personal autonomy and individuality. Children are seen as separate individuals, making and breaking friendships with one or more individuals. By contrast, in so-called collectivist cultures, greater importance is placed on group identity and collective responsibility for the welfare of group members. Friendships arise in the context of shared activity and they are less personalized. Traditional Chinese society is a good example of a collectivist culture and, while generalizations should invariably be treated with caution, it has been observed that Chinese society values the rejection of verbal aggression, the avoidance of direct expression of feelings, and the use of mediation as a way of resolving conflict. These values have their roots in the principles to be found in Buddhism, Taoism and Confucianism.

A study which compared five year olds in China and Canada found that the Chinese children helped one another more and shared more with one another – so called *prosocial behaviour* – than did the Canadian children (Orlick *et al.* cited in Schneider, 2000). The Canadian children co-operated less with one another and more of their behaviour involved conflict. The experience of Chinese children also offers interesting insights into the relative value placed on shyness in different cultures. In most cultures shy and sensitive children typically experience difficulties in making friends and being accepted by their peers. However, a study of Chinese children aged between seven and ten years found that shy and sensitive children gained greater acceptance from their peers (Chen *et al.*, 1992). The researchers suggest that this may be because being soft spoken and well mannered is considered virtuous in Chinese culture. However, the advantage appears to be short lived, for the same researchers also found that, by the age of twelve, shyness and sensitivity in Chinese children were associated with the rejection by peers that is characteristic of many other societies. Why the change? One explanation offered is that once children have entered the secondary school system the advantage lies with those who exhibit independence, responsibility and self-control. Another response is to question whether the valuing of shyness by younger children is actually as widespread in China as was initially claimed. A study by Hart *et al.* (cited in Schneider, 2000) failed to replicate Chen *et al.'s* earlier findings.

One feature of many collectivistic cultures is the significance of the extended family – grandparents, uncles, aunts and cousins – which has the potential to provide the emotional support, advice and practical help that is a core function of friendship. Does this alternative source of support have implications for the voluntary formation of relationships with friends?

Allow about 10 minutes

A C T I V I T Y 3 **Family and friends**

Reflect, briefly, on your experience of the contrasting roles of family members and friends, where children are concerned. If you can, draw on observations of extended families where there is greater scope for relationships which parallel – and maybe conflict with – friendship with peers.

Does a rich family life mean an impoverished social life with peers? Or do the relationships within the family provide positive models for engaging in relationships outside the family?

Some evidence with a possible bearing on these questions comes from research which compared a sample of English Canadian children with children in Italy, often considered to be a very family-oriented country. One study (Schneider *et al.*, 1997) found that the friendships among eight-year-old Italian girls were more stable than those of their counterparts in Ontario. The Italians were also more likely to agree with one another about the quality of their relationships, which the researchers took as a positive sign of the quality of the communication between the friends.

The same research team also observed the children from these two groups in situations which offered the potential for conflict between friends (Schneider *et al.*, 2000). When playing a competitive car racing game with their friends, the Canadian children broke the rules more often while the Italian friends were more involved in the race. In another task, when the friends where presented with a chocolate egg with a toy hidden inside and were asked to discuss how they would share it, the Italian children demonstrated superior skill at negotiation and compromise. Why these differences?

One explanation suggested by the researchers was that the Italian children's more extensive contact with members of the extended family afforded them greater exposure to compromise within relationships. Of course, this is not the only possible interpretation, but it serves to illustrate the ways in which experiences within families may impact on friendships and the ways in which different cultural values attached to relationships impact on the quality of children's interactions with their friends.

Picturing friendship

Although the studies we have cited suggest differences in the lives of children on either side of the Berlin Wall and in family experiences in Canada and Italy, these children would also seem to share much in common. What is to be found when the differences between cultures appear, on the surface at any rate, to be more pronounced? One study compared children in five locations across three countries in different parts of the world (Pinto *et al.*, 1997). The settings differed on the individualism/ collectivism continuum, on the extent of ethnic homogeneity or heterogeneity, and on whether they were at peace or at war. The five locations were Rome, the capital of Italy; Villafranca, a smaller Italian town; Camiri, a town in Bolivia, South America; Ipitacito del Monte, a Bolivian forest village; and Beirut in Lebanon.

Pinto and her colleagues employed a different approach to the study of friendship from those introduced so far in this chapter – children's pictorial representation of their friends. This falls within one tradition of research in developmental psychology which regards children's drawings as providing a 'window on the mind', including being a valid way of gauging emotions and of indicating relative feelings toward significant interpersonal relationships. In this context, drawings have been regarded as particularly useful when comparing children in different cultures because they seem to overcome some of the problems associated with comparing meanings expressed through language. At the same time, powerful cultural conventions apply to children's drawings as well as to their language, so it would be unwise to assume that they offer a literal window on the mind.

In Pinto's study the children were asked to draw a picture of themselves with a friend and the researchers scored the similarities between the figures depicted in terms of their 'dimensions' (e.g. height, width), their 'position' (standing, sitting, frontal, in profile, etc.), the 'body' (shape of trunk, facial features), and 'attributes' (clothes, accessories). So, for example, the eight-year-old Italian boy's drawing of himself and his friend, illustrated in Figure 1, shows high levels of similarity, particularly for 'position'.

Figure 1   An eight-year-old Italian boy's drawing of himself and his friend. What can be deduced from their relative positions?

One of Pinto *et al.'s* hypotheses was that in collectivistic cultures children would emphasize sharing and affinity with friends, whereas those in individualistic cultures would give more importance to maintaining a personal sense of uniqueness. This led to the prediction that children from Ipitacito del Monte, a highly collectivistic culture, would create more similar pictorial representations of themselves and their friends. An analysis of all the children's drawings revealed that children from the Bolivian forest village did indeed exhibit the greatest overall degree of similarity in their drawings of themselves and their friends. The researchers concluded that, of the three different aspects of the settings they studied, individualism/ collectivism was the only one that affected similarity between friends. That said, the main conclusion from the study was a confirmation that 'universal characteristics of friendship exist, as the analogies between the groups considered seemed stronger and more pervasive than the divergencies' (Pinto *et al.*, 1997, p. 467).

That conclusion from one particular study is echoed in the following observation, based on a review of a wider spread of research:

> Despite the possibilities that the functions of friends are not identical in all societies, and that children's behaviour with friends differs across cultures, enough data do exist to indicate, at the most fundamental level, that children around the world regard friendship as an intimate relationship based on reciprocal personal commitment.

(Schneider, 2000, p. 183)

SUMMARY OF SECTION 3

- The development of children's friendships may be influenced by factors such as: where they live, which school they attend and the role of parents and other adults in their lives.
- The characteristics of friendships are culturally specific, reflecting the social practices and values of the culture in which children live.
- Children's friendships usually involve relations of intimacy and reciprocity.

4 GENDERED FRIENDSHIPS

The underlying significance of the 'intimate relationship based on reciprocal personal commitment' referred to at the end of Section 3 serves as a reminder of the importance of children's experiences around friendship for the development of their personal identity. To map such effects in a comprehensive way is an enormous challenge, and here I will focus on just two aspects: the contrasting experiences of boys and girls, and the ways in which friendship relations can be the site of powerful negative emotions. The studies selected for consideration also provide examples of the different ways in which researchers have sought to gain access to the worlds of children and young people as they work at their friendships.

If you look back to the conversations between the three-to-four year olds recorded by Corsaro (Section 2.3) you may note that, even at this age, Jenny is engaging in friendship talk with Betty, and Peter with Graham. This is indicative of the general finding that, even among pre-schoolers, opposite-sex friendships are comparatively rare. They are rarer still, for Western children at any rate, as they become further absorbed into the culture of elementary school. Here, patterns of play tend to be segregated by gender and this is replicated in children's friendship relations. As Allison James notes:

> In this sense, gender has a double significance for children. Its differentiating potential both reinforces and is reinforced by particular forms of play and patterns of friendship which, in turn, generates cultural models of and for particular gendered identities.

(James, 1993, p. 224)

James distinguishes between the tightly bound and structured form of the games that seven, eight and nine-year-old girls typically play and the looser team structure of those played by boys which places less emphasis on the personal. The former she sees being reflected in the pattern of intensive one-to-one relationships involving considerable emotional commitment which are characteristic of girls' friendships.

Minna and Elizabeth: 'the most special friendship in Bangladesh'.

4.1 Girls and friendship

The sort of girls' friendship described by James (1993) is well exemplified by two thirteen-year-olds interviewed as part of our research for this book. Minna and Elizabeth come from middle-class homes in Chittagong, Bangladesh. Here they talk about their close, two-year-long friendship – what they describe as 'the most special friendship in Bangladesh'.

ELIZABETH: A best friend can understand you best, like when two people stay together for a long time they get to know the people and know their feelings. So it's easier to talk about a problem to a best friend than to talk about it with someone else.

MINNA: We agree to each other's decisions always. Yeah. That's what the main thing is. She likes what I like, she dislikes what I dislike, so that's why we're best friends. We're just a photocopy of each other, that's what I think.

(The Open University, 2003a)

Minna and Elizabeth's understanding of the basis for their relationship and of its value to them illustrates the sorts of ways in which the particular relationship of friendship – here between girls – may provide the context for wider personal explorations. Box 3 presents a rather different perspective on how talk between friends offers the potential for wider personal developments.

Box 3 'He's still for me'

The setting for this research project is a primary school in the West Midlands of England in the late 1990s. A group of eight to nine-year-old girls, most of South Asian heritage, met regularly in the school playground during breaks and discussed issues of mutual interest, such as friends, boyfriends and puberty. Of their own accord, the girls developed a format for these meetings: they would decide on a topic for discussion and then take it in turns to ask questions of one another. Their self-imposed rules said that they had to answer the question and they couldn't give a misleading answer. At first sight this may appear rather contrived, but the format seems to have been modelled on the 'circle time' discussions which are a feature of the personal, social and health education curriculum in UK schools, when both talk on particular themes and turn-taking are used to encourage social learning.

One of the researchers, Mary Jane Kehily, became an 'honorary member' of this group of girls over a period of seven months. With their agreement she participated in their discussions and activities and recorded their conversations. During this time the girls' discussions centred around three themes: imagined futures, puberty and periods, and erotic attachments. The latter related to male celebrities such as footballers, pop musicians and 'soap' stars; their teachers; and boys in their class. The following extract is from a conversation between three of the girls about Sunil and Ben, the two most desired boys in their class:

> LAKBIAH: [referring to Sunil] If he killed me I don't care but I still love him.
>
> SELENA: [referring to Ben] I love him, I love him, I love him.
>
> LAKBIAH: I don't mind 'cos it's me who likes him. I don't care if he doesn't like me, he's still for me.
>
> SARAH: [to Selena of Ben] Do you mind, do you mind if you never see him again in secondary school?
>
> SELENA: I don't mind, I still know that I love him.
>
> (Kehily et al., 2002)

Kehily and her co-researchers suggest that exchanges such as this have a wider significance. The subjects of their conversation – here, two boys in their class – provide a resource for the girls' friendship talk and simultaneously a 'fantasy space' within the group where they can articulate different forms of desire. These conversations provide opportunities for the girls to try out different identities and to project themselves into situations, including sexual relationships, which may not be part of their actual experience. The structure of the friendship group provides these girls with a relatively 'safe' performance space for fantasizing and articulating different forms of intimacy in relation to young men.

Discourses: ways of talking about people and events which encode particular assumptions, beliefs and values.

Kehily and her colleagues propose that the *discourses* that these girls engage in, of which the above is but one example, demonstrate what it means to be both a girl and a friend in the context of their group. They also suggest that the rules that the group established for the conduct of their discussions serve as the friendship rules that consolidate their links with each other and their membership of the group.

(Source: Kehily et al., 2002)

Allow about 10 minutes

ACTIVITY 4 **A methodological diversion**

The approach to research taken here by Kehily and her colleagues should be familiar to you as an example of an ethnographic method (see Section 2.3).

What are the particular strengths of this approach in this context and what are its possible limitations?

COMMENT

Kehily observed the group at first hand and participated in their interactions. This is similar to the example of Corsaro's work with pre-school children which is referred to in Section 2.3. You may also have noted similarities with Iona Opie's approach to observing children in the school playground as described in Reading A in Chapter 1.

There are differences, however. Although Opie did get drawn into conversation with the children, her predominant role was as an observer and recorder of their activities. Kehily, by contrast, was keener to engage with the children and become as much part of their activities as possible. Her perception was that 'my presence as researcher and "grown-up girl" was quickly integrated into the structure and ritual of group meetings. Within this space I would be called upon by girls at different moments as group member, invited audience, moral arbiter and source of knowledge about the adult world' (Kehily *et al.*, 2002).

The exchange quoted in Box 3 is typical of other extracts from these girls' conversations and, on the strength of that, it would appear that they were not overly inhibited by Kehily's presence. But to what extent might they have played up to impress the 'grown-up girl' and performed for the tape-recorder?

Positive and negative

One common image of girls' friendships, in particular, is that they are characterized by a capacity for sharing, caring and mutual support. This is exemplified by Christine, a sixteen-year-old girl living in Cape Town, South Africa, who was interviewed, along with her female friends, during the preparation of this book:

> I think friends are important, to be there for you, to comfort you in times of need. And sometimes they have to be there, like to fill that space, that need, that you are a person who's special, and you are wanted.

> (The Open University, 2003a)

Christine's words indicate how those who rank as her friends have a special role and responsibilities to support her and to provide positive affirmation of her personal worth and of her actions. This is of particular significance during the adolescent period when young people are, typically, questioning and being questioned about their developing selves in more intensive ways, and when personal identities are being shaped. Although for many children and young people the family provides one important site for such work, friends offer a framework which has different properties.

Katherine Read has expressed this clearly:

> We must measure ourselves against others who are like us, finding our strengths and facing our weaknesses, winning some acceptance and meeting some rejection [...] A favourable family situation helps us to feel secure, but experiences with our own age group help to develop an awareness of ourselves and of social reality which family experience alone cannot give.

(Read quoted in Rubin, 1980, p. 15)

As Read notes, this awareness of self develops from facing weaknesses and meeting rejection as well as from the more positive aspects of the relationship. Later in the interview, Christine from Cape Town makes clear that she regards arguments between friends as a necessary part of establishing what it is that maintains friendship relationships:

> If you don't argue with your friends sometimes, there is something wrong. Then you know that, no, this person is just saying 'I'm your friend' but not really ... If you recover from the argument and then they are still your friend, then you know that they are a true friend.

(The Open University, 2003a)

In this respect it is one of the hallmarks of 'true' friendships that within the relationship friends can criticise and challenge and disagree in ways which have a particular force and significance *because* they come from a friend – if this person, who is my friend, sees things differently to me then I need to take notice and work through the implications. The personal identity development function is fulfilled via other routes than the positively supportive.

But does even this recognition of the place of negative actions and emotions within friendships go far enough? The Canadian writer Margaret Atwood has presented a telling account of remembered childhood in her novel *Cat's Eye*. The central character, Elaine, recounts the importance of friendships in her life in Toronto forty years previously, and in particular her relationship with Cordelia. Though fictional, the power of such narratives resides in their almost certain origin in personal experience.

> On the way home from school I have to walk in front of them, or behind. In front is worse because they talk about how I'm walking, how I look from behind. 'Don't hunch over,' says Cordelia. 'Don't move your arms like that'.

> They don't say any of the things they say to me in front of others, even other children: whatever is going on is going on in secret, among the four of us only. Secrecy is important, I know that: to violate it would be the greatest, the irreparable sin. If I tell I will be cast out forever.

> But Cordelia doesn't do these things or have power over me because she's my enemy. Far from it. I know about enemies. There are enemies in the schoolyard, they yell things at one another and if they're boys they fight. In the war there were enemies. Our boys and the boys from Our Lady of Perpetual Help are enemies. You throw snowballs at enemies and rejoice if they get hit. With enemies you can feel hatred, and anger. But Cordelia is my friend. She likes me, she wants to help me, they all do.

They are my friends, my girlfriends, my best friends. I have never had any before and I'm terrified of losing them. I want to please.

(Atwood, 1990, p. 120)

Atwood's fictional depiction illustrates how power can be deployed within the confines of a friendship, where the very existence of the friendship is the prize. Equivalent real-life accounts are to be found in Valerie Hey's ethnographic study of girls, aged eleven to eighteen, in two secondary schools in London (Hey, 1997). She documents the frequent interactions between the girls that centre on the less than supportive practices of bitching, falling out and rituals of exclusion. This view challenges that of some feminist researchers who tend to romanticize girls' friendship and to celebrate their capacity for sharing, caring and mutual support. By contrast, girls whom Hey observed were engaged in patterns and practices of friendship that were fuelled by tensions and conflict as much as by support and care.

One closely-knit group of eleven-year-old girls included Erin, the acknowledged leader, Samantha, Saskia, Anna and Natalie. Hey observed that these girls *do* friendship in a constant and frenetic bout of activity, by talking and hanging out inside and outside school and by exchanging notes when they are in lessons. A particular social practice for this group was the issuing, accepting and rejecting of invitations in the form of notes that were passed between them. By these means they could include and exclude, and so negotiate their relations with each other. Saskia appeared particularly keen to identify herself as the main manager of the group's social life. At first sight this suggested that she was a popular, central member of the group. However, Hey's observations suggested that, despite her efforts, Saskia never achieved the status she so desperately wanted. She identified popularity with becoming Erin's best friend, but in desiring and not achieving this outcome she conceded rather than accumulated power within the group.

Allow about 10 minutes

A C T I V I T Y 5   Passing notes

Below is an extract from Hey's field notes of an episode concerning some members of this group of girls. Saskia, not for the first time, had excluded Anna from an arrangement by which the group would all meet at lunchtime at Samantha's house. Read the following exchange of written notes, which included drawings, and suggest an interpretation of what is going on.

ANNA/NATALIE TO SASKIA:	Saskia we are not your friend because you are a snide and you are not very nice.
SASKIA TO ANNA/NATALIE:	I did not [rest of this obliterated]
NATALIE TO SASKIA:	because I am not OK GOT THE MESSAGE
SASKIA TO NATALIE/ANNA:	Why did Anna write the first one. Anyway I don't care what you say because words don't hurt. But I still like you both. Can't you answer.
NATALIE/ANNA TO SASKIA:	Don't you come cheeky to me girl.
SASKIA TO NATALIE/ANNA:	I'm allowed to say what I want to, it's a free world

NATALIE TO SASKIA:	Don't bubble up your mouth on me girl. Get it slag.
SASKIA TO NATALIE/ANNA:	Why don't you try shutting up.
SASKIA TO ANNA:	Is Natalie my friend?
NATALIE TO SASKIA:	NO!
SASKIA TO NATALIE/ANNA:	If NO you don't like me. Then I don't have to do anything you say. If you were my friend then I would but you're not so I won't.
	[A naturalistic, relatively neutral drawing of Anna]
ANNA TO SASKIA:	If you must draw my wonderful complexion draw it properly
NATALIE TO SASKIA:	But shut your mouth cheeky
SASKIA TO NATALIE/ANNA:	I know but I have never been good at art. PS. Is Nattie still my friend
NATALIE TO SASKIA:	NO
ANNA TO SASKIA:	*[A drawing of Saskia with sticky up hair – teenage style – with arrows pointing to her chest with the phrase 'Saskia Stevens' and 'flat as a pancake']*
SASKIA TO ANNA/NATALIE:	I don't care if that's what I look like. I like the hair cut though.

(Hey, 1997, pp. 62–3)

COMMENT

At one level this exchange can be viewed as a written slanging match in which insults are traded back and forth. However, Hey applies further layers of interpretation. For example, she notes the references to 'slag' and the flat-chested depiction of Saskia in the picture as evidence of 'the capacity of girls to reposition other girls within the regime of the male gaze' (Hey, 1997, p. 63). In this way, too, the other girls effectively 'exclude her from the pleasures of girlhood and feminine approval' (p. 64). Nor was this some quickly forgotten exchange; Saskia was practically and effectively excluded from the group, she was ill for two weeks and never returned to the school.

Hey summarizes these girls' friendships relations as follows:

> The desire to become and the fear of being displaced as a girl's significant other appears to be what Erin, Samantha, Saskia and Anna bring to the negotiations. However, girls' tangible desires for power through friendship have to be reconciled with its ethical rules. These social rules are premised on the exact opposite of undisciplined individualism … The central premises of girls' friendship are: reliability, reciprocity, commitment, confidentiality, trust and sharing. The repertoire of emotions that are provoked if these rules are broken are as powerfully felt as those that have characteristically been claimed as the sole prerogative of sexualised relations … Girls' 'divorces' are messy, as we can see in what happened to Saskia.

(Hey, 1997, p. 65)

4.2 Boys and friendship

If girls are seemingly willing to talk – both to one another and to researchers – about their friends and about friendship, the same appears to be less true of boys. James (1993) found that the eight and nine-year-old boys at Hilltop School in the English Midlands, where she did her research, rarely allowed others to enter into the world of their friendships. This, she thought, was not because they did not have valued male friends but rather because they had learnt not to be demonstrative about them in the public context of the classroom or the playground.

Though it may be more difficult to access the world of boys' friendships, it is not impossible. For example, Christine Skelton has investigated features of boys' friendship groups in primary schools in the north-east of England (Skelton, 2001). She noted that the six to seven-year-old boys she observed tended to form large, loosely connected groups and there was a general absence of tight friendship groupings. However, these loose connections did not mean that the groups were without a structure, as the following example illustrates.

Her observations of a group in one school identified one boy, Luke, as an obvious outsider and two others, Carl and Rick, as being marginalized on account of their physical appearance and personal habits. Rick was regarded as 'smelly' and Carl dribbled, and as a consequence of being avoided by many of the children in the class these two tended to seek each other out at 'choosing time'. Skelton observed that the relationships of the remaining ten boys were best understood in terms of their standing with John and Shane, the two boys who instigated the majority of competitive, challenging behaviours both to authority and among their peer group. Gary, Tommy and Matt were always the first to join in with John and Shane and, occasionally, they attempted to initiate and take the lead in various challenging actions. By contrast, Bobby, Adam, Dean, Sean and Martin always took part in group actions but were unlikely to lead.

Skelton drew an analogy between the relationships among these boys and a military hierarchy:

- John and Shane were the generals who organized the action and led the initial assault;
- Luke, Gary, Tommy and Matt were the regular soldiers who were quick to see what was required and proficient in supporting the action of the leaders;
- Bobby, Adam, Dean, Sean and Martin were the conscripts who realized they had to join in but their involvement was minimal and they sought to position themselves on the periphery of the action;
- Rick and Carl might be regarded as conscientious objectors. Recognizing their marginal position they preferred to avoid contact with the rest of the group. Nevertheless, they always took some role in any action, possibly because the alternative was more personally threatening.

This example presents a further perspective on the patterns of friendship that can exist within groups, a pattern in which children themselves construct and organise friendships in a hierarchical fashion, often based on their own notions of power and status. These friendships operate in ways which produce both individual and collective identities, and in the particular example provided by Skelton's research the boys' collective identity was defined by their oppositional stance to authority.

A boy's best friend is his cat.

Allison James's observation that it is more difficult to gain access to boys' friendships is supported by a study of boys, aged eleven to fourteen, also in the UK, which suggests that their relationships with each other are structured around the contradictions of masculine identities (Frosh *et al.*, 2002). Many of the boys the researchers spoke to saw masculinity and toughness as inextricably linked, thus making it difficult for them to discuss feelings of emotional closeness and intimacy within male friendship groups.

In one-to-one interviews with one of the researchers, however, many of the boys did discuss their feelings of intimacy and vulnerability at school and within the family. A notable feature of this was the ways in which they spoke with affection about their pets, about the pleasure they derived from caring for them, being able to stroke them and cuddle up to them and being loved by them. In many instances this was not something they would talk about with other boys at school for fear of being seen as 'wimpish'. A few of the boys contrasted the sorts of relations they had with their pets with the much less intimate relations they had with people. These findings point to the ways in which conforming to masculine norms may constrain boys.

SUMMARY OF SECTION 4

- Children's experiences of friendship play a part in the development of their identity.
- Gender difference may have an impact upon friendship groups in many Western cultures. Boys and girls commonly form single-sex friendship groups characterized by large informal networks for boys and more tightly bound structures for girls.
- Friendship may involve the playing out of powerful negative emotions such as jealousy, hatred and fear as well as positive feelings of support and care.
- Children may use friendship as a way of regulating and controlling each other.

5 THE LONGER TERM SIGNIFICANCE OF FRIENDS

The accounts in this chapter of the place and significance of friendship in children's social and cultural worlds have assumed that they play more than an ephemeral part. Lorna Sage's recollection of her childhood friends when she was eight years old, and Elaine's account of how memories of her best friend and tormentor Cordelia continue to haunt her forty years on, both raise the expectation that childhood friendships have an enduring influence well into adulthood. The task of investigating these influences is one for psychologists and sociologists, but it is not a straightforward one and, as Allison James warned, it remains 'but haltingly documented' (James, 1993, p. 203).

Although it is possible to ask adults to attempt to recall significant features of childhood friendship – much as you did in Activity 1 – and then to seek correlations between those and their relationships as adults, this *retrospective* approach produces data which are subject to similar selectivity of memory and distortions as those which afflict the biographer. One option is to gather data on the same individuals at two or more points in their lives, separated by a period of time, and then to analyse the relationship between them. In this approach there can be greater confidence in the validity and reliability of the data. Box 4 outlines an example of a *longitudinal study* that explores the relationship between the friendship patterns of ten year olds and features of their subsequent adult lives.

Box 4 Enduring consequences?

Catherine Bagwell, Andrew Newcomb and William Bukowski were able to follow up a sample of young adults, average age just over 23, who had been participants in an earlier study of theirs when they were aged ten and attending school in a suburban community in the American mid-west. Sixty adults were involved, 30 of whom (15 males and 15 females) had had a stable, mutual best friend at the time of the earlier study. When they were ten, the members of this *friended group* had chosen the same best friend on two occasions, one month apart, and this best friend had chosen them in return. The other 30 (15 males and 15 females) were drawn from the group who had been *chumless* at the age of ten – they had not received any reciprocal nominations, on either occasion, from the children they had chosen as their best friend.

Other measures were made at the age of ten, including how the children perceived their competence in four domains – cognitive, social, physical and general self-worth.

Thirteen years later these 60 people completed a questionnaire which asked them about their life since the earlier study. They provided information about how they had got on at school and in their jobs, their family interactions, their aspirations, their social life and involvement in activities, any trouble with the law, and any mental health difficulties. Further scales assessed their perceptions of their self-worth and competence in a variety of areas including their job, their friendships and their romantic relationships, and their self reports of psychopathological symptoms.

In addition, they were asked to take part in a short interview about the quality of the friendship they had identified when they were ten. They were asked to describe the relationship and what they did together and to identify any negative features. These interviews were then rated according to the overall quality of the relationship in terms of intensity and intimacy.

Finally, they were asked to give details of their present same-sex best friend who was then contacted and invited to complete a questionnaire about them.

Statistical analysis of this large mass of data revealed a number of interconnections and correlations of which the following is a selection:

- there was clear association between pre-adolescent friendship and positive relations with family members;
- feelings of positive self-esteem as a young adult were well predicted by pre-adolescent friendship status;
- the presence of depressive symptoms in adulthood were associated with a failure to form a close friendship in pre-adolescence.

Some associations that might have been anticipated were not borne out by the analysis, for example:

- those who had had positive pre-adolescent friendship experiences were no more competent in their adult friendly and romantic relationships than those who had not;
- reports by the participants' current best friends on the quality of their relationship and the participants' level of social competence in their friendship were not related to the pre-adolescent peer experience.

(Source: Bagwell et al., 1998)

ACTIVITY 6   Identifying causes

Allow about 5 minutes

The study by Bagwell *et al.* (1998) was designed to look for associations over a longish period of development – thirteen years – according to whether the participants were *friended* or *chumless* at the age of ten. Among other questions, it sought to investigate whether intimate friendships at the pre-adolescent stage are the forerunner of positive self-esteem in adulthood. There was some evidence of such an association, but how satisfied are you that a causal link has been established?

COMMENT

Here is what Bagwell *et al.* have to say on this matter:

> Clearly, the design of the current study prohibits the evaluation of the causal model. The study is correlational in nature, and no matter how convincing the results, the conclusion that poor pre-adolescent peer and friendship relations cause poor adult outcome cannot be made. We are thus left with the possibility that poor peer relations are only a marker for underlying difficulties that will produce maladaptive outcomes, or that they moderate the emergence of these difficulties into more extreme adjustment problems. ·

(Bagwell *et al.*, 1998, pp. 151–2)

Although there are statistical associations between some of the measures made when the children were ten and those made when they were 23, it is unsafe to regard this necessarily as a *causal* link. It could be, for example, that features of their personality which made them attractive or unattractive as potential friends at the age of ten continued to have an equivalent effect in early adulthood. A further limitation of the study, in the context of this chapter, is that little is recorded about the nature and quality of the childhood friendships – that they either existed or didn't exist was the feature that distinguished the two groups.

You may find this a disappointing conclusion to such an extensive study, but it serves to underline some of the problems that researchers face when attempting to substantiate and generalise the links that biographers and others make with such apparent ease when dealing with individual cases.

SUMMARY OF SECTION 5

- If friendships play a central part in children's lives, do they have enduring consequences through into adulthood?
- One longitudinal study found some positive relationships between childhood friendships and quality of life in adulthood.
- However, establishing clear causal relationships between childhood experiences and adult outcomes is far from straightforward.

6 CONCLUSION

This chapter has explored various aspects of the friendship relationships which are a significant feature of the worlds of children and reflected on the degree to which they provide experiences of particular importance at this stage of the life cycle. We questioned how far and by what means it is possible for adults to gain access to these worlds, either through personal reminiscence or active research, and considered the issue of continuity and change over time.

The chapter discussed some of the different ways in which children's friendships provide them with an important source of emotional, social and physical support. For example, different forms and patterns of friendship exist between children in different locations and different cultural contexts. The street children in South Africa and Brazil, for example, appear to have intense and closely-binding friendships, while friendship among the !Kung in Southern Africa is transitory, dependent on the seasonal cycles of a hunter-gatherer society. These and other examples indicate the ways in which friendships are culturally specific, reflecting the values and social practices of the society in which children live as well as the children's own concerns and interests in the here and now.

We also considered the functions of friendships for children's identity. Children's friendships generally provide them with opportunities for intimate relations based upon forms of reciprocity. Experience of friendship is one of the ways in which individual children develop a sense of identity, defining who they are in relation to others. Friendship, however, is not always a positive experience. There can be a darker side to children's friendship, illustrated by some of the examples in this chapter in which powerful negative feelings are acted upon.

The chapter went on to consider ways in which gender may impact upon patterns and practices of friendship, particularly in Western societies where same-sex friendship groups remain the norm for most children. Finally, the chapter discussed the long-term significance of friends and concluded, somewhat inconclusively, that links between childhood friendships and quality of life in adulthood are difficult to determine.

REFERENCES

AMIT-TALAI, V. (1995) 'The waltz of sociability: intimacy, dislocation and friendship in a Quebec High School' in AMIT-TALAI, V. and WULFF, H. (eds) (1995) *Youth Cultures: a cross cultural perspective,* London, Routledge.

ATWOOD, M. (1990) *Cat's Eye,* London, Virago.

BAGWELL, C. L., NEWCOMB, A. F. and BUKOWSKI, W. M. (1998) 'Pre-adolescent friendship and peer rejection as predictors of adult adjustment', *Child Development,* **69**, pp. 140–53.

BIGELOW, B. J. and LA GAIPA, J. J. (1980) 'The development of friendship values and choice' in FOOT, H. C., CHAPMAN, A. J. and SMITH, J. R. (eds) *Friendship and Social Relations in Children,* Chichester, John Wiley.

CAMPOS, R., RAFFAELLI, W., UDE, W., GRECO, M., RUFF, A., ROLF, J., ANTUNES, C. M., HALSEY, N., GRECO, D. and THE STREET YOUTH STUDY GROUP (1994) 'Social networks and daily activities of street youth in Belo Horizonte, Brazil', *Child Development,* **65**, pp 319–30.

CHEN, X., RUBIN, K. H. and SUN, Y. (1992) 'Social reputation and peer relationships in Chinese and Canadian children: a cross-cultural study', *Child Development,* **63**, pp. 1336–43.

CORSARO, W. (1985) *Friendship and Peer Culture in the Early Years,* Norwood, NJ, Ablex.

CROCKETT, L., LOSOFF, M. and PETERSEN, A. C. (1984) 'Perceptions of the peer group and friendship in early adolescence', *Journal of Early Adolescence,* **4**, pp. 155–81.

DAMON, W. (1977) *The Social World of the Child,* San Francisco, Jossey-Bass.

FROSH, S., PHOENIX, A. and PATTMAN, R. (2002) *Young Masculinities,* Basingstoke, Palgrave Macmillan.

HARTUP, W. (1992) 'Friendships and their developmental significance' in MCGURK, H. (ed.) *Childhood Social Development: contemporary perspectives,* Hove, Lawrence Erlbaum Associates.

HEY, V. (1997) *The Company She Keeps,* Buckingham, Open University Press.

JAMES, A. (1993) *Childhood Identities: self and social relationships in the experience of the child,* Edinburgh, Edinburgh University Press.

KEHILY, M. J., MAC AN GHAILL, M., EPSTEIN, D. and REDMAN, P. (2002) 'Private girls and public worlds: producing femininities in the primary school', *Discourse,* Special issue on friendship, **23**(2), pp. 167–78.

KONNER, M. J. (1981) 'Evolution of human behaviour development' in MUNROE, R. H. and WHITING, B. B. (eds) *Handbook of Cross-cultural Human Development*, New York, Garland STPM Press.

LARSON, R. W. and BRADNEY, N. (1988) 'Precious moments with family members and friends' in MILARDO, R. M. (ed.) *Families and Social Networks*, Newbury Park, California, Sage.

LITTLE, T. D., BRENDGEN, M., WANNER, B. and KRAPPMANN, L. (1999) 'Children's reciprocal perceptions of friendship quality in the sociocultural contexts of East and West Berlin', *International Journal of Behavioural Development*, **23**, pp. 63–89.

NEWSON, J. and NEWSON, E. (1976) *Seven Years Old in the Home Environment*, London, George Allen & Unwin.

OPIE, P. and OPIE, I. (1959) *The Lore and Language of Schoolchildren*, Oxford, Oxford University Press.

OSWALD, H. and KRAPPMANN, L. (1995) 'Social life of children in a former bipartite city' in NOACK, P., HOFER, M. and YOUNISS, J. (eds) *Psychological Responses to Social Change: human development in changing environments*, Berlin, de Gruyter.

PINTO, A., BOMBI, A. S. and CORDIOLI, A. (1997) 'Similarity of friends in three countries: a study of children's drawings', *International Journal of Behavioural Development*, **20**(3), pp. 453–69.

RUBENSTEIN, J. and HOWES, C. (1976) 'The effects of peers on toddler interaction with mother and toys', *Child Development,* **47**, pp. 597–605.

RUBIN, Z. (1980) *Children's Friendships*, Glasgow, Fontana Paperbacks.

SCHNEIDER, B. H. (2000) *Friends and Enemies: peer relations in childhood*, London, Arnold.

SCHNEIDER, B. H., FONZI, A., TANI, F. and TOMADA, G. (1997) 'A cross-cultural exploration of the stability of children's friendships and predictors of their continuation', *Social Development*, **6**, pp. 322–39.

SCHNEIDER, B. H., FONZI, A., TOMADA, G. and TANI, F. (2000) 'A cross-national comparison of children's behaviour with their friends in situations of potential conflict', *Journal of Cross-Cultural Psychology*, **31**, pp. 259–66.

SELMAN, R. (1980) *The Growth of Interpersonal Understanding*, New York, Academic Press.

SHOSTAK, M. (1983) *Nisa: the life and words of a !Kung woman,* New York, Vintage Books.

SKELTON, C. (2001) *Schooling the Boys: masculinities and primary education*, Buckingham, Open University Press.

THE OPEN UNIVERSITY (2003a) U212 *Childhood*, Video 3, Band 4, 'Friendship', Milton Keynes, The Open University.

THE OPEN UNIVERSITY (2003b) U212 *Childhood*, Video 2, Band 2, 'Kinship', Milton Keynes, The Open University.

WOODHEAD, M. (2003) 'The child in development' in WOODHEAD, M. and MONTGOMERY, H. (eds) *Understanding Childhood: an interdisciplinary approach*, Chichester, John Wiley and Sons Ltd/The Open University (Book 1 of the Open University course U212 *Childhood*).

Bad Blood

Lorna Sage

Try as I might to lose myself in the landscape, however, I was still only an apprentice misfit and self-conscious in the part. Other kids who hung about at all hours turned out to have errands – big brothers or sisters to fetch, a message to carry to someone working down the fields, or to Dad in the pub. You loiter with a lot more conviction if you've even the shadow of a purpose to neglect and that I lacked. And the truth was that often no amount of trudging would get me to the state of dreamy abstraction I craved. Then I was simply lonely. I wanted friends desperately and, as it happened, the move to The Arowry held out hope, for it gave me a second chance with two girls from school who'd had nothing to do with me when I'd lived in the vicarage – Janet Yates and Valerie Edge, who were now neighbours. Valerie, brown, rosy, curly-haired and tall for eight, lived at the first council house to be finished, which already had a proper garden with dahlias in the borders. Janet – slighter like me, but unlike me, neat and tidy – came from a smallholding down the lane, with a bush of pungent, grey 'Old Man' at the gate and a path made of red-and-blue bricks. Gates and gardens figured large in our friendship because we spent at lot of our time together leaning or swinging on one or other of our gates. With Valerie and Janet you didn't wander off, not because they weren't allowed to, exactly, but because they were too grown-up, they saw no point in it.

They were busy being big girls, practising for real life, which meant not so much mothering dolls or playing house or dressing up (although we must have done all these things), as whispering in a huddle, sharing secrets, giggling behind our hands and linking arms around each other's waists. It was like a dance, a dance of belonging with no private space in it, all inside-out intimacy, and I found it euphoric, intoxicating. And then we would quarrel, for the magic number three is a formula for dissension: two against one, two whispering together, turning away and giggling, the third shamed and outcast. It's obvious now that this was the real point of the whole elaborate dance, its climactic figure, but back then, of course, each quarrel seemed a disaster and I'd run home, tears streaming, and howl on my own back doorstep for hours. My mother, dismayed in the first place by my obsession with such ordinary (if not common) little girls and even more put out by the intensity of my grief when they turned their backs on me, would say, 'It's not the end of the world.' But she unwittingly provided me with exactly the right words. That's what it was, the end of the world, every time

I cast myself as the odd one out, but in truth it wasn't always so at all. The real shame that sticks to this memory comes when I recall the pang of pleasure I felt when Valerie and I shut out Janet. Our emotional triangle was a very good rehearsal for the world, the mimic anticipation of group psychology was perfect, even down to the fact that Valerie was never excluded. She was more sure of herself to start with and she remained innocent of the needy jealousy the other two of us suffered, so became ever more blithely, unconsciously cruel, our unmoved mover. Valerie for her part adored her mum.

[...]

It was Valerie's mum's example that inspired a game that was not – for once – part of the dance of rejection. True, it just involved Valerie and me, but Janet was away for the summer holidays, staying with some auntie or cousin, not a shadowy rival waiting in the wings. This game – *Doing the Flowers for the Dolls' Wedding* – developed a mimic reality and depth our other games lacked. *[note: Mrs Edge supplemented the family income by making wreaths and 'doing flowers for weddings']* It didn't seem like play at all, in fact, that was its charm. We planned for weeks, discussed exactly what the dolls wanted, made lists of the different bouquets and sprays we'd need for the bridesmaids and matron of honour, as well as the bride herself (who'd ordered flowers for her hair too) and priced them all, including buttonholes for the families, strictly graded in order of kinship and importance, with mothers top. We were confined to wild flowers mostly, and of course we had to miniaturise everything for the dolls, but these additional problems only enhanced the busy, anxious pleasure of the whole thing. In the days before the big day we picked our flowers and ferns, and put them in separate jam jars ready to be made up into bunches of different sizes and splendour, which was something you had to do at the last minute.

We even arranged to borrow a camera, to take a group picture of the happy event, in order to immortalise our handiwork, although I don't think we managed to take one, for I never remember seeing it. Perhaps it was an overcast day, or possibly no one would lend us a camera for they were expensive, temperamental, grown-up toys back in 1952. Nonetheless, although the wedding itself hasn't left much trace, it was a great success, for it was the background *Doing* of the flowers over all that time (we were only nine, it must have seemed an age) that counted. So much so that neither the dolls nor their clothes figured at all prominently in our professional calculations about how to get things exactly right – although the dolls were all the wrong sizes and baby-shaped (we were pre-Barbie, let alone Ken). This was fantasy at work, with the emphasis on work. And the other thing that made it idyllic was that we plotted and staged it all on my back doorstep, since Valerie's mum didn't want us under her feet.

Source

SAGE, L. (2000) *Bad Blood*, London, Fourth Estate, pp. 105–108.

Chapter 3
Language, relationships and identities

Janet Maybin

CONTENTS

LEARNING OUTCOMES

When you have studied this chapter, you should be able to:

1   Understand how children and young people use different languages, dialects and language styles for their own purposes.

2   Recognize the important role of narrative in children's conversation and the collaborative uses of turn-taking in expressing friendship.

3   Understand how children's language use is sensitive to context and how they can also use language to change the context.

4   Identify children and young people's use of different media to negotiate relationships and explore and express aspects of their own identity.

5   Recognize the dual role of language in providing children with a cultural resource which shapes their knowledge, beliefs and values and also with a tool which they can use in shaping their own lives and their sense of self.

I INTRODUCTION

Allow about 15 minutes

ACTIVITY I   Children's language

Think back over the first two chapters in this book and briefly note down two or three ways in which language plays an important role in children's play, their friendships and in the creation of their personal cultural worlds.

COMMENT

You may have thought back to the playground lore collected by Iona and Peter Opie, and the rhymes, chants, jokes, riddles, nicknames and rituals of inclusion and exclusion which have been used by children for hundreds of years. You may remember that William Corsaro identified six different categories of talk about friendship used by three to five year olds in the course of their play. For older children, friendship often involves sharing secrets and talking through problems, and you may recall the example of the group of girls who met regularly at school lunch-times to discuss imagined futures, puberty and periods and erotic attachments. Oral and written language may also be used in solitary play, for instance in the creation of imaginary alternative worlds.

Language is frequently mentioned in the discussion of friendship and play in Chapters 1 and 2, and in this chapter we bring into the foreground children's talk and informal personal writing to examine more closely how language provides such a powerful resource for children and young people in so many different aspects of their lives. I shall start by looking at what children say about using the different languages and dialects in their repertoire, and discussing how language style can also be an important marker of identity.

Story telling is an intrinsic part of conversation at all ages, and in Section 3 I look at the different ways in which children learn to tell stories and also examine other conversational strategies used in managing relationships and expressing identity. Finally, in Section 4 I shall examine children and young people's use of different media, for instance the mobile phone and the internet, for social and personal purposes.

Language has been seen as the link between the individual and society. Children learn to use a language or languages in culturally shaped ways and through language are introduced to a particular tradition of oral and written literature and to particular sets of knowledge and values. In this sense, language is a cultural resource. As we saw in Chapters 1 and 2, children also use language to manage activities and to negotiate relationships with other children. In this way language is an important tool for getting things done in everyday life. Finally, language is important in inner thought and imagination and in children's growing sense of their own identity. These three aspects of language – cultural resource, everyday tool and means for internal reflection – are closely interrelated in children's lives.

2 LANGUAGES AND LANGUAGE VARIETIES

A dialect is a language variety with distinctive patterns of vocabulary, pronunciation, grammar and conversational style. Technically speaking, standard English is also a dialect.

A majority of children in the world speak more than one language; often these languages are associated with different parts of their lives, and with different aspects of themselves. Monolingual children also vary their use of language; for example, they may use a different accent or dialect depending on where they are and to whom they are speaking. Activity 2 explores how two young people in different parts of the world see the role of various languages or language varieties in their lives.

Allow about 20 minutes

ACTIVITY 2   **Language choices**

Below are comments from young people talking about the languages they speak which we recorded during the preparation of this book. The first is from fourteen-year-old Sarah who lives in Cape Town, South Africa. She speaks Xhosa, Sotho, English and Afrikaans. The second comment comes from twelve-year-old Terina in California, who speaks standard English and Ebonics, a variety or dialect of English spoken by African American people which includes some different vocabulary, different ways of using grammar and different conversational styles from standard English.

What reasons do the girls give for using different languages or dialects when speaking to different people, and in different parts of their lives? How does their use of language and dialect relate to their sense of identity and hopes for the future?

Sarah (Cape Town)

At home I speak Xhosa and Sotho and then sometimes I speak a little bit of English. If there's someone who doesn't understand Xhosa we *(Sarah and her friends)* try to mix it with English, because sometimes we get over-excited and forget that there's someone who doesn't understand Xhosa. There are some things which I can't say in English but I can say in Xhosa. If I don't know the hard word in English then I'll just say it in Xhosa. You can't speak English in Afrikaans class and you can't speak Xhosa in Afrikaans class, you have to use that language in that class. Let's say a teacher is walking down the corridor and they tell you 'You're not supposed to speak Xhosa' and I say 'Yes, we know that but we're speaking to our friends', if she doesn't understand, we're not even speaking to her … I think it's important to speak an African language because people of today, they go to places overseas and when they come back their way of speaking has changed. She'll be speaking a different tongue. It's to basically know where you come from, your roots.

Terina (California)

I wouldn't say that Ebonics was a big part of my life because I don't use it that often, I use it probably when I'm talking to my friends. It's kind of cool having your own separate language … Most of the day I would say about 89 per cent I'm using standard English because I'm in my classes most of the day … You don't use slang in class, it's just not right. We have morals. We know better than to use slang in class … If I'm trying to get into a college or something and I can't turn the Ebonics off that's going to be really bad because they're going to think that I'm just so ghettofied that I can't turn off the Ebonics that I'm using.

I feel more myself when I'm using standard English, maybe with a couple of Ebonics words at times. Ebonics is just a different part of me. Some people say I talk white and I really don't mind. I know how to talk to people when they're not always my same culture. I like to stay diverse.

(The Open University, 2003a)

COMMENT

The reasons the girls give for using a particular language or language variety relate to:

1   Context: Sarah uses Xhosa and Sotho at home and Africaans in her classes at school – each have their own appropriate language. Terina uses standard English at school and she feels it would be 'just not right' to use Ebonics in class. Ebonics would also not be appropriate for a college interview.

2   Audience: Sarah and her friends try to use some English if they are with someone who doesn't understand Xhosa. They can also use Xhosa to exclude people, for example, teachers. Terina says she wants to be able to use standard English to mix with people from different cultures.

3   Language and identity: Sarah says that it's important for African people to speak an African language, to express their roots. Terina says it's 'cool' to have a separate language to use with friends, but that she feels more herself using standard English 'maybe with a couple of Ebonics words at times'.

'Code switching' refers to the way speakers will sometimes switch between different languages or dialects within the one conversation. These switches are significant for the meaning of what is said, and the relations between speakers.

Notice how, for Sarah, some contexts are definitely associated with a particular language while at other times, for instance when she is with a multilingual group of friends, she will mix English and Xhosa within the same conversation. When we recorded Sarah talking with friends who spoke both Xhosa and English, they still switched between the two languages during their conversation. Multilingual speakers often use their home language when they switch to talk about a personal family matter, or want to emphasize a shared ethnic identity with their listeners. They may also change the language they're using to reflect an area of life associated with a particular language, for example, using English to refer to school procedures, or when talking about popular music and films. We might imagine that Terina inserts 'a couple of Ebonics words' into her standard English when she wants to refer to peer group matters or confirm a shared African American identity with her listeners. Code switching between different languages or dialects may be a routine way of talking in a particular community, or a switch may be used by a speaker to alert the listener to a significant shift in topic, or to foreground a particular aspect of their relationship with the speaker. Switching between different languages or dialects adds another layer of meaning to the conversation.

The girls' feelings about the different languages they speak are related to the kind of person they imagine themselves becoming. For Terina a command of standard English is vital for going to college, while Sarah does not like the way some Africans who go overseas lose touch with their language and their roots. The status of Terina and Sarah's languages is also important. The political climate of the new South Africa, with its eleven official languages, has produced a resurgence of pride in African languages and African identity. In the United States, in contrast, despite a number of efforts to raise its status and introduce it into schooling, Ebonics or African American English has been generally seen as having a lower status than standard English, a kind of slang appropriate only to informal occasions.

Terina and Sarah each represent just one possible way of relating to their respective language environments. Some African American youths, for instance, attach much more importance to a group and language identity which is in opposition to the dominant political and educational system.

All children and young people have a repertoire of language or languages which they draw on for different occasions and purposes in their lives, according to complex personal, social and political criteria. In racially mixed

areas of South London, England, for instance, some white teenagers who
socialize and are friendly with British teenagers of Afro-Caribbean origin
have learnt to speak Caribbean-based Creole, or patois. Hewitt (1986)
suggests that using Creole is an important way of expressing inter-racial
friendship in a community where there is also a considerable amount of
racism. The ability to 'talk black' was a source of pride for these white
teenagers. As one boy put it, looking back on his early teens:

> I was the sort of person who liked to stand out, and being able to speak
> patois seemed as a form of being able to stand out. And they was all
> white kids at school. Because I went round with black kids I was
> different. They was all the ones saying you can't walk down Brixton *(an
> Afro-Caribbean neighbourhood),* you know what I mean. Whereas I
> was the one who could say I go round with 'em.

(Hewitt, 1986, p. 143)

White teenagers who speak Creole also have to be careful, however,
because many black teenagers are suspicious or dislike the taking on of
Creole speech by an outsider. One black girl explained:

> It's offensive 'cos, like, a white boy might say something in joke to
> another, and then he'll see a black person and say, 'Wa'appen', or make
> some joke, or say 'Oh, rass!', but he's taking the piss out of you, you
> know? So when you hear two of them talking it, you think, 'What they
> trying to do now? What they trying to prove now?'

(Hewitt, 1986, p. 151)

Language and style

In addition to choosing and switching between languages and dialects, quite
subtle aspects of language use can be a signal of young people's personal
and group identity. Penelope Eckert, an American linguist, has documented
the language styles of students in American high schools who call
themselves Jocks, Burnouts or 'In betweens' (Eckert, 2000). Teenagers in the
schools she studied took part in different kinds of social activities, had
different personal styles and different kinds of aspirations for the future
depending on which group they belonged to. Jocks participated
enthusiastically in extra-curricular activities, played sports, served on the
school council and hoped to graduate to college. When Penelope Eckert did
her research in the 1980s they wore smart designer jeans, the girls used
candy-coloured make-up and the boys had short hair. The Burnouts, in
contrast, did not participate in school social activities and resisted the
corporate identity of the high school and what it stood for. They wore
bellbottom jeans, rock concert T-shirts, sweatshirts and auto plant jackets,
and expected to work in local industry when they were older. They were
more likely to be out at an all-night party in the town than at the school
dance. Jocks and Burnouts hung out in different parts of the school, and
Eckert found that they used language in distinctively different ways. Jock
girls used a wider range of pitch when they talked (to produce a bright,
vivacious 'cocktail party' style) while Burnout girls, who saw the Jocks'
friendliness as fake, used a much more serious tone with less range in pitch.

Burnouts used more profanities and non-standard grammar (like 'I didn't do nothing'), and adopted a particular exaggerated pronunciation of certain vowels which Eckert came to recognize as an unmistakable sign of being a Burnout. Using language in this way to talk about key Burnout cultural themes such as alienation from school, drugs, trouble and fights was a central part of the construction of Burnout identity. Young people who saw themselves as somewhere between a Jock and a Burnout would use a modified form of Burnout linguistic style, and were involved in a mixture of Jock and Burnout type activity.

Eckert argues that Jocks and Burnouts are essentially class-based groups, and in fact that these young people are recreating the class divisions of their parents' worlds through what appears to be a specifically teenage style of rebellion. A middle-class teenager can become a Burnout and a working-class teenager a Jock, but this involves all sorts of personal sacrifices and compromises in resisting what seems a natural positioning.

Allow about 10 minutes

ACTIVITY 3   Style and context

Thinking back to your own childhood and youth, in what ways were different languages, dialects or language styles associated with different parts or different stages of your life? For instance, did you make different use of dialect, accent or slang when you were with friends and when you were with adults? In and out of school?

COMMENT

As a monolingual child growing up in a professional family in rural Northern Ireland, I remember speaking with a much stronger local accent and using more local idioms when I was playing out with friends in the neighbourhood than when I was with my parents or at school in the nearby town. Speaking 'posh' with a more English accent was definitely an obstacle to being accepted in the local community. As an adult living and working in England, my Northern Irish accent has virtually disappeared but comes back when I am talking to someone who has a strong Northern Irish accent themselves.

Many people associate changes in their own language with other significant turning points in their lives, for example, moving home, going to secondary school, or becoming involved with a particular group of friends. Generally speaking, we consciously or unconsciously moderate our way of speaking to more closely resemble the style of people we want to affiliate with, and to contrast more strongly with the style of people from whom we want to distance or dissociate ourselves.

Speech style, as well as clothes and other aspects of personal appearance, can be an important expression of idendity..

Translation into a new language

So far I've been looking at children and young people's facility and flexibility in using different languages, dialects and styles of language. Sometimes, however, children who migrate to live in a different country may experience a particularly difficult disjuncture between the world and the language they have left behind and the demands of their new environment. Eva Hoffman, who left Poland in 1959 at the age of thirteen with her parents and younger sister to live first in Canada and later in the USA, has written in her autobiography about her development as a writer and speaker in English and the losses and gains which this entailed. As a teenager she struggled to reconcile herself to the loss of the places, people, language and taken-for-grantedness of her childhood in Poland. At quite a profound level, learning to speak and write in English were an integral part of translating herself, and her sense of her own identity, into a new language and into her new context in Canada.

READING

Read Reading A, an extract from Hoffman's autobiography *Lost in Translation: life in a new language*. As an adult, Hoffman is reflecting back on how she remembers her fifteen-year-old self.

How does having to use a second language and adapt to a new cultural environment shape Hoffman's feelings, as she remembers them, about her own identity as a fifteen year old? When she is given a diary, why does she decide 'If I'm to write about the present, I have to write in the language of the present, even if it's not the language of the self'?

Hoffman's autobiography conveys a sense of her intense frustration as she rails against the false persona she feels 'stuffed into' through her lack of ease and familiarity with either the English language or the world of Canadian teenagers. This sense of a splitting of different parts of the self, connected with the person she was when she left Poland at thirteen, the person she might have become had she stayed there, and the person she is now in Canada, is reflected in the imaginary dialogue with herself. But although Hoffman identifies her Polish self from the past as 'the real one' in her inner dialogue, her compulsion in her diary is to write in English, even if this means writing rather impersonally about thoughts rather than emotions. Although English is still a public rather than a private language in Hoffman's life, Polish has become the language of an 'untranslatable past' and she has to use English to simultaneously update what might have been her Polish self and also carve out a new existence, an identity in English. Hoffman's reflections about which 'I' is expressed in Polish and which in English address the division in her experience at that point in her life between the past and the present, between the public and the private and between thought and feeling (Miller, 1996).

The struggle to create a coherent sense of self out of diverse and distinctive experiences is echoed also in the lives of many young people who are not necessarily migrants or bilingual but who are in various ways exploring and experimenting with different aspects of self and identity in relation to their developing sense of personal biography. We shall return later, in Section 4, to young people's use of writing and other media within this process.

SUMMARY OF SECTION 2

- Children and young people choose between using different languages or dialects depending on the context, the people they are talking to, their purposes and their sense of who they are, or who they want to be.

- 'Code switching' between languages or dialects within the same conversation contributes to the meaning and social purpose of the talk.

- Language styles adopted by young people may be closely related to other aspects of personal style such as clothes, preferred social activities and aspirations for the future.

- Changes in language use and style are related to other life changes, and can be involved in complex ways with the exploration and construction of new identities.

3 RELATIONSHIPS AND IDENTITY IN CONVERSATION

While Section 2 dealt with choices and switches between different language varieties, this section will look more closely at how children use talk to represent and reflect on their experience, pursue and manage relationships and negotiate their own identity. I shall first discuss children's use of narrative in conversation, then examine some particular patterns of co-operation in their talk, and finally illustrate how children's use of talk is sensitive to context and can change quite dramatically across different settings.

One of the most easily recognizable patterns in children's and adults' talk is the conversational story. What counts as a good story and the appropriate way to tell it is strongly dependent on the speaker's audience and may vary across different situations and different cultures. The most basic definition of a narrative is that it recapitulates a sequence of events. For instance, in Chapter 2, Section 3.1, we referred to the friendship between three boys, Shane, Steven and Wilfred, who live on the streets of Cape Town. We asked Steven:, 'How did you and Wilfred first become friends?' His answer was in the form of a story relating a series of actions. Like the majority of the coloured population in South Africa, Steven's first language is Afrikaans but he is also fairly fluent in English.

Under the apartheid regime in South Africa, mixed race people were categorized as 'coloured', and most still refer to themselves by this term.

Steven.

Steven's story

One time I saw Wilfred, he's hungry, then he's by the home. Then I don't know Wilfred, then I stay by his house, next to his house. Then he come to me, then he ask me some bread. Then I give him two slice of bread and that's why we are – he's my friend. See. (Steven, twelve years old, Cape Town)

(The Open University, 2003b)

There is a clear sequence of events: Steven saw Wilfred, Wilfred came up to Steven and asked him for bread, Steven gave Wilfred bread and now they are friends. In addition to conveying this simple story, Steven's narrative follows the common narrative structure in English (Labov, 1972), which includes three main elements:

1   an *orientation* setting the time and place (the first three sentences)

2   a *complication* which gets the action going (Wilfred asks for bread)

3   a *resolution*, which closes the story (Steven gives him two slices of bread and they became friends).

Stories may also include an *abstract* at the beginning which introduces the nub of the story, for example, Steven might say to a friend 'Did you hear about how I met Wilfred?'. This was not necessary in the example above where our question 'How did you and Wilfred first become friends?' had, in effect, provided the focus of Steven's account. A story may also finish with a *coda* which provides a link back into the conversation. In Steven's story he provides an explicit link at the end, back to the question we had asked: 'that's why we are – he's my friend. See'. Notice how Steven presents himself in this story as someone who responds generously to those in need. People often use narratives to represent themselves as generous, courageous, clever, witty or resourceful.

Children learn to tell stories from listening to people around them, and they develop different story-telling styles depending on those used in their local community. The American anthropologist Shirley Heath studied young children's language and literacy learning in two contrasting nearby communities in the Piedmont Carolinas in the United States in the 1970s. She suggests that these pre-school children learnt different 'ways with words', including different expectations about story telling. In a white working-class community of mill workers, which she calls Roadville, Heath found that adults told parable-like stories in conversations with friends and neighbours that made fun of themselves or a close friend who was present, usually pointing up some way in which they had broken a community norm, for example, how they had failed to be a 'good cook', 'good handyman' or 'good Christian'. Heath suggests that these stories test the strength of relationships, declare bonds of kinship and friendship and confirm that the teller accepts the values of the local community. In Roadville, young children were introduced to traditional fairy stories, stories from the Bible and 'true' stories or parables about children like themselves which stress a particular moral message. Fictional stories and exaggerations were seen as 'lies'. Children were not encouraged to tell their own stories, unless an adult announced that something had happened to them which made a good story and invited them to tell it. In these cases children were expected to get the facts right and were corrected if their version didn't match what the adult wanted them to tell. For instance, here is how five-year-old Wendy is probed into telling a particular story by her Aunt Sue, who has been looking after her. Wendy's mother has just arrived to pick her up from Sue's house. In her account, Wendy also refers to Aunt Sue as 'Mamma'.

Note: = indicates where one speaker follows another without any break between the utterances.

SUE:	Tell yo' mamma where we went today.
WENDY:	Mamma took me 'n Sally to the Mall. Bugs Bunny was=
SUE:	=No, who was that, that wasn't Bugs Bunny.
WENDY:	Uh, I mean, Peter, no, uh a big Easter bunny was there, 'n we, he, mamma got us some eggs=
SUE:	='n then what happened?
WENDY:	*(turning her head to one side)* I don't 'member.
SUE:	Yes, you do, what happened on the climbing=
WENDY:	=me, 'n Sally tried to climb on this thing, 'n we dropped, I dropped, my eggs, some of 'em.
SUE:	Why did you drop your eggs? What did Aunt Sue tell you 'bout climbin' on that thing?
WENDY:	We better be careful.
SUE:	No, 'bout the eggs 'n climbing?
WENDY:	We better not climb with our eggs, else 'n we'd drop 'em.

(Heath, 1983, p. 158)

While children in Roadville were taught to tell true stories 'on themselves' with particular morals, the situation was very different in a nearby black community that Heath calls 'Trackton'. Adults in Trackton (who grew up working on the land) might base their own story telling on an actual event, but they were expected to creatively fictionalize it and 'talk junk', that is, use exaggerated descriptions and comparisons. Their stories were humorous and imaginative, full of metaphors and analogies and narrators often invited the audience to join in. These stories didn't carry the direct moral messages of the Roadville stories, but focused on events and personalities, conflict and attempts at resolution. In Trackton most community life went on out of doors, on the porches and in the plaza, and children were not excluded from hearing stories about adult affairs. Young children could create and tell stories about themselves and often tried to break into adult conversation with a story, but they had to use witty and clever descriptions and analogies in order to hold the attention of their audience. Heath summarizes the very different stance in these two communities to what counts as a story: 'for Roadville, Trackton's stories would be lies; for Trackton, Roadville's stories would not even count as stories' (Heath, 1983, p. 189).

From the age of two, children in Trackton started producing their own stories about events or situations in their lives spontaneously during play, in the presence of other children or an adult. The following rhythmic 'story-poem' was produced by Lem, a two-and-a-half-year-old boy who was playing outside with his older brother and sister when he heard the church bell in the distance:

> Way
> Far
> Now
> It a church bell
> Ringin'
> Dey Singin'
> ringin'
>
> You hear it?
> I hear it
> Far
> Now

(Heath, 1983, p. 170)

Lem had been taken to his family's Pentecostal church the previous Sunday where he was very impressed by the church bell and had enthusiastically joined in the hymn-singing, rocking to and fro on his grandmother's lap and clapping his hands in time to the music. Now, as he hears the sound of a bell again, he recites this rhythmic 'story' to his brother and sister. Lem's exploitation of rhyme, rhythm and repetition in recalling a pleasurable event echoes the kind of verbal style particularly valued by conversationalists and raconteurs in Trackton. Heath points out that Lem's story contains elements of narrative structure, for example, some orientation at the beginning and a verbal outline of the sequence of the bell ringing and people singing. But she suggests that very young children's stories are often more like a musical poem, with a theme and variation structure, rather than a complication and resolution. Lem's story could be seen as a variation around the theme of the church bell, with the echoing of his beginning in the repetition of 'far, now' at the end providing a rounding off and sense of closure.

Allow about 1 hour

ACTIVITY 4   Conversational story telling

When you have the opportunity, record or note down a conversational story or anecdote told by a child, young person or adult. What kind of narrative structure can you identify? Is there an orientation, complication and resolution, or a theme with variations? Is the narrator using the story to present a particular view of themselves and, if so, how do they do this? How do the listeners react?

COMMENT

Labov (1972) suggests that stories in conversation always have what he calls an 'evaluative function', that is, they are told to make a particular point. Narrators use various devices like comparisons or stepping momentarily outside the story to make a comment to the audience, in order to get their intended point or perspective across. You may have noticed this happening in the story you recorded. Whether they are successful or not depends on the listeners' response. A 'so what?' response might indicate a badly told or inappropriate story, or a lack of shared values between the teller and the audience. Think of the possible misunderstandings if a Roadville child told a story to children in Trackton, or vice versa. Researchers have also been interested in the frequent use of creative and poetic language in stories and other aspects of ordinary conversation, suggesting that there is not such a rigid division between everyday and artistic forms of language as is sometimes assumed.

Story telling is an integral part of everyday conversation.

Duetting and mirroring

We saw in Section 2 how a choice of language or dialect may indicate a particular relationship with the listener, for instance the use of a home language to emphasize a shared ethnic identity. Patterns in the ways in which people take turns in dialogues also reflect aspects of the relationship between them. Think of the typical pattern in many school classrooms where the hierarchical relationship between teacher and students is expressed through the question and answer pattern of teacher–student dialogue. The teacher asks the questions, the student answers and the teacher evaluates the answer. Turning to a very different kind of conversation, a more equal relationship may be expressed through rather different patterns in speakers' turn-taking.

During the preparation of this book, two thirteen-year-old brothers, Yasir and Yamin, gave the following reply when asked by an interviewer whether they were looking forward to being grown up. Notice how, although they take turns, what they say could be read through as a single utterance.

YASIR: I look forwards to work

YAMIN: because the job we want to do is interesting. We want to be an astronomical

YASIR and YAMIN: engineer.

YAMIN: We'll be working in NASA

YASIR: or any other space stations. And we'd like to go to space

YAMIN: and that's a good industry.

Yasir and Yamin: twins.

'Duetting', where one speaker starts a sentence and another extends or completes it, is a turn-taking pattern often found among people who feel close to each other. Here, the boys use the connectives 'because', 'or' and 'and' to extend what the other has said. At one point they literally become a single voice. Yasir and Yamin's friendship and closeness is expressed not just through what they say, but also in the closely collaborative way they express themselves. Here's another example of duetting from an interview conducted in the preparation of this book, this time between two teenage best friends, Elizabeth and Minna who you have already met in Chapter 2:

INTERVIEWER:	Do you share the same tastes?
MINNA:	Yeah, most of the things.
ELIZABETH:	Like we have the same taste in most of the things like music, clothes,
MINNA:	ice cream, like we both like the same flavour and then we like the same sort of ornaments, clothes,
ELIZABETH:	shoes,
MINNA:	bags, everything.

Elizabeth and Minna: best friends.

Elizabeth and Minna also illustrate another common pattern in talk among friends, where one speaker mirrors another speaker's words or phrases, together with the theme of what they are saying. Notice how Elizabeth mirrors Minna's phrase 'most of the things'. Like Yasir and Yamin, Minna and Elizabeth are obviously tuned in to each other's lives and are confident in their assumptions about what they share. While language can sometimes be used to say 'We're friends, right', this sentiment can also be expressed, as in these examples, through collaborative structures like duetting and mirroring.

Context, gender and communicative competence

When children learn language, they have to learn how to use it appropriately in different contexts, according to local cultural expectations. As the American anthropologist Dell Hymes put it, communicative competence involves knowing 'when to speak, when not … what to talk about with whom, when, where, in what manner' (Hymes, 1972, p. 277).

Particular languages also encode societal norms about power structure, for instance in some languages people are addressed in the third person and children have to learn to call older people by more respectful titles. In different cultures expectations about how language should be used may differ according to the age, gender and class of the child. In the next Reading Bronwyn Davies, an Australian educationalist, argues that an intrinsic part of children's development is learning the right kind of behaviour and language use for a girl or a boy. She also suggests that in any one cultural context there are different ways of 'being a boy', or 'being a girl', depending on situation and audience.

READING

Read Reading B, an extract from Davies' chapter 'Becoming male or female'. Davies uses the term 'discourse' in a similar way to Mary Jane Kehily, cited in Chapter 2: it refers to ways of using language which encode particular assumptions, beliefs and values.

How do you respond to Davies' analysis of her encounter with the boys in the yellow raincoats? Would you agree that they were in some ways 'robbed of their personhood' when their mother was present?

COMMENT

The description of the boys' riotous transformation once they were left alone with Davies in the car and instant switch back into 'good child' mode when their mother returned demonstrates how children can appear to be quite different people in different situations, and also shows the boys' skill at adopting different behaviours. I'm not so sure, however, that I see the boys as quite so repressed in their conversations with adults as Davies does; they strike me as already very skilled at performing different ways of being (upper-class) boys to their own best advantage, including the charming way in which one of them thanks Davies for her discretion.

Davies argues that there are two different ways of being a boy: one when their mother is there and one when she's not (their apparent ignoring of Davies' own presence is intriguing). One could also imagine girls behaving riotously once their parent's back is turned, but the implications of Davies' argument is that boys and girls would do their rioting differently, and be treated differently if they were caught. Would you agree with this?

Another researcher who has looked at these issues, Valerie Walkerdine, a psychologist, is particularly interested in how women and girls are often positioned as less powerful than men and boys. She also argued that this positioning can be challenged and resisted. The following example comes from her research in a children's nursery where the children were playing doctors and nurses. The girls had all been dressed up as nurses and were urged by their teacher to 'help' the boy doctors. However, one girl, Jane, suddenly stopped being a nurse and started to make imaginary cups of tea for the patients. When Derek, who was one of the 'doctors', arrived in the Wendy House, Derek and Jane had the following exchange:

JANE: You've gotta go quickly.

DEREK: Why?

JANE: 'Cos you're going to work.

DEREK: But I'm being a doctor.

JANE: Well, you've got to go to work doctor 'cos you've got to go to hospital and so do I. You don't like cabbage do you? (he shakes his head) … well you haven't got cabbage then. I'm goin' to hospital. If you tidy up this room make sure and tell me.

(Walkerdine, 1981 p. 20)

Jane appears to switch her imaginary identity from a nurse, through a hospital tea-lady, to 'woman of the house', changing the imaginary context from a 'hospital' into a 'home'. Thus, Walkerdine argues, she manages to

Children's role play may replicate or challenge power relationships in the adult world.

convert the situation from one where she was stuck in the subservient role of a nurse at the beck and call of 'doctors' like Derek into one where the power relationship between them is reversed. By the end of this exchange she is the one giving the orders. Interestingly, Jane chose to take on another stereotypical female role in her community (housewife/ mother) rather than challenge the boys and the teacher by claiming that she too could be a doctor. As in much research on children, the interpretation of Jane's behaviour here rests partly on the assumptions of the adult researcher about what she is doing. It seems clear that Jane subverts the 'helping' she was asked to do by the teacher, but it is less clear whether she understands enough about social positioning in the adult world to be using her 'identity-hopping' in the strategic way which Walkerdine suggests.

We've seen how, as with their switching between different languages and dialects, children can be flexible in the ways they use language in different contexts and can also use language in their play to create new imaginary contexts where they can take on more powerful roles. Sometimes, however, children are faced with contexts which they find so unfamiliar or disabling that they can only participate in a minimal way, or sometimes even not at all. The quotation below describes the experience of the novelist Maxine Hong Kingston, whose parents migrated from China to San Francisco. Hong Kingston started school in San Francisco in the 1950s.

During the first silent year I spoke to no one at school, did not ask before going to the lavatory, and flunked kindergarten. My sister also said nothing for three years, silent in the playground and silent at lunch. There were other quiet Chinese girls not of our family, but most of them got over it sooner than we did. I enjoyed the silence …

It was when I found out I had to talk that school became a misery, that the silence became a misery. I did not speak and felt bad each time that I did not speak. I read aloud in first grade, though, and heard the barest whisper with little squeaks come out of my throat. 'Louder' said the teacher, who scared the voice away again. The other Chinese girls did not talk either, so I knew the silence had to do with being a Chinese girl.

(Hong Kingston, 1981, pp. 149, 150)

School is often a place where children are required to use different languages or language varieties from those they are used to at home, or to use language in new and unfamiliar ways which in some cases may conflict with what they have learnt in their own community. The children Heath studied in Trackton, for instance, like Lem, whose story was discussed earlier, did not usually have any books at home, other than the Bible, and were not read to by their parents. Their parents didn't read on their own either, but discussed letters or newspaper articles collaboratively with family and neighbours. Heath suggests that because Trackton children did not experience school-like reading practices in their own community, they had difficulties in understanding what the teacher wanted them to do in the classroom. They could not understand the point of the sorts of questions they were asked about written texts, for example, questions about the number or colour of objects. While children from Trackton had fluent oral skills and could create imaginative metaphors and analogies, they found it difficult to pick up the composition and comprehension skills needed to translate these into an acceptable channel at school. Heath sees this mismatch between home and school language practices as part of the reason why many of these children lost confidence and later switched off school altogether.

Other researchers have found that in communities where children are expected to learn at home by watching, listening and imitating, demands in the classroom to publicly answer questions and display proficiency through talk may run counter to how they believe they should behave. Although these children lack communicative competence in the classroom, however, they may be perfectly competent in other contexts.

SUMMARY OF SECTION 3

- Children, like adults, use stories and anecdotes to describe their experiences and also to present themselves as particular kinds of people.

- Children express their relationships to other people through interactional strategies in conversation such as mirroring and duetting, as well as through what they say.

- Children are socialized into specific ways of using language to express social categories such as gender. While on the one hand language pushes children towards particular positions and identities, on the other hand they may actively seek to renegotiate these positions.

- Children can adapt their language use flexibly between different contexts, but they may be faced with situations, for example at school, where they are unfamiliar with language practices and show much less communicative competence.

4 MEDIATED VOICES

In Section 3 we focused on different aspects of children's language use in face-to-face interaction and talk. Many children, however, especially in more affluent circumstances, may also communicate regularly through a variety of other media. While much of the discussion in Section 4 will apply mainly to children and young people in affluent societies, the current rapid spread of new technology such as the mobile phone and the internet suggest that more and more children in the future will be using such media.

Grafitti on a door in an alley behind a supermarket.

One of the longest established media is the written text. Many children today are surrounded by a vast array of different kinds of written texts in their environment, from advertisement hoardings, street signs and labels on food packets and medicine to newspapers, books, religious texts and the internet. From their earliest experiences of literacy, as well as being inducted into educational activities and local cultural practices, children use reading and writing for their own private purposes, for example, they may leave their mark on public places.

They also send personal messages to each other through notes, letters and, where the technology is available, e-mail and texting. Adolescents like Eva Hoffman (Reading A) may keep diaries in which they reflect on and explore their thoughts and feelings. You may remember how Hoffman's diary included a kind a dialogue between different aspects of herself. Diaries may also be addressed to an imaginary 'other'. Zlata Filpović, an eleven-year-old girl who kept a diary while she was living through the heavy shelling of Sarajevo in the 1991–93 Bosnian war, started out with brief accounts of her daily activities but soon began to address her entries to an imaginary friend called 'Mimmy'. She refers to the fact that the famous child diarist, Anne Frank (1997), called her diary 'Kitty', as a reason for deciding to adopt a similar practice herself. Zlata may have felt a particularly close link with another young girl who had experienced the privations and terror of war and recorded her intimate thoughts and feelings in writing. Zlata also seems to feel more comfortable writing in her diary once she is addressing her thoughts to someone else, even if this friend exists only in her imagination.

Zlata Filipović in the ruins of Vijenecaica Library, Sarajevo.

Zlata's diary

Sunday, 5 April 1992

Dear Mimmy,

I am trying to concentrate so that I can do my homework (reading), but I simply can't. Something is going on in town. You can hear gunfire from the hills. Columns of people are spreading out from Dobrinja. They're trying to stop something, but they themselves don't know what. You can simply feel that something is coming, something very bad. On TV I see people in front of the B–H parliament building. The radio keeps playing the same song 'Sarajevo, My Love'. That's all very nice, but my stomach is in knots and I can't concentrate on my homework any more.

Mimmy, I'm afraid of WAR!!

Zlata

(Filipović, 1993, pp. 29–30)

When children use writing they are engaging in a medium with a long history of different genres, associated with different social practices. Thus Zlata could link herself in to a tradition within diary writing, through her reference to Ann Frank, because she was familiar with an earlier example of the genre.

The telephone is another medium with which children in the North are often familiar from an early age.

Allow about 15 minutes

A C T I V I T Y 5   Telephone talk

In the following extract Doreen (three years, ten months), Justine (three years, four months) and Amy (two years, eight months) are playing with an old disconnected telephone in a British family day-care centre. Note down a list of the evidence in their talk which suggests that:

1   They know how a telephone works.

2   They know what it's used for.

3   They can use language appropriately for this medium.

JUSTINE: (*Speaking into the phone*) Hello

DOREEN: (*Takes phone from Justine and dials number.*) One o nine nine three. Hi. (*To Justine*) I'm ringing my mummy up.

JUSTINE: (*Takes phone back*) Hello

DOREEN:	(*Speaks into phone pretending to be day-care transport.*) I pick Luke up 9.30 this morning. Thank you.
JUSTINE:	(*Talking to Doreen*) It was only transport.
DOREEN:	(*Pretends to answer the phone.*) Hello, hello. (*To Justine*) It's Nicola's mum Hello. Yeah, yeah. Bye. (*Talks into 'phone then dials a number.*) Eight, eight, nine, two. I've only got the answer machine.
JUSTINE:	I ring eight, eight, nine, seven, four, six, three.
DOREEN:	Are you a good girl, Amy? (*Picks up the receiver and holds it for Amy.*) Come on, Amy, say hello.
AMY:	(*Speaks into the phone.*) Hello, hello. Is Kevin coming later?
JUSTINE:	(*Takes over the phone.*) Hello, yes.
DOREEN:	No, Justine off. Have a quick word. Say bye, quick.
JUSTINE:	Hello Natalie, going to jump. (*Jumps over the telephone wire and runs out of the room.*)

(Adapted from Kennedy, 2000, p. 92–3)

COMMENT

The girls' pretend dialogue on the telephone suggests that they know it can be used to speak to absent family and friends, and to make and check social arrangements. They can simulate brief imaginary conversations and know about dialling numbers, answerphones and the kinds of people who might be on the other end of the line. Because the other person is not present and there are no visual cues, verbal openings and closings are particularly important on the telephone, a point Doreen seems to have grasped in her minimalistic representation of a conversation: 'Hello. Yeah, yeah. Bye'. Children appropriate words and expressions from their immediate social environment and phrases like 'It was only transport', 'Are you a good girl Amy?' and 'Have a quick word' may have been imitated from the overheard conversations of parents and day-care staff.

From an early age, many children are familiar with different communication media.

Doreen and Justine play with the telephone using approximations of the language routines which they have observed are connected with its use. This kind of role play, when children pretend to be somebody else, including talking like somebody else, is an important part of their social and personal development because they are beginning to try out the roles and perspectives of other significant people in their social environment like parents and day-care centre staff. The children here can also respond imaginatively to each others' pretended identities. Notice how Justine acknowledges Doreen's role as the transport organizer ('It was only transport'), and how Amy responds to Doreen's request, in role, to 'Say hello'.

4.1 Mobile phones

In addition to the long established modes of communication, children and young people with access to new technology are increasingly using new ways of communicating with adults and with each other. In some cases children are far quicker than adults in taking up and adapting technology for their own purposes, and are in the vanguard of the development of new social practices around its use.

At the end of the twentieth century there was a rapid and momentous increase in the number of mobile phone users, especially among children and young people in industrialized parts of the world like Europe and Japan. From the young people's perspective, their mobile phone provided a new flexibility, privacy and independence in personal communication and social arrangements. They could contact each other directly, without having to go through a parental intermediary, at any time of the day or night (although mobile phones were quickly banned from many classrooms!). The next Reading discusses the findings of research at the beginning of the twenty-first century into the use of mobile phones by teenagers living in a range of contrasting localities in Britain and Northern Ireland. The researchers were interested both in what the mobile phone meant to young people as a consumer object, and also how it fitted into, or changed, their social activities and relationships as they negotiated the transition into adulthood.

> ### READING
>
> Read Reading C, 'In touch: young people and the mobile phone' by Sheila Henderson *et al*.
>
> What differences did the researchers find between the way mobile phones were used in different localities? What gender differences did they find?

In this reading the researchers describe how young people's use of mobile phones in Britain and Northern Ireland is one element in the current transformation of 'public' and 'private' areas of their lives. Young people conduct their social life from the bedroom via the mobile and the internet, and, conversely, parents can speak to their children directly via the mobile in arenas of their lives which were previously parent-free. The ways in which the mobiles are used, however, depends on existing patterns of social life and communication in the young people's neighbourhood. The researchers contrast the use of mobile phones by young school leavers in a number of commuter villages with their use by young people in more socially deprived Northern Irish and English towns. They found that young people from the commuter villages used mobiles to keep in touch and organize social activities with their old school friendship network. In contrast, the social life of the young people in the towns was organized face to face in more physically bounded communities, and mobile phones were initially treated as fashion accessories and status symbols.

The researchers emphasize that there were significant gender differences, not so much in who owned phones and how they were used, but in the meanings that young people attached to this use. The traditional association of the bedroom with girls' rather than boys' social life may be breaking down, but the researchers found that ownership of a mobile phone is particularly important for young people who feel in some way trapped in their homes, and they give examples of young women whose phones gave them the freedom to join in friends' social activities at a distance and, in one case, to pursue a relationship with a boyfriend, which they could not otherwise have done. In general the researchers found that young women tended to see the mobile phone as potentially liberating, giving them more access to the public sphere, while young men were more likely than the women to mention the constraining affect of constantly being available to others.

4.2 Texting

In Reading C Henderson *et al.* refer to an additional form of communication provided by mobile phones, text messaging or texting, where the sender keys a short message into a touch pad on their phone and transmits it to another mobile phone user.

Managing social networks.

Allow about 15 minutes

A C T I V I T Y 6 Texting

Below are three messages that were exchanged between two seventeen-year-old friends, Helen and Natalie, in the north of England in 2000, when texting was just becoming popular in the UK. In what ways have the girls adapted language to fit the medium? What functions do you think this form of communication is having, over and above conveying information and making arrangements?

NATALIE TO HELEN: Did he say owt to U? Just do wot Freddie says B silent be still. Don't feel down 2nite. Im sendin u a Nat hug from aydok. Luv u! Brie!

HELEN TO NATALIE: Fanx Nat ur a gr8 m8. talk to me anytime too. Speak to you 2mrw. Say hi to Al 4 me R U both comin out on Friday?

NATALIE TO HELEN: Did Nic say you weren't the only one with problems? Thats a bit harsh coming from a mate. We'l make a pact we can cry c moan 2 each other bout boys any time. Ok!

(Long, 2000, Appendix B, p. 2)

COMMENT

Natalie and Helen include abbreviations commonly used in text messaging in 2000 (and often recommended in telephone instruction booklets at that time), for example, 'ur' for 'you are', 'B4' for 'before' and 'gr8' for 'great'. They also incorporate spoken slang or dialect: 'mate' for 'friend' and the northern English dialect word 'owt' for 'anything'. 'Aydok' is an adapted spelling of where they live, which reflects the local pronunciation. In addition, words can be used that have a private meaning for the girls, for example, 'brie', which the girls said was their code for 'smile' as in smile = Cheshire cat = Cheshire cheese = French cheese = brie). Despite this style of 'writing', which some British commentators fear will lead to a degeneration of the language (e.g., Henry, 2000), the fact that Natalie and Helen were both successful students expecting to go on to university suggests that they were quite capable of using more standard formal written English in other contexts.

These text messages seem to be very much about feelings and emotions, both in connection with the girls' relationships with boys and between the girls themselves. Natalie gives Helen reassuring advice and sends love and a hug and tells her in the final message that they can cry and moan together about boys any time. The messages also contribute to a shared checking out and sanctioning of appropriate strategies and behaviour ('B silent be still', 'That's a bit harsh coming from a mate'). I would suggest that the code-like nature of the language, with its creative uses of spelling and private words, reinforces feelings of group solidarity and the girls' creation of a private, supportive social network.

Answering a text message from a friend.

Messaging seems to be functioning in the example above as anthropologists suggest gossip does in small communities, to regulate behaviour and values through support, advice and discussions of other people's actions and activities. Remember also Heath's point in Section 3 about the function of conversational stories in Roadville. This regulatory aspect of young people's private written communications with each other has been explored by Valerie Hey (1997) in her ethnographic study of teenage girls' friendships in two secondary schools in London. You have already read about this study in Chapter 2, Section 4.1. It is especially relevant here because of what it says about the ways the young people communicate. Chat between students was forbidden in their classroom, but they still managed to maintain some informal communication through the surreptitious passing of notes. The notes were described by teachers as 'garbage' and by the girls themselves as 'silliness'. Hey argues, however, that these notes were key sites for negotiating intimacy, secrecy and struggle and were enormously important in transmitting the cultural values of friendship. A note was passed to the recipient who wrote an answer underneath which was then passed back and so on, so that the chain of messages ended up looking something like the following (between younger teenagers). This note involved four 'turns':

> Bernice if you must know I don't like you. And I know what you are going to do tomorrow tell your sis.

> No, I'm not going to tell my sis of you. Marcia's started again (not really). Bernice.

> Oh Yeh I bet you are. If you feel like being moody go ahead.

> I like you, you are being childish.

> (Hey, 1997, p. 1)

Another example of such exchanges is given in Chapter 2, page 77. These notes very often centred around gender issues, but the girls sometimes added in a racist dimension to insult girls thought to associate with boys outside their own racial group. Hey suggests that the notes reveal the pressure on the white girls in her study to position themselves as white, non-boffin (not over-studious) and not slaggy, and encouraged them to evaluate themselves in terms of their 'racialized heterosexuality'. Do you remember any note-passing from your own school days? If so, would you agree with Hey that they play an important part in transmitting cultural values?

4.3 Chat on the web

Positioning and identity have been key themes in the analysis of young people's use of the internet. Since the early 1990s young people with access to a computer have been using the internet to join in on-line chat with friends and others, to send and receive messages by e-mail, and to create personal home pages to present themselves and their interests to a virtual world. In the early days the medium was particularly popular with boys, who often started playing collaborative simulation games in Multi User Domains (MUDs) and then moved on to visiting chat rooms. Inran Choi (2002), who researched Korean teenagers' personal uses of literacy at the turn of the twenty-first century, found that these teenagers widened their social circle by creating personal home pages, with a guest book where visitors could post messages, on their school web sites. Most Koreans attend single-sex senior high schools, and visiting personal pages on the web sites of schools for students of the opposite sex was a popular pastime. Young Koreans also registered to join in on-line chat rooms, choosing between rooms organized by age group, theme (for instance music, film, TV) and geographical region. They adopted an 'ID' to use in on-line chat, and many said they enjoyed the anonymity this conferred. Sometimes a friend's ID was used, with or without their permission, so that on-line identities could be assumed and manipulated. Young people used chat rooms to exchange views and opinions, or simply to joke and mess about. Others wanted to establish contact with others of the opposite sex, and would sometimes then arrange a meeting in real life (known as 'lightning', to reflect its speed and unpredictability).

An 'ID' is an assumed name used for meeting and talking to people on-line.

When Choi watched teenagers using a chat room, she found it impossible to follow the language on the screen. Sentences were stripped down, words contracted and acronyms and emoticons frequently inserted. Choi found that the teenagers were creating a new form of the language, different from either speech or writing. The following are some of the emoticons used by Korean teenagers in computer mediated communication.

Emoticons used by Korean teenagers

^ _ ^	smile
^O^	laughter
*^_^*	blush
-_-;;;	embarrassment

(Source: Choi, 2002, pp. 182–3)

4.4 Home pages

While some teenagers use the anonymity of chat room personae to assume fictitious identities, research suggests that young people's personal home pages provide a more direct and serious expression of their feelings about who they are.

Allow about 15 minutes

ACTIVITY 7   **Personal home pages**

Below are a number of comments by teenagers. Quotations 1–2 come from interviews about their home pages and extracts 3–5 are from the home pages themselves.

What does creating a home page on the web offer these young people which more traditional forms of communication may not?

Comments about personal home pages

1   You can … tell a lot about us from our links page … we only put links to pages that we like and we use. [*Two seventeen-year-old females who share a home page*]

2   People should be able to know what other people think about life.
    Also because the Internet is vast and I would like to be part of it.
    [*Thirteen-year-old male*]

(Chandler and Roberts-Young, 1998, p. 8 and 15)

Extracts from home pages

3   If any of you have any ideas for a theme to my page, then send 'em
    in Matee'o's and if ya' 'ave any pics ta go wiv'em, den by all means
    giv 'em 'ere! DUDE!

    What I meant was, if you can think of a good theme for me to base
    my page on, then I would be grateful for them. [*Fourteen-year-old
    male*]

4   I once was isolated and lonely, and the 'net really helped give me
    solace and find some value in a world that sometimes seems
    tempestuous. The advent of homepages gives me an outlet to
    distribute my thoughts, ideas, and feelings – something so many
    people on here gave me so much of. Don't begin to think that I
    believe the net is a supplement for real human interaction. I think
    it's a complement that can sometimes be a little detrimental.
    Computers are great when you're just beginning to see light and
    building the confidence to come out of your shell. But one
    shouldn't stagnate in the web – it's not some opiate form of human
    interaction. Computer interaction is so paradoxical – you feel so
    close yet so far. When one begins to embrace fonts a little too much,
    it's time to return to reality. [*Seventeen-year-old male*]

5   Each day of my life has become an inner fight for me, but it is a fight
    that I will not quit fighting until I win. It is a fight with no way out
    but winning. I fight against an inner fear, afraid of comments people
    might make, afraid of discrimination or worse because of who I am.
    This fear is so strong that it sometimes consumes all of what I feel.
    Yet this is precisely why I must keep fighting.

    I am bisexual; I am very sure of myself and comfortable with my
    own identity. But still I fear, every time I come out farther, every
    time I say something more, will this be my last chance? Will my
    world fall apart because of the hatred someone else carries? And so I
    keep talking, I keep coming out, and I keep fearing what might
    happen. But each time I come a out a little farther, I feel an inner
    success. I have won at least one more battle, and actually I have
    won two: one outward battle against homophobia and one inward
    battle against the separation I feel from the world. [*Eighteen-year-
    old female*]

(Abbott 1998, pp. 94, 95 and 102)

COMMENT

One immediately exciting aspect of publishing on the web is the possibility
of communicating with a far larger audience than most of us could ever
reach in ordinary print (the counters on some pages register many
thousands of visitors). To have a home page is to be part of a vast, anarchic
universe, and to make contact with other fellow travellers (quotes 2 and 4).

Chandler and Roberts-Young (1998) suggest that, like mobile phones, the web is changing the relations between the private and the public: authors may include intimate diaries and journals on publicly accessible web pages, and they appropriate icons and other material from the public internet domain to use for their own private purposes. The 'bricolage' of a teenager's web page, with its extracts of journals, music, favourite jokes, publicity images of sportsmen and musicians, and photographs is not dissimilar to the bricolage in some teenagers' bedrooms but, unlike the bedroom, it is accessible to an audience across the world.

A home page is far more interactive than a real world text. Home pages often invite visitors to contact the author through e-mail or on-line chat. They may list links to other sites of particular significance to the author (quote 1) and they often invite comments, reactions and advice from 'visitors', which may result in a radical refashioning of the page (quote 3). Personal home pages can also provide a virtual space for young people to explore quite intimate thoughts and feelings, which they may not yet feel confident enough to express in either speech or writing in the real world (quote 5).

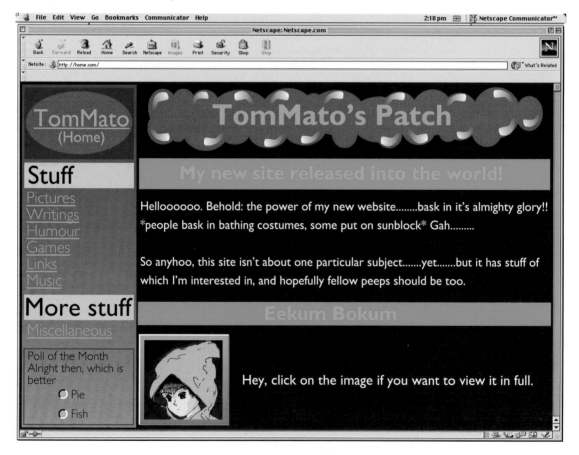

A thirteen-year-old boy's home page.

It has been pointed out that what are often taken to be key aspects of identity in the real world – age, race, class and gender – are not necessarily visible on the net, thus freeing individuals from the usual baggage of social expectations. It has, however, also been argued by some critics that identity on the web is rather too much tied up with consumer taste and technical wizardry.

One of the most distinctive features about home pages is the frequency with which their authors update them. This means that teenagers can constantly confront the images of themselves that they presented the previous week or month so that they become more conscious of ways in which they are changing. The identities presented by young people on their home pages are not frozen in time as in the printed word, or constrained by shared histories and everyday contexts as in communications with family and friends. The shifting, changeable virtual selves which are expressed seem particularly well suited to teenagers' explorations and experimentations with appearance, taste and values (Abbott, 1998; Chandler and Roberts-Young, 1998).

Anime: Japanese style of animation for film and television, often on science fiction/fantasy themes.

As well as reflecting changing aspects of the self on a home page, it is also possible to use the internet to make personal changes which may then feed back into the real world. Wan Shun Eva Lam (2000) has documented the case of Almon, a sixteen-year-old immigrant from Hong Kong living in California who was very worried about his future life and career because of his lack of progress in English. All his friends were Chinese speakers and he told Lam 'It's like this place isn't my world, I don't belong here' (p. 467). When Lam met Almon a year later, however, he told her that he felt much more positive about his situation as the result of learning about the internet and corresponding with a number of on-line chat mates and e-mail pen-pals. He also reported a considerable improvement in his command of English. Almon had used an international server, 'Geocities', to construct his personal home page. This server allows users to choose an imaginary geographical area to connect their page to, for example, 'Paris is the neighbourhood of romance, poetry and the arts' or 'Wellesley: a community of women' (p. 469). Almon chose 'Tokyo: Anime and all things Asian' (p. 469), and designed his page to feature information about a young Japanese popular singer, Ryoko Hirosue, in order to entice other surfers who shared his interest in Japanese pop culture to visit his page. Almon used information and images from magazines and other web sites on J-pop music to construct his page, which included an invitation for 'visitors' to contact him via e-mail or on-line chat. In this way, and through exploring other sites in 'Tokyo', Almon was able to make contact with other Asian youths in different parts of the world.

An alternative world.

Lam points out that in contrast to other parts of Almon's everyday life, where his limited use of English marginalized and stigmatized him, on the web he was able to present himself as an expert in the J-pop world and to use English in establishing correspondences with supportive and helpful new friends. While there already seemed to be a payoff in the real world in his improvements in English, Almon was struggling to reconcile his rather different sense of his own identity in the virtual and the real worlds. Here is a quotation from a conversation with one of his e-mail pen-pals:

> I believe most people has two different 'I', one in the realistic world, one is in the imaginational world. There is no definition to define which 'I' is the original 'I', though they might have difference. Because they both are connect together. The reality 'I' is develop by the environment changing. The imaginative 'I' is develop by the heart growing. But, sometimes they will influence each other. For example me, 'I' am very silent, shy, straight, dummy, serious, outdate, etc. in the realistic world. But, 'I' in the imaginational world is talkative, playful, prankish, naughty, open, sentimental, clever, sometimes easy to get angry etc. … I don't like the 'I' of reality. I'm trying to change myself.
>
> But, I think you usually would see 'I' in imaginational world because I'm very open to writing email to people. ^-^ How about you?? Do you have two different 'I'?? hee, hee.

(Lam, 2000, p. 474–5)

SUMMARY OF SECTION 4

- In using media like writing and the telephone for their own purposes, children and young people draw on the established social practices and traditions which are connected with them. These are reflected in young children's play.

- Some children and young people also have an increasing range of new media to use in communicating with each other and in expressing and exploring their own changing identities. Children and young people are actively involved in the development of new social practices around technology such as mobile phones and the incorporation of this technology into their existing social practices.

- Young people's use of secret notes in class and text messaging shows how these function to negotiate and confirm social values.

- The internet is used by some young people to reflect on their experience, to step outside inhibiting factors in their lives and to create social networks, locally and across national boundaries, with new possibilities for the development or recreation of the self.

5 CONCLUSION

Throughout this chapter we've moved back and forth between looking on the one hand at how language shapes children and young people's knowledge, interactions and sense of self and on the other hand at how they very actively use language as a resource to get things done, pursue relationships and negotiate identity. Children learn local languages and dialects. They also learn local ways of using language, for instance how to tell stories, and discourses which encode particular beliefs and values. Children and young people have access to various kinds of literary genres and communication technology with associated language forms and routines. The language practices and texts in a child's environment, therefore, provide culturally-shaped resources for meaning-making. Language, however, is also used on a practical level as a tool by children and young people to build relationships with people around them, to gain social control, to negotiate friendship and to pursue individual goals and purposes. Finally, language also enables reflection on personal experience, for example, within conversational narrative or diaries or journals, or through e-mail correspondences and personal home pages on the internet. Becoming a member of a particular society, developing personal relationships and negotiating individual identity are all closely intertwined.

Language provides a web of meaning within which children are positioned and defined, but it is also the most important tool children have to create a distinctive cultural world, and a sense of their own place and identity within it. One of the most complex and fascinating aspects of language is how it mediates the transformation of the individual into the social, and at the same time provides a tool through which the individual can act on and change the nature of both their social environment and themselves.

REFERENCES

ABBOTT, C. (1998) 'Making connections: young people and the internet' in SEFTON-GREEN, J. (ed.) *Digital Diversions: youth culture in the age of multimedia*, London, UCL Press.

CHANDLER, D. and ROBERTS-YOUNG, D. (1998) 'The construction of identity in the personal homepages of adolescents' (www document) URL: http://www.aber.ac.uk/media/Documents/short/webident.html (accessed December 2002)

CHOI, I. (2002) 'Their own voices: vernacular literacies in the lives of young people', unpublished PhD thesis, Lancaster University.

ECKERT, P. (2000) *Language Variation as Social Practice*, Oxford, Blackwell.

FILIPOVIĆ, Z. (1993) *Zlata's Diary: a child's life in Sarajevo*, London, Viking.

FRANK, A. (1997) *The Diary of a Young Girl*, the definitive edition edited by FRANK, O. H. and PRESSLER, M., London, Penguin.

HEATH, S. B. (1983) *Ways with Words*, Cambridge, Cambridge University Press.

HENRY, J. (2000) 'Email style is :-) for writing', *Times Educational Supplement,* 1 September 2000.

HEWITT, R. (1986) *White Talk Black Talk: inter-racial friendship and communication amongst adolescents,* Cambridge, Cambridge University Press.

HEY, V. (1997) *The Company She Keeps: an ethnography of girls' friendship,* Buckingham, Open University Press.

HONG KINGSTON, M. (1981) *The Woman Warrior: memoirs of a childhood among ghosts,* London, Picador.

HYMES, D. (1972) 'On communicative competence' in PRIDE, J. and HOLMES, J. (eds) *Sociolinguistics,* Harmondsworth, Penguin.

KENNEDY, P. (2000) 'Freedom for speech: outdoor play and its potential for young children's conceptual, linguistic and communicative development', unpublished EdD dissertation, The Open University.

LABOV, W. (1972) *Language in the Inner City,* Philadelphia, University of Philadelphia Press.

LAM, W. S. E. (2000) *'L2 literacy and the design of the self: a case study of a teenager writing on the internet',* TESOL Quarterly, **34**(3), pp. 457– 82.

LONG, T. (2000) 'An explanation of the social practices and linguistic structures which characterise text messaging by a select group of adolescents', unpublished research assignment for The Open University MA module E825 *Language and Literacy in Social Context.*

MILLER, J. (1996) 'A tongue, for sighing' in MAYBIN, J. and MERCER, N. (eds) *Using English: from conversation to canon,* London, Routledge.

THE OPEN UNIVERSITY (2003a) U212 *Childhood,* Audio 5, Band 3, 'Code switching', Milton Keynes, The Open University.

THE OPEN UNIVERSITY (2003b) U212 *Childhood,* Video 3, Band 4, 'Friendship', Milton Keynes, The Open University.

WALKERDINE, V. (1981) 'Sex, power and pedagogy', *Screen Education,* 38, pp.14–24.

Lost in translation

Eva Hoffman

A life in a new language

The car is full of my new friends, or at least the crowd that has more or less accepted me as one of their own, the odd 'greener' tag-along. They're as lively as a group of puppies, jostling each other with sharp elbows, crawling over each other to change seats, and expressing their well-being and amiability by trying to outshout each other. It's Saturday night, or rather Saturday Night, and party spirits are obligatory. We're on our way to the local White Spot, an early Canadian version of McDonald's, where we'll engage in the barbarous – as far as I'm concerned – rite of the 'drive-in'. This activity of sitting in your car in a large parking lot, and having sloppy, big hamburgers brought to you on a tray, accompanied by greasy french fries bounding out of their cardboard containers, mustard, spilly catsup, and sickly smelling relish, seems to fill these peers of mine with warm, monkeyish, groupy comfort. It fills me with a finicky distaste. I feel my lips tighten into an unaccustomed thinness – which, in turn, fills me with a small dislike for myself.

'Come on, foreign student, cheer up,' one of the boys sporting a flowery Hawaiian shirt and a crew cut tells me, poking me in the ribs good-naturedly. 'What's the matter, don't you like it here?' So as the car caroms off, I try to get in the mood. I try to giggle coyly as the girls exchange insinuating glances – though usually my titter comes a telling second too late. I try to join in the general hilarity, as somebody tells the latest elephant joke. Then – it's always a mistake to try too hard – I decide to show my goodwill by telling a joke myself. Finding some interruption in which to insert my uncertain voice, I launch into a translation of some slightly off-color anecdote I'd heard my father tell in Polish, no doubt hoping to get points for being risqué as well as a good sport. But as I hear my choked-up voice straining to assert itself, as I hear myself missing every beat and rhythm that would say 'funny' and 'punch line,' I feel a hot flush of embarrassment. I come to a lame ending. There's a silence. 'I suppose that's supposed to be funny,' somebody says. I recede into the car seat.

[…]

I've never been prim before, but that's how I am seen by my new peers. I don't try to tell jokes too often, I don't know the slang, I have no cool repartee. I love language too much to maul its beats, and my pride is too quick to risk the incomprehension that greets such forays. I become a very serious young person, missing the registers of wit and irony in my speech, though my mind sees ironies everywhere.

Perhaps the extra knot that strangles my voice is rage. I am enraged at the false persona I'm being stuffed into, as into some clumsy and overblown astronaut suit. I'm enraged at my adolescent friends because they can't see through the guise, can't recognize the light-footed dancer I really am. They only see this elephantine creature who too often sounds as if she's making pronouncements.

[...]

If you had stayed there [Poland], your hair would have been straight, and you would have worn a barrette on one side.

But maybe by now you would have grown it into a ponytail? Like the ones you saw on those sexy faces in the magazine you used to read?

I don't know. You would have been fifteen by now. Different from thirteen.

You would be going to the movies with Zbyszek, and maybe to a café after, where you would meet a group of friends and talk late into the night.

But maybe you would be having problems with Mother and Father. They wouldn't like your staying out late.

That would have been fun. Normal. Oh God, to be a young person trying to get away from her parents.

But you can't do that. You have to take care of them. Besides, with whom would you go out here? One of these churlish boys who play spin the bottle? You've become more serious than you used to be.

What jokes are your friends in Cracow exchanging? I can't imagine. What's Basia doing? Maybe she's beginning to act. Doing exactly what she wanted. She must be having fun.

But you might have become more serious even there.

Possible.

But you would have been different, very different.

No question.

And you prefer her, the Cracow Eva.

Yes, I prefer her. But I can't be her. I'm losing track of her. In a few years, I'll have no idea what her hairdo would have been like.

But she's more real, anyway.

Yes, she's the real one.

For my birthday, Penny gives me a diary, complete with a little lock and key to keep what I write from the eyes of all intruders. It is that little lock – the visible symbol of the privacy in which the diary is meant to exist – that creates my dilemma. If I am indeed to write something entirely for myself, in what language do I write? Several times, I open the diary and close it again. I can't decide. Writing in Polish at this point would be a little like resorting to Latin or ancient Greek – an eccentric thing to do in a diary, in which you're supposed to set down your most immediate experiences and unpremeditated thoughts in the most unmediated language. Polish is becoming a dead language, the language of the untranslatable past. But writing for nobody's eyes in English? That's like doing a school exercise, or performing in front of yourself, a slightly perverse act of self-voyeurism.

Because I have to choose something, I finally choose English. If I'm to write about the present, I have to write in the language of the present, even if it's not the language of the self. As a result, the diary becomes surely one of the more impersonal exercises of that sort produced by an adolescent girl. These are no sentimental effusions of rejected love, eruptions of familial anger, or consoling broodings about death. English is not the language of such emotions. Instead, I set down my reflections on the ugliness of wrestling; on the elegance of Mozart, and on how Dostoyevsky puts me in mind of El Greco. I write down Thoughts. I Write.

There is a certain pathos to this naïve snobbery, for the diary is an earnest attempt to create a part of my persona that I imagine I would have grown into in Polish. In the solitude of this most private act, I write in my public language, in order to update what might have been my other self. The diary is about me and not about me at all. But on one level, it allows me to make the first jump. I learn English through writing, and, in turn, writing gives me a written self. Refracted through the double distance of English and writing, this self – my English self – becomes oddly objective; more than anything, it perceives. It exists more easily in the abstract sphere of thoughts and observations than in the world. For a while, this impersonal self, this cultural negative capability, becomes the truest thing about me. When I write, I have a real existence that is proper to the activity of writing – an existence that takes place midway between me and the sphere of artifice, art, pure language. This language is beginning to invent another me. However, I discover something odd. It seems that when I write (or, for that matter, think) in English, I am unable to use the word 'I'. I do not go as far as the schizophrenic 'she' – but I am driven, as by a compulsion, to the double, the Siamese-twin 'you'.

Source

HOFFMAN, E. (1991) *Lost in Translation: life in a new language*, London, Minerva, pp. 117–21.

READING B

Becoming male or female

Bronwyn Davies

In order to become recognizable and acceptable members of the society they are born into, children must learn to think with and act in terms of the accepted, known linguistic forms. This is not just a skill they must acquire in order to communicate, but an acquisition of the means by which they constitute themselves as persons in relation to others in the social world. In learning the language they learn to constitute themselves and others as unitary beings, as capable of coherent thought, as gendered, and as one who is in particular kinds of relation to others. Language is both a resource and a constraint. It makes social and personal being possible but it also limits the available forms of being to those which make sense within the terms provided by the language …

Adults require children to adopt their linguistic practices, not just for the child's own benefit but as a way of confirming the rightness of the world as they understand it. Until children have accepted the terms of reference embedded in the language, they are potentially a disruptive force, undermining 'what adults claim is "obvious" and "known" to "everybody" ' (Waksler, 1986, p. 74).

Part of what is 'obvious and known to everybody' is that people are either male or female. In learning the discursive practices of their society children learn that they must be socially identifiable as one or the other, even though there is very little if any observable physical difference in most social situations. Dress, hairstyle, speech patterns and content, choice of activity – all become key signifiers that can be used in successfully positioning oneself as a girl or a boy.

[…]

Of course taking oneself up as a boy or a girl is not a unitary process. How one 'does' masculinity or femininity with one's parents, say, may differ profoundly from how one 'does' masculinity with one's friends, or from one friend to another. A fascinating episode that I became involved in quite by chance during the period that I was undertaking this study illustrates the coercive nature of adult discourse in relation to children. It also shows how children learn both to position themselves to advantage within that discourse and to develop quite a different discourse for use with each other in the absence of adults.

The episode took place when I accepted a lift in the car of an acquaintance who was on her way to pick her children up from an elite private boys' school. The boys, two brothers aged five and seven, and a friend aged seven, were waiting quietly with their peers and their teachers in a rain shelter at the front of the school as the mothers drove up in their Porsches and Mercedes. The scene was very orderly with each boy neatly attired in a yellow raincoat and rain hat. As each mother drove up, the required routine was that each child say 'good afternoon' to his teacher, or shake her hand, and then climb without haste into his mother's car. The boys jumped into the back seat (I was in the front) and the five-year-old announced that he hadn't said good afternoon to his teacher. His mother observed that he would be in trouble tomorrow. The children were each introduced to me. They greeted me very politely, seat belts were fastened and we drove off. The mother asked them about what had happened at school that day and managed to elicit almost no information other than whether they had played inside or outside at lunchtime. The children were nevertheless very 'well spoken' and polite. There was some friction between the parent and the youngest child when he took off his seat belt in order to remove his raincoat. She pointed out that she would, as she had on previous occasions, stop the car, even though we were on a freeway, if he did not immediately fasten his seat belt. She pointed out that this would be to the great irritation of the other drivers. He fastened his seat belt.

The day was overcast and hot, and the heater in the car was full on. The conversation turned to which games they would play when they got home and what they would have to eat. A potential conflict between whether they would play table tennis or model trains ensued. The mother announced that the youngest child, who asked for table tennis, had first choice as he had asked first. The other two quietly discussed how he was going to be able to play table tennis if they would not play with him, and the mother counteracted this by saying that she would play with him. They decided to play table tennis today and trains tomorrow. It was a long, hot drive and I was amazed at how quiet and polite the children were, especially given the discomfort they must have felt in their sweaty raincoats. I began to wonder whether these boys were in fact different from any of the other boys I had worked with, and whether this had something to do with their class membership. Eventually we stopped and the mother got out to go to the bank, leaving me and the boys in the car. They immediately adopted a totally different way of behaving, and I, as stranger, was totally ignored. They pressed all the buttons in the car, they romped, they threw their raincoats off, and then they started a wild game which involved grabbing each other's genitals. There was a noisy mixture of pleasurable squeals of laughter and screams of pain. They jockeyed for power, for control, for an ally, not to be one against two and not to be hurt too much. It was wild and exciting and painful. After ten minutes or so of this riotous and noisy behaviour I spotted the mother coming back and told them so. They settled down rapidly. When she got into the car she asked me had they been behaving themselves. There was a tense pause and then I said, 'They were delightful'. One of the boys said 'thank you' with obvious relief in his voice, charming and polite, entirely relocated as child in the particular form of adult–child discourse that he clearly knew well.

There was a little bit of wriggling in the back as we took off, and the youngest child whinged in a pathetic voice to his mother that one of the others was pushing him. Power now resided not in who was smartest at grabbing whose genitals and in protecting his own, but on who could get his mother on side, and off side with the other two. The transformation was profound and dramatic and the boys were completely in command of it, producing the small, sweet, powerless child required by their mother. Although the switch was almost automatic, it felt to me like an uncomfortable, somehow 'unreal' switch, not because of some lingering humanist presumptions about the unitary nature of the person, but because the extent to which they were so visibly 'under control', 'behaving themselves' seemed to rob them in some sense of their personhood. My sympathy with their 'wild' state, despite the fact that it had been excruciatingly noisy, probably had a lot to do with the similarities between adult–child and male–female relations. Children are defined as *other* to adults in much the same way that women are other to men. Children have to learn to be both outside adult discourse and to participate with adults both in terms of adult's concepts of children and of adult–child relations (Davies, 1982).

Much of the adult world is not consciously taught to children, is not contained in the *content* of their talk, but is embedded in the language, in the discursive practices and the social and narrative structures through which the child is constituted as a person, as a child and as male or female … [W]hat children learn through the process of interacting in the everyday world is not a unitary, non-contradictory language and practice – and it is not a unitary identity that is created through those practices, as the example of the boys in the yellow raincoats makes clear. Rather, children learn to see and understand in terms of the multiple positionings and forms of discourse that are available to them. More, they learn the forms of desire and of power and powerlessness that are embedded in and made possible by the various discursive practices through which they position themselves and are positioned.

References

DAVIES, B. (1982) *Life in the Classroom and Playground: the accounts of primary school children,* London, Routledge and Kegan Paul.

WAKSLER, F. (1986), 'Studying children: phenomenological insights', *Human Studies,* 9.

Source

DAVIES, B. (1989) *Frogs and Snails and Feminist Tales,* London, Allen and Unwin.

READING C

In touch: young people and the mobile phone

Sheila Henderson, Rebecca Taylor and Rachel Thomson

> It seems the chirp of mobile phones is set to drown out the whirl of yo-yos and the scraping of knees in the schoolyards of the 21st Century. (BBC News, 2000)

Keeping in touch with friends and family is an important part of contemporary young people's lives. Traditionally, moving from the private world of childhood into the public world of adulthood was seen as a critical transition in young people's lives (Fornas and Bolin, 1995; Thompson, 1990; Habermas, 1989). Adult status was defined by entry into public institutions and roles – such as worker, parent and citizen. However, with the extension and fragmentation of the different strands of the transition there is no longer a clear sense of movement from the private to the public in the process of becoming an adult (Jones and Bell, 2000). Commentators are increasingly pointing to a realignment in the relationship between the individual and the social that transforms the *meaning* of the public/private divide (Fahey, 1995).

Information and communication technologies, such as the mobile phone, have increasingly been recognized as an important medium for the management of social networks with family and friends and for the reworking of public and private boundaries (Silverstone *et al.*, 1992). Bedrooms can no longer be understood as the epitome of the private, being wired to global networks (Reimer, 1995) and transformed by young people into club style 'chill out zones' (Lincoln, 2000). Technologies such as the internet, video games and mixing decks have redefined the traditionally feminine nature of bedroom culture (Henderson, 1997; MacNamee, 1998).

This reading will draw on findings from a recent longitudinal study of young people's transitions to adulthood [Economic and Social Research Council, 1999-2005] in order to explore the uses and social meaning of the mobile phone. The young people in the study were living in five contrasting locations within the UK: a leafy Home Counties commuter town that was predominantly middle class and white; a working class and ethnically diverse inner London borough; a white working-class estate in the north of England; an isolated rural village that was mixed in terms of social class and a city in Northern Ireland drawing on communities that were mixed in terms of social class and religion. We briefly examine how mobile phones are used differently according to social and geographical location, how they become integrated into different practices of social networking and how they contribute to romantic and parenting relationships. We also consider gender differences in this context.

ECONOMIC AND SOCIAL RESEARCH COUNCIL (ESRC) (1999-2005). An ESRC funded study 'Inventing adulthoods: young people's strategies for transition' (L134251008). Research commenced 1999 and is due to run until 2005.

Differences in meaning and usage of mobiles

Our first round of interviews with young people in 1999 showed that leaving school and moving into further/higher education or work was experienced as a collective transition, a 'critical moment' in the maintenance and/or transformation of their social networks. As young people became more independent and mobile, they acquired mobile phones. However, while ownership in all sites increased, their use was shaped by the local cultures.

Young people in the Home Counties town were particularly concerned to keep in touch with friends from school. Susannah told of a friend who found a job instead of going into the sixth form and now phoned her up 'every other night' in an attempt to maintain contact with his old friendship group. She explained that all of her friends were from school, 'so it's sort of from school that all your contacts come, it's quite hard to meet people otherwise'.

In this location, young people's transitions were shaped by a lifestyle where 'mobility and flexible scheduling are central' (Gillard *et al.*, 1996). For these young people who lived dotted across a landscape of commuter villages, mobile phones were a tool that transcended the boundaries of geographical distance, facilitating the 'micro organization' of social activities. Not having a mobile could mean exclusion from new forms of sociality. Stan described the chain of calls that took place in his group of friends in relation to a trip to the pub.

> Normally what'll happen is if someone's going out we'll make one phone call and someone phones someone else and by the time you get down the pub, they'll all be waiting for you.

In sharp contrast, hanging out on the street and 'popping round' were still the usual method of keeping in touch outside school for those living in physically bounded (and less affluent) communities. Ruth in Northern Ireland described a complex process of social organization involving neither phones nor mobiles. She and her friends met 'in each others' houses really … one friend goes out gets another one and then another one'. Belinda from London's inner city had a mobile, but its use was dictated by her financial situation – with little effect on her friendships. She explained 'When I've got money I ring up loads of people, but when I ain't, I just go round to their house or something'.

For young people in the Northern Irish city and the northern English estate, both communities with high levels of social deprivation and unemployment, leaving school often led to a fragmentation of friendship groups as they moved between jobs and courses at different FE colleges. Tara from Northern Ireland echoed other young people in these locations when she said of her school friends: 'I've lost all touch with them and they only live beside me'. This break-up of old networks was rarely presented as traumatic. Indeed most of them welcomed the opportunity to make more relevant friendships with people at college or work.

Mobile phones were predominantly discussed in these two sites in terms of material culture. In the north of England estate, they constituted just one more aspect of material one-upmanship – where young people were under intense pressure to blend in by wearing designer labels. Young men in this site displayed a detailed knowledge and interest in the various deals available for financing the phones as well as the latest technological and design developments. In Northern Ireland young people also talked about mobile phones as a fashion accessory. Lucy reported that, 'They're really in at the minute'. Luke admitted that he bought his to show off to his friends.

> I seen the phone for seventy pounds, pay as you talk, and I went, 'That there's good', just for show like. I walked around and showed all my friends … then we started going mad with them and then they ran out of … and there's only two of us now that don't have phones.

Mediating gendered boundaries between the public and the private

Although the ownership and use of mobile phones was not significantly gendered, we found differences in the meanings young men and women attached to them. While young women emphasized the potential freedoms provided by the telephones in the form of access to the public sphere, young men emphasized the more constraining dimensions of being available to others.

The mobile phone was of particular relevance to the young people in the study who felt 'trapped' in the domestic sphere. This was the case for Monique (aged seventeen), who was particularly small for her age and unable to join in with the social life of her peer group that centred on attending films, clubs and pubs for over-eighteens. Monique argued that her family took advantage of this, giving her responsibility for babysitting younger siblings and cousins. Her mobile telephone facilitated access into the social life of her friends in a vicarious way, keeping her in touch with what was happening elsewhere.

The mobile phone's potential for mediating the lines between the domestic sphere and a more 'public' world of teenage leisure is illustrated by the case of seventeen year old Jasmine for whom the acquisition of a phone marked a transformation of her social life. As the only daughter of a British/ Turkish family she had suffered the protective surveillance of brother, father and mother and, when we first met her aged sixteen years, was relatively restricted in her ability to socialize. Although her brother had previously taken responsibility for 'keeping an eye on her', he had bought her the mobile phone that enabled her to have a 'private life', receiving her own telephone calls from her newly acquired boyfriend – 'Well because he can't ring my house that's one of the reasons why I've got to have one'. She opted for a pay-as-you-go phone for particular reasons: 'I don't get like the bills. No numbers or anything'. In this way, Jasmine escaped the embodied surveillance of the domestic sphere and, in so doing, subverted the operation of a particular set of gendered power relations.

By the second and third round interviews (July 2000–June 2001), voicemail and text messages had become popular media for making, maintaining and breaking romantic relationships. Mal, for example, who lived in Northern Ireland, maintained a relationship by mobile phone with a young man in London. They met in a gay chatroom on the internet. Monique, when asked in the interview if she was still seeing her boyfriend, demonstrated the breakdown of the relationship by phoning him there and then saying 'watch if I don't phone him and he don't answer', 'he'll put me to voice mail'. He did. Texting also operated as an erotic practice in its own right. At her second interview, Sandy read out a 'database' of saved text exchanges with her boyfriend. An initial flurry of erotic banter had been facilitated by the free messaging that formed part of their phone 'deals'. When this ended, she explained, 'we condensed our messages down a bit. To the occasional dirty text every now and again'.

In an exploration of the 'coining of new forms of social interaction' arising from the use of mobile phones, Rich Ling observes that the telephone, like all symbolic relics, is open to multiple interpretations. 'While some see it as a way to mark their departure from the home, others use it symbolically to integrate themselves further with their parents' (2000, p. 108). Moreover, parents themselves play an active role in inventing these new forms of interaction, 'trying to reassert their control'. In our study, we found that mobile phones gave parents access to arenas of young people's lives that would formerly not have been available to them. For example, Tara described her mother calling her at her new job as a podium dancer in a local bar to make sure that she was 'there'.

Young men were particularly resistant to this kind of contact. Sixteen year old Luke explained that having a phone was 'a bit of a curse with my mother and father they can always get you wherever you are'. By the second interview, Luke had got rid of his phone, explaining that 'people can get to you too easily'. Paul had learned to screen his calls. He explained that his mother only phoned him on his mobile if he had done something wrong. So, when he saw she was calling, he simply turned his phone to voicemail, then listened to her message.

Another way in which young people used the mobile phone to bypass parental authority was in relation to reconstituted families. Monique, for example, talked about how her acquisition of a mobile facilitated contact with her father after a period of estrangement. Reluctant to come to the house as he and her mother were not on speaking terms, he was now able to ring her direct and say, 'Monique, I'm outside, come'.

Conclusions

Our study illustrates how young people realize the potential of the mobile phone in different ways: as a means of 'buying' forms of privacy and independence from parental control; of accessing social networks; and of positioning themselves within social hierarchies. Its contrasting usage in our different research sites suggests differences in the underlying patterns of sociality and particular spatial configurations of the public and private spheres. The mobile phone becomes a tool for both developing new friendships and maintaining old ones – whichever is the most appropriate within a particular pattern of sociality. Such practices are gendered in that young women appear to utilize their potential for moving beyond the domestic sphere, while for young men, they hold the danger of being constrained by it. Here it is possible to see how the tool of the mobile telephone facilitates a reworking of public and private boundaries, as the individual becomes the centre of a network of communicative practices.

References

FAHEY, T. (1995) 'Privacy and the family: conceptual and empirical reflections', *Sociology,* **29**(4), pp. 687–703.

FORNAS, J. and BOLIN, G. (eds) (1995) *Youth Culture and Late Modernity,* London, Sage.

GILLARD, P., BOW, A. and WALE, K. (1996) *Ladies and Gentlemen, Boys and Girls: gender and telecommunications services,* Melbourne, Telecommunications Needs Service.

HABERMAS, J. (1989) *The Structural Transformation of the Public Sphere: an enquiry into a category of bourgeois society,* trans. Thomas Burger, Cambridge, Polity Press.

HENDERSON, S., (1997) *Ecstasy: case solved,* London, Pandora.

JONES, G. and BELL, R. (2000) *Balancing Acts: youth, parenting and public policy,* York, York Publishing Services for the Joseph Rowntree Foundation.

LINCOLN, S. (2000) 'Teenage girls' "bedroom culture" and the concept of zoning in socio-spatial configuration', paper presented at BSA youth study group conference 'Researching youth: issues, controversies and dilemmas', 12 July 2000, University of Surrey.

LING, R. (2000) '"We will be reached": the use of mobile telephony among Norwegian youth', *Information technology and people,* **13**(2), pp. 102–20.

MacNAMEE, S. (1998) 'Youth, gender and video games: power and control in the home' in SKELTON, T. and VALENTINE, G. (eds) *Cool Places: geographies of youth culture,* London, Routledge.

REIMER, B. (1995) 'The media in public and private spheres' in FORNAS, J. and BOLIN, G. (eds) *Youth Culture in Late Modernity,* London, Sage.

SILVERSTONE, R., HIRSCH, E., MORLEY, D. (1992) 'Information technologies and the moral economy of the household' in SILVERSTONE, R., and HIRSCH, E. (eds) *Consuming Technologies: media and information in domestic spaces,* London, Routledge.

THOMPSON, J. (1990) 'The theory of the public sphere: a critical appraisal' in *Polity Reader in Cultural Theory: from ideology to modern culture,* Cambridge, Polity Press.

Source

Adapted from HENDERSON, S., TAYLOR, R. and THOMSON, R. (forthcoming) 'In touch: young people, communication and technology', *Information, Communication and Society,* **5***(3).*

Chapter 4
Children's literature

Christine Hall

CONTENTS

When you have studied this chapter, you should be able to:

1 Understand the ways in which children's literature embodies certain views about the nature of children and childhood.

2 Consider what counts as suitable literature for children, and how this has varied in different historical and cultural contexts.

3 Consider some of the purposes ascribed to literature for children, and how these too are historically and culturally variable.

4 Evaluate ideological debates about the values inherent in children's books, and the effects these have had on recent literature for children.

5 Critically evaluate the different views about children's literature discussed in this chapter.

6 Offer your own analyses of the views of childhood embedded in specific literary texts.

1 INTRODUCTION

Chapters 1 to 3 have considered how children draw on a range of cultural resources – play, friendship and language – to negotiate relationships with others and to develop their own identities as children (or certain types of children). In this chapter and the next, the emphasis shifts slightly. These chapters look at two types of cultural resource – children's literature and certain forms of media – in their own right. Literature and media are of interest partly because of the ways they represent children and childhood, and the cultural messages they make available to children who engage with them. In the case of literature, in this chapter, I shall look at the historical development of a literature aimed specifically at children – and at how what counts as suitable reading for children has varied at different points in time and in different cultural contexts. I shall look also at recent debates about the values inherent in children's books; and at children as 'active' readers who are able to bring their own interpretations to literary texts (children as readers – or viewers – are considered more fully in the next chapter).

A good way into this discussion may be to consider your own experiences of reading as a child.

Allow about 10 minutes

A C T I V I T Y 1   **Your childhood experience of books**

Think back on your own childhood experiences:

1 If you can, identify one or two books that were important to you as a child.

2 With hindsight, why do you think these particular books appealed to you?

3 Were they 'good' books? Would you recommend them to children now? Would you class them as children's literature?

COMMENT

Responses to the first and second questions will, of course, be very personal. Your favourite books will depend to some extent on your age, where you grew up, your social class, cultural background and sex. Your choice will also depend on your personality and the kind of child you were. If you weren't able to name a book that was important to you as a child, some of these same factors will no doubt have been in play. Perhaps you come from a family or culture that gave precedence to oral storytelling over reading; perhaps books weren't available to you, or perhaps you were never drawn to books as a child. For any books you identified, there may have been several things that appealed to you: certain characters or events in the story; or the look or the feel of the books – for instance the quality of the illustrations, or the feel of the paper; or the act and context of reading (e.g. cuddling up to a parent while reading a favourite book).

The third set of questions was included to help you think about issues of quality in children's literature. You might have found that books you considered good as a child don't match up to the criteria you've developed for judging children's literature as an adult. The answers you give to these questions will depend to some extent on what you think children's literature is *for*. You may think that reading is primarily about enjoyment, for instance, or you may ascribe more serious purposes to it, as in this statement by the British author Anne Fine:

> Children do want to read. The enchantment is undimmed. Characters in books still rise from the page to accompany the child through life. And 'tell me a story' is a constant plea …
>
> The child who misses the best in children's fiction is impoverished. To have no tools to reflect on your own emotional responses is to be ill-equipped for life, and set fair for recurring stupidities. Reading increases the sense of things beneath, the complex layers under the specious soap opera surface of what people do and say. Books are a spur to thought, reflection and self-knowledge – always a virtue – and the more we all read, the richer and safer is our society.
>
> Extracts from the novelist, Anne Fine's acceptance speech on becoming the second British Children's Laureate in 2001: http://www.childrenslaureate.org/afspeech.html, last accessed January 2003.

Views about the purposes of children's literature are closely bound up with our understanding of what childhood is. We know that ideas about children and childhood vary enormously from place to place and from group to group and over time. Since ideas about childhood are fundamental to both the content of children's literature and its function in society, understanding of what counts as children's literature and what it is for depend in large part upon the definition of childhood which is being employed.

The phrase 'children's literature' is often associated with writing that is deemed to be of a high quality. One of the best known historians of children's literature, John Rowe Townsend (1990), for example, distinguishes between 'children's literature' and 'children's reading matter'. He excludes from his own discussion examples of the latter such as 'popular series-books and other material of insignificant literary merit', which he equates with '[e]phemeral matter produced to catch a market' (p. xii). In this chapter, however, I adopt a broader definition of literature, which encompasses popular culture as well as high cultural or classic texts. While literature in this broader sense could include a range of print genres as well as oral literature, theatre, film, television, I shall limit myself here to printed literature, and mainly to fiction in narrative form (stories, and novels for older children and teenagers). Media forms such as children's television are considered in the next chapter.

Most of the examples I draw on are from English language texts, often, especially in the historical sections of the chapter, in British settings. I have chosen these examples because the ideas under discussion need to be understood in specific cultural and historical contexts, and because this is the tradition that I know about. But there are rich and diverse traditions of children's literature in many countries and among many different cultural and ethnic groups, and as you read the chapter you may well be able to draw upon examples from other contexts with which you are familiar.

2 A HISTORY OF CHILDREN'S BOOKS IN ENGLAND

2.1 Starting points: John Locke and John Newbery

John Rowe Townsend in *Written for Children*, a history of children's literature, writes about the 'prehistory' of children's literature in England, pointing out that it had two branches: ' … material that was intended specially for children or young people but was not story, and the material that was story but was not specially used for children' (1990, p. 4). Townsend is identifying a time when in England it was not considered necessary to create stories specifically for children. There was no shortage of *stories* (lots of them, such as those about Robin Hood, the outlaw hero, are still around today). These stories would almost always have been told orally and adapted to the audience in the way that oral stories can be. But the view of childhood operating in English society did not lead people to think that children should be regarded as a separate audience and offered different stories. This is a view that has been and still is held by many people around the world.

There was, however, plenty of *instruction* for children, often written in rhyming verse to make it easier to remember. These lessons were often recorded in 'courtesy books', which were popular in the fifteenth century. They reveal that fifteenth century parents' worries about their children were not altogether different from those of twenty-first century parents.

Child, climb not over house or wall
For no fruit nor birds nor ball.
Child, over men's houses no stones fling
Nor at glass windows no stones sling,
Nor make no crying, jokes nor plays
In holy Church on holy days … .
Child, keep thy book, cap and gloves
And all things that thee behoves,
And but thou do, thou shalt fare worse
And thereto be beat on the bare erse.

(From *The Babees' Book*, a fifteenth-century courtesy book reproduced by F. J. Furnivall in 1868. Text modernized by John Rowe Townsend, 1990, p. 4)

Historical changes in conceptions of childhood are considered in an earlier book in this series (Woodhead and Montgomery, 2003).

The general view at that time, influenced by the teachings of the Church, was that children were naturally sinful and in need of correction. Some commentators felt that exposure to stories would exacerbate innate tendencies towards wrongdoing. Hugh Rhodes, in his 1545 *Book of Nurture*, an early guide to childcare, encouraged the reading of 'the Bible and other Godly Bokes, but especyally keepe them [your children] from reading of fayned fables, vayne fantasyes, and wanton stories, and songs of love, which bring much mischiefe to youth' (quoted in Darton, 1932/1982, p. 43). This attitude towards fiction, particularly fantasy, can be traced through the history of children's literature to its present day forms, which are probably most obvious amongst certain fundamentalist groups. Implicit in the attitude, of course, are notions of what should constitute 'literature' and the nature of children and childhood.

The combined effect of regarding children as naturally sinful and fiction as potentially dangerous was the production of instructional texts that did not flinch from detailing the dire consequences of misbehaviour. Cotton Mather, addressing American children in 1699, explained why they should obey their parents:

Undutiful Children soon become horrid Creatures, for Unchastity, for Dishonesty, for Lying, and for all manner of Abominations … And because these undutiful Children are Wicked overmuch, therefore they Dy before their time … Children, if by Undutifulness to your Parents you incur the Curse of God, it won't be long before you go down into Obscure Darkness, even into Utter Darkness: God has reserved for you the Blackness of Darkness for ever.

(Cotton Mather (1699) *A Family Well Ordered, or An Essay to render Parents and Children Happy in one another*, quoted in Townsend, 1990, p. 9)

A counter influence to these attitudes came from the philosopher John Locke who wrote *Some Thoughts Concerning Education* in 1693. Locke held the view that, in terms of ideas (though not personality and abilities), children were born with minds that were like 'blank slates' ready to be written upon (*tabula rasa* in Latin). He recognized the differences between children and emphasized their individuality rather than their similarities.

He therefore advocated a process of education that was a gentler and more enjoyable one than Cotton Mather envisaged: children could be 'cozened [coaxed] into a knowledge of their letters … and play themselves into what others are whipped for'. A child should be given 'some easy pleasant book, suited to his [*sic*] capacity … wherein the entertainment he finds might draw him on and reward his pains in reading … and yet not such as should fill his head with perfectly useless trumpery, or lay the principles of vice or folly.' Locke's interest in teaching methods resonates with modern educational concerns, and was also influential in his own day. Of particular interest for this discussion is the influence of Locke's views on John Newbery, one of the best known early publishers of children's books.

Newbery was born in 1713 in Berkshire in England. In 1745 he moved his printing business to London to St Paul's Churchyard from where he printed, wrote and sold books for the rest of his working life. His business continued successfully in the same location for at least a century after his death in 1767. In 1744, Newbery published the *Little Pretty Pocket-Book* which, although not the first children's book of its kind, is credited with tremendous significance, as marking the start of the production and trade in English-language children's literature as it has developed in contemporary European and North American societies.

Allow about 5 minutes

A C T I V I T Y   2   An early example of children's literature

The frontispiece and title page for *The Little Pretty Pocket-Book* are reproduced opposite. Before you read on, it's worth looking carefully at this early example of children's literature. How does it set out to appeal to children as readers? What views about children and childhood does it seem to represent?

The Little Pretty Pocket-Book is clearly an example of literature directed at children as a readership. It assumes parental or adult involvement and oversight, but the text aims to capture the child's interest and engagement (as demonstrated by the letters from Jack the Giant Killer and the 'free gifts' – the ball or pincushion cost two pence extra).

Authorship of this literature is not considered an issue: no author is credited with having written this, or most of the other thirty or more children's books that Newbery published (Townsend, 1994). Neither is the distinction between bookselling and book publishing a marked one at this stage – booksellers both published and sold work and often (as is true in Newbery's case) wrote it as well. The available technology and the economics of the trade had, then as now, an important influence on the nature of what was produced and distributed for children. The absence of named authors tends to indicate the status of the literature as *popular culture*; a modern equivalent might be that authors of Disney versions of stories tend not to be given prominence, whereas the author of a more 'serious' text would always be cited.

The text also seems to indicate a shift in the view of childhood that is taking place around this time in eighteenth-century England (and, as we shall see later, in France as well). There is increased acceptance of the idea of childhood as a separate and distinct phase in which learning can occur through play (Plumb, 1975). Jokes and frivolity are not necessarily seen as

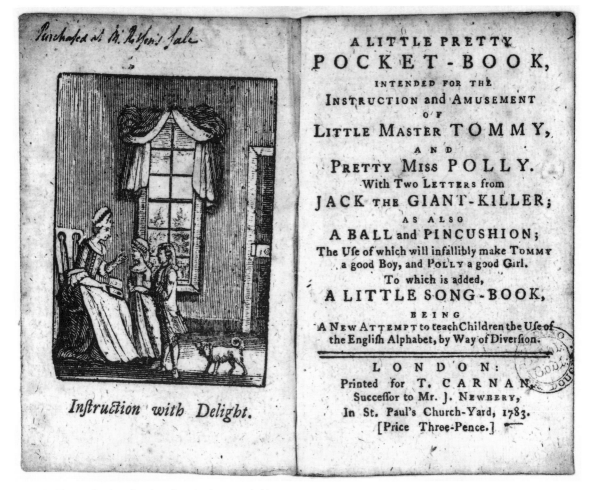

A Little Pretty Pocket Book – frontispiece and title page.

detrimental to moral development and there is more acceptance of the idea that a degree of naughty behaviour could be expected – and forgiven – in children. Documenting changes in social attitudes is, necessarily, an imprecise matter, and views of childhood such as those given above would have been contested in Newbery's day, just as they have been contested by some groups in English society ever since. And, of course, many children lived in material conditions that rendered such attitudes insignificant or meaningless – the luxury of being able to view childhood as a separate and distinct phase and to value the educational potential of play was denied to many children who were forced to work to stay alive. Opportunities to acquire literacy and to gain access to books were extremely limited for working class children. In relation to children's literature, however, we are tracing not the huge variation in the circumstances of childhoods experienced by children from different social classes, but the prevalent ideologies of childhood in a given society – that is, the widely held views which become 'common sense' about what people want for their children, how they want them to be, and how they think they should be brought up. The study of children's literature offers windows onto what various societies at different times consider as desirable for children and distinctive about them.

The formula '1932/1982' indicates that the work was originally published in 1932, but that the author has used a more recent edition – 1982 in this case.

In discussing the starting points of children's literature I have drawn a distinction between 'instruction' for children and 'literature'. This is a distinction commonly made in academic writing about children's literature; it was probably most famously asserted by Harvey Darton, whose authoritative study *Children's Books in England* written in 1932 is still widely respected today. Darton (1932/1982, p. 1) used the distinction as a central feature of his own definition: 'By "children's literature" I mean printed works produced ostensibly to give children spontaneous pleasure and not primarily to teach them, nor solely to make them good, nor to keep them profitably quiet.'

Despite its merits in helping map out the field of study, the distinction between instruction and literature designed to give 'spontaneous pleasure' is not always easy to maintain. A strongly didactic and moralistic streak has run through children's literature since the earliest days. We might consider, for example, Newbery's most famous legacy in terms of an individual book: *The History of Little Goody Two-Shoes*, first published in 1765. The title page sets the tone of ironic good humour (including the attribution to an original manuscript in the Vatican archives with '[wood]cuts by Michael Angelo'). But, as the plot summary indicates, the tale is also a didactic one with a clear set of moral values about hope, faith, industry and education.

Frontispiece and title page of *The History of Little Goody Two-Shoes.*

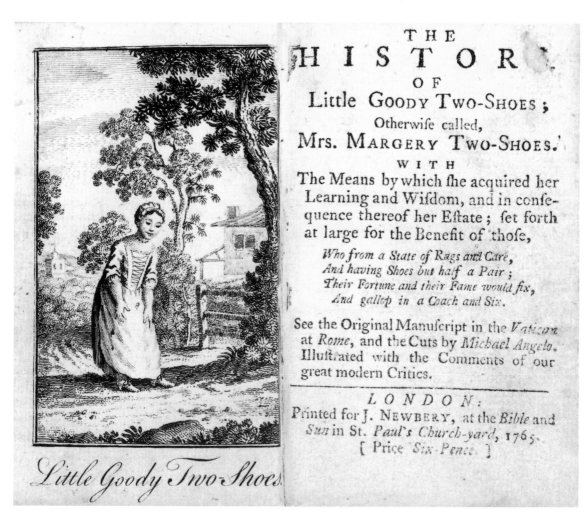

The History of Little Goody Two-Shoes

At the start of the story proper, the heroine Margery and her brother Tommy are orphaned … Ignored by relatives and in a ragged state – Margery has only one shoe – the children are befriended by a charitable gentleman, who offers to take Tommy to London and make a sailor of him, and orders new shoes for Tommy's sister. Margery, staying with a local clergyman, is inconsolable at the loss of her brother until her new shoes arrive. She then repeatedly cries out, 'See, two shoes', and earns her nickname. [Forced to] leave the clergyman's home, … Margery decides to learn to read by borrowing books from children coming back from school, and reading till they return. Margery is soon more knowledgeable than the parish children, and becomes an itinerant tutor to them … Margery demonstrates the folly of believing in ghosts, and eventually succeeds [the teacher] on her retirement from the local 'College for instruction in the Science of ABC'. There, Mrs Margery – 'for so we must now call her' – is a model of enlightened teaching, kindness to animals, and patience in adversity. The school roof falls in but the children escape, warned by Margery's dog … Margery … is arrested as a witch because she uses a barometer to forecast the weather … Finally she marries a wealthy widower … Her brother Tommy comes back from sea after making his fortune. Margery buys up the estate of the tyrannical squire, returns it to its separate tenancies, and leads a life of unparalleled generosity. After her death the poor weep at her monument.

(Carpenter and Prichard, 1984, pp. 213–214)

2.2 Didacticism and moralism

The tensions between wanting to teach children and wanting to amuse them are inherent in children's literature, and while they might sometimes pull in opposite directions, there is no reason why a book should not both teach *and* amuse its readers. Not everyone would agree with the categorical tone of Fred Inglis's assertion that 'Only a monster would not want to give a child books she will delight in and which will teach her to be good. It is the ancient and proper justification of reading and teaching literature that it helps you to live well' (Inglis, 1981, p. 4). Nevertheless, Inglis's concerns about the importance of the values reflected in children's books will strike a chord with many people.

If we adopt Darton's definition of children's literature, discussed above, we discount instructional texts that are *entirely* didactic in nature. But as the forms of children's literature become established in a society, the texts produced will reflect the range of dominant views about what and how children are to be taught. As we have seen, beliefs about the nature of children and childhood are a fundamental determinant of the types of text produced for children. So, Newbery acknowledged his respect for 'the great Mr Locke' and wrote children's books that aimed to be entertaining and gently didactic.

Alternative views of the nature of childhood co-existed. John Wesley, the Methodist leader, (1703–91) advised parents to 'break the will of your child' in order to 'bring his will into subjection to yours that it may be afterward subject to the will of God' (Wesley [1872], in Ward and Heitzenrater, 1986, p. 354). In 1799 the *Evangelical Magazine* urged parents to teach children that they 'are sinful polluted creatures' (quoted in Hendrick, 1997, p. 38). These views are also reflected in children's literature whose aims were, clearly, to 'teach [the child] to be good' as well as to entertain. The views are represented in eighteenth and nineteenth century British and American children's literature whose traditions persisted into the twentieth century (and, some would argue, to the present day).

Allow about 5 minutes

ACTIVITY 3 Teaching the child to be 'good'

The History of the Fairchild Family is an early nineteenth century example of this tradition in children's literature – see the extracts below. How do children, and relations between children and parents, seem to be represented in these extracts? Do you think this would count as 'literature' according to Darton's definition?

A History of the Fairchild Family

Mary Martha Sherwood (1775–1851) wrote *The History of the Fairchild Family* in 1818. It was a bestseller and continued to be reprinted until the early twentieth century. In the following extract, entitled 'Fatal Effects of Disobedience to Parents', Mrs Barker, after ensuring that the family have eaten their breakfast, breaks the news of Miss Augusta Noble's premature death.

> 'You know that poor Miss Augusta was always the darling of her mother, who brought her up in great pride, without fear of God or knowledge of religion: nay, Lady Noble would even mock religion and religious people in her presence; and she chose a governess who had no more of God about her than herself.'

> 'I never thought much of that governess,' said Mrs Fairchild.

> 'As Miss Augusta was brought up without fear of God,' continued Mrs Barker, 'she had, of course, no notion of obedience to her parents … '

This lack of obedience leads Miss Augusta to play with candles and burn herself to death. The funeral is described in detail. In the coach home, Mr Fairchild concludes:

> '… what a dreadful story is this! Had this poor child been brought up in the fear of God, she might now have been living, a blessing to her parents and the delight of their eyes. "Withhold not correction from the child; for if thou beatest him with the rod, he shall not die: thou shalt beat him with the rod, and shalt deliver his soul from hell." '

> (Sherwood, 1818, pp. 155, 160)

COMMENT

My own responses would be that children are clearly meant to be in a subservient position in the family, owing strict obedience to their parents. The extracts exemplify Wesley's view that there is a religious imperative behind such family structures. They offer a succinct illustration of adult/child power relations presented in a narrative context, while at the same time claiming moral authority for the opinion from religion.

I am not sure if a strict interpretation of Darton's definition would allow this to qualify as children's literature: the text is overtly didactic and may well be designed '*primarily* to teach'. On the other hand, it is story (rather than a purely instructional text) and children may well have gained 'spontaneous pleasure' from the sometimes gruesome details of others' misfortunes.

Clear (or crude, depending on your point of view) morals and didactic intentions were also evident in the children's literature produced for religious groups during the eighteenth and nineteenth centuries. Hannah More, evangelical founder of the Sunday School movement, launched a series of Cheap Repository Tracts in the 1790s. These stories were read by millions of children and adults, and spawned many similar publications both in Britain and in America. Townsend quotes from one such story, called *The Glass of Whiskey*, issued by the American Sunday School Union in 1825:

> There is a bottle. It has something in it which is called whiskey. Little reader, I hope you will never take any as long as you live. It is poison. So is brandy, so is rum, so is gin, and many other drinks. They are called strong drink. They are so strong that they knock people down and kill them.

> (Townsend, 1990, p. 32)

2.3 Rousseau and Romanticism

In 1762, in *Emile, ou de l'éducation,* Jean-Jacques Rousseau proposed a new set of theories, advocating a 'natural' upbringing for boys: in the countryside, roaming freely, in conversation with a tutor but without moral instruction until the age of fifteen. The aim was to create a strong, healthy child, with a mind uncluttered by prejudice, who could move forward confidently into adulthood. Rousseau also considered girls' education (in relation to Sophie, a companion for Emile). Some similar themes emerged (e.g. the value of outdoor life) but Rousseau was concerned primarily to ensure girls accept subservience to men and learn how to please their husbands.

In *Emile*, Rousseau recommended just one book for reading during the teenage years – Daniel Defoe's *Robinson Crusoe*, in which the hero survives shipwreck and lives on an island until his eventual rescue by a passing ship. Book-reading generally was classed as an unnatural activity, however, likely to corrupt the purity of the child's education. Rousseau's emphasis was on the child as a child ('Nature wants children to be children before they are men'); he saw childhood as a separate state to be valued in its own right, not just as a launch-pad to adulthood.

These ideas were attractive to many thinkers and writers across Europe and North America. Ironically, Rousseau's strictures against book reading did not diminish children's authors' desires to write fiction that embodied his view of childhood and learning. The Romantic movement, particularly the nineteenth-century English poets Blake, Coleridge and Wordsworth, adopted Rousseau's notion of the 'natural' child and the concept of 'original innocence' (rather than the 'original sin' emphasized strongly in the teachings of some Christian sects). William Wordsworth, for instance, saw

THE FOOTPRINT IN THE SAND.

Robinson Crusoe discovers a human footprint. Illustration by J. Finnemore from the 1895 edition.

the innocence of childhood as an ideal but fragile state, never to be regained once childhood is over. Growing up, therefore, becomes in Christian metaphor like leaving the paradise of the Garden of Eden, moving from an ideal and protected space to a corrupt and imperfect wider world.

The influence of these conceptions of childhood on English-language children's literature has been enormous. The popularity of *Robinson Crusoe*, even before Rousseau's endorsement of the book's qualities, is evident from the numerous abridged versions which appeared in 'chapbooks' (cheap pamphlets sold by peddlers or 'chapmen') after it was first published in 1719. Since that time stories of survival on desert islands have become a major theme for children's and adult literature, film and television, to the extent that the word 'Robinsonnade' has been coined to describe such survival adventure stories. Two nineteenth-century 'classics' you may know of are *The Swiss Family Robinson* (1814) by J. D. Wyss, in which an entire family – a pastor, his wife and four boys – are shipwrecked on a deserted island; and *The Coral Island* (1857) by R. M. Ballantyne, which details the adventures of four boys shipwrecked on a South Sea island. A more recent example is *Slake's Limbo* (1974) by Felice Holman, a story which details how a boy survives underground in the New York subway.

The Secret Garden by Frances Hodgson Burnett is a metaphor of childhood innocence and growth in a protected natural space. Illustration by Robin Lawrie from the 1994 Puffin Books edition.

Stories of children's innocent adventures in rural settings became a staple of twentieth century children's fiction. The child protagonists of Arthur Ransome's *Swallows and Amazons* novels (published between 1930 and 1947) or Enid Blyton's *Secret Seven* series (published between 1949 and 1963), conduct their adventures in circumscribed yet independent (and largely adult-free – and book-free) environments. Anthropomorphic animals and toys live in idyllic rural settings, which are sites of innocence and simple pleasures (*Winnie-the-Pooh*, 1926, by A. A. Milne) until threatened by grown-up life in the form of new technologies and class politics (*The Wind in the Willows*, 1908, by Kenneth Graham). Gardens – particularly secret gardens – are used metaphorically to symbolize the growth of the child in a place which is separate and organic (*The Secret Garden*, 1911, by Frances Hodgson Burnett; *Tom's Midnight Garden*, 1958, by Philippa Pearce). Children's innate goodness shines through, despite tribulations and grumpy and difficult adults (*Anne of Green Gables*, 1908, by L. M. Montgomery; *Rebecca of Sunnybrook Farm*, 1903, by Kate Douglas Wiggin). And in Johanna Spyri's novel *Heidi* (1881) we witness Heidi's innocence and innate goodness combine with a rural, mountain setting to heal the physical, emotional and spiritual problems of Heidi's friends and family.

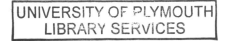

In summary then, much of the children's literature produced in England at the end of the nineteenth century and in the first half of the twentieth century, builds on ideas from Romanticism and Christianity, which have coalesced in the public consciousness to suggest a conception of childhood as a separate state. Generally, children are no longer seen as apprentice adults; they have identities of their own, an innocence which adults should respect and a natural environment which it is healthy for them to inhabit and useful to learn about. This 'natural' environment is rural. The strident didacticism of some earlier children's literature is muted, though perhaps the will to teach and to 'make children good' can still be detected. Certainly, the adult (author's) nostalgia for the 'lost realm' of childhood innocence can be readily detected in some of these texts. The conception of childhood as a separate state has made the segmentation of the child readership easier to envisage for twentieth century writers than it was for Defoe, who did not see himself as writing a 'children's book.' And perhaps one result of this more closely defined sense of the audience is a greater self-consciousness on the part of the author, a stronger sense of the differences between adults and children which has its effects in the qualities of the writing produced.

2.4 Social reformers

Changes in the conception of childhood are not, of course, simply matters of how characters are portrayed in books. The social, political and ethical logic of these views of childhood was opposition to the exploitation of children's labour. Hendrick puts this well:

> Prior to the closing decades of the eighteenth century, there were few voices, if any, raised against child labour. For most children labouring was held to be a condition which could teach them numerous economic, social and moral principles. By the end of the century, however, this view was being challenged as first climbing-boys and parish apprentices in cotton mills and then factory children in general came to be regarded as victims, as 'slaves', as innocents forced into 'unnatural' employment and denied their 'childhood'. During the course of the debates, between, say, 1780 and 1840, a new construction of childhood was put together by participants, so that at the end of the period the wage-earning child was no longer considered to be the norm. Instead childhood was now seen as constituting a separate and distinct set of characteristics requiring protection and fostering through school education.

(Hendrick, 1997, p. 39)

Children's literature played its part in transforming, reflecting and debating these societal changes. Campaigning Christian authors drew attention to the conditions in which many children were forced to live and work. A well-known example is Charles Kingsley's *The Water Babies* (1863), a fantasy story in which Tom, a young orphan working as a chimney sweep, is cruelly treated by his master until he runs away and is transformed into a water baby. The story was first serialized in a magazine before being published as a book. It can be seen as popular culture written with a moral and didactic purpose. The fact that Kingsley is now generally seen as inhabiting the ranks of 'classic' children's authors returns us neatly to the issue of how we define 'literature' for children.

Allow about 10 minutes

ACTIVITY 4   Children's literature and social reform

Consider the quotations and illustrations from *The Water Babies* (below). How do they support the idea that Charles Kingsley was a social reformer?

The Water Babies

Under the snow-white coverlet, upon the snow-white pillow, lay the most beautiful little girl that Tom had ever seen … She never could have been dirty, thought Tom to himself. And then he thought, 'Are all people like that when they are washed?' … And looking round, he suddenly saw, standing close to him, a little, ugly, black, ragged figure, with bleared eyes and grinning white teeth. He turned on it angrily … And behold, it was himself, reflected in a great mirror …

(pp. 20–21)

Tom as a chimney sweep. Illustration by Jessie Wilcox Smith from the 1916 edition of Kingsley's *The Water Babies*.

[Mrs Doasyouwouldbedoneby] took Tom in her arms and … kissed him, and patted him and talked to him, tenderly and low, such things as he had never heard before in his life, and Tom looked up into her eyes, and loved her, and loved, till he fell asleep from pure love … 'Don't go away,' said little Tom. 'This is so nice. I never had anyone to cuddle me before.'

(pp. 139–40)

Tom as water baby, with Mrs Doasyouwouldbedoneby. Illustration by Jessie Wilcox Smith from the 1916 edition of Kingsley's *The Water Babies*.

COMMENT

The first quotation and illustration point up the dramatic and unfair differences in the material circumstances of the two children. Tom not only *is* dirty from the soot of the chimneys; he also feels dirtied and impure from the life he has had to lead. The mirror is used to illustrate Tom's moment of self-awareness; he feels alienated and angry, and knows that he has intruded upon a calm and attractive private world that is not for him. Yet that other world is no more than the comfortable and clean bedroom of a sleeping child.

The second quotation and illustration show Tom as a water baby, innocent, clean and tiny, being nurtured and loved by a larger than life mother figure. The language of the text and the illustration emphasize the closeness of the moment; the direct speech underscores the fact that Tom has not experienced this maternal love in his earthly life. The name – Mrs Doasyouwouldbedoneby (sister of Mrs Bedonebyasyoudid!) – has a clear didactic purpose which suggests that Kingsley was aiming to persuade his readership of the need for reform of the conditions in which orphans like Tom were brought up.

The focus so far has been largely on locating the discussion of the chapter's key questions and themes in terms of the development of children's literature in England. Each country, and different cultural groups within countries, will have its own particular history to tell. Tracing the development of children's literature in different countries will reveal views of childhood, definitions of literature and a good deal about the social history of that country. As we have seen, stories are used to instruct and explain and to entertain, and the political context for those stories will be important in determining whose stories are written down and how they are interpreted. However, one type of story, strongly associated with children's literature – the fairy tale – is often considered to stand apart from its political and social context. I'd therefore like to consider these stories next.

SUMMARY OF SECTION 2

Evidence from the history of children's literature in England suggests that:

- Children's literature is historically variable: the types of stories considered appropriate for children have changed over time.
- These changes represent changing conceptions of children and childhood (compare the images evident in *Little Goody Two-Shoes*, *The Fairchild Family*, *The Secret Garden* and *The Water Babies*).
- Children's literature has often been designed explicitly to instruct children in accordance with contemporary social or religious values.
- Even literature that is designed primarily to entertain conveys certain sets of values.

3 FAIRY TALES, FOLK TALES AND OTHER TRADITIONAL NARRATIVES

3.1 The features of folk and fairy tales

John Rowe Townsend offers a very clear definition which helps distinguish fairy from folk tales:

> Fairy tales, ancient and modern, are stories of magic, set in the indefinite past and incorporating traditional themes and materials; they may be about giants, dwarfs, witches, talking animals, and a variety of other creatures, as well as good and bad fairies, princes, poor widows and youngest sons. Folk tales are the traditional tales of the people. They are often fairy tales, but they do not have to be; 'folk' indicates the origin, 'fairy' the nature of the story.
>
> (Townsend, 1990, p. 67)

Generally, fairy tales are not very specific about where or when a story is set, preferring the vague 'Once upon a time … ' (or the Armenian equivalent 'There was a time and no time … '). They don't aim to make you believe in them on a literal level. They don't tend to sketch in much character detail or suggest much in the way of motivation, even for the most extreme of acts. Consider, for example, the over-reaction of the old fairy who hadn't been invited to a party to celebrate the birth of a princess in *The Sleeping Beauty*: 'The old Fairy's turn coming next, with a head shaking more with spite than old age, she said, that the Princess should have her hand pierced with a spindle and die of the wound …' (Opie and Opie, 1974, p. 85).

The stories focus upon good and evil, right and wrong, and action. Transformations and resolutions often occur with the aid of magic. And similar fairy stories crop up, with amazing regularity, in many different parts of the world, at different times and in different societies. A basic human impulse towards storytelling is observable in every society. These factors have led some critics to ask whether there are universal story elements, which might be seen as binding people together on a spiritual or psychological or even biological level.

3.2 Fairy tales and psychoanalysis

Folk and fairy tales have proved a source of tremendous interest to psychologists and psychiatrists, and there is a well-established body of psychoanalytic criticism, of fairy tales in particular. The author Angela Carter, a notable collector of fairy tales, suggested why this might be the case:

> The loose symbolic structure of fairy tales leaves them so open to psychoanalytic interpretation, as if they were not formal inventions but informal dreams dreamed in public.
>
> (Carter, 1991, p. xx)

Freud himself wrote about the impact of fairy tales on the mental life of the child, asserting that their influence was so profound that adults will use fairy tales in later life as 'screen memories' to block some of the experiences of childhood (Freud, 1913/1958). Particularly influential in the field of fairy tales is the work of Bruno Bettelheim, a Freudian psychoanalyst whose work was deeply coloured by the time he spent in the concentration camps of Dachau and Buchenwald during the Second World War. Bettelheim believed that fairy stories hold a place of unparalleled importance in a child's psychological growth. In *The Uses of Enchantment*, he sets out the rationale for his psychoanalytical interpretation of fairy tales:

> In order to master the psychological problems of growing up – overcoming narcissistic disappointments, oedipal dilemmas, sibling rivalries; becoming able to relinquish childhood dependencies; gaining a feeling of selfhood and of self-worth, and a sense of moral obligation – a child needs to understand what is going on within his conscious self so that he can cope with that which goes on in his unconscious. He can achieve this understanding, and with it the ability to cope, not through rational comprehension of the nature and content of his unconscious, but by becoming familiar with it through spinning out daydreams – ruminating, rearranging, and fantasizing about suitable story elements in response to unconscious pressures ... It is here that fairy tales have unequalled value, because they offer new dimensions to the child's imagination which would be impossible for him to discover as truly on his own.
>
> (Bettelheim, 1976, pp. 6–7)

Bettelheim's interpretations of fairy tales relate to the workings of the unconscious mind, to psychosexual, moral and imaginative development. His primary interest is in the therapeutic power of the tales. It is probably best to get the flavour of Bettelheim's interpretations, which often surprise readers when they first encounter them, by looking at a short extract from his work on *Hansel and Gretel*.

Allow about 10 minutes

A C T I V I T Y 5   Interpreting Hansel and Gretel

The first quotation below gives a brief account of the first part of *Hansel and Gretel*, followed by an extract from Bettelheim's interpretation of the story. What would you see as Bettelheim's main concerns in offering this interpretation?

> A brother and sister, Hansel and Gretel, are abandoned in the forest by their parents, who cannot afford to feed them. Thanks to Hansel's foresight, the children find their way home, but the parents make a second attempt, and this time Hansel and Gretel are well and truly lost. After wandering about, they are near dying of starvation when they find a cottage which is 'made of bread and cakes, and the window-panes were of clear sugar'. They are busily biting pieces off when an old woman hobbles out and invites them inside, gives them a good meal, and puts them to bed. In the morning she reveals that she is a witch ...
>
> (Carpenter and Prichard, 1984, p. 238)

> The fairy tale expresses in words and actions the things which go on in children's minds. In terms of the child's dominant anxiety, Hansel and Gretel believe that their parents are talking about a plot to desert them. A small child, awakening hungry in the darkness of the night, feels threatened by complete rejection and desertion, which he experiences in the form of fear of starvation. By projecting their inner anxiety onto those they fear might cut them off, Hansel and Gretel are convinced that their parents plan to starve them to death … The mother represents the source of all food to the children, so it is she who now is experienced as abandoning them, as if in a wilderness …
>
> (Bettelheim, 1976, p. 159)

COMMENT

My own response to this would be that Bettelheim clearly goes far beyond the literal meaning of the story. He sees fairy stories as an expression of children's inner fears and anxieties – in the case of Hansel and Gretel, their fears of abandonment by their parents. Fairy stories offer children a means to work out and resolve these fears, and in that sense they are cathartic.

The interpretation seems to focus on the 'universal' in fairy tales – the idea that fairy tales have universal elements and that children respond to these in similar ways. There is little acknowledgement of the possibility that children may take different meanings from stories – or that stories themselves may change through history and in different cultural contexts.

3.3 The social history of fairy tales

Critics of this psychoanalytic approach tend to object to the view of childhood upon which it draws and/or the definition of literature upon which it is based. Jack Zipes, for example, comments:

> The fairy tales we have come to revere as classical are not ageless, universal, and beautiful in and of themselves, and they are not the best therapy in the world for children. They are historical prescriptions, internalized, potent, explosive, and we acknowledge the power they hold over our lives by mystifying them.
>
> (Zipes, 1983, p. 11)

Zipes' own concern, along with other scholars, has been to document the social history of the fairy tale genre, showing how popular tales have been adapted by writers from the seventeenth century onwards and refashioned to conform to changing social beliefs and values.

READING

Please now consider Reading A, Geoff Fox on *Little Red Riding Hood*. The reading illustrates some of the transformations that have taken place in one particular story. As you read, note in particular:

1   How the story has been rewritten at different historical periods and in different cultural contexts.

2   Geoff Fox's argument that these retellings reflect different sets of
    values and beliefs about children and childhood.

In your view, would the initial oral version of the story be suitable for
contemporary child readers?

I'd like to conclude this brief review of fairy tales by thinking about how the
discussion in this section relates to some themes that are threaded through
this chapter: changing views about the nature of children and childhood,
and about what counts as suitable literature for children; and the question of
what children's literature is for.

The origins of fairy tales are in the oral tradition. We can assume that story-
tellings would be adapted to different audiences and places, but before they
were written down, there was no sense that fairy tales were, as a genre, stories
just for children. If we accept the analysis of Zipes and others engaged in
scholarly research on fairy tales, we can think of the collecting and writing
down of folk and fairy tales, which began at the end of the seventeenth
century, as part of a social and cultural project related to the economics and
politics of the period. Central to this was the rise in the economic and
political power of the middle class, and we can trace, in the stories of the
Brothers Grimm in Germany and Perrault in France for example, changes
that were made to the oral stories, or choices about which stories to include
in collections – and these choices can be seen as reflecting values and
attitudes associated with the middle classes (such as industry, delayed
gratification, respectability, differentiated gender roles). Once written down,
stories such as *Little Red Riding Hood* were quickly accepted as 'literature',
often getting a clear stamp of approval from royal or aristocratic patrons.
However, they were increasingly marketed for use with children, at a time
when childhood was being conceptualized as distinct from adulthood. The
morals and messages of the collected tales reflected, and perhaps helped to
form, contemporary ideas of how children should be educated and entertained.

By the mid-twentieth century, fairy tales were firmly established in Western
Europe and North America as inhabiting the realm of 'children's literature.'
Within that realm, some of the older written versions of tales were accorded
'classic' status. Meanwhile, Walt Disney's film versions of the tales
consolidated the status of the tales as part of contemporary children's
culture. *Snow White and the Seven Dwarfs*, Disney's first feature length
animation, was released in 1937 and a steady flow of fairy tale animations
followed (for example, *Cinderella*, 1950; *Beauty and the Beast*, 1991).
Research in the field reinforced the sense that fairy-tale elements are
universal, ageless, and wise in unfathomable ways. The Western view of
childhood had shifted under the influence of psychological and educational
theory: childhood was no longer understood simply as a separate state, but
as a formative, intensely vulnerable period which provided the foundations
for healthy development in later life. Some stories were seen as having
therapeutic value for certain children. And if some stories can heal, mustn't it
be the case that others can harm children? There were fears in some quarters
about what that harm might be and how it might occur. Questions were
raised about who is represented in children's literature, how they are
represented and the values that permeate the stories. These are issues I
return to in the next section.

3.4 New markets and new projects

From the middle of the twentieth century onwards, there was a further distinction drawn in common thinking about childhood, as teenagers came to be seen as a separate group, developmentally, socially and as consumers. Fairy tales had established their stake as children's literature, but in the further segmentation of childhood into different phases, the readership for fairy tales was redefined as younger rather than older children. A survey conducted amongst members of girls' clubs in the UK during the 1940s suggested that 25 per cent of fourteen-year-old girls were still reading fairy tales, as were 10 per cent of eighteen-year-old girls who were still in school, statistics which sound surprising now (Trease, 1949). Later surveys of children's reading habits (see, for example, Hall and Coles, 1999) suggest that relatively few fairy tales are being read, even amongst ten to fourteen year olds, and that those which are read tend to be linked to film titles, such as a new Disney release.

'Classic' tales were under attack on two fronts, however. Some commentators found the characters unrepresentative and the values of the tales unpalatable for children. Furthermore, the whole idea of 'classic literature' was itself under attack, because it was seen as representing the work of a relatively narrow and elite group of writers, and for being hostile to work from other perspectives. The debates about these issues resulted in two areas of work – two challenges, in fact – which have become important in the late twentieth and the early twenty-first centuries.

The first challenge is the project of recovering suppressed and forgotten texts: texts about working people, texts rejected because they were classed as popular culture, texts by and about women and other under-represented or under privileged groups. The second challenge for children's literature was to produce new texts that included a wider range of perspectives and challenged stereotypical views and attitudes. This project would involve the generation of texts from people in under-represented groups, as well as encouraging more diverse perspectives and subject matter from established writers. These are not projects exclusive to children's literature, of course, but they have had marked effects on children's literature.

With regard to folk and fairy tales, one of the effects of the 'recovery' project has been an increase in the publication of tales from different parts of the world. Some of these are straightforward retellings of folk or fairy tales for young children. Many UK school reading programmes, for example, now include *Anansi* stories from Africa and the Caribbean. But, inevitably, folk and fairy tales from other times and from diverse regions of the world will embody different values and ways of seeing the world. They will not all fall neatly into current Western ways of thinking, which assume that such tales are for children. In her collection of tales with female protagonists, for example, Angela Carter includes stories which many people would consider unsuitable for children. *Blubber Boy*, an Inuit tale, begins:

> Once there was a girl whose boyfriend drowned in the sea. Her parents could do nothing to console her. Nor did any of her other suitors interest her – she wanted the fellow who had drowned and no one else. Finally she took a chunk of blubber and carved it into the shape of her

drowned boyfriend. Then she carved the boy's face. It was a perfect likeness. 'Oh, if only he were real!' she thought. She rubbed the blubber against her genitals, round and round, and suddenly it came alive. Her handsome boyfriend was standing in front of her …

(Carter, 1991, p. 31)

Angela Carter's commitment to the publication of suppressed, ignored or forgotten stories, and to hearing a wide range of voices, is clear:

> … the content of the fairy tale may record the real lives of the anonymous poor with sometimes uncomfortable fidelity – the poverty, the hunger, the shaky family relationships, the all-pervasive cruelty and also, sometimes, the good humour, the vigour, the straightforward consolations of a warm fire and a full belly …

(Carter, 1991, p. xi)

> I haven't put this collection together from such heterogeneous sources to show that we are all sisters under the skin, part of the same human family in spite of a few superficial differences. I don't believe that anyway. Sisters under the skin we might be, but that doesn't mean we've got much in common … Rather, I wanted to demonstrate the extraordinary richness and diversity with which femininity, in practice, is represented in 'unofficial' culture: its strategies, its plots, its hard work.

(Carter, 1991, p. xiv)

Other writers committed to recovering suppressed or marginalized stories weave the traditional tale into a more complex and self-conscious narrative framework which seeks to acknowledge the modern context of the retelling. Reading B provides an example of this process.

READING

Please look at Reading B by Clare Bradford. The reading discusses a contemporary picture book based on a traditional Aboriginal story. As you read, note in particular the following points:

1   The social and political context in which texts such as *The Story of the Falling Star* have been produced – and what particular reasons there are for 'recovering' such stories.

2   How stories may embody certain Aboriginal values – in this case, note the particular importance of 'country'.

3   The traditional storytelling practices that are evident in *The Story of the Falling Star*.

4   How the story is said to offer a reinterpretation of colonial discourses about Aboriginal people.

The Story of the Falling Star differs in many respects from the European tradition of folk takes I have referred to earlier in this section, first because it is regarded as true (rather than 'fiction') and it relates to important events of the Aboriginal Dreaming. It is a version of an ancient story which the narrator, Elsie Jones, is authorized to tell as its custodian and as a Paakantji elder, but it also relates to other stories about the same events which are sacred/secret and which are passed on to initiated Paakantji during ritual ceremonies. Such stories are not subject to the same kind of variation and change over time as European folk tales: they have to be transmitted as they were handed on by a former custodian. The book therefore represents, and makes available to its readers, an important Aboriginal cultural tradition.

In the next section I'd like to think more about what I referred to previously as the second challenge for children's literature – that of producing new texts that included a wider range of perspectives and undermined stereotypical views and attitudes.

SUMMARY OF SECTION 3

- Folk and fairy tales have been seen as timeless, containing universal themes that are important for children's psychological development (e.g. Bettelheim).

- An alternative approach (e.g. Zipes, Reading A by Geoff Fox) emphasizes the historical and cultural specificity of different versions of traditional tales: these are seen as 'products of their time', promoting culturally specific sets of values.

- Contemporary concerns about limitations in the range of books and stories available to children have led to attempts to 'recover' stories from different, often marginalized traditions. *The Story of the Falling Star* represents an example of this.

4 REPRESENTATION, POLITICS AND CHILDREN'S LITERATURE

4.1 Ideological debates

In 1949, Geoffrey Trease commented on the conservative bias of historical fiction for children. In the 1950s and 60s in Britain, concerns were expressed about a class bias in children's books, particularly focused on a concern that representations in books did not reflect the realities of working class children's lives. In 1965 in the United States, an influential article in the *Saturday Review* complained that ' ... most of the books children see are all white' (Larrick, 1965). In the 1970s the Children's Rights Workshop was formed in Britain to promote non-racist and non-sexist books; and the Writers and Readers Publishing Co-operative published *Racism and Sexism in Children's Books* in 1976, critiquing the stereotyped portrayal of black characters, and of female and male characters, in children's books.

Some commentators suggested that children's authors should challenge the *status quo* rather than reflect it in their writing. There were fierce debates about values and about what children's books are *for* – both in the sense of

" Let me go, you savage!"

'Attitudes to race as shown through illustration': an illustration from
Mary Poppins, cited in *Racism and Sexism in Children's Books,*
Writers and Readers Publishing Co-operative, 1976, p. 7.

what their purposes are and what they stand for. Although posed in the
language of the day, these were not entirely new debates. The political,
ideological and educational discussions about children's books, which have
taken place from the 1960s onwards and continue in the present day, are
recognizably linked to earlier discussions of the moral and didactic purposes
of children's literature.

The response to these challenges has been a huge increase in the variety
and range of books produced for children over the last decades of the
twentieth century and into the new century. The explosion in publishing for
children has been affected by ideological debates, but also by technological
change, educational change, and economic interests. New technologies have
revolutionized the appearance and form of books as new relationships

between text, graphics and illustrations have become possible. Educationalists agree upon the benefits to children of reading widely and for pleasure, and home/school partnerships have been encouraged to promote reading in and out of school. School and public libraries have developed enormously since the 1970s. The production and marketing of books for teenagers and for babies has increased dramatically. In Europe and North America, the promotional superstructure of literary prizes, reviews, advertizing campaigns and media tie-ins has been established for children's literature in its own right. The most dramatic recent example of the effect of these promotional strategies is probably the enormous success of the *Harry Potter* books (by J. K. Rowling), which have benefited from globalizing marketing strategies, media tie-ins and innumerable spin-offs in the form of toys, games, items of stationery, bathroom products, clothing, etc.

The debates about representation in children's books, started in the 1960s and 1970s, could be said to have had four main effects on children's literature. Firstly, by highlighting the importance of including different perspectives, the debates resulted in a wider circle of people becoming authors of children's books. Secondly, the debates affected the types of stories that were written. The protagonists in recent stories, for example, are from a wider variety of backgrounds than had previously been the case. More stories have been written 'against the grain', to subvert stereotypes related to gender, ethnicity, ability, sexuality, religion … or even genre stereotypes. If we return to thinking about fairy tales, for example, and

Harry Potter merchandise, including duvet cover, toys, puzzles, games, video and audio tapes, birthday cards, calendars, t-shirts and 'every flavour beans'.

A contemporary princess? *Princess Smartypants* by Babette Cole, first published in 1988.

consider the princesses of the new fairy tales of the 1970s and 1980s, we would almost certainly find more tomboyish, wrestling, motorbike riding, practical, strong, messy princesses than traditional ones!

The third main effect of the debates about representation has been, I think, the establishment of a lively critical readership for children's literature, amongst both children and adults. In school, even very young children are encouraged to critique their books, to identify the features of their favourite texts and to think about what they would want to say to the book's author. Adults have been encouraged to take an interest in children's literature – the public debates have shown that what children read is no longer an uncontroversial and anodyne area which parents don't need to bother about. Box 1 shows the books that were most frequently criticised in American newspapers and elsewhere in 2001, and the reasons for the challenges. Teenage fiction, particularly, regularly provokes arguments about the suitability of the issues that are considered. For instance, Melvin Burgess's Carnegie Medal winning novel *Junk* (1996) provoked heated discussions because of its focus upon drugs. The 'Author's Note' at the beginning of the novel ends dramatically: 'The book isn't fact; it isn't even faction. But it's all true, every word..'

> ## Box 1 The most frequently challenged books in the USA, 2001
>
> 1 *Harry Potter* series, by J.K. Rowling, for its focus on wizardry and magic.
>
> 2 *Of Mice and Men* by John Steinbeck, for using offensive language and being unsuited to age group.
>
> 3 *The Chocolate War* by Robert Cormier (the 'Most Challenged' fiction book of 1998), for using offensive language and being unsuited to age group.
>
> 4 *I Know Why the Caged Bird Sings* by Maya Angelou, for sexual content, racism, offensive language, violence and being unsuited to age group.
>
> 5 *Summer of My German Soldier* by Bette Greene for racism, offensive language and being sexually explicit.
>
> 6 *The Catcher in the Rye* by J.D. Salinger for offensive language and being unsuited to age group.
>
> 7 *Alice* series, by Phyllis Reynolds Naylor, for being sexually explicit, using offensive language and being unsuited to age group.
>
> 8 *Go Ask Alice* by Anonymous for being sexually explicit, for offensive language and drug use.
>
> 9 *Fallen Angels* by Walter Dean Myers, for offensive language and being unsuited to age group.
>
> 10 *Blood and Chocolate* by Annette Curtis Klause for being sexually explicit and unsuited to age group.
>
> (American Library Association, 2001, http://www.ala.org/bbooks/challeng.html, last accessed October 2002)

Controversy is highlighted in the marketing of Burgess's fiction. His 2001 novel *Lady: My Life as a Bitch*, in which the flirtatious heroine is accidentally turned into a dog, carried on the front cover a quotation that emphasized the controversial nature of the story: 'Melvin Burgess is about to trigger an earthquake in the publishing world with his new book – *The Guardian*.'

The fourth effect of opening up a debate about the ideological impact of children's literature is that it also, necessarily, raises questions about whether we really are influenced by what we read. If readers *weren't* influenced at all, it wouldn't much matter what children read. Since the debate is posited on the premise that what is in books does matter, we soon arrive at new questions about exactly *how* readers are influenced and how the reading process works. Developing theory about reader response and the processes of making meaning from texts is an important area of ongoing research in education, literary theory and psychology. These are complex fields of study in which ideas change as, for example, more is understood about the way the brain works, or as researchers help us develop our understanding of how meanings are made in different social and cultural contexts. But, faced with immediate and very practical decisions about whether to encourage or to ban the reading of *Mary Poppins*, or whether to try to deter your child from getting caught up in the latest superhero comic or cartoon craze, there is a need for a working theory about how books influence readers.

4.2 Children as readers

One of the working theories which underpinned much of the criticism of children's literature in the 1970s centred on the idea of identification. The assumption was that readers 'identified with' the main characters and therefore took on, at least temporarily, their viewpoints and values. This fairly simple view of how the process worked was questioned, not least because it was clear from empirical research that readers often produced 'aberrant' readings, that is readings that were different from the ones anticipated by the writer. In a study of young people reading pulp violence and horror, for example, Charles Sarland found readers importing their own ideologies and taking meanings from the texts in ways that were far more complex than are envisaged in models which depend upon the idea of identification (Sarland, 1991). Readers' responses are complex and often contradictory; ideologies are inscribed in fictional texts, which are not tracts or propaganda, in complex and often contradictory ways.

However, pointing out the complexity and complications of the issues does not necessarily help in deciding where you stand when making decisions on these matters! One way of thinking about it is to accept that children in the twenty-first century are bombarded with stories and images. The volume of the bombardment, and the sophistication of the stories and images, are more intense than has ever been the case before. Adults cannot entirely regulate what children read and see, and even the best intentioned texts will be read in contradictory ways, as Bronwyn Davies's research illustrates (see Box 2 overleaf).

Allow about 10 minutes

A C T I V I T Y 6   **Responding to children's reading**

This is a good point at which to pause and gather your thoughts about where you stand on these issues. Do you think that responsible adults should attempt to regulate children's reading? How should we prepare children to meet the challenges presented by new technologies in terms of the volume of unregulated material available to them in print and through the electronic media?

Decisions on these matters will be based on personal moral codes and principles. They will relate to what you think reading is for, and to your own views of childhood. But perhaps one responsibility that adults need to accept is the responsibility of helping children question the books they read, by encouraging them to develop their confidence as critical thinkers and by offering them opportunities to read widely and independently. Peter Hollindale, whose article 'Ideology and the children's book' has been influential in this whole area of discussion, puts it this way:

> Our priority in the world of children's books should not be to promote ideology but to understand it, and find ways of helping others to understand it, including the children themselves.

(Hollindale, 1988, p. 10).

Box 2 The Paper Bag Princess

Bronwyn Davies' interest in gender and meaning-making led her to research the varied ways that different five-year-old children understood the story *The Paper Bag Princess* (Munsch, 1983). Davies's own summary of the story is followed by Gabrielle's (a five-year-old girl) and then Robbie's (a five-year-old boy). The way the story is heard is different for each of the child listeners. Davies suggests that the differences relate, in part, to how the listener positions herself/himself in the story (i.e. with Elizabeth or Ronald or the dragon) and in part on the understanding of gender relations that is being drawn upon.

Bronwyn Davies's summary

This is an amusing story about a princess called Elizabeth who goes to incredible lengths to save her prince from a fierce dragon. At the beginning of the story, Princess Elizabeth and Prince Ronald are planning to get married, but then the dragon comes along, burns Elizabeth's castle and clothes and flies off into the distance carrying Prince Ronald by the seat of his pants. Elizabeth is very angry. She finds a paper bag to wear and follows the dragon. She tricks him into displaying all his magic powers until he falls asleep from exhaustion. She rushes into the dragon's cave to save Ronald only to find that he does not want to be saved by a princess who is covered in soot and has only an old paper bag to wear. Elizabeth is quite taken aback by this turn of events, and she says: 'Ronald, your clothes are really pretty and your hair is very neat. You look like a real prince, but you are a bum.' The last page shows her skipping off into the sunset alone and the story ends with the words: 'They didn't get married after all'.

(Davies, 1989, p. viii)

Gabrielle's summary

Princess Elizabeth is a 'nice' and 'beautiful' princess who is going to marry Prince Ronald.

The dragon burns her castle and clothes and crown and carries off Prince Ronald.

Elizabeth plans to 'follow the dragon on these trails'. 'She wants to talk to the dragon' and 'she is going to trick him'.

Princess Elizabeth is pleased that she is not going to marry Ronald because he is not a nice person. This is the correct decision.

Gabrielle says she would like to be like Elizabeth, though preferred her at the beginning rather than the end.

(Davies, 1989, p. 61).

Princess Elizabeth rescues Prince Ronald in *The Paper Bag Princess* by Robert Munsch. Illustration by Michael Martchenko.

Robbie's summary

Prince Ronald is a tennis player. 'He's got a tennis jumper and he won the tennis gold medal.' He is 'shy' and he doesn't want to marry Princess Elizabeth.

The dragon burns off Elizabeth's clothes, breaks her tower and burns the trees and flies off with Prince Ronald.

Elizabeth is 'cross'.

Elizabeth 'follows the trail' to 'look for him' 'because she wants to get Prince Ronald back'.

Ronald quite rightly tells her she is messy. He is angry that she is so dirty. He tells her to go away because he doesn't want to marry her.

Robbie would like to be Prince Ronald.

(Davies, 1989, p. 62).

SUMMARY OF SECTION 4

Debates from the 1960s onwards about the ideological impact of children's literature have led to:

- A wider range of people becoming authors of children's books.
- The availability of alternative stories, and attempts to challenge or subvert traditional values in children's books.
- Increasing interest in how children understand and respond to literature.

Traditional models of children as readers simply 'taking on' the values in books have given way to models of children as more active interpreters of texts, to some extent creating their own meanings as they read.

5 REVIEW AND CONCLUSIONS

This chapter has been able to offer only a brief account of some of the central questions in what is a wide, multidisciplinary field of study. It has been impossible in one chapter to discuss children's poetry or plays, or indeed many forms of children's fiction. Three themes have run through the chapter: how children's literature reflects and represents certain views of children and childhood; changing ideas about what counts as suitable literature for children; and the whole question of what children's literature is for. I have also considered recent debates about the social and cultural values inherent in children's books. The aim of the chapter was to help you clarify your own views on these issues, so it seems appropriate to end by thinking about how to relate these ideas to particular children's books. I have chosen extracts from three highly acclaimed picture books, a genre which has, in my view, been particularly creative and responsive to new ways of thinking in recent years.

Allow 20–30 minutes

A C T I V I T Y 7 **Children and childhood: contemporary views**

Look carefully at each of the pictures on the next two pages and read the accompanying contextual notes. Then consider:

1 Do these extracts tell you anything about views of children and childhood in contemporary European and American societies?

2 Do they tell you anything about what counts as suitable literature for children, and about what children's literature is for?

Where The Wild Things Are

From *Where The Wild Things Are*, by Maurice Sendak (1963).
Max begins the wild rumpus.

Max, wearing his wolf suit, has been sent to bed for 'making mischief'. A forest grows in his bedroom and Max sails away on a boat to a land of Wild Things who acclaim him as their king, 'the most wild thing of all'. This is one of six wordless pages showing their 'wild rumpus'. After the rumpus Max becomes lonely, sails home and finds 'his supper waiting for him' in his room. The final page, which contains no illustration, reads 'and it was still hot'.

Where The Wild Things Are was first published in the USA in 1963. It won the Caldecott Medal for the Most Distinguished Picture Book of 1963. It has remained in print ever since, and is widely written about as a classic of the genre.

Rose Blanche

From *Rose Blanche*, illustrated by Roberto Innocenti (1985).

The text and illustrations describe the everyday life of Rose Blanche and her mother in a town in Germany during the Second World War. After seeing soldiers recapture a child who tries to escape from a lorry, Rose follows and discovers a prison camp. The inmates appeal for food. Rose saves and steals food and regularly takes it to the camp. In the panic as the war is ending, Rose disappears. She has returned to the camp. 'As Rose Blanche turned to walk away, there was a shot … ' Her mother never finds her. Nature – and colour – begin 'another, gentler, invasion' of the site.

Roberto Innocenti was born in 1940 near Florence in Italy. *Rose Blanche* was the name of a group of German citizens who protested against the war. The book was first published in 1985 and is still in print.

Black and White

Each double page of *Black and White* is divided into quarters, which contain words and pictures, or just pictures, or just words. Separate stories can be tracked through from page to page. It is not immediately clear whether the four stories are linked, whether they are part of the same story, or whether they are occurring at the same time. The cover contains a 'warning' that points this out. The story illustrated here is one of the four strands, called 'Udder Chaos'. The opening images are of a pink-faced burglar figure, wearing a black mask and a black and white striped jumper, in a herd of black and white cows. The images have gradually disintegrated into patches of colour on preceding pages, suggesting that the burglar is being carried along with the cows towards a choir festival which is sign-posted on the page immediately before the one shown here.

Black and White was first published in 1990. It won the 1991 Caldecott Medal. David Macauley is well known for his non-fiction, as well as his fictional, picture books, particularly *The Way Things Work*.

From David Macauley's *Black and White* (1990).

COMMENT

Where the Wild Things Are can be interpreted as an exploration of Max's anger. The fact that Max is being punished for antisocial behaviour is established at the start of the book. His 'journey' to become the wildest of the Wild Things is a journey into his fury, which is, symbolically, acted out with abandon in the six full pages of wordless rumpus. Here is a child who is being given a chance to 'get it out of his system' in a safe and loving environment, symbolized by the orderly room and the hot food at the end. This acceptance of childhood anger is rooted in twentieth century psychological views of childhood. A young child reading the book is likely to interpret the story much more literally, of course, but perhaps the unexpressed, unconscious emotions that drive the story are part of what attracts children to it. The book is marketed as literature for very young children but nevertheless it has a multi-layered structure, which leaves it open to different readings. The artwork is used boldly to carry the narrative forward – it works in conjunction with the rather elliptical and poetic language of the text, rather than as simply an illustration of the written text.

Rose Blanche acknowledges that childhood innocence cannot exist outside of history. The reader stands with Rose, looking at desperate children across an incomprehensible divide. As a child, Rose is courageous, stealthy, stoical, and knows instinctively that talking is both dangerous and fruitless. Her presence provides splashes of colour in an increasingly monotone world. The children in this book have dignity and courage, but they are ultimately victims of adult brutality. The book carries with it an expectation that a child reader will be able to understand and to tolerate this view of children – that the child does not need to be protected from knowing the brutal facts of history. Clearly the publishers felt that 'children's literature' – and indeed, picture books – could accommodate a topic of such seriousness and sensitivity. Again, the artwork is more than an illustration of the words. It carries much new information – here, for example, the Star of David on the prisoners' clothing – and evokes the sombre mood of the book.

The humour in *Black and White* is highly visual and quite sophisticated, relying upon the reader to appreciate the embarrassment of the choir member whose clothes have been stolen, to note the surprise of the man who has noticed the udder and to pick out the burglar figure. The whole image of a herd of black and white cows lost amongst a group of such serious choristers is absurd and depends for its humour on the reader having some background knowledge about how occasions like choir festivals are usually conducted. The child here is expected to be quite knowing, with a sense of humour sophisticated enough to appreciate the ironies of the burglar's progress. The text as a whole contains fragmented narratives and images, and there is a strong sense of playfulness and the need for the reader to work out what is going on, rather than be told it directly by the author.

All three books demand high levels of visual literacy from their child readers. Even in *Where the Wild Things Are*, the book which is aimed at the youngest age group, readers are expected to draw inferences and employ quite sophisticated sense-making strategies. The books are challenging, and their subject matter is not cosy, domestic or especially 'safe'. These examples of children's literature encourage readers to ask questions and develop their own opinions.

REFERENCES

BALLANTYNE, R. M. (1994) *The Coral Island,* London, Wordsworth (first published 1857).

BETTELHEIM, B. (1976) *The Uses of Enchantment: the meaning and importance of fairy tales,* Harmondsworth, Penguin Books.

BLYTON, E. (2000) *The Secret Seven,* London, Hodder and Stoughton (first published 1949).

BURGESS, M. (1996) *Junk,* London, Andersen Press.

BURGESS, M. (2001) *Lady: my life as a bitch,* London, Andersen Press.

BURNETT, F. H. (1987) *The Secret Garden,* Oxford, Oxford University Press (first published 1911).

CARPENTER, H. and PRICHARD, M. (1984) *The Oxford Companion to Children's Literature,* Oxford, Oxford University Press.

CARTER, A. (ed) (1991) *The Virago Book of Fairy Tales,* London, Virago.

COLE, B. (1988) *Princess Smartypants,* London, Picture Lions.

DARTON, F. J. H. (1982) *Children's Books in England: five centuries of social life.* 3rd edn, revised by Brian Alderson, Cambridge, Cambridge University Press (first published 1932).

DAVIES, B. (1989) *Frogs and Snails and Feminist Tales: preschool children and gender,* Sydney, Allen and Unwin.

FREUD, S. (1958) 'The occurrence in dreams of material from fairy tales' in *Character and Culture,* New York, Macmillan (first published 1913).

FURNIVALL, F. J. (1868) *The Babees' Book,* London, Trubner.

GRAHAME, K. (1978) *The Wind in the Willows,* London, Methuen (first published 1908).

HALL, C. AND COLES, M. (1999) *Children's Reading Choices,* London, Routledge.

HENDRICK, H. (1997) 'Constructions and reconstructions of British childhood: an interpretative survey, 1800 to the present day' in JAMES, A. AND PROUT, A. (eds) *Constructing and Reconstructing Childhood,* London, Falmer.

HOLLINDALE, P. (1988) 'Ideology and the children's book' *Signal,* **55**, pp.3–22.

HOLMAN, F. (1996) *Slake's Limbo,* London, Heinemann (first published 1974).

INNOCENTI, R. (1985) *Rose Blanche,* London, Jonathan Cape (text by Ian McEwan).

INGLIS, F. (1981) *The Promise of Happiness,* Cambridge, Cambridge University Press.

KINGSLEY, C. (1970) *The Water Babies,* London, Samuel French (first published 1863).

LARRICK, N. (1965) 'The all-white world of children's books', *Saturday Review,* September, pp.84–5.

LOCKE, J. (1989) *Some Thoughts Concerning Education,* Oxford, Clarendon Press (first published 1693).

MACAULEY, D. (1990) *Black and White,* New York, Houghton Mifflin.

MILNE, A. A. (1965) *Winnie-the-Pooh,* London, Methuen (first published 1926).

MONTGOMERY, L. M. (1994) *Anne of Green Gables,* Harmondsworth, Puffin Books (first published 1908).

MUNSCH, R. (1983) *The Paper Bag Princess,* Toronto, Annick Press.

OPIE, I. and OPIE, P. (1974) *The Classic Fairy Tales,* Oxford, Oxford University Press.

PEARCE, P. (1984) *Tom's Midnight Garden,* Harmondsworth, Puffin (first published 1958).

PLUMB, J. H. (1975) 'The new world of children in eighteenth century England' *Past and Present,* **67**, pp. 74–95.

RANSOME, A. (1961) *Swallows and Amazons,* London, Cape (first published 1930).

ROUSSEAU, J-J. (1911) *Emile, ou de l'éducation,* London, Dent (first published 1762; English translation, BLOOM, A. (2001) *Emile, or On Education,* Harmondsworth, Penguin Books).

ROWLING, J. K. (1997 onwards) *Harry Potter* series, London, Bloomsbury Children's Books.

SARLAND, C. (1991) *Young People Reading: Culture and Response,* Milton Keynes, Open University Press.

SENDAK, M. (1992) *Where the Wild Things Are,* London, Picture Lions.

SHERWOOD, M. M. (1818) *The History of the Fairchild Family,* London, Hatchard.

SPYRI, J. (1995) *Heidi,* Harmondsworth, Penguin Books (first published 1881).

TOWNSEND, J. R. (1990), *Written for Children* London, The Bodley Head.

TOWNSEND, J. R. (1994) *Trade and Plumb Cake For Ever, Huzza! The Life and Work of John Newbery, 1713–1767,* Cambridge, Colt Books.

TREASE, G. (1949) *Tales Out of School,* London, Heinemann.

WARD, W. R. and HEITZENRATER, R. P. (eds) (1986) *The Works of John Wesley* Vol. 3: Sermons III, pp. 71–114, Nashville, Abingdon Press.

WIGGIN, K. D. (1994) *Rebecca of Sunnybrook Farm,* London, Wordsworth (first published 1903).

WOODHEAD, M. and MONTGOMERY, H. K. (eds) (2003) *Understanding Childhood: an interdisciplinary approach,* Chichester, John Wiley and Sons Ltd/The Open University (Book 1 of the Open University course U212 *Childhood*).

WRITERS AND READERS PUBLISHING CO-OPERATIVE (1976) *Racism and Sexism in Children's Books,* London, Writers and Readers Publishing Co-operative.

WYSS, J. D. (1996) *The Swiss Family Robinson,* Harmondsworth, Puffin (first published 1814).

ZIPES, J. (1991) *Fairy Tales and the Art of Subversion,* New York, Routledge (first published 1983).

Little Red Riding Hood

Geoff Fox

Introduction

Surely no heroine has met her audience in so many guises as Little Red Riding Hood. Her tale might be told simply as a bed time story, but she also features in pantomimes, musicals and plays, in reading primers, movable books and comic verse, in moralizing pamphlets and scratch-and-sniff paperbacks. Her story is told on tape, film, radio, television, records and CDs. Most commonly, children first encounter her in picture-books, where she might be anything from a moppet of three or four to a self-assured young woman of sixteen or seventeen. She has been all kinds of animal, from Walt Disney's Minnie Mouse to Colin MacNaughton's Preston Pig in a red duffel coat.

She is published literally all over the world. Even in Outer Mongolia, where bookshops of any kind are hard to find, she was discovered on a market stall in a version which may have originated elsewhere (she is a blonde, unlike any of her local readers in Ulan Bator) but with a Mongolian text.

Scholars with backgrounds in literature, fine art, psychoanalysis or education have been fascinated by her continuing appeal as generations and cultures reinterpret her story. Beneath the surface of the tale, they have found such issues as the male domination of women (some see the tale as a parable of rape), gender stereotyping or initiation into womanhood. Such matters inevitably lead any reader directly engaged with children, whether relative, teacher or librarian, to the questions: Is this a story I want children to know? If so, which version? And what do I think my chosen version offers to the reader/listener in my care?

By way of background to such concerns, the following sections consider: the tale's origins; versions by two of the most influential retellers, Perrault and the Brothers Grimm; and the development of the tale in more recent times.

The tale's origins: the story of grandmother

The earliest oral versions of the tale seem to originate in the South of France and the North of Italy. Jack Zipes (1993) draws upon the work of the French folklorist, Paul Delarue, who collected the following oral story in the Nivernois, in about 1885. Very probably, versions such as this had been handed down from teller to teller for several centuries.

> There was a woman who had made some bread. She said to her daughter: 'Go carry this hot loaf and a bottle of milk to your granny'.
>
> So the little girl departed. At the crossway, she met bzou, the werewolf, who said to her:
>
> 'Where are you going?'

'I'm taking this hot loaf and a bottle of milk to my granny.'

'What path are you taking,' said the werewolf, 'the path of needles or the path of pins?'

'The path of needles,' the little girl said.

'All right, then I'll take the path of pins.'

The little girl entertained herself by gathering needles. Meanwhile the werewolf arrived at the grandmother's house, killed her, put some of her meat in the cupboard and a bottle of her blood on the shelf. The little girl arrived and knocked at the door.

'Push the door,' said the werewolf, 'it's barred by a piece of wet straw.'

'Good day, granny. I've brought you a hot loaf of bread and a bottle of milk.'

'Put it in the cupboard, my child. Take some of the meat which is inside and the bottle of wine on the shelf.'

After she had eaten, there was a little cat which said:

'Phooey! A slut is she who eats the flesh and drinks the blood of her granny.'

'Undress yourself, my child,' the werewolf said, 'and come lie down beside me.'

'Where should I put my apron?'

'Throw it into the fire, my child, you won't be needing it any more.'

And each time she asked where she should put all her other clothes, the bodice, the dress, the petticoat, and the long stockings, the wolf responded:

'Throw them into the fire, my child, you won't be needing them any more.'

When she laid herself down in the bed, the little girl said:

'Oh, Granny, how hairy you are!'

'The better to keep myself warm, my child!'

'Oh, Granny, what big nails you have!'

'The better to scratch me with, my child!'

'Oh, Granny, what big shoulders you have!'

'The better to carry the firewood, my child'

'Oh, Granny, what big ears you have!'

'The better to hear you with, my child!'

'Oh, Granny, what big nostrils you have!'

'The better to snuff my tobacco with, my child!'

'Oh, Granny, what a big mouth you have!'

'The better to eat you with, my child!'

'Oh, Granny, I've got to go badly. Let me go outside.'

'Do it in the bed, my child!'

'Oh, no, Granny. I want to go outside.'

'All right, but make it quick.'

> The werewolf attached a woollen rope to her foot and let her go outside. When the little girl was outside, she tied the end of the rope to a plum tree in the courtyard. The werewolf became impatient and said:
>
> 'Are you making a load out there? Are you making a load?'
>
> When he realized that nobody was answering him, he jumped out of bed and saw that the little girl had escaped. He followed her but arrived at her house just at the moment she entered.

Zipes opens up the metaphors and symbols of the tale for us. He notes that the references to pins and needles imply that the girl has embarked upon the needlework apprenticeship undergone by young French peasant girls as they take their places within an adult society. The girl 'replaces' her grandmother by eating her flesh and drinking her blood. Whilst her attacker may be seen as the embodiment of male oppression, he may also be seen quite literally as a werewolf, for there were numerous trials in France in the fifteenth, sixteenth and seventeenth centuries of men accused of being werewolves. Stories of cannibalism in mountain villages suffering harsh winters were not unknown.

The dialogue between the girl and the wolf in this tale may suggest to the reader a meeting on equal terms. She seems not unwilling to discard her clothes, and the wolf's repeated 'You won't be needing them any more' implies some kind of transition for the girl. Her decision to leave the wolf is equally deliberate, however, and her return to her own house depends entirely upon her own determination and wits.

Perrault and 'Little Red Riding Hood'

Scholars largely agree that the first printed version of the tale was that of Charles Perrault (1628–1703) in his *Histoires ou contes du temps passé (Stories or Tales of Past Times)* published in 1697. Perrault had been a civil servant during the reign of Louis XIV – he served, for example, as Controller General of the King's Buildings, Gardens, Arts and Manufactories, an important position in the administration of a ruler as concerned with self-aggrandisement as 'le roi soleil'. Perrault was also a well-regarded poet and essayist, frequenting the literary salons of Paris. In 1671, he was elected to the Académie Française. He was almost seventy years old when he began the work for which he is best remembered. Taking several popular folk tales (including Sleeping Beauty, Puss-in-Boots and Cinderella as well as the tales on which he based Little Red Riding Hood), he transformed them into stories for the polite adult audience of the court and salons who would appreciate the political and social comment he introduced into the old tales of the countryside. If Perrault's sources were oral versions similar to 'The Story of Grandmother', he clearly decided upon several changes. The girl is no longer the attractively independent heroine of the oral tale. In Perrault, her mother 'doted on her and her grandmother even more'. It is her grandmother who makes her little hood the colour of which, scholars suggest, a listener of the day would have associated with sinfulness. She is childlike in the way she gathers nuts, runs after butterflies and makes bouquets of small flowers. Most importantly of all for Red Riding Hood, when she gets eaten up her story ends, apart from the moral which Perrault appends to his tale:

One sees here that young children,
Especially young girls,
Pretty, well brought-up, and gentle,
Should never listen to anyone who happens by,
And if this occurs, it is not so strange
When the wolf should eat them.
I say the wolf, for all wolves
Are not of the same kind.
There are some with winning ways,
Not loud, nor bitter, or angry,
Who are tame, good-natured, and pleasant
And follow young ladies
Right into their homes, right into their alcoves.
But alas for those who do not know that of all the wolves
The docile ones are those who are most dangerous.

Little Red Riding-Hood.

TALE I.

 ONCE upon a time there lived in a certain village, a little country girl, the prettiest creature ever was seen. Her mother was excessively fond of her; and her grandmother doated on her much more. This good woman got made for her a little red Riding-Hood; which became the girl so extremely well, that every body called her *Little Red Riding-Hood.* One

Little Red Riding Hood. The first English edition of Perrault's stories appeared in 1729.

So, Perrault seems to imply, the responsibility for the girl's death is largely her own. She ought to have known better, she should not have listened to a wolf who, after all, was only doing what a wolf has to do. Perrault had lived among courtiers and visited salons long enough to know his audience, and the enthusiastic welcome his tales received reflects the attitudes which prevailed in polite Parisian society.

The Brothers Grimm and 'Little Red Cap'

Jakob and Wilhelm Grimm (1785–1863 and 1786–1859 respectively) produced their collection of tales, *Kinder und Hausmärchen (Children and Household Tales)* in two volumes (1812 and 1815). Over the next 40 years, they refined and republished their work 17 times, sometimes incorporating scholarly notes but also producing an illustrated 'Small Edition' of 50 tales intended for children.

A dramatic 'tragedy' by Ludwig Tiech (1800) based on the tale had included a flirtatious huntsman ('Give me a kiss, you silly little urchin') who is too late to save the victims but slays the wolf as a warning to others. The Grimms took the avenging huntsman a step further. His curiosity aroused by the replete wolf's snores as he passes the cottage, he decides to look inside. Finding the bloated creature, he slits open the belly to see 'the glowing red cap' and releases the girl and her grandmother. Despite the invasive nature of the operation, the wolf slumbers on and Little Red Cap loads the wolf's stomach with stones. When he finally wakes, the wolf is too heavy to jump up and falls over, dead. The hunter skins the wolf, grandma enjoys the cake and wine and Little Red Cap tells herself; 'Never again in your life will you stray by yourself into the woods when your mother has forbidden it'.

The Grimms were not finished yet. To demonstrate that Little Red Cap and her grandmother had really learned their lessons, the meeting in the wood is repeated with another wolf. This time, however, the generations work together to lure the second visitor onto the roof, drawn by the smell of frying sausages. Here he overbalances, falls from the tiles and drowns in a handy stone trough. Little Red Cap 'went merrily on her way home'.

More recent retellings

Over the two centuries since the Grimms' retelling, the tale has been reinterpreted literally thousands of times. Modern publishing practices allow the production of international editions, so that the illustrations for a contemporary Greek edition, for example, are identical to those of a Portuguese text. The influence of Disney is as evident in some Russian editions as in others produced in Italy or Canada. Almost always, the ending of the tale is sanitized, with the bloodless execution of the wolf (usually 'off page') and the resurrection of the unsullied girl and her grandmother. Sometimes, the wolf is even allowed a second chance. A 1992 British retelling concludes with grandma stuffing the wolf's tummy with a sack-load of onions. 'When the wolf woke up he felt terrible. His head hurt and his tummy felt as though it was on fire. "Ooooh," he said to himself, "I'll never eat another grandma again." He never did and he never talked to strange girls either.' (Langley, 1992)

Occasionally, versions are produced where the author's eye seems to be on an adult reader. Here, for example, is the final page of the text from a movable book produced by Child's Play (International) UK. The page is filled with the 'popped-up' heads of the Woodcutter puffing away on his pipe and the little girl; in the background, granny looks on with a smile and the wolf lies outside the cottage door with his legs in the air and his arms spread-eagled:

RED: Oh, Sir, you got here just in time!

WOODSMAN: It was lucky I was passing. Otherwise, the wolf would have just got his dessert, instead of his just deserts.

RED: I have learned once and for all not to talk to strangers. Thank you for saving Grandma and me.

WOODSMAN: Think nothing of it, my dear. Perhaps I could come and share your delicious health food lunch.

RED: I am sorry, Sir, but you are a stranger too. And you should give up smoking. It is bad for you.

THE END

A US edition of this book with identical cover and illustrations carries a wholly conventional verbal reworking of the tale.

Maria Tatar (1999) believes that in the story of Little Red Riding Hood, 'the feeling of dread, coupled with a sense of enchantment, captures the fascination with matters from which children are usually shielded'. Certainly, each retelling rewards attentive and discriminating reading of word or image.

References

CARPENTER, H. and PRICHARD, M. (1984) *The Oxford Companion to Children's Literature*, Oxford, Oxford University Press.

LANGLEY, J. (1992) *Little Red Riding Hood*, London, HarperCollins.

ROUGER, G. (1967) *Contes de Perrault,* Paris, Garnier.

TATAR, M. (1999) *The Classic Fairy Tales*, New York and London, W.W.Morton & Co. p.10

ZIPES, J. (1993) *The Trials and Tribulations of Little Red Riding Hood*, New York and London, Routledge.

Source

This reading was specially commissioned for this chapter.

READING B

Aboriginal narratives for children:
The Story of the Falling Star

Clare Bradford

Writing for children has been an important facet of Aboriginal publication since the 1970s, and is integral to the contemporary politics of Australia's postcolonial culture. Aborigines do not currently enjoy a postcolonial state in which they have achieved recognition, compensation and political autonomy – these are yet to come – but it is no longer possible within political, academic or popular discourses to ignore the facts of invasion and dispossession integral to Australia's foundation, or the significance of Aboriginality to national identity. It was not until 1967, following a nation-wide referendum, that Aboriginal people were given the right to vote. From this decade Aboriginal authors and artists increasingly turned to cultural production in order to protect and celebrate their traditions, notably through texts for children. Indigenous publishers and community groups consciously aim at producing texts which are located within the assumptions, beliefs and practices of Aboriginal culture, so offering Aboriginal children an empowered sense of Aboriginal identities, and non-Aboriginal children an experience of cultural difference. By publishing texts for children, Aboriginal people recover traditional stories which have been neglected, use Aboriginal languages which are in danger of dying out (in dual-language texts) and retell the history of Aboriginal people from the point of view of Aborigines and not the dominant culture.

In this reading I will be concentrating on one Aboriginal text, *The Story of the Falling Star,* told by Elsie Jones. This text, first published in 1989, has been reprinted numerous times, most recently in 2001. It has been purchased mainly by schools, both primary and secondary, and has been widely read by children, but it has also found a readership among the general public, because it is a book suitable both to children and to adults. Among Aboriginal communities it has been particularly important, because it shows how one group of Aboriginal people have reclaimed an ancient story and retold it in a contemporary style. It is thus a book which traverses Aboriginal and non-Aboriginal audiences of children and adults.

The Story of the Falling Star tells two related stories. One is a modern story about a falling star which was observed in the 1950s and which was followed by an episode of bad weather, with heavy rain and wind. The other story is set in exactly the same place, in the country of the Paakantji people in northern New South Wales, but it tells about events which took place in ancient times, and is a narrative handed down through many generations of Paakantji. When the events of the ancient story occurred, a magician or 'cleverman' called Malkarra was living with the Paakantji, but he was not of their clan and they did not like him, believing him to be treacherous. Thus, when he warned them of a disaster to come and advised them to move off their land, they did not believe him. The falling star caused great loss of life, with many people burned. It was followed by terrible floods so that the Paakantji had to flee their country carrying people who were injured, and shelter in caves in higher country.

Cave paintings relating to this episode still exist. When the danger was over, the Paakantji had a great corroboree (celebration) to commemorate their survival.

As well as reading Aboriginal texts for their aesthetic values, it is important to read them politically, in the light of the long struggle by Aboriginal people for access to and ownership of their ancestral lands. The idea of 'country' is crucial to Aboriginal formulations of identity, and plays an important part in *The Story of the Falling Star*. In Aboriginal English, the word 'country', as in 'my country', refers not to the Australian nation but to the particular tract of land to which people belong because of kinship and association. People derive their sense of identity from their connections with country and from the rituals, clan relationships and traditional knowledge associated with country. The process of colonization involved large-scale appropriation of Aboriginal lands, so that many Aboriginal people have lost access to their country. Over the last few decades Aboriginal clans have sought restitution of their lands, but it has been difficult for indigenous people to gain land rights because of the rival claims of pastoralists and mining companies, and because laws relating to land have generally favoured settlers and their descendants. Non-Aboriginal people have slowly come to understand how important country is to Aboriginal people, so that mainstream publishers producing Aboriginal narratives are generally careful to include maps or explanations showing where such narratives originate, and the peoples and individuals to whom they belong.

A distinctive aspect of Aboriginal textuality is that of notions of authorship. Traditional Aboriginal narratives are not owned by individuals, but are subject to the collective ownership of a kinship group and associated with a particular stretch of country and often with ceremonial occasions. Within a kinship group, individuals become custodians of certain narratives. Older people will pass on custodianship to those who have the correct familial relationships to them, and the right associations with country, and serious consequences may occur if a person tells a story without authorization. Sometimes narratives (notably song cycles) are serial in form; a narrator will tell a story as far as a certain point, and then defer to another narrator who is responsible for telling the part of the story that takes place in the next stretch of country. Many narratives originate from the Dreaming, a time or place when ancestor spirits created the land and its features, instituted groups of people and taught them rites and songs. The Dreaming is not an ancient event now over, but continues in the seasonal renewal of the country and in the rituals of humans.

In *The Story of the Falling Star* modes of transmitting narratives are represented visually; for this is a text as much about how narratives are passed from one person to another as about the events it describes, which involve two episodes of falling stars, one in the 1950s and one in ancient times. The more recent family story is told by a grandfather, Frankie, to his grandchildren, and the illustration you see in Picture 1 captures a moment of transition from one storyteller to another. Frankie and his audience are placed in the background of the page; in the centre is the figure of Elsie Jones, the custodian of the second (ancient) story, looking out of the page directly at her audience, her words in a speech balloon. She holds a hand-drawn map produced, as its scroll form suggests, by a school student,

NOW, THIS STORY THAT FRANKIE'S TELLING HIS GRANDCHILDREN IS VERY INTERESTING. IT REMINDS ME OF **ANOTHER** STORY THAT STARTS AT THE EXACT SAME PLACE...BUT THIS STORY IS SO OLD, WE DON'T EVEN KNOW HOW OLD IT IS. BUT IT'S A PAAKANTJI STORY, ABOUT PAAKANTJI LAND AND PAAKANTJI PEOPLE.

SCALE 1:250,000

"MOUNT MURCHISON"

0   5   10

MILES

0   5   10

KILOMETRES

WILCANNIA

"MURTEE"

THIS IS WHERE ELIZA JOHNSON SAW A STAR FALL. IT IS ALSO THE PLACE WHERE A STAR FELL IN A VERY OLD PAAKANTJI STORY.

Picture 1

fourteen-year-old Murray Butcher, who is mentioned in the acknowledgements. Indeed, the book as a whole presents as a disarmingly naive work, home-made and unpretentious, but in fact it is a sophisticated and layered text. In this page, one storyteller (Frankie) cedes to a more senior one, Elsie Jones, whose authority is shown by her position on the page, her bodily presence and her knowledge of country and people, encoded in the map she shows and in her repetition of the name of the group to which the story belongs: 'it's a Paakantji story, about Paakantji land and Paakantji people'.

As the narrative proceeds, its communal nature is represented through collages showing its audience, who model to readers of the book how the narrative should be received—that is, with attention and respect. The faces seen in Picture 2 perform a further semiotic function: they play out the living tradition within which narratives are handed on. Elsie Jones refers to

Picture 2

a former custodian, the old Paakantji clever-man, Dick Willow; and as the audience members participate in the narrative by exclamations and questions they too are linked in the line of custodianship and identified with the place where the narrative is told. Thus, this retelling of the story insists both on the presence of the past, and on the fact that Aboriginal culture is continually transformed as ancient stories are retold for contemporary audiences.

The cultural theorist Stephen Muecke says that 'the postcolonial problematic … is based on the notion of (re)attributing value to the Aboriginal discourses' (1992, p. 15). That is, if Australia is to reach a state of decolonization where Aboriginal culture is valued and respected, non-Aboriginal people need to understand and 'reattribute value to' Aboriginal narratives and Aboriginal narrative practices, and this involves rereading colonial discourses through Aboriginal perspectives. This is exactly what

Picture 3

happens in Picture 3, where children descended from the Paakantji people are photographed in and in front of a shelter which they have constructed along the lines of those used by their ancestors. These photographs are placed beneath a colonial engraving of Aboriginal people in a similar shelter. The hunched shoulders of the woman on the right and of the man squatting in front of the shelter, and the immobility of the scene, construct this as a picture of the doomed race living out its primitive life; such scenes of pathos are common in early colonial artworks, where they convey a mixture of pity and voyeuristic pleasure. Transposed here into an Aboriginal text, the drawing takes on other meanings. Most obviously, its gloom is overturned by the liveliness and poise of the children; but it also 'reattributes value to' the figures in the drawing, reclaiming them as kinsfolk and as people and rescuing them from their representation as specimens of the dying race. Strategies like this are commonly used by

Picture 4

Aboriginal authors and illustrators to overturn colonial representations of Aborigines.

As I said earlier, Aboriginal narratives operate through complex systems of custodianship, involving forms of knowledge, rights and obligations which are specific to individuals and to groups of people. For instance, *The Story of the Falling Star* shows that Elsie Jones is the custodian of specific knowledges, rights and obligations in a sequence in which she shows her audience inscriptions in the rocks around the site of the falling star (Picture 4). Here she links the ancient story with hand stencils made by certain of the survivors of the cataclysmic events (fire and flood) associated with the falling star. In the top third of the page, one of the Paakantji people asks Elsie Jones how the inscriptions relate to the narrative; in the middle of the page is her response, which identifies which families out of the contemporary Paakantji are descended from those who left their handmarks in the rock. In the lower third of the page, the stencilled rock links young and old members of these families. From the top to the bottom of the page, then, ancestral rights to place and signs are progressively narrowed and refined. But this is not all, because the book's readers, looking at the faces of the descendants, are also reminded that they do not necessarily have the right to 'put their hands there to show they [belong] to that place'. With great subtlety, then, the visual narrative affirms the continuing potency of ancient practices of custodianship and their inscription on the land.

In Aboriginal Dreaming narratives, the land is created by mythological beings, ancestors who travel through a blank space and fill it with features (rocks, mountains, rivers, gorges) as they proceed. The landscape is thus a vast text, rich with the inscriptions of the ancestors. These traditions of ritual and narrative continue in spoken narratives and songs, and in published works such as *The Story of the Falling Star*. But as Elsie Jones makes very clear, non-Aboriginal consumers should not imagine that they can ever fully know, let alone own, the meanings inscribed in this and other Aboriginal texts. In *The Story of the Falling Star*, Aboriginal textuality engages with Western forms and practices in order to make Aboriginal traditions available to Aboriginal and non-Aboriginal readers. Above all it affirms the centrality of country to narrative traditions. Thus, it carries political messages about the attachment of Aboriginal people to their ancestral lands, and their contemporary struggles for land rights.

References

JONES, E. (1989) *The Story of the Falling Star*, Canberra, Aboriginal Studies Press.

MUECKE, S. (1992) *Textual Spaces: Aboriginality and cultural studies*, New South Wales, Sydney, University Press.

Source

This reading was specially commissioned for this chapter.

Chapter 5
Multimedia childhoods

David Buckingham

CONTENTS

LEARNING OUTCOMES

When you have studied this chapter, you should be able to:

1 Identify and debate contrasting views of children's relationships with the media, in relation to broader perspectives on childhood and children's culture.

2 Develop an awareness of the technological and economic forces that influence children's relationships with the media.

3 Identify some of the changing formal and thematic characteristics of media texts produced specifically for children.

4 Identify some of the theoretical and methodological issues at stake in studying children as media audiences, in relation to broader debates about media power.

5 Reflect systematically on the differences between your own childhood uses of media and those of contemporary children.

I INTRODUCTION

The media are self-evidently a central aspect of contemporary children's lives. Surveys consistently show that most children in industrialized countries spend more time watching television than they spend in school, or in interacting with their families or friends. If we add to this the time they spend reading books and magazines, watching films and videos, listening to recorded music, playing computer games and surfing the internet, it is clear that the media are far and away children's major leisure-time pursuit. This phenomenon often provokes anxiety among adults who claim to be concerned for children's welfare. The media, they argue, have a negative influence on children's psychological – and indeed physical – well-being. 'Too much' exposure to the media is commonly seen to lead to violence and delinquency, sexual promiscuity, educational underachievement, obesity, apathy and cynicism, and a whole host of anti-social behaviours. At times, these anxieties rise to the level of 'moral panics', in which the media are seen to be primarily responsible for the demise of moral standards and civilized behaviour (Barker and Petley, 2001).

Sociologists of childhood have largely neglected the role of the media in children's lives. Yet it is now impossible to understand contemporary childhood without taking account of the media. Indeed, it could be argued that children today are living 'media childhoods' – that children's experiences, and indeed the *meanings* of childhood itself, are largely defined and determined by the electronic media. And yet children are also often celebrated as 'active consumers', who are self-confident, wise and discriminating in their dealings with media. Of course, debates about these issues are particularly prevalent in industrialized countries; and it is the experience of children growing up in these 'media-saturated' societies that forms the primary focus of this chapter. However, widespread access to electronic media is increasingly a global phenomenon, which is affecting children in developing countries as well.

This chapter begins by looking at some of the arguments that recur in public debates about these issues – arguments that typically overstate the negative and (less frequently) the positive influences of media in children's lives. I argue that we need to understand the role of the media as a dynamic and multi-faceted process, a matter of the interaction between *production, texts* and *audiences*. A discussion of these three elements forms the core of this chapter; and in the final section, by means of a particular case study, I consider some of the ways in which they are related. Threaded through the chapter is a series of activities designed to encourage you to reflect on your own childhood experiences of the media, and the changing role they play in children's lives. We begin with the first of these.

Allow about 45 minutes

ACTIVITY I   A media autobiography

Most readers of this chapter are likely to have grown up with some form of media – or can remember the advent of 'new' media (such as television or video) at some point in their lives. Before you read further, try to recall your earliest memories of television and the cinema.

1   Which programmes or films do you remember watching? What do you particularly recall about them? Did you have favourite characters or stars, theme tunes, catch phrases, and so on? Do you recall watching things which really scared or shocked you, or made you upset?

2   Did you have particular rituals associated with TV viewing, or with cinema-going – for example, favourite times to watch, people you liked to watch with, things you might do at the same time (like eating)?

3   Did your parents ever try to control your exposure to particular types of media, or to encourage you to watch or read particular things? Did similar rules apply to other members of your family? Do you remember watching your first 'forbidden' film or programme?

4   Do you remember anything you might have done as a result of television, the cinema or other media – for example, made or bought something, played a particular game, read a book, imitated or dressed like a favourite character?

5   Finally, think about how representative you are of people who are like you – for example, in terms of gender, ethnicity, social class, the place or community in which you live, your generation. To what extent are your tastes and preferences typical of your social group?

COMMENT

The attractions of media nostalgia are of course a growing preoccupation in the media themselves. It is hard to avoid TV retrospectives of 1970s cop shows or soap operas, or best-forgotten pop performers. The nostalgia surrounding children's programmes is particularly powerful: several channels are now re-running children's shows from earlier decades, not least for the benefit of adult audiences, and there are countless fan web sites devoted to cataloguing the more obscure details of adults' earliest screen memories.

Family viewing – media nostalgia may be dewy-eyed or ironic.

While permitting a degree of dewy-eyed – or perhaps ironic – nostalgia, a 'media autobiography' of this kind should raise some broader issues. In my experience, there are three general points that frequently emerge:

1 Our experiences of media are often impossible to separate from our everyday lives – from the rituals and relationships that surround and define media use. We don't just remember TV programmes, for example; we remember who we used to watch them with, when and where we watched them, and what it *meant* to us to do so.

2 The media help to define what *counts* as 'childish' or 'adult'; and this is reinforced by the ways in which parents regulate their children's viewing. Most of us can probably remember aspiring to watch particular programmes that we didn't completely understand, or watching 'forbidden' films that somehow promised us access to a more adult world.

3 Media use is inextricably tied up with the process of identity formation. However temporarily and even superficially, the media give us access to new identities, or fantasy identities: we use them as 'symbolic resources' with which – and against which – we come to define who we are.

Before you move on, you might like to consider whether or not these generalizations apply to your own childhood memories of media. To what extent do you think they apply, not just to *children's* relationships with media, but also to those of *adults?*

2 CHILDHOOD AND THE MEDIA

It is possible to identify two contrasting views of the relationship between children and media, both of which have been influential in popular and academic debate. On the one hand, there is the idea that childhood as we know it is dying or disappearing, and that the media are primarily to blame for this. On the other, there is the idea that the media are now a force of liberation for children – that they are creating a new 'electronic generation' that is more open, more democratic, more socially aware than their parents' generation. In some ways, these two views are diametrically opposed; yet there are also some similarities between them. Both also invoke fundamental assumptions and questions about the nature of childhood that have been addressed in previous chapters.

2.1 The death of childhood?

The notion that the media are destroying childhood is most popularly associated with the American critic Neil Postman's book *The Disappearance of Childhood* (Postman, 1983), although it is a theme that recurs in several other works (e.g., Elkind, 1981; Sanders, 1995; Winn, 1984). Essentially, Postman holds the electronic media responsible for the decline of modern civilization. Television, he argues, undermines our capacity to think critically, and reduces politics, culture and morality to mere entertainment. In *The Disappearance of Childhood*, Postman argues that our modern conception of childhood was a creation of the print media; and that new media, particularly television, are destroying it. According to him, this is primarily to do with children's access to information. Whereas acquiring print literacy took a long period of apprenticeship, we don't have to learn to read or interpret television. Television is, he argues, a 'total disclosure medium': through television, children are increasingly learning about the 'secrets' of adult life – sex, drugs, violence – that would previously have been hidden in the specialized code of print. As a result, they are increasingly coming to behave like adults, and to demand access to adult privileges.

Thus, Postman points to the demise of children's traditional games and distinctive styles of dress; the increasing homogenization of children's and adults' leisure pursuits, language, eating habits and tastes in entertainment; and the increase in child crime, drug-taking, sexual activity and teenage pregnancy. He is particularly dismayed by the erotic use of children in advertisements and films, the prevalence of 'adult' themes in children's books and what he sees as the misguided emphasis on 'children's rights'. Significantly, Postman's concern about childhood is also a concern about the changing nature of *adulthood*: television not only forces children into 'premature' adulthood, it also infantilizes adults (Postman, 1986).

One can certainly challenge Postman on the grounds of his evidence – both about the incidence of the phenomena he is describing and about his explanation of the causes. For example, does the fact that adults now wear similar clothes to children (at least in some social settings) or eat the same kinds of food necessarily mean that the fundamental differences between them have disappeared? And is there really any evidence that television is a major cause of changes in family structures, or that it encourages precocious sexuality, as he alleges?

Furthermore, there are a number of underlying assumptions here that one might wish to question. First, there are assumptions about *childhood*. Postman does not believe that our contemporary definition of childhood is a timeless phenomenon; but he clearly views the 'invention of childhood' as a highly positive development, indeed as a kind of civilizing process. This is a view that many historians of childhood would challenge or qualify. Second, there are assumptions here about *media* – both about the uses of media and about the skills or competences that are required to make sense of them. To what extent, for example, can one say that making sense of television is a natural, rather than a learned, process? Third, there are assumptions about the *relationships* between these things. Ultimately, Postman's position is that of a technological determinist: technology is seen to produce social (and indeed psychological) change, irrespective of how it is used, or the representations it makes available. Finally, there are implications of the argument in terms of *social policy*. Postman wants to eradicate technology, or find a way of living without it (see Postman, 1992); and while he distances himself from the so-called 'moral majority', he clearly wants to return to an imaginary golden age of traditional moral values – and thereby to reinforce adult authority and control.

2.2 The electronic generation

The second argument I want to consider here is in some respects a mirror image of the first. One of its leading exponents is the American journalist and media consultant Don Tapscott (1998), although several of his views are echoed by other recent authors (e.g., Katz, 1997; Papert, 1996; Rushkoff, 1996). In some ways, these authors support Postman's diagnosis, although they interpret it in a very different way. They agree that the boundaries between childhood and adulthood are blurring; and they agree that media technology – particularly digital technology – is primarily responsible for this. But rather than regretting this development, they see it as a form of liberation or 'empowerment' for

Around the computer.

young people. Thus, Tapscott (1998) argues that the internet has given children a range of new tools to think with, speak with and play with. Furthermore, these tools can play a powerful part in young people's lives.

The differences between these two positions are partly about the differences between technologies. If Postman and others are seeking to blame television, these authors see the computer as the hope for the future. Tapscott in fact sets up a direct opposition between television and the internet. Television is seen as passive, while the net is active; television 'dumbs down' its users, while the net raises their intelligence; television broadcasts a singular view of the world, while the net is democratic and interactive; television isolates, while the net builds communities; and so on. Just as television is the antithesis of the net, so the 'television generation' is the antithesis of the 'net generation'. Like the technology they now control, the values of the television generation are increasingly conservative, 'hierarchical, inflexible and centralized'. By contrast, the members of the 'net generation' are 'hungry for expression, discovery and their own self-development' (Tapscott, 1998): they are savvy, self-reliant, analytical, creative, inquisitive, accepting of diversity, socially conscious, globally-oriented – all, it would seem, because of their intuitive relationship with technology.

Not all the writers mentioned agree with this opposition between technologies; although all of them see the contemporary media as agents of a kind of children's liberation. Katz (1997), for example, sees rap music, talk shows and cable television – along with the internet – as 'one of the great creative explosions of modern culture' (p. 10), and argues that they represent a growing challenge to centralized adult control.

Here again, one might challenge these arguments on the grounds of evidence. Much of the evidence here is anecdotal and unrepresentative – although this may be inevitable, given that these writers are looking to predict the future rather than describe the present. Nevertheless, there is a great deal missing from the picture. One could argue, for example, that talk shows and cable TV do not represent a democratization of political debate (as Katz implies), but merely the decline of the public sphere. And is the internet in fact any more 'democratic' than earlier media? One could point, for example, to the growing commercial uses of the internet (Center for Media Education, 1997) and to the enormous inequalities in access between different social groups.

As with the 'death of childhood' thesis, these arguments reflect a kind of *'media determinism'* – albeit of a very different kind. Postman and others see children as vulnerable and in need of protection from the corrupting influence of media technology; while Tapscott and others see children as naturally wise, and as having an innate thirst for knowledge which media technology can satisfy. Where Postman wants to return to a situation in which children knew their place, Tapscott and others argue that adults should try to 'catch up' with their children. Where Postman places his faith in adult authority, Tapscott looks to technology alone as the solution to social problems. In some respects, therefore, these apparently contrasting arguments could be seen as two sides of the same coin. Both have an undeniable appeal: they tell simple stories that speak directly to our hopes and fears about our children's futures. Yet, ultimately, we are bound to question their generalized views of childhood and of media technology, and of the relationships between them.

However, there are clearly some truths in both positions. Joshua Meyrowitz's book *No Sense of Place*, published in the United States in 1985, provides a more even-handed account of the argument. Meyrowitz argues that, unlike older media, television makes 'backstage' behaviour visible to all. It reveals facts that contradict dominant social myths and ideals. In the process, it makes it impossible for powerful groups to keep 'secrets', and hence undermines much of the basis of their authority. In this way, Meyrowitz argues, television has blurred the boundaries between men and women, between individual citizens and their political representatives – and between children and adults.

READING

Read Reading A, 'The blurring of childhood and adulthood', which is an extract from Joshua Meyrowitz's *No Sense of Place*. As you read, consider the following questions:

1 Do you agree with Meyrowitz's estimation of the power of television, as compared with other factors (such as the family)?

2 What would you see as the positive and negative consequences for children of the developments Meyrowitz describes?

3 Is there any evidence that – contrary to Meyrowitz's argument – the separation between children and adults is being *reinforced* in contemporary societies? And what role might the media be playing here?

4 Do Meyrowitz's arguments – and the others considered here – apply only to Western, industrialized societies?

COMMENT

Meyrowitz is more cautious than the more popular authors discussed above. His aim is not to judge whether such changes are good or bad, or whether they represent an unnatural deviation from 'proper' adults' and children's roles: indeed, he strongly refutes universalist accounts of child development. The notion of childhood 'innocence', he suggests, does not reflect an essential state of being: on the contrary, it was deliberately produced in order to justify the social separation between adults and children. In so far as it undermines this separation, he suggests, the advent of television represents a further shift in the balance of power – a shift whose consequences are decidedly double-edged.

Nevertheless, one can think of many exceptions to Meyrowitz's argument, particularly if we look beyond the context of the United States. Even within industrialized countries (for example, if we compare Northern and Southern Europe), there are wide variations in the degree of separation between adults and children. Furthermore, it could be argued that children are increasingly being defined as a 'special' group, with needs and tastes that are quite distinct from those of adults – both in terms of social policy, and specifically in relation to the media and consumer culture. To some extent, children and adults can now live in quite separate 'media worlds'; and for many adults, 'children's culture' has become increasingly inaccessible. Do contemporary children really have 'an image of society and roles that differs markedly from that held by children of earlier generations'? And, even if they do, how far do they carry this into their adult lives?

Allow about 20 minutes

A C T I V I T Y 2   Changing childhoods?

In different ways, Meyrowitz, Postman, Tapscott and others all suggest that there have been significant changes in the definition – and experience – of childhood over the past few decades; and that the media have played a significant part in producing these changes. Before moving on, try to compare your own media autobiography with one that might be written by a child like yourself growing up today (you can use a real child if you wish). What are the differences and similarities, for example in terms of:

1   their level of access to media;

2   the technological possibilities at their disposal;

3   the degree of 'commercialism';

4   the extent to which their use of media is regulated or controlled by adults;

5   the kinds of media content (or 'adult secrets') they are likely to encounter;

6   the extent to which they can actively participate in media-related activities.

To what extent do you believe these differences either reflect or produce broader changes in childhood?

C O M M E N T

Children today undoubtedly do have access to a wider range of media, and (at least potentially) to more 'adult' content. Yet the consequences of this can be seen as damaging in some ways, and empowering in others. To what extent – and for how long – *should* we keep children ignorant of 'adult secrets'? Likewise, children are increasingly recognized as consumers in their own right; yet this can be seen either as a pretext for commercial exploitation or as offering new opportunities for creativity and agency – or indeed as both simultaneously (see Chapter 7).

The following sections of this chapter review recent changes in the media environment in the light of these broader arguments. We look in turn at three key aspects of children's relationships with the media: *production*, *texts* and *audiences*. As I shall argue, these changes have ambivalent consequences for our views of childhood.

SUMMARY OF SECTION 2

Two contrasting views of children's relationships with media:

- The death of childhood (Postman, 1983; 1986; 1992): television reveals hidden information, and undermines adult authority.
- The electronic generation (Tapscott, 1998): the internet empowers children, enabling them to create their own culture.

Three questions for debate:

- Are the media really so powerful?
- Are children innocent and vulnerable, or naturally competent?
- Are the boundaries between adults and children blurring – or are they being reinforced?

3 PRODUCTION: TARGETING CHILDREN

3.1 Technologies

As we have seen, discussions of young people's relationships with the media often attribute a determining power to technology. Such arguments are problematic for several reasons. Technologies do not produce social change irrespective of how they are used; nor are the inherent differences between technologies as absolute as is often supposed. In this case, we need to consider how technological changes are related both to economic developments and to changes in the behaviour of audiences.

Recent developments in media technologies can be understood, first, as a matter of *proliferation*. Since the advent of television, the domestic TV screen has become the delivery point for an ever broader range of media. The number of channels has grown, both on terrestrial television and (more spectacularly) with the advent of cable, satellite and digital TV; while the screen is also being used for video in various forms, as well as for the ever-broadening range of digital media, from computer games and CD-ROMs to the internet.

Second, there has been a *convergence* between information and communications technologies. Over the coming decade, the advent of digital TV, internet set-top boxes, on-line shopping, video-on-demand and other developments will increasingly blur the distinctions between linear broadcast media such as television and 'narrowcast', interactive media such as the internet. Like the other developments identified here, this has been commercially driven; but it has also been made possible by digitization.

These developments have implications, third, in terms of *access*. Hitherto expensive aspects of media production, and a whole range of new media forms and options, have been brought within reach of the domestic consumer. The price of video camcorders, digital cameras and multimedia PCs has steadily fallen as their capabilities have increased; and, at least in principle, the internet represents a means of communication that cannot be exclusively controlled by a small elite. In the process, it is argued, the boundaries between production and consumption, and between mass communication and interpersonal communication, are beginning to break down.

These changes have several specific implications for children; and while these are currently most apparent in industrialized countries, they are also increasingly manifested in the developing world. Children and parents are among the most significant markets for these new technologies. Cable and satellite television, for example, have been strongly targeted towards the younger audience; while much of the advertising and promotion for home computers trades in a popular mystique about children's natural affinity with technology (Nixon, 1998). In the UK, for instance, the take-up of satellite and cable television, video, camcorders and home computers has been much higher in households with children. Technology is also being used in more individualized ways. Thus, a majority of children in the UK have televisions in their bedrooms, and a significant proportion have VCRs. These tendencies are encouraged by the general democratization of relationships within the family; although collective uses of media – 'family viewing' – are very far from disappearing (Livingstone and Bovill, 1999).

Similarly, many of the new cultural forms made possible by these technologies are primarily identified with the young. Computer games, for example, are predominantly addressed to the children's and youth market; while popular music (particularly dance music) is increasingly generated by digital technology, via sampling, editing and other software. The increasing accessibility of this technology is also enabling some young people to play a more active role as cultural producers. More and more teenagers have home computers in their bedrooms that can be used to create music, to manipulate images or to edit video to a relatively professional standard.

Of course, we should not exaggerate the scale of these developments. Levels of access to technology will increase significantly in the coming years, as prices fall; yet there is also a polarization between the 'technology rich' and the 'technology poor', both within societies and in global terms (van der Voort *et al.*, 1998). As with other new technologies (such as television in the 1950s), those with greater disposable income are almost always the 'early adopters': they have newer and more powerful equipment, and more opportunities to develop the skills that are needed to use it. This polarization has been apparent for several years in the United States, where there is an enormous divergence between children who have access to cable television, whose parents can afford to buy or rent videos, and who live in areas where a broad range of material is available to them, and those who do not (Wartella *et al.*, 1990).

Meanwhile, children's growing access to media is generating increasing concern about their exposure to material hitherto largely confined to adults – most obviously to 'sex and violence' (both of which are often very loosely defined). When compared with older technologies such as the cinema or

Games, games, games – the mass marketing of media products for children and young people.

The paraphernalia of multimedia childhoods.

broadcast television, media such as video and cable/satellite television significantly undermine the potential for centralized control by national governments. Video, for example, makes it possible to copy and circulate material to a much greater extent than has ever been the case with moving images. It also makes it possible to view it, not in a public space to which access can be controlled, but in the private space of the home; and to do so at a time chosen by the viewer, not by a centralized scheduler working with ideas about what is appropriate for children to watch. A large majority of children have seen material on video which they should not legally have been able to obtain (Buckingham, 1996).

This anxiety about control is accentuated by the advent of digital technology. It is now possible not only for material to be easily copied and circulated, but also for it to be sent across national boundaries on the telephone line. At present, the internet is a relatively decentralized medium: anyone with access to the technology can 'publish' anything they like, and anyone else can get access to it. Via the internet, children can communicate much more easily with each other and with adults, without even having to identify themselves as children. And, of course, the privacy and anonymity afforded by the internet particularly lends itself to the easy dissemination and sale of pornography. This situation has led to growing calls for stricter regulation and censorship; and to the search for a 'technological fix' in the form of the V-chip or so-called 'blocking software' that will prevent children from gaining access to material that is deemed undesirable. Yet evidence of the effectiveness of such initiatives is decidedly limited (Waltermann and Machill, 2000).

3.2 Institutions

The technological developments described in Section 3.1 have helped to reinforce – and been reinforced by – fundamental institutional and economic changes in the media industries. The past two decades have been characterized by growing *privatization*. The large majority of new media outlets and forms identified above are commercially driven; and even those which initially were not – such as the internet – are increasingly subject to commercial imperatives, such as the need to carry advertising. Meanwhile, public sector provision – for example in broadcasting – has gradually been commercialized from within; and regulation concerned with the social and cultural functions of the media is gradually being abandoned in favour of a narrower concern with morality. These tendencies have been fostered by the 'free-market' ideologies of national governments.

One inevitable consequence of this development has been the *integration* of the media industries. The media market is now dominated by a small number of multinational conglomerates; and for nationally-based companies, success in the international market is increasingly necessary for survival. Significantly, most of these corporations are cross-media empires: they integrate broadcasting, publishing, media and digital technology, and in many cases have interests in both hardware and software. Yet integration does not necessarily mean homogenization: growing competition has also resulted in the fragmentation of audiences, and the rise of 'niche marketing'. Media are increasingly targeted towards specialized fractions of the mass audience, albeit on a global scale.

These developments affect children in quite ambiguous ways. Children have effectively been 'discovered' as a new target market only in the past few decades. In the case of commercial television, for example, children were not initially seen as an especially valuable audience. In the early decades of the US commercial system, programmes would be provided for children at minimum cost only, and at times when other audiences were not available to view (Melody, 1973); and even in the UK, where the public service tradition has been very strong, children's television has been comparatively underfunded. In the contemporary era of niche marketing, children have suddenly become much more valuable: they are seen to have significant influence on parents' purchasing decisions, as well as substantial disposable income of their own. Thus, the advent of cable television in the UK has led to a plethora of specialist channels competing to attract the child audience; and both on terrestrial and non-terrestrial channels, there has been a significant increase in the *amount* of provision for children, if not necessarily in its quality or diversity (Buckingham *et al.*, 1999). These developments have led to a significant (and decidedly double-edged) shift in thinking about the child audience, at least within the media industries: the vulnerable child in need of protection has increasingly given way to the child as 'sovereign consumer'.

However, we should be wary of economic determinism here. It is far too easy to fall back on traditional notions of children as vulnerable to commercial exploitation or to the seductions of media imperialism. In the UK, as in many other countries, domestically-produced media remain popular among children as well as adults; and particular British television programmes continue to serve as a form of 'common culture', both among children and between the generations. While new media technologies are steadily being more widely disseminated, significant numbers of children do not have access to cable or satellite television – let alone to the internet – in the first place. Furthermore, a large proportion of commercial products aimed at children simply fail to generate a profit: the market is highly competitive and uncertain. To this extent, there is some justification in producers' recurrent claim that children are a volatile, complex market, which cannot easily be known and controlled.

Allow about 30 minutes

A C T I V I T Y 3   Empowerment or exploitation?

The changes described above raise many dilemmas for policy-makers. Try to identify the arguments *for* and *against* the following (partly imaginary) proposals:

1   The complete abolition of age-related classifications for film and video (in the UK, for example, these are currently U – universal, PG – parental guidance, 12A – under twelves must be accompanied by an adult, 12, 15 and 18).

2   The compulsory use of blocking software to prevent children gaining access to web sites containing sexually explicit images or language.

3   The banning of advertising and other commercial promotions during children's television programmes.

4   A tax on the profits of technology companies, with the revenue to be directed towards providing computers and internet access for children in poorer areas, and in developing countries.

5   A requirement for television stations to allocate a specified amount of their production budgets to children's programming.

What assumptions about childhood inform your arguments?

C O M M E N T

For some, the technological and economic changes described here are merely an opportunity for exploitation; while for others, they offer children a kind of empowerment – a liberation from adult control. How we respond to these changes inevitably depends upon our broader assumptions about the nature of childhood itself. Do we continue to regard children as vulnerable and in need of protection – or can we trust them to make their own decisions? Can children still be considered as a special audience, with specific needs or entitlements in relation to the media? On what basis do we decide what is appropriate or harmful for them? And even if we can agree on such matters, how effectively can we exercise control over the material they encounter?

SUMMARY OF SECTION 3

The main technological and economic changes in children's media environment are:

- proliferation: the appearance of increasing choice;
- convergence and integration: multi-media marketing;
- increasing access to media, both for consumption and production;
- privatization and deregulation.

The consequences for children include:

- access to previously forbidden material;
- polarization between rich and poor: the digital divide;
- children discovered as a valuable new market;
- 'dumbing down' or 'consumer empowerment'?

4 TEXTS: CONSTRUCTING CHILDREN

Perhaps the most obvious manifestation of the developments I have described is in the changing characteristics of media texts – that is, the television programmes, films, games and other artefacts children are engaging with. On one level, this can be seen as a further consequence of technological and economic *convergence*. Here, too, there has been a significant blurring of boundaries. More and more media texts are somehow 'spin offs' or advertisements for other texts or commodities; and the media have become much more closely bound up with the merchandizing of a whole range of other products.

As a result, *intertextuality* has become a dominant characteristic of contemporary media: texts are constantly referring to and drawing upon other texts, often in ironic ways. Many contemporary cartoons, for example, self-consciously draw upon other media in the form of pastiche, homage, or parody; they juxtapose incongruous elements from different historical periods, genres or cultural contexts; and they play with established conventions of form and representation. In the process, they implicitly address their readers or viewers as knowing, 'media literate' consumers.

Finally, many of these new media forms are characterized by types of *interactivity*. As we have seen, some of the more utopian advocates of interactive multi-media (such as Tapscott) have seen it as a means of liberation from the constraints of more traditional 'linear' media such as film and television. Hypertext, CD-ROMs and computer games have been seen to abolish the distinction between 'reader' and 'writer': the reader (or player) is no longer passively manipulated by the text – and indeed the only text is the one the reader chooses to 'write'.

Many of these developments are dictated by a primarily economic logic. As media have become increasingly commodified, producers need to exploit successes across a wider range of media within a shorter time scale, and are bound to use the same material in different forms. Meanwhile, 'irony' has become a useful marketing device, enabling media corporations to secure additional profit by recycling existing properties, and 'interactivity' is often little more than a form of packaging.

Nevertheless, many of these characteristics apply with particular force to media texts that are aimed at children and young people (see Bazalgette and Buckingham, 1995; Kinder, 1991). As children's access to technology increases, they no longer have to watch or read what their parents choose. As the 'niche market' of children grows in importance, they are increasingly able to confine themselves to media that are produced specifically for them. Indeed, the new 'postmodern' cultural forms that characterize children's and youth culture often exclude adults: they depend upon particular cultural competences and on a prior knowledge of specific media texts (in other words, on a form of 'media literacy') that are only accessible to the young. While children may increasingly be sharing a global media culture with children from other parts of the world, they may be sharing less and less with their own parents.

Thus, many of the most popular cartoons and children's magazine programmes – from *The Simpsons* to *SMTV Live* – are permeated with references to other texts and genres, sometimes in the form of direct quotation or 'sampling'. They raid existing cultural resources – both from high culture and from the popular culture of the past and present – in a fragmentary and often apparently parodic manner. Comparing current animation series with those of thirty years ago, one is struck not just by their rapid pace, but also by their irony and intertextuality, and their complex play with reality and fantasy (Wells, 2002).

Yet television programmes are not just television programmes: they are also films, records, comics, computer games and toys – not to mention T-shirts, posters, lunchboxes, drinks, sticker albums, food, and a myriad of other products. Children's media culture increasingly crosses the boundaries between texts and traditional media forms – most obviously in the case of phenomena such as *Teenage Mutant Ninja Turtles*, *Super Mario Brothers*, *Mighty Morphin Power Rangers* and, most spectacularly, *Pokémon*. In this process, the identity of the 'original' text is far from clear: these commodities are packaged and marketed as integrated phenomena, rather than the text coming first and the merchandizing following on. And this development is not confined to the work of exclusively 'commercial' corporations – as is illustrated by the success of public service productions such as *Sesame Street, Barney* and the BBC's *Teletubbies*.

The Disney Store, Milton Keynes, UK.

Disney is of course the classic example of this phenomenon (see Bryman, 1995). Right from the early days of the Mickey Mouse clubs, merchandizing and subsequently theme parks have been a key dimension of the enterprise – and in fact it is these aspects which have guaranteed its continuing profitability (Gomery, 1994). However, this horizontal integration is now moving to a different scale. Once you have seen the latest Disney movie, you can catch the spin-off episodes on the Disney Channel, or meet the characters at the theme park; you can visit the Disney store at your local mall, or shopping centre, and stock up on the video, the posters, the T-shirts, and other merchandize; you can collect the 'free gifts' of character toys in cereal packets and fast-food restaurants; and you can buy the animated storybook on CD-ROM, play the computer game, visit the web site, and so on. Children are very much in the vanguard of what Marsha Kinder (1991) calls 'trans-media intertextuality' – and, as she argues, the logic of this development is primarily driven by profit.

It is also important to recognize changes at the level of *content*, which, as in the case of Postman (1983), are often those that cause most alarm among adult critics. At least in the UK, children's television has steadily changed over the past twenty years to incorporate topics such as sex, drugs and family breakdown that would previously have been considered taboo. Likewise, magazines and books aimed at the early teenage market have attracted widespread criticism for their frank and explicit treatment of such issues (see Jones and Davies, 2002; Rosen, 1997). Even cartoons aimed at very young children – from *Ninja Turtles* to *Biker Mice From Mars* – play on 'adult' anxieties about environmental pollution, social decline and global destruction.

Indeed, it could be argued that the age at which childhood *ends* – at least as far as the media industries are concerned – seems to be steadily reducing. Children's television producers, for example, now acknowledge that the bulk of older children's viewing is given over to 'adult' programmes; and the content and style of programmes aimed at them clearly reflects this. The social issues addressed in children's dramas have much in common with those in adult soaps; while the visual style and pace of kids' magazine shows have clearly influenced the approach of 'adult' programmes. While some critics have always complained about the precocity of children's programmes, others are beginning to bemoan what they see as the infantilization of 'adult' television.

Several authors have discussed the implications of these changes in contemporary children's television. In Reading B, Stephen Wagg focuses on historical shifts in one area of programming, the Saturday morning 'magazine' show. Such programmes date back to the mid-1970s, and continue to be a focus of intense competition for ratings. On one level, they are a kind of scheduling device – a way of holding together a diverse menu of material in order to keep the audience watching. Across a two- or three-hour show, viewers will be led through a sequence of music videos, cartoons, game shows, comedy sketches, informational sequences, studio guests, competitions, and so on, linked by youthful presenters.

READING

Read Reading B, ' "One I made earlier": media, popular culture and the politics of childhood' by Stephen Wagg. As you read, consider the following questions:

1 Compare Wagg's account (written in the early 1990s) with contemporary examples of the magazine show. Are the characteristics he identifies any more or less apparent today?

2 To what extent do the changes Wagg describes in children's television reflect broader changes in the social position of children over this period?

3 In what ways are these developments 'empowering' for children, or 'exploitative' – or indeed both?

4 To what extent might the changes Wagg describes be seen as merely superficial – a matter of style rather than substance?

eletubbies was launched in 1997.

Watch with Mother – Trumpton, 1967.

Allow about 40 minutes

A C T I V I T Y 4   **Reconstructing childhood**

In order to test out some of Wagg's arguments, compare a programme you recall from your own childhood with a contemporary counterpart. For example, if I were doing this activity, I might compare a contemporary pre-school programme (such as *Teletubbies*) with an earlier one (*Watch with Mother*, perhaps); or a modern cartoon (such as *The Simpsons*) with an older one (such as *The Flintstones*). Alternatively, I might select a current edition of a long-running programme such as *Blue Peter*, *Grange Hill* or *Sesame Street*. See how far you can detect differences and similarities, for example, in the following areas:

1   the visual style;

2   the pace and editing;

3   the roles played by adults and children;

4   the nature of the humour;

5   the ways in which children are spoken to, or addressed.

Do modern programmes in fact make different assumptions about childhood – for example, about children's skills as TV viewers or about their understanding of the world?

C O M M E N T

The changes Wagg identifies will probably have been quite apparent – particularly if you have not seen children's television for several years. Even the longest-running, most conservative children's programmes appear significantly more hyperactive than you might recall. In the magazine shows Wagg describes, the boundaries between one item and another are increasingly blurred, and often several things will be happening at once, as though the viewer must not be given the opportunity to hit the remote control. Meanwhile, the avuncular, schoolteacherly approach of children's presenters of earlier decades has given way to the anarchic, 'hip' approach of their contemporary counterparts. The blurring of boundaries between children and 'youth' also means that the 'worthy' educational or informational elements of these programmes have largely disappeared; and, as Wagg points out, they have become increasingly 'media-centric', orienting children not towards the real world of purposeful activity, but to the glamorous world of the media themselves.

Yet we should not ignore the significant continuities here. For all the differences between them, *The Simpsons* has much in common with *The Flintstones* (Wells, 2002): the apparent cynicism of the former may only superficially disguise its status as a warm-hearted family sitcom. Likewise, *Teletubbies* represents a continuation of the tradition of *Watch with Mother* (Buckingham, 2002): for all its 'postmodern hyper-reality', it presents a safe, enclosed world that has much in common with the gardens inhabited by Andy Pandy and Bill and Ben. As Wagg suggests, a great deal of children's television struggles to avoid 'talking down' to children – although it does not necessarily always avoid being patronizing. Indeed, as popular texts from the past are increasingly recycled and appropriated in different ways by new generations, the similarities between them may be much more apparent than the differences.

SUMMARY OF SECTION 4

Changes in media texts aimed at children:

- convergence of media; integrated marketing;
- 'trans-media intertextuality';
- interactivity.

Some questions raised:

- To what extent are these new developments?
- Are they merely changes in form, or in content, or both?
- Is 'children's culture' blurring into 'youth culture'?

5 AUDIENCES: CHILDREN AS READERS

5.1   Changing audiences

As the media have evolved, they have come to assume quite different kinds of competence and knowledge – and to encourage very different forms of 'activity' – on the part of audiences. Contemporary media are increasingly addressing children as highly 'media literate' consumers. Whether they actually *are* more media literate, and what we might mean by that, is a rather more complex question, however.

As we have seen, advocates of the 'communications revolution' have argued that audiences are increasingly 'empowered' by these new media, while critics have suggested that they are simply more open to manipulation and commercial exploitation. Yet the consequences of these developments are difficult to predict. Thus, it is frequently claimed that there is now much greater *choice* for consumers, while others argue that such choice is merely spurious. For example, the proliferation of television channels has led to a significant increase in the quantity of television available for children, even taking account of the fact that much of it is frequently repeated. Whether this increase will be sustained over the longer term is more debatable, however: the amount of new product cannot keep pace with the increase in outlets for it – not least because the audience for each channel is decreasing as more become available, and hence the funding for new production will decline. In practice, therefore, what viewers are more likely to be offered is ever-increasing opportunities to watch the same things (Buckingham *et al.*, 1999).

These issues are to some extent compounded by *interactivity*. Leaving aside the question of whether surfing the web actually is more 'active' than surfing TV channels or browsing through a magazine (for example), there are significant questions about whether audiences actually *want* greater 'activity'. Even for regular users, there is room for scepticism about the 'empowerment' that is apparently offered here. The web clearly allows users much greater control over the selection of content and the pace at which it is 'read'. Yet in the process it also permits much more detailed surveillance of consumer behaviour: it is now very easy to track users' movements between and within particular web sites, and thereby to build up consumer profiles which can subsequently become the basis for electronic advertising. Children have become key targets in this respect (Center for Media Education, 1997).

Finally, there are questions about the growing *fragmentation* of audiences, as texts are increasingly targeted at specialized groups of consumers. Multi-channel television, for example, may bring about the decline of broadcasting (and the 'common culture' it makes possible) in favour of 'narrowcasting'; while the internet is the medium *par excellence* for those with specialist or minority interests. Yet, in the longer term, it remains to be seen how far consumers actually *want* to pursue wholly individualized or 'customized' uses of media, or whether they want a more shared experience – at least to the extent of being able to talk the following day about what they have seen. Here, too, the idea that new media necessarily offer a form of 'empowerment' is open to question.

5.2 Constructing the child audience

Nevertheless, these changes have specific implications for our views of the child audience. At least in the English-speaking world, sensational stories about the harm the media allegedly inflict on children have increasingly come to dominate the headlines. Significantly, much of this concern focuses on children's exposure to 'adult' media. There is a clear acknowledgement that children are no longer restricted to material that is designed for them – although research suggests that in fact they have always preferred 'adult' media, at least insofar as they could gain access to them (Abrams, 1956).

Yet if public debates about children and the media have become more and more preoccupied with defending children from harm – with a kind of moral protectionism – the discourses that circulate within the media industries seem to be moving in a rather different direction (Del Vecchio, 1997). Here, children are no longer predominantly seen as innocent and vulnerable to influence. On the contrary, they are increasingly regarded as sophisticated, demanding, 'media-wise' consumers. This shift is certainly apparent in the recent history of children's television (Buckingham *et al.*, 1999). The broadly 'child-centred' ethos that flourished in the UK during the 1960s and 1970s is increasingly losing ground to an essentially consumerist approach. The child viewer is no longer seen as the developing consciousness of the psychological imagination, but as a sophisticated, discriminating, critical consumer. Children have become 'kids'; and kids, we are told, are 'smart', 'savvy' and 'street wise'. Above all, they are 'media literate'. They are hard to please; they see through attempts at deception and manipulation; and they refuse to be patronized.

This discourse is in turn often connected with arguments about *children's rights*. Internationally, the most successful exponent of this discourse has been the dedicated children's channel Nickelodeon (owned by the US media giant Viacom). What we find here is a rhetoric of empowerment – a notion of the channel as a 'kid-only' zone, giving voice to kids, taking the kids' point of view, as the friend of kids (Laybourne, 1993). This discourse reinforced in the channel's publicity and on-screen continuity material. Significantly, children seem to be defined here primarily in terms of being *not adults*. Adults are boring; kids are fun. Adults are conservative; kids are fresh and innovative. Adults will never understand; kids intuitively *know*. Yet despite its emphasis on 'children's rights', this discourse does not define children as independent social or political actors, let alone offer them democratic control or accountability: it is a discourse of consumer sovereignty masquerading as a discourse of cultural rights. As Nickelodeon's company slogan puts it, 'what's good for kids is good for business'.

TV shows - a 'kid-only' zone.

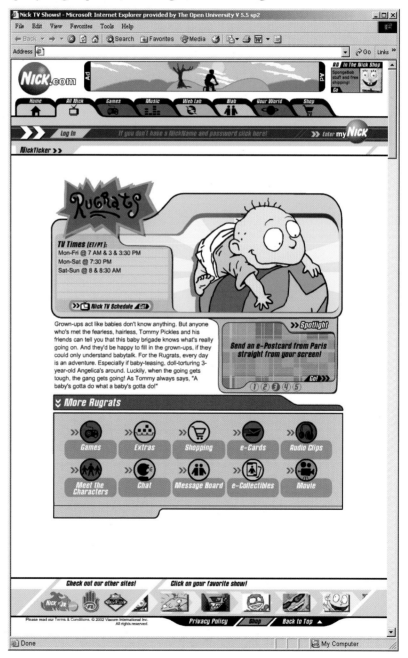

5.3 Researching the child audience

Ultimately, however, the question of whether children can be seen as an 'active' audience or as 'passive' victims of the media – and whether these new developments encourage either tendency – cannot be answered in the abstract. We need to take account of the diverse ways in which audiences use and interpret the media, and the social contexts in which they do so.

Historically, research in this field has been dominated by the search for evidence of negative effects. Based on a form of behaviourism or 'social learning theory', this research sought to demonstrate causal connections between violent stimuli and aggressive responses; and it was this approach that subsequently came to inform research on areas such as sex role stereotyping and the influence of advertising. Over the past two decades, however, psychological researchers have increasingly moved away from a behaviourist to a constructivist (or cognitive) perspective – from the study of stimulus and response to the study of how children understand, interpret and evaluate what they watch and read (Dorr, 1986; Durkin, 1985; Young, 1990). Children are seen here not as passive recipients of media messages, but as active processors of meaning. The constructivist approach provides a valuable alternative to the behaviourism of 'effects' research. Yet it still tends to conceive of children's relationships with media in *individualized* terms: the main focus is on the isolated encounter between mind and medium, rather than the social contexts in which the media are used and interpreted (Buckingham, 2000, Chapter 6).

Meanwhile, researchers in media and cultural studies have begun to develop a more *sociological* analysis of the child audience. Broadly speaking, these researchers share the cognitive view of children as active agents, rather than passive recipients of adult culture. They set out to investigate children's experiences in their own terms, rather than judging them in terms of their inability to use or understand the media in appropriately 'adult' ways. However, the central focus here is on the ways in which children use and interpret media in the context of their everyday lives. The production of meaning from the media is therefore seen not as a *psychological* process, but as a form of *social negotiation* (Tulloch, 2000).

This position has significant consequences in terms of research method. How children interpret a cartoon, for example, and what they choose to say about it in the company of other children and an adult interviewer, depends upon how they perceive their own social position and their relations with others. Children's judgements are seen here not as evidence of their cognitive abilities, but as inherently social processes. Thus, for example, I have analysed how boys' talk about soap operas – and their judgements about what is realistic or plausible – is inextricably related to their construction of their own masculinity; or how black and white children's discussions of 'positive images' in a programme like *The Cosby Show* are bound up with the dynamics of inter-racial friendships (Buckingham, 1993a; 1993b). In effect, therefore, this research is investigating how children define and construct their social identities – or perform a kind of 'identity work' – through talk about television. Reading C provides a brief illustration of this kind of research.

The Cosby Family, c. 1986.

READING

Read Reading C, 'In the worst possible taste: children, television and cultural value'. This extract provides an edited account of Davies *et al.*'s research on the question of children's *taste*, and how they perceive the differences between themselves and adults. As you read, consider the following questions:

1   What would you see as the advantages and disadvantages of the methods used here (focus group activities conducted in schools)?

2   To what extent can children's observations be taken at face value – that is, as honest reflections of what they think and feel?

3   How do these children use talk about television to define their own social position as children? How does this differ between the two age groups?

Allow 1 hour

A C T I V I T Y 5   Researching the child audience

If possible, you could attempt at this stage to gather some 'data' about children as an audience. You might choose to observe your own or somebody else's children watching television or playing computer games for an hour or so; you might talk to a child or group of children you know about their favourite programme or media 'craze'; or you might ask them some autobiographical questions of the kind raised in Activity 1. Don't attempt anything too ambitious: this should be very small scale.

When you have gathered your 'data', think about the following questions:

1   What does this data tell you? What does it *not* tell you? What more would you like to know in order to obtain a more complete picture?

2   What questions or hypotheses are raised here which you might like to investigate more systematically? How might you go about doing this?

3   Was there anything surprising about your data? How does it relate to the arguments you have been encountering on the course so far?

C O M M E N T

The questions raised here relate back to the methodological issues addressed in earlier chapters. There are several ways in which the context of the research can affect the results that are obtained; but this may be particularly acute where there is a significant gap between the researcher and the researched, for example, in terms of age and social status. Adults are inevitably outsiders in relation to children's culture; and how children respond to their investigations is bound to reflect this. While some may choose to 'play the researcher's game', others may deliberately attempt to subvert it.

Conducting research with *groups* of children may help to alleviate the effects of this differential in power; and it provides insights into the social negotiations that surround the use and interpretation of media. However, it also constrains what it is possible for children to say, and makes it harder to assess what is going on for children on a more personal level. Both within the peer group and in relation to the adult researcher, children are effectively constructing a 'child' identity – or indeed seeking to refuse or to redefine it. As the children's responses in Reading C clearly show, what it *means* to be a child is not fixed or given, but socially constructed – not least by children themselves.

SUMMARY OF SECTION 5

- Economic and technological changes result in greater choice, interactivity and fragmentation of audiences.
- Public debates are becoming preoccupied with the need to protect children from harm.
- Academic research has moved away from the search for negative effects. The focus now is on children as 'active' users and meaning-makers.
- Research methodology: how children define what it means to be a child.

6 INTEGRATING THE ANALYSIS: A CASE STUDY

In this chapter, we have considered three dimensions of children's relationships with the media: production, texts and audiences. I have argued that the 'power' of the media lies not in the hands of any one of these dimensions but in how they interact. In analysing any contemporary media phenomenon, we should be addressing all three, and recognizing the dynamic complexity of the relationships between them. I conclude with a brief illustration of how this approach might be applied to a single case study. (For more details, see Buckingham and Sefton-Green, forthcoming; Tobin, 2002.)

6.1 Production

At the time of writing, the Pokémon phenomenon has already waned in popularity; yet at its peak in 2000 it was undoubtedly the most profitable children's 'craze' of all time. In that year, it reputedly generated over seven billion dollars world-wide. Beginning as a computer game, and quickly 'spinning off' into a TV series, a trading card game, feature films, books, magazines, toys and a plethora of other merchandize, Pokémon is a paradigm example of the 'multimedia intertextuality' or cross-media marketing identified above (Kinder, 1991). Yet there are different ways of accounting for its success.

To some extent, Pokémon can be seen as a very calculated commercial strategy on the part of its originators, the Nintendo Corporation of Japan. In targeting the game at the child market, rather than the youth market dominated by Sony, and in devising a product that would effectively exploit the unique qualities of its Game Boy hand-held console, Nintendo was playing to its strengths. Taken as a whole, Pokémon products seem to have been designed to maximize appeal across the increasingly fragmented child market. The products combined traditional 'girl appeal' (via an emphasis on nurturing and 'cuteness') with traditional 'boy appeal' (via the emphasis on collecting and competition). Different types of products were also targeted at different age groups – soft toys for younger children, TV cartoons for six to eight year-olds, the computer game for older children – allowing children to 'graduate' from one to the next. And the products were also designed to cross cultural boundaries: while some elements appeared distinctively Japanese, the visual style was a combination of Japanese and 'Western' conventions. Described in this way, Pokémon appears to be precisely the kind of commercial manipulation of children of which Kline (1993) and others complain.

On the other hand, Pokémon is also often described as the product of an individual 'creator', Satoshi Tajiri; and in designing the game, Tajiri set out to recapture elements of his own childhood (such as his fascination with collecting insects). According to this account, the success of Pokémon was somewhat unpredictable: it 'took off' because children somehow instinctively recognized and responded to Tajiri's vision. There is obviously an element of mythology about this account. Nevertheless, as with previous

Pokémon products - cards, books and toy characters.

'crazes' of this kind, the companies involved were somewhat slow to respond to this immediate popularity; and the eventual demise of Pokémon – which was even more precipitous than its rise – was far from accurately predicted. These patterns of rise and fall in children's 'crazes' are difficult to explain if we regard them simply as a matter of corporate manipulation.

6.2 Texts

The central narrative of Pokémon is that of the hero's quest. Ten-year-old Ash leaves home in search of the mythical creatures that will eventually bring him adult mastery. Assisted by various helpers and donors, he travels uncharted lands encountering a series of obstacles and enemies, until (at least in the computer game) he finally arrives at his goal and defeats his rival trainers. In doing so, he must learn to overcome his emotional side, and achieve self-control. In this respect, the appeal of Pokémon is similar to that of other stories of masculine maturation, which recur not just in classic children's literature but also in martial arts films, role-playing games and fantasy novels. It could be seen as a form of training in the characteristic cultural forms of male adolescence – although, as I have noted, it also has things in common with 'girl culture', such as the 'maternal' appeal of collectable toys and Tamagotchis.

Knowledge – or at least the acquisition of information – is central to the game. Significantly, much of this knowledge is inaccessible and meaningless to non-initiates – most obviously, adults. This knowledge is designed to be portable across different media or platforms: what you learn from the TV cartoon can be usefully applied in the card game, and vice-versa. This 'portability' also allows different aspects of the phenomenon to be enjoyed in different social contexts, either alone or with others: it provides a useful way of 'filling in time' when no alternative options are available, and a 'ticket of entry' to play and friendship groups.

A further key characteristic of Pokémon texts is their 'interactivity': they are designed to generate cognitive activity and social interaction of various kinds. Playing the computer game, for instance, involves making choices and predictions, recalling key information, planning strategy, and so on. More broadly, becoming part of the Pokémon culture involves actively seeking out new information and new products from a range of sources. Pokémon is not just something you 'read' or 'consume', but something you *do*. It positively *requires* and depends upon an 'active audience'.

6.3 Audience

Research into the uses of Pokémon illustrates the diverse – and in some instances, highly creative – ways in which children consume and re-work media texts in their everyday lives (Tobin, 2002). In our research, we found examples of children producing their own Pokémon-style cards, writing original stories featuring Pokémon characters, and creating imaginary 'play worlds' in which Pokémon featured alongside other (seemingly randomly assembled) toys and artefacts. Far from being passive consumers, children were using these texts selectively in their play, and re-inventing them for their own purposes. Yet the unavoidable question arises: in what ways is this 'good' or 'bad' for children?

On the positive side, it could be argued that some aspects of Pokémon are intellectually challenging for children. Becoming a 'master' of the computer game involves a whole range of cognitive skills; and in this respect, there are many parallels between Pokémon and other (more culturally approved) 'brain-teasing' games like chess. Whether or not these skills can be transferred to other contexts or activities is more debatable, although some certainly argue that they can (Greenfield, 1984).

A further positive argument here follows from my point about marketing. The appeals of Pokémon crossed significant boundaries of age, gender and culture; and, in this respect, it could be seen to have created or facilitated a 'common culture' among children, as well as enabling them to develop social skills. Like other fan phenomena (Jenkins, 1992), it generated 'interpretive communities', although it would be false to imply that these communities were necessarily cosy or tolerant. Knowledge is power in the world of Pokémon, and children were more than capable of using their superior knowledge to bully or deceive those less well-informed than themselves.

On the negative side, there are familiar arguments about commercial exploitation. Children were encouraged to spend large amounts of money in their efforts to collect rare trading cards – although this 'rarity' was of course artificially created by the trading card companies. For some, this process enabled children to learn valuable lessons about economic life; although for others, it was tantamount to extortion. As we shall see in more detail in Chapter 7, the broader question of children's relationship with the commercial market place is decidedly double-edged.

A further negative argument here is to do with cultural value. The Pokémon films and the TV cartoon in particular were widely reviled by adult critics on the grounds of their poor production values and predictable narratives. However, there are significant difficulties here. To what extent are children's aesthetic tastes *necessarily* different from those of adults, as we implied in Reading C? And if they are, on what basis should adults be making judgements about the aesthetic value of children's culture?

6.4 Integrating the analysis

To what extent is Pokémon simply a case of powerful corporations manipulating vulnerable children? Or do children in fact have the power to determine how the phenomenon evolves and the purposes it will serve? Of course, this should not be seen as an either/or choice; and *activity* on the part of audiences should not necessarily be equated with *power*. Yet in this respect Pokémon raises new issues for the study of children's culture. Many aspects of the phenomenon – the narrative themes, the role of merchandizing, the significance of collecting – are obviously far from new; yet the fact that children themselves are the active participants, and the ways in which that activity is mediated entirely through commercial processes, are at least quite different in scale from otherwise comparable phenomena. Commercial culture of this kind clearly *feels* 'empowering' – and therefore pleasurable – for children, many of whose other experiences are largely of *dis*empowerment. Yet the extent to which it genuinely *is* empowering – and indeed, what we might mean by that – is a complex question.

SUMMARY OF SECTION 6

Issues raised by the Pokémon phenomenon:

- Children's 'crazes' are difficult to explain as simply a matter of corporate manipulation.
- In contemporary media phenomena such as Pokémon, knowledge is portable across different media or platforms.
- Interactivity is a key characteristic of such texts; children do not passively consume them.

A question:

- Are the contemporary media 'empowering' children, or just exploiting them more effectively?

7 CONCLUSION

Recent developments in the media appear to reinforce – and to be reinforced by – broader changes in childhood of the kind identified in previous chapters. The metaphor of 'blurring boundaries' encapsulates many of these changes. Here, as in many other areas of social life, previously distinct boundaries between children and adults appear to be breaking down. And yet, as I have suggested, such boundaries are simultaneously being reinforced or redrawn. The separation between children's and adults' media worlds is becoming more apparent, even if the terms of that separation are changing. Older children can no longer be so easily 'protected' from experiences that are seen to be morally damaging or unsuitable. The walls that surround the garden of childhood have become much easier to climb. And yet children – particularly younger children – are increasingly participating in cultural and social worlds that are inaccessible, even incomprehensible, to their parents. In this respect, the media are playing an increasingly important role in defining the changing meanings of contemporary childhood – and, by extension, of 'adulthood' as well.

REFERENCES

ABRAMS, M. (1956) 'Child audiences for television in Great Britain', *Journalism Quarterly,* **33**, pp. 35–41.

BARKER, M. and PETLEY, J. (eds) (2001, second edn) *Ill Effects: the media/ violence debate,* London, Routledge.

BAZALGETTE, C. and BUCKINGHAM, D. (eds) (1995) *In Front of the Children: screen entertainment and young audiences,* London, British Film Institute.

BRYMAN, A. (1995) *Disney and His Worlds,* London, Routledge.

BUCKINGHAM, D. (ed.) (1993a) *Reading Audiences: young people and the media,* Manchester, Manchester University Press.

BUCKINGHAM, D. (1993b) *Children Talking Television: the making of television Literacy,* London, Falmer.

BUCKINGHAM, D. (1996) *Moving Images: understanding children's emotional responses to television,* Manchester, Manchester University Press.

BUCKINGHAM, D. (2000) *After the Death of Childhood: growing up in the age of electronic media,* Cambridge, Polity.

BUCKINGHAM, D. (2002) '*Teletubbies* and the educational imperative' in BUCKINGHAM, D. (ed.) *Small Screens: television for children,* Leicester, Leicester University Press.

BUCKINGHAM, D., DAVIES, H., JONES, K. and KELLEY, P. (1999) *Children's Television in Britain: history, discourse and policy,* London, British Film Institute.

BUCKINGHAM, D. and SEFTON-GREEN, J. (forthcoming) '"Gotta catch 'em all": structure, agency and pedagogy in children's media culture', *Media, Culture and Society.*

CENTER FOR MEDIA EDUCATION (1997) *Web of Deception: threats to children from online marketing,* Washington, DC, Center for Media Education.

DEL VECCHIO, G. (1997) *Creating Ever-Cool: a marketer's guide to a kid's heart,* Gretna, Louisiana, Pelican.

DORR, A. (1986) *Television and Children: a special medium for a special audience,* Beverly Hills, Sage.

DURKIN, K. (1985) *Television, Sex Roles and Children,* Milton Keynes, Open University Press.

ELKIND, D. (1981) *The Hurried Child: growing up too fast too soon,* Reading, Mass., Addison Wesley.

GOMERY, D. (1994) 'Disney's business history: a reinterpretation' in SMOODIN, E. (ed.) *Disney Discourse,* London, British Film Institute.

GREENFIELD, P. (1984) *Mind and Media: the effects of television, computers and video games,* Cambridge Mass, Harvard University Press.

JENKINS, H. (1992) *Textual Poachers,* London, Routledge.

JONES, K. and DAVIES, H. (2002) 'Keeping it real: *Grange Hill* and the representation of the "child's world" in television drama' in BUCKINGHAM, D. (ed.) *Small Screens: television for children,* Leicester, Leicester University Press.

KATZ, J. (1997) *Virtuous Reality,* New York, Random House.

KINDER, M. (1991) *Playing With Power in Movies, Television and Video Games,* Berkeley, University of California Press.

KLINE, S. (1993) *Out of the Garden: toys and children's culture in the age of marketing,* London, Verso.

LAYBOURNE, G. (1993) 'The Nickelodeon experience' in BERRY, G. L. and ASAMEN, J. K. (eds) *Children and Television,* London, Sage.

LIVINGSTONE, S. and BOVILL, M. (1999) *Young People, New Media,* London, London School of Economics.

MELODY, W. (1973) *Children's Television: the economics of exploitation,* New Haven, Yale University Press.

NIXON, H. (1998) 'Fun and games are serious business' in SEFTON-GREEN, J. (ed.) *Digital Diversions: youth culture in the age of multimedia,* London, University College London Press.

PAPERT, S. (1996) *The Connected Family,* Atlanta, GA, Longstreet.

POSTMAN, N. (1983) *The Disappearance of Childhood,* London, W.H. Allen.

POSTMAN, N. (1986) *Amusing Ourselves to Death,* London, Methuen.

POSTMAN, N. (1992) *Technopoly: the surrender of culture to technology,* New York, Knopf.

ROSEN, M. (1997) '*Junk* and other realities: the tough world of children's fiction', *English and Media Magazine,* **37**, pp. 4–6.

RUSHKOFF, D. (1996) *Playing the Future,* New York, Harper Collins.

SANDERS, B. (1995) *A is for Ox: the collapse of literacy and the rise of violence in an electronic age,* New York, Vintage.

TAPSCOTT, D. (1998) *Growing Up Digital: the rise of the net generation,* New York, McGraw Hill.

TOBIN, J. (ed.) (2002) *Nintentionality: or Pikachu's global adventure*, North Carolina, Duke University Press.

TULLOCH, J. (2000) *Watching Television Audiences*, London, Edward Arnold.

VAN DER VOORT, T., BEENTJES, J., BOVILL, M., GASKELL, G., KOOLSTRA, C., LIVINGSTONE, S. and MARSEILLE, N. (1998) 'Young people's ownership of new and old forms of media in Britain and the Netherlands', *European Journal of Communication*, **13**(4), pp. 457–77.

WALTERMANN, J. and MACHILL, M. (eds) (2000) *Protecting Our Children on the Internet*, Gutersloh, Germany, Bertelsmann Foundation.

WARTELLA, E., HEINTZ, K. E., AIDMAN, A. J., and MAZZARELLA, S. R. (1990) 'Television and beyond: children's video media in one community', *Communications Research,* **17**(1), pp. 45–64.

WELLS, P. (2002) '"Tell me about your id, when you was a kid, yah?" Animation and children's television culture' in BUCKINGHAM, D. (ed.) *Small Screens: television for children*, Leicester, Leicester University Press.

WINN, M. (1984) *Children Without Childhood*, Harmondsworth, Penguin.

YOUNG, B. (1990) *Children and Television Advertising*, Oxford, Oxford University Press.

READING A
The blurring of childhood and adulthood

Joshua Meyrowitz

Television and child integration

[D]istinctions in social status are supported, in part, by separating people into different informational worlds. The movement from one social status to another generally involves learning the 'secrets' of the new status and going to places or situations where that information is available.

Each step in the socialization process from childhood to adulthood involves exposure to some new information and continued restriction from other social information. Traditionally, for example, we tell third graders things we keep hidden from second graders, and we continue to keep hidden to third graders things we will tell them when they become fourth graders. Children are walked up the ladder of adult information, but slowly and in stages. A child's cognitive development helps in the climb, but it is not the only factor that affects children's learning or social status. Another significant variable is the amount and type of information made available to children of different ages. If a society is able to divide what people of different ages know into many small steps, it will be able to establish many stages or levels of childhood. Conversely, if a society does not have sharp divisions in what people of different ages know, there will be fewer stages of socialization into adulthood. If we always taught second, third and fourth graders in the same classroom, for example, we would have a very difficult time clearly dividing them into three different social statuses.

This perspective suggests that traditional notions of childhood 'innocence' may have been related to children's exclusion from the social situations, or information-systems, of adults; and, conversely, that adults' seeming 'omniscience' in the eyes of children may have been related to the extent to which adults were able to keep secrets from children and maintain a private 'backstage' area to rehearse their 'onstage' roles, hide their fears, doubts, anxieties, and childish behaviours, and 'privately' discuss techniques for handling children. When the distinctions in information-systems for people of different ages becomes blurred, however, we would expect a blurring in the differences between child and adult behaviour.

[...]

The impact of television on the redefinition of 'home' is all but lost in the dominant, message-orientated approach to the study of television. The focus on content rather than on situational structure has obscured the ways in which television bypasses the filters of adult authority and decreases the significance of the child's physical isolation in the home. In one sense, it makes little difference whether television programs reinforce the message that 'adults always know best' or the message that 'adults don't always know best', or whether a commercial tells children to buy a product themselves or to ask their parents to purchase it for them. For regardless of the specific messages in programs and advertising, the pattern of information flow into the home has changed.

Certainly, today's parents still control much of the atmosphere of the family home, yet home life is no longer the base of all a child's experiences. Children who have television sets now have outside perspectives from which to judge and evaluate family rituals, beliefs, and religious practices. Parents could once easily mould their young children's upbringing by speaking and reading to children only about those things they wished their children to be exposed to, but today's parents must battle with thousands of competing images and ideas over which they have little direct control. As a result, the power relationships within the family are partially rearranged. The influence of parents and family life continues to be seen: children still differ markedly by class, religion, and ethnic background. But the family is no longer an all-powerful formative influence.

Unable to read, very young children were once limited to the few sources of information available to them within or around the home: paintings, illustrations, views from a window, and what adults said and read to them. Television, however, now escorts children across the globe even before they have permission to cross the street.

[...]

What is revolutionary about television is not that it necessarily gives children 'adult minds', but that it allows the very young child to be 'present' at adult interactions. Television removes barriers that once divided people of different ages and reading abilities into different social situations. The widespread use of television is equivalent to a broad social decision to allow young children to be present at wars and funerals, courtships and seductions, criminal plots and cocktail parties. Young children may not fully understand the issues of sex, death, crime, and money that are presented to them on television. Or, put differently, they may understand these issues only in childlike ways. Yet television nevertheless exposes them to many topics and behaviors that adults have spent several centuries trying to keep hidden from children. Television thrusts children into a complex adult world, and it provides the impetus for children to ask the meanings of actions and words they would not yet have heard or read about without television.

[...]

Exposing the 'secret of secrecy'

In printed communication, it is common to have books for parents that discuss what books are suitable for children. This book-about-books is an adult–adult interaction in which young children cannot participate. Further, children do not usually even know about the existence of this type of book.

With the help of such private adult 'discussions', children were once shielded from certain topics such as sex, money, death, crime, and drugs. Even more significant, however, children were shielded from the fact that they were being shielded. Print allowed for an 'adult conspiracy'. In terms of knowledge and awareness, the child was in a position of some one hypnotized to forget something and also hypnotized to forget the hypnosis.

The same thing does not apply to television. Television, it is true, often offers parents advice. Talk shows discuss children's television, and warnings are placed at the beginning of programs to let parents know that a program may contain material 'unsuitable for pre-teenagers'. Yet while the manifest content is similar to the content of parents' advice books, the structure of the communication situation is radically different. Television discussions and warnings are as accessible to children as they are to adults. Ironically, such advice on television often cues children to which programs they are not supposed to see and increases children's interest in what follows. Even if such warnings are heard by parents, and even if parents act to censor the program, parental control is nevertheless weakened because the control becomes overt and therefore often unpalatable to both children and adults. For these reasons, perhaps, studies over several decades have found that parents exercise surprisingly little control over what children watch on television.

Through books, adults could keep secrets from children, and they could also keep their secret-keeping secret. Television, in contrast, exposes many adult secrets to children and also reveals the 'secret of secrecy'. And while today's parental advice books remain private adult interactions, the secrets they contain (and compromise) are exposed daily on television.

Source

Meyrowitz, J. (1985) *No Sense of Place: the impact of electronic media on social behavior*, Oxford, Oxford University Press, pp. 235–47.

READING B

'One I made earlier': media, popular culture and the politics of childhood

Stephen Wagg

Going live: the battle for Saturday morning

The pattern of BBC programming for children in the 1970s and 1980s has to be seen in its political and cultural context. Politically, ever since the campaign for commercial television in the early 1950s, the tradition of 'public service broadcasting', and the institution which upheld it, the BBC, had been on the defensive. From the 1960s onwards, with the established popularity of ITV programmes, the BBC was likely to be told by government, whether Conservative or Labour, that continued support would be conditional upon winning a greater share of the national audience. At the BBC, in many areas, this led over time to a more full-hearted pursuit of the popular.

Children's programming was particularly important, in this context, for two reasons. First, the BBC was felt to produce better programmes for children, so this was a sphere of operations where ITV might still be shown a clean pair of heels. Second, more credence was being given to the arguments that children were a means to capturing a whole household of viewers for the evening: if the children could be persuaded to watch BBC TV at teatime, maybe the family would stay with the BBC until bedtime. By the mid-1970s this consideration had been extended to morning time at the weekend. In 1978, Brian Cowgill, Controller of BBC 1 informed the Head of Children's Programmes: ' You're doing alright in the week, but you're not doing much on Saturday mornings' (Baxter and Barnes, 1989, p. 141). This admonition led to the Saturday morning magazine programme *Multi-Coloured Swap Shop*, and its subsequent mutations, *Saturday Superstore* and the current *Going Live* and the *The 8.15 From Manchester.* These shows, and their kindred programmes around the networks (notably ITV's *Disney Club* and *Motormouth*), illustrate a number of important and decisive departures from the traditional childhood of the broadcasting 'hearth', which I'd like briefly to discuss.

First, the traditional paradigm of autonomous *activity* is largely abandoned in these shows. Children are now assumed to be active principally in relation to *consumption* (equated with passivity in the 'hearth' paradigm). This consumption is principally of media products; pre-eminently, therefore, it involves buying, listening and watching rather than the previously valued pursuits that entailed making or doing. Thus much of the show features pop stars with a new album or video to promote, people who appear in other TV programmes, and so on. Doing-things-for-oneself is, as a theme, very much subordinate to these matters and, if it is pursued at all, this may be in the context of a media promotion: the golfer Nick Faldo, for instance, dropped into the *Going Live* studio one morning (21 September 1991) and helped a handful of young golfers with their technique, but his appearance was principally in connection with TV coverage of the Ryder Cup golf competition, forthcoming on BBC.

Similarly, these programmes often include cartoons such as *Teenage Mutant Hero Turtles* and *Masters of the Universe* whose characters are available in toy form. The BBC will not normally buy cartoons which have actually been financed by toy companies (Taylor, 1990) but, given the promotional value of broadcasting the cartoon in any event, the distinction seems arbitrary. This centrality of commercial discourse … in *Going Live* was acknowledged in 1990 by the Office of Fair Trading who published a magazine called *VFM* (Value for Money), which was aimed at the 'Young Consumer'. The stars of *Going Live* were used to promote it: '*VFM*' they informed readers, 'tells you all you need to know about money and shopping' (Office of Fair Trading 1990:2).

Second, as I've said, these programmes borrow heavily from, and mesh into, pop culture. The presenters of *Swap Shop* and *Superstore,* Noel Edmonds and Mike Read respectively, were both, initially, disc jockeys. Timmy Mallett, presenter of *Wacaday,* TVam's programme for the school holidays, released a record in 1990 which entered the top ten. In this sense, the programmes presuppose children as *fans* and, especially in the case of girls, the spontaneous squeals of the 1950s and 1960s have become routinized: they're expected. When the pop duo Bros come out to be interviewed by presenter Ross King on an edition of *8.15 From Manchester* in 1991, the screams had a prescribed ring about them. The boys looked suitably humble and sheepish. Having some star or other as an object of adoration was as normal for a pre-teenage girl in the 1980s and 1990s as having a pet rabbit was in the 1950s: on *Going Live* in 1990 presenter Philip Schofield suggested to a young woman who had just put a question to TV/pop star Jason Donovan that she might care to spend the remaining time 'gazing into his eyes'.

A third element is satirical humour. This was imported into children's television by ITV in the late 1960s, notably with *Do Not Adjust Your Set* (1968), a programme written and performed by Oxbridge comedians later to form the *Monty Python* team. In the 1970s ATV developed *Tiswas,* a children's magazine programme based on pop, irony and self-conscious mayhem. More recently, such magazine programmes, most of which are approximations of *Tiswas,* have often featured Oxbridge or 'alternative' comedians and the discourse of the presenters has become reflexively ironic. *Going Live,* for example, has resident comedians who, for several series up to 1991, were Trev and Simon, a double act recruited from the alternative cabaret circuit. Much of Trev and Simon's comedy plays off the idea of the young, media-wise consumer-fan: their routines invariably include references to the stars in this week's show, whose names and sources of celebrity they are Always Getting Wrong: no, no, silly, it's *Kylie* Minogue, not Kelly, and so on.

This resident skittishness can be taken together with a fourth element – a mock cruelty – which, again, seems to have originated with ATV's *Tiswas.* In *Tiswas* there were seldom more than a few minutes before the next custard pie or bucket of whitewash. In the 1980s and early 1990s children's magazine programmes usually ran competitions wherein the losers (or even the winners) were variously slid into tanks of brightly coloured gunge, dropped into swimming pools, hit over the head with soft mallets or required to pay some such forfeit. On the BBC 1's *The 8.15 From Manchester* (a summer show) teachers, wearing archaic garb of gown and mortar board, are tipped, ceremonially, into swimming pools. All this illustrates how contemporary TV programmes for the young *take the part of the child,* attempting to appropriate elements of his/her culture. Previously, broadcasters, when they addressed children, took the part of the parent/teacher/adult. Away from adults, children had, as they still have, a social world of their own – out playing, in school corridors, in their bedrooms, up town – and this world always had a harder edge to it than the sentimental childhood-of-the-hearth notion suggested. The duckings and the tubs of gunge represent an attempt to capture this edge, with its constituent sense of opposition and subversion. The forfeits are determinedly unsentimental; they say, just as the paternalists said, 'We don't talk down to children'.

This process is also reflected in the changing face of the children's broadcaster. In the 1920s and the 1930s such people were men and women of early middle age who styled themselves 'Uncle' and 'Auntie'. By the late 1950s, this age group was beginning to be considered unviable for the task: the first presenters of *Blue Peter,* in 1958, were a male of twenty-five (Christopher Trace) and female of twenty-one (Leila Williams). By the 1980s, this age, or the appearance of it, was the norm for children's magazine programmes: when Yvette Fielding was recruited to present *Blue Peter* in 1987 she was only eighteen. 'Right now', said Andy Crane, twenty-seven-year-old (but looking younger) presenter of *Children's BBC* and *Motormouth* recently, 'I think that me and Philip Schofield are like older brothers to the viewers' (*Guardian*, 27 September 1991:98). Comparative youth is, moreover, allied to a radically changed presentation of self, as noted with some acerbity by Georgia Campbell: Jean Morton, of ITV's *Tinga and Tucker Club* (1950s and 1960s), is remembered as 'wearing clothes that are creaking with starch and propriety, and her hair has been freshly pin-curled, rococo style. She is not, please note, trying to pretend she is five years old.' Similarly

> On bygone *Blue Peter,* Val is wearing a polite blouse and sensible flats, while Pete 'n' John look crestfallen because they were forced to leave their club ties in the dressing room.

Today's presenters, by contrast, 'look like a gang of inner city crack-dealers … hyper-groovers filling in time before the next acid party' (Campbell, 1991).

Lastly, as I've already observed, these programmes are substantially about the media themselves. The subject matter (the latest records, CDs, videos, films and TV programmes) and the discourse – the phrase 'going live', for example – are drawn from the media. Indeed, a regular feature of *Going Live* involves one of the presenters telephoning a viewer so that they can talk 'live on television'. There are regular trips 'behind the scenes' to see producers and control panels, technicians are frequently hauled on screen, cameras whirl around to reveal other cameras and their crew. On *The 8.15 From Manchester* (14 September 1991) presenter Ross King talks to other 'children's presenters' Andi Peters and Simon Parkin (both of *Children's BBC*) and then interviews his fellow *8.15* presenter, singer Sonia, about her new record, asking her ultimately: 'What was your most wonderful moment – apart from working with me?' Sonia is then complimented by *her* fellow presenter, Diane Oxberry, on her 'brilliant new image'. Similarly, on *Going Live*, presenters and children have a 'Press Conference' where they interview celebrities: in the programme of 21 September 1991 presenter Philip Schofield asks both Bros and Kylie Minogue if they think they sell more newspapers (through being famous) than records. Likewise, the show's resident furry animal, Gordon the Gopher, is asked how did he 'get into presenting'?

This self-referential media culture reflects what might be called a postmodern childhood, wherein children's TV troubles less and less to mediate the world to the child, or to impact knowledge or skills. Instead, TV (along with other mass media) *is* the world, and it happily discusses itself.

References

BAXTER, B. AND BARNES, E. (1989) *Blue Peter: the inside story*, Letchworth, Ringpress Books.

CAMPBELL, G. (1991) 'Watch with horror', *Guardian*, 18 February.

OFFICE OF FAIR TRADING (1990) *VFM*, London, OFT.

TAYLOR, P. (1990) 'Beeb in soup over Turtles', *The Guardian*, 10 December.

Source

Wagg, S. (1992) '"One I made earlier": media, popular culture and the politics of childhood' in Strinati, D. and Wagg, S. *Come on Down: popular media culture in post war Britain*, London, Routledge.

READING C

In the worst possible taste: children, television and cultural value

Hannah Davies, David Buckingham and Peter Kelley

One of the implicit concerns in debates [about children and television] is with the question of children's *taste*. It seems to be assumed that, if left to their own devices, children will choose to watch material that is not only morally damaging but also inherently lacking in cultural value. Dietary metaphors are common here: children, it is often asserted, will opt for chips and chocolate bars in preference to the nourishing cultural food that adults consistently tell them is good for them. Children's 'natural' taste, it is argued, is for vulgarity and sensationalism, rather than restraint and subtlety; for simplistic stereotypes rather than complex, rounded characters; and it is led by the baser physical instincts rather than the higher sensibilities of the intellect. Children and 'good taste' are, it would seem, fundamentally incompatible.

[...]

Talking taste

The data presented in this article are drawn from a larger study of changing views of the child audience for television (Buckingham *et al*, 1999). In addition to looking at how the television industry defines and constructs the child audience – through practices such as programme production, scheduling and research – we wanted to understand how children perceived *themselves* as an audience (cf. Buckingham, 1994). We decided to focus this aspect of our research around one key question: how do children define what makes a programme either 'for children' or 'for adults'?

We took this question to two classes of children in a socially and ethnically mixed inner-London primary school. Year 6 – the top year of primary school – was selected because of its transitional position. At the age of 10 or 11, these were the most senior or 'grown-up' children in the institution, looking towards secondary school, where they would be the least grown-up (cf. de Block, 1998). We chose to compare this with a Year 2 class of six to seven-year-olds, for whom we expected their position as 'children' would be more secure and less problematic.

[...]

What makes a children's programme?

In effect, our research activities deliberately set up the opposition child–adult and asked the children to negotiate it. For various reasons, they found this very difficult. New categories emerged such as 'in between' or 'for everyone'. The older group of children in particular were uneasy about defining their favourite programmes as 'children's'; while some of the younger children constructed the category 'babies' to differentiate their tastes from those of their younger siblings. In this respect, the process of classifying programmes explicitly served as a means of social self-definition. For example, when a group of Year 2 boys collapsed into laughter at the mention of the pre-school programme *Teletubbies*, they were clearly distancing themselves from the younger audience for whom the programme is designed – and from the girls in their class who had appropriated its 'cuter' aspects. Similarly, when a group of Year 2 girls covered their ears every time football was mentioned, they were self-consciously constructing their own girlishness by rejecting the male world of football. In this respect, our activity effectively dramatised Bourdieu's (1979) famous statement: 'classification classifies the classifier'.

In the children's explorations of what makes a programme 'for children', a number of quite predictable factors emerged. Perhaps unsurprisingly, the strongest arguments were negative ones. Programmes featuring sex, violence and 'swearing' were singled out by both year groups as being particularly 'grown-up'. Likewise, children's programmes were predominantly defined in terms of absences – that is, in terms of what they do *not* include.

[...]

[T]he most obvious criterion for selecting a programme as being 'for children' was that of personal preference (I like it, so it must be for children). Such expressions of preference often involved contrasting their own personal taste with that of parents, most noticeably in relation to news or current affairs programmes. However, this opposition between parents and children was often expressed in quite complex ways. In some cases, the children made a clear distinction between 'parents' in the abstract and their *own* parent(s). While parents in general were seen to like 'boring stuff' such as the news, talk about their own family lives often involved anecdotes about their parents watching and enjoying the same kinds of programmes that they liked. Two six-year-old boys, for example, referred to the comedy show *Mr. Bean* in this way:

DANIEL: My mum likes watching it and she's nearly 29.

PAUL: My dad loves it, my dad laughs at it!

In the lived reality of these children's lives, then, the viewing preferences of the 'grown-ups' (parents) are not independent of the tastes of their children, nor do they necessarily correspond to what are seen as adult norms.

To a large extent, this could be regarded as simply a consequence of the daily routines and structures of family life: people (parents included) do not always choose what they watch, and they may decide to watch programmes together for the experience of companionship rather than because they actually prefer them. In this sense, the opposition between parent and child is not necessarily fixed and stable.

Aspirational tastes

This parent/child distinction had greater currency among the younger children, who were generally more inclined to accept their dependence on parental and adult authority. The ten- and eleven-year-olds, looking forward to adolescence and secondary school, tended to make more nuanced distinctions between ages *within* the category of 'childhood'. On the brink of becoming teenagers themselves, they associated particular programmes or types of programmes with this age group. These choices were clearly informed by a broader sense of a 'teen' lifestyle, to which many of them aspired, even though they didn't see themselves as teenagers quite yet. Being a teenager was seen to offer a degree of autonomy and control over their lives which was just around the corner. Thus, they recognised that situation comedies like *Sister Sister* or *Sabrina the Teenage Witch* might feature teenage characters, but they were quite clearly claimed as programmes for people like them. Unlike older people, however, it was felt that teenagers – the actual bearers of this projected future identity – might also share some of their own tastes:

INTERVIEWER:	Do you think it *(Sister Sister)* is a programme for teenagers?
ALL:	No.
INTERVIEWER:	Why is that? Aren't the characters sixteen?
SHARON:	Yes, but they're the sort of age where, you know, we can understand…
ANNIE:	I think teenagers can like it as well.

Certain lifestyle options were consistently associated with this slightly older age-group. Teenagers, it would seem, have social and emotional lives, characterised by boyfriends, girlfriends, fashion and music. During our group interviews, conversations around these subjects were frequent and unsolicited. These conversations clearly had a social, performative role and were used partly as a way of articulating their own (heterosexual) gender positions (for a fuller discussion, see Kelley *et al.*, 1999). However, the identity of the teenager was not only differentiated through sexual and romantic knowledge; it was also about having greater access to the public world …

However, looking forward to being teenage was not at all the same thing as wanting to be grown-up. Certain programmes that were seen as the kinds of things that teenagers would like – notably the comedy quiz show *Shooting Stars* – were enjoyed because of their almost 'childish' silliness and rebellion against adult authority. For example, one boy singled out the character George Dawes as a particular reason for liking this programme, because he was a grown man dressed as a baby:

INTERVIEWER:	What's so funny about him?
SIMON:	He's a baby and he plays the drums with his hand up and he says 'silly git' and everyone laughs on the show.

The juxtaposition between babyishness and adult humour and swearing is clearly a source of enjoyment to this boy. In cases like this, enthusiasm for the 'childish' and silly aspects of comedy were also combined with a sense of exclusivity. In discussion, it was important for certain children to show that they could 'get' the joke (as it were), in order to show that they were grown up and sophisticated.

In a sense, then, these were clearly *aspirational* preferences. As Liesbeth de Block (1998) notes, comedies like *Friends* and *Men Behaving Badly* seem to be particularly popular with children in this age group, partly because they allow them to rehearse a kind of adulthood that is both independent, autonomous and self-sufficient (living in your own flat with your friends, having control over your own space and time) while at the same time allowing irresponsibility, irreverence and immaturity (watching lots of television, getting into trouble with more 'responsible' grown-ups). Yet, unlike characters in more serious adult soaps or dramas for instance, the male characters in these comedies are not portrayed (or indeed perceived by children) as particularly mature. As de Block suggests, their appeal rests largely on the fact that they are men behaving like boys. Such programmes thus offer children a version of 'adulthood' that combines elements of autonomy and freedom with irreverence and irresponsibility.

It was these qualities, as much as the music or the clothes the characters wore, that defined such programmes as inherently 'cool', as opposed to 'old-fashioned'. As one boy with a particular self-esteem problem explained:

LUKE: I have to admit this, but I'm quite – I'm not a cool guy. I don't watch *Friends*.

In this aspirational world of 'cool', there seems to be an almost narcissistic relationship between reader and text. It is partly that the qualities of the programme are seen to transfer across to the individuals who watch it; but also that one's existing qualities are somehow necessarily reflected in what one chooses to watch in the first place. In Luke's account, classification very definitely classifies the classifier.

How uncool can you get?

If the cultural identity labelled 'teenage' is characterised by fun, rebellion and sex, it was necessary for a contrasting identity to be constructed – as something that was none of these things, and indeed was actively opposed to them. This category was identified by several groups of girls in particular as that of 'grannies'. Given the highly gendered nature of this classification, it is interesting that it was more clearly formulated by the girls. The identity of the granny was defined as boring, old-fashioned and censorious. The representative programmes associated with it included *Songs of Praise* (religion), *Ready Steady Cook* (cookery), *Countdown* (a quiz show) and *The Antiques Roadshow*:

INTERVIEWER: Why do you think it (*Countdown*) is so boring?

ANNIE: Because it's full of all these words that you have to make.

INTERVIEWER:	Who do you think would like those kinds of programmes?
JULIA:	Grannies.
ANNIE:	Yeah, grannies!

Likewise, 'grannies' or (more charitably) 'people in their sixties' were also seen as the least appropriate audience for the children's own favourite shows. This renouncement of old age was also used as a strategy in arguments about programmes. In a mixed group, one girl expressed a preference for the sit-com *Frasier*, only to be put down by one of the boys with the withering comment: 'What, old people living in a flat? That's not funny.'

In this way, certain types of adults and adult viewing are very explicitly rejected. Being old and female, it would seem, is the ultimate cultural stigma. Of course, this expression of cultural taste is not unrelated to questions of social power and status, not least as defined by the media themselves: when younger women are valued for their physical desirability, older women are frequently invisible – and, when they are represented at all, often serve as the butt of young people's humour. This might go some way to explaining why it was the girls rather than the boys who were so hostile to 'grannies' and all that they were seen to represent: on some level, perhaps, they recognised that they couldn't be Spice Girls for ever.

You've got to laugh

In response to our somewhat earnest questions about why a programme was chosen or preferred, the most common answer across both age groups was simply that it was 'funny'.

[...]

While children's expressions of enthusiasm for comedy are, on one level, simply an assertion of 'personal' pleasure, there are also social functions in talking about what makes them laugh. Different kinds of comedy had different kinds of value in this respect. *Mr. Bean* or the 'video bloopers' show *You've Been Framed* are primarily physical, slapstick humour; although the children's accounts of them focused particularly on the subversive or 'carnivalesque' element of adults behaving like children and making fools of themselves. On the other hand, programmes such *as Shooting Stars* or *Have I Got News for You* (a news quiz) were valued for different reasons. Central to their appeal for the older children was the idea that in 'getting the joke', they were gaining access to an exclusive world of irony and media-references, not suitable for younger children:

ANDREW:	*Friends* is – it's not a little kids thing. Like *Shooting Stars* is a show for older people.
JAMES:	Little kids don't have the patience to watch them.
ANDREW:	Yeah, someone younger won't find *Friends* or *Shooting Stars* funny.

For James and Andrew, the 'older people' identified here are implicitly people like them.

Talking about these kinds of programmes seemed to be more important for the boys in the group – which may reflect an aspirational identification with the men who tend to dominate these shows. Particularly in the case of programmes like *They Think It's All Over* (a sports quiz) and *Have I Got News For You*, the humour often involves a characteristically male form of 'banter' and one-upmanship. To some extent, being seen to be 'in on the joke' was more important than actually finding it funny. As one boy explained in relation to *Shooting Stars* and *Have I Got News For You*:

DAVID: You see them maybe once and sometimes you don't get the jokes, but you still laugh because you know it's meant to be funny … But you don't really know why.

Laughing with the big boys, as it were, has the most social and cultural currency: this is what you *should* find funny. For one particular boy – who clearly saw himself as a taste leader in the class – this became apparent when he discussed the US sit-com *Sabrina the Teenage Witch*. As a less sophisticated, more girl-oriented show, he almost apologised for liking it:

INTERVIEWER: So what's good about *Sabrina*?

JAMES: It's just good.

ALAN: I have to admit, it's not the kind of thing you'd think is good. But it's good, it's funny.

Particular kinds of comedy, then, clearly have a social function, which is again associated with being more sophisticated and 'teenage'. To this extent, talking about comedy is a serious business: it can be used to mark out social status and knowledge as well as simply expressing pleasure.

If what is 'funny' was seen to be particularly appropriate for children, then what is 'boring' (and hence lacking in pleasure) was consistently equated with adults – and particularly with 'grannies'. For this group of six-year-old girls, being boring is a defining characteristic of adult programmes:

INTERVIEWER: So what makes it [the news] a grown-ups programme?

TONI: It's boring.

INTERVIEWER: So does that mean that grown-ups are boring?

RUTH: Yes, because they like the news.

TONI: I hate the news.

INTERVIEWER: Why do you think grown-ups like the news?

TONI: Because they want to know what's happening?

INTERVIEWER: And aren't you interested?

TONI: No!

[…]

[T]he association between what was 'boring' and what was identified with 'adults' was very consistent. Thus, for a group of girls in Year 6, *Shooting Stars* – which was a preferred programme among their male peers – is defined as boring, in part because it is associated with one of their parents:

SHARON: My dad would laugh at *Shooting Stars* … sometimes I think it's really boring.

INTERVIEWER: Is there anything in particular about the programme that makes it for grown-ups?

SHARON: It's boring. And it's –

JULIA: They laugh about stupid, dumb things.

Being boring – while it means different things for different children – is thus a cardinal signifier of a lack of cultural capital. In contrast, being funny (and 'getting the joke') is seen to convey value on these children as individuals as well as on the programmes that they consume. In the process, the cultural hierarchy that elevates 'seriousness' and civic responsibility is effectively inverted.

References

BOURDIEU, P. (1979) *Distinction: A Social Critique of the Judgment of Taste*, London, Routledge and Kegan Paul.

BUCKINGHAM, D. (1994) 'Television and the definition of childhood' in B. MAYALL (ed.) *Children's Childhoods: Observed and Experienced*, London, Falmer.

BUCKINGHAM, D., DAVIES H., JONES, K. and KELLEY, P. (1999) *Children's Television in Britain: History, Discourse and Policy*, London, British Film Institute.

DE BLOCK, L. (1998) 'From childhood pleasures to adult identities', *English and Media Magazine*, **38**, pp. 24–9.

KELLEY, P., BUCKINGHAM, D. and DAVIES, H. (1999) 'Talking dirty: children, sexual knowledge and television', *Childhood*, **6**(2), pp. 221–42.

Source

Adapted from DAVIES, H., BUCKINGHAM, D. and KELLEY, P. (2000) 'In the worst possible taste: children, television and cultural value', *European Journal of Cultural Studies*, **3**(1).

Chapter 6
Youth cultures

Mary Jane Kehily

CONTENTS

LEARNING OUTCOMES

When you have studied this chapter, you should be able to:

1   Demonstrate an understanding of the concept of youth cultures and its usefulness for studying the cultural worlds of children and young people.

2   Apply the concept of youth culture to young people's lives and the social practices they engage in.

3   Critically evaluate the concept of subculture and its significance to the study of young people's lives.

4   Discuss some of the strengths and limitations of seeing young people in terms of cultural and subcultural movements.

I AN INTRODUCTION TO YOUTH CULTURES

In earlier chapters in this book, you looked at the cultures of children and young people and considered how they develop and are maintained through games, friendship and language. This chapter further explores and develops an idea that has already been introduced – that children and young people create their own distinct cultures and that these can be observed and studied. In the Western world, the age group frequently referred to as 'youth' has engaged in activities and movements over the years that come to be regarded as forms of *youth culture*. However, the distinctive cultures of young children and of youth are often seen differently. Whereas the cultural worlds of children at play are usually regarded as a benign feature of childhood, youth cultures are often seen as dangerous and challenging. This chapter will explore different aspects of youth culture as well as looking at specific examples of youth cultures. We will be focusing on the cultures of older children or young people in the thirteen to eighteen age range.

Over time, young people's engagements in cultural activities have acquired names and identities such as teddy-boys, skinheads, punks and goths. There is a rich vein of research that develops the idea that youth constitutes a distinct cultural group. These studies frequently illustrate the many ways in which young people in this age group relate to and participate in society. It is through the concept of youth culture that the activities of many young people become visible. The first section of this chapter will explore the concept of youth cultures and consider some features of youth culture. In subsequent sections you will be introduced to some key themes and features within youth cultures as well as studying some specific examples. Section 2 considers the concept of youth subcultures within the wider youth culture. Section 3 looks at three of these subcultures – skinheads, ducktails and Rastafarians – while Section 4 focuses on the status of girls in relation to youth cultures. Section 5 takes the punk subculture as a case study, giving you the opportunity to compare two accounts of the world of punk written from different perspectives. In conclusion, Section 6 looks at the advantages and limitations of considering young people as a separate cultural group.

Allow about 10 minutes

A C T I V I T Y I   Subcultures in your youth

Look back on your own youth and identify any youth cultures of which you were a part. Did they have a distinctive name or label? What were their particular characteristics – dress, hair-style, music, behaviour? How old were you at the time of your involvement? If you weren't yourself a member of such a culture, what do you remember of those that were? What do you see as the equivalent cultures that attract young people today?

C O M M E N T

The youth cultures available to you as a young person depend to a large extent on the period you grew up in and other factors such as where you grew up, socio-economic background and ideas that you identified with at the time. The two youth cultures that were prominent during my teenage years in a small town in Warwickshire, England were mods and rockers, neither of which appealed. I saw them as a choice between obsessively neat but ugly clothes or an excess of leather and grease. I was more influenced by the legacy of the hippy culture than by youth cultures that offered the possibility of membership in Leamington Spa. The idea of being a hippy was on the wane but the hippy ethos was much in evidence. My friends and I were against wars, governments and 'selling out', and for all things mind expanding. We wore long hair, long dresses, lots of velvet and patchouli oil – and having a purple bedroom wall was compulsory. Despite smelling like cat's wee, intimacy was very much in vogue and I recall many tender moments huddled up with friends listening to The Velvet Underground. While I am tempted to make fun of this time in my life and see it as a resource for humour, I also recognize that identification with a youth culture can be formative and generative.

Peace and love – the hippy era.

Anti-capitalism
demonstration,
Brussels, 2001.

But what about youth cultures today? If I were young now would I be part
of a cultural group, and if so which one? Well, the appeal of new-age
hippies is an obvious one for me. Environmental protest movements,
animal rights activism and the global anti-capitalist demonstrations of
recent years owe a great deal to the hippy era and can be seen as a
reworking of earlier themes and issues.

Cultural groupings, however, as a particular feature of children's cultural
worlds are not necessarily the preserve of the older age group. In a study of
a middle school in the UK, Andrew Pollard (1984) found that children aged
between eight and twelve could be identified according to their membership
of child groups within the school. Pollard suggested that there were three
sub-groups and defined them as 'goodies, jokers and gangs'. Goodies,
Pollard indicated, were a large group of children – boys and girls – who had
a positive attitude to school and were of moderate ability. Jokers were
another large, mixed gender group who were seen to be academically able,
good at sport and popular with teachers and peers as members of sporting
teams or the school choir and as house captains. The gang was a group of
girls who were less academically successful, played rough and tumble
games, often with boys, and drew upon sexual themes in many of their
exchanges. Collectively, Pollard's study suggests that younger children in
school may position themselves within groups that can be defined by their
different approaches to schoolwork, sport, academic achievement and play.
Pollard indicates that the cultural groupings children affiliate with in school
play an important role in shaping their lives and futures.

Other research shows that such groups are also an abiding feature of life in
secondary and high schools. In an Australian study, Bob Connell (1989)
identified and documented the divisions within male peer groups as 'cool
guys, swots and wimps' and Pamela Nilan's (1992) ethnographic study of
girls in Sydney, Australia describes four categories of female friendship
as 'kazzies, DBTs, tryhards and originals'. These groups were identified by

the young women that Nilan spoke with and were characterized in the following way:

- *kazzies* – girls from ethnic minority backgrounds, usually Greek, who live in less fashionable parts of town and dress in ways that emphasize their femininity;
- *DBTs* – Double Bay Trendies – middle- and upper-middle-class girls, living in exclusive suburbs, attending private schools and dressing in casual but expensive clothes to achieve an American college look;
- *tryhards* – girls in either of the above categories who simply try too hard to possess style and achieve the look, but never quite get there;
- *originals* – girls who embody a style and a look that is recognized as individual, distinctive and eclectic, setting fashion rather than following fashion.

Based on her discussions with these young women, Nilan presents a very particular cultural world – of femininity and adolescence – that provides a way of making sense of everyday experience. All groups can be defined and identified by their *style*. Style in this sense can be seen as more expansive than the appropriation of fashion, make-up and other forms of adornment. In the lives of these young women, style can also encompass issues of social class and ethnicity. Key markers of style can include: ways of talking; ways of dressing and self-presentation; and, finally, issues of location – where you live and what your neighbourhood is like. Nilan's analysis illustrates the ways in which the intimate cultural world of girls is linked to and shaped by broader social structures. This approach has points of connection with the work of Penelope Eckert discussed in Chapter 3.

In this chapter, we will be looking at a range of youth cultures that extend beyond the school. The rest of this section is intended to introduce you to the idea of looking at young people as a cultural group and considers some contrasting approaches to the study and analysis of young people in society.

It is commonplace to suggest that young people in the North challenge many of the norms and values of mainstream society. A widespread assumption among adults is that young people have a difficult time adjusting to the social demands of developing an identity as a young adult. The stereotype of the teenager as moody, difficult and estranged from adults is ubiquitous in soap operas, comedies and other media representations. Concerns expressed by adults about young people frequently refer to non-conformist events such as the Sex Pistols' 1977 performance on the Thames or 'worrying' activities and practices such as shooming or Slipknot's encounter with the beaver (See Box 1).

But such concerns are not new. Griffin (1993) makes the point that young people are always seen in relation to their society. Her analysis suggests that the disquiet expressed about young people at any given time can be understood as a comment upon broader social changes affecting the population as a whole. Researchers who have studied youth cultures often refer to key moments of cultural activity that help to define young people as a distinct cultural group. The hippy movement associated with 1960s' counter-culture and the phenomenon of Beatlemania are frequently referred to as influential activities that a cohort of young people participated in and through which they defined themselves.

Box 1 Non-conformist events

Generation X?

The Sex Pistols were banned from playing on land, and their song 'God Save the Queen' banned from being played on the airwaves. So the only place left was the water. One of the most delirious memories I have is of seeing crowds of artful dodgers – punk rockers – jamming London's bridges… 'God save the Queen/she ain't no human being/she made you a moron/a potential H-bomb/God save the Queen/we mean it maaan!' It was a frenzied, cacophonous, exhilarating, inspired moment.

(McLaren, 2002)

Slipknot – the teenagers' latest idols

At one gig in the US late last year, they took out a dead beaver, sucked its tail and head, squeezed its guts on to their faces and spent the next ten minutes vomiting all over the stage and on to the audience. One fan claimed she would never wash the puke from her hair.

(Hari, 2002)

Shooming

'Shooming' is the state of ecstasy dancers aspire to, losing themselves in Bam Bam's rhythms in order to leave the real world behind.

(Godfrey, cited in Redhead, 1993, p. 62)

Slipknot – expressing the negativity of contemporary youth.

Subsequent youth cultures such as punk and rave can be seen as a response to these earlier forms of youth culture. The rave culture of the late 1980s/early 1990s has been described as chemically enhanced young people taking ecstasy and dancing all night in a bid to escape the real world. Redhead (1993) refers to this phenomenon as 'hedonism in hard times' (p. 4). Young people in the North in the current period have been referred to as 'Generation X', a nihilistic, gloom-stricken group with more than a passing interest in despair, hatred and self-destruction. The negativity of contemporary youth has been explained in societal terms as a reflection of the crisis to be found in post-industrial societies. For instance, the band Slipknot wear barcodes and rubber masks to conceal their identity; they refer to each other using numbers rather than names. Fans of Slipknot are attracted to hell and death rather than the nirvana-like appeal of shooming in rave culture.

Slipknot's lyrics are laced with imagery of self-harm and suicide: 'I've felt the hate rise up in me …/kneel down and clear the stone of leaves …/I wander over where you can't see …/Inside my shell I wait and bleed …/Goodbye!' But do these characterizations of young people relate to the way they think and feel? This chapter aims to address this question.

2 YOUTH CULTURES AND SUBCULTURES

In Section 1, we discussed the idea of young people as a distinct group defined by their age, activities and position within society. However, young people do not exist as a homogeneous group. Inevitably, there will be differences between young people, often inflected through social categories such as class, ethnicity and gender. Sometimes these differences may be marked by a set of different interests, values and aspirations. Researchers who have studied the activities and behaviour of young people in Western societies developed the concept of *subculture* as part of an attempt to understand youth culture from the perspective of young people themselves. Participants in a subculture usually have things in common with one another that serve to distinguish them from other social groups and from other young people. Tim O'Sullivan *et al.* (1994) and Sarah Thornton (1997) offer alternative ways of defining subculture (see Box 2).

These definitions make it clear that subcultures exist in relationship to the society from which they emerge and that their existence may provide an insight into the experiences of young people, especially in the areas of education, work and leisure.

The prefix *sub* in the word subculture signals that these groups have a position which is subordinate to the broader culture. It also captures the sense in which participants in subcultures often see themselves, and are seen by others, as different or oppositional in some way. The sociologist Albert K. Cohen was one of the first to explore the concept of subculture and the ways in which it can aid an understanding of the social world (Cohen, 1955). For Cohen, subcultures arise when people with similar problems get together to look for solutions. Through their interactions with one another, the members of a subculture come to share a similar outlook on life and evolve collective solutions to the problems they experience. In the process, a distance is created between the subculture and the dominant culture. Indeed, achieving status within a subculture may entail a loss of status in the wider culture.

Box 2 Definitions of subcultures

As the prefix implies, *sub*cultures are significant and distinctive negotiations located within wider cultures ... The term and its supporting theory have developed almost exclusively in the study and explanation of youth ... youth negotiate and advance 'their own' distinctive and especially symbolic *subcultural* responses to the problems posed not only by age or generational status, subordination and control, but also by class position and inequality, particularly as they are experienced and combined in the spheres of education, work and leisure.

(O'Sullivan *et al.*, 1994, p. 307)

Subcultures have generally been seen to be informal and organic ... The defining attribute of 'subcultures', then, lies with the way the accent is put on the distinction between a particular cultural/social group and the larger culture/society. The emphasis is on variance from a larger collectivity who are invariably, but not unproblematically, positioned as normal, average and dominant.

(Thornton, 1997, pp. 4–5)

As you will see in the following section, youth subcultures frequently seek to define themselves as against the culture that exists around them and particularly against its values. It could be argued that there is a tendency in studies of subcultures to emphasize the unconventional, deviant and non-conformist aspects of subcultural groups. However, within the context of non-conformity, participation in subcultures also demands a considerable amount of conformity. Subcultural groups are commonly marked by distinctive modes of appearance, dress and adornment that make the participants look different, sometimes even spectacular and shocking. In the context of youth cultures, style takes on a particular meaning as 'the means by which cultural identity and social location are negotiated and expressed' (O'Sullivan *et al.*, 1994, p. 305). Membership of a subculture may also bring with it a certain emotional experience – something to which we will return later in the chapter.

It is important to stress that being a member of a subculture is not about being a victim. Individuals involved in subcultural activity often speak of the highs and lows of life as part of a subculture; the mundane inertia of 'doing nothing' (Corrigan, 1979, p.103) and the moments of risk and excitement, getting a buzz, having your kicks, feeling turned-on. A final point of definition is that many contemporary subcultures are involved in the act of self-definition. In other words, groups of young people may collectively develop ways of differentiating themselves from others and, in the process of doing so, constitute and define themselves as a group set apart from the rest of society.

SECTION 2 SUMMARY

- Young people may be seen as a distinct cultural group within society.
- The term subculture can help us to understand differences between young people as well as offering some insight into the views of young people themselves.
- Some subcultural groups may have underground or marginal status within society that may challenge the conventions of the wider society.
- Subcultural activity may be regarded as transgressive or oppositional.
- Subcultural groups may be marked by a distinctive style.
- Members of a subculture do not regard themselves as victims.
- Subcultural activities and practices may be exciting and pleasurable.

3 YOUTH CULTURES IN ACTION

So far, we have discussed youth cultures and the notion of subculture in general terms. In this section, we will explore further the concept of youth cultures as developed by researchers working in the UK and South Africa. In particular, we will look at examples of three different youth subcultures, all of which can be seen to be involved in some form of subcultural activity: skinheads, ducktails and Rastafarians. In each case, there is a need to read and analyse these subcultures in the context of the societies in which they took shape.

3.1 Skinheads

Skinhead style emerged in 1960s Britain at a time of social and economic change. Phil Cohen (1972) has described the scene in the East End of London: the breakdown of traditional working-class communities, as old, run-down and cramped terraces were demolished and replaced by new housing developments. Long-established communities were uprooted, dispersed and finally rehoused in new environments which, although brighter and more hygienic, were often considered to be unfriendly and even alien. Workplaces and traditional forms of employment were also disrupted and many young men had no choice but to find work outside the area. The disruption of family life, kinship patterns and working relations have been well documented. In this literature, the focus on the East End prior to redevelopment often conjures up an imaginary past, the 'classic white slum' as Hebdige (1979) describes it.

At the same time, the structure of British society underwent change due to the impact of post-war immigration from former colonies in the Asian subcontinent and the Caribbean. Changes in social relations were also taking shape that can be understood in terms of the emergence of a new sexual agenda.

Questions were being asked about the position of women in society and their rights in relation to men. Such questions inevitably challenged the dominance of the white heterosexual male. Within this context, the skinhead appeared to represent the concerns of the present couched in the myth of the past. Cohen describes the skinhead style of dress as 'a kind of caricature of the model worker', ready for manual work but actually taking up leisure time.

John Clarke's (1975) study of 'Skinhead Mobs' in the West Midlands area of England further explores skinhead youth subculture, suggesting that they emerged as a response to the decline of traditional working-class communities in the UK in the post-war period. For Clarke, skinhead groups defining themselves as 'mobs' represented an attempt not just to mourn the loss of working-class community but actually to recreate it. The term 'mob' and its associations with revolutionary zeal and criminal activity captured a sense of proletariat energy and protest that was forceful and purposeful. Skinheads had things to be angry about and this anger provided them with a collective cause, or 'solidarity' as Clarke puts it.

Clarke and Cohen document the many ways in which skinheads felt oppressed by the environment they found themselves in and the people around them: the police and the legal system; schools and youth clubs; social workers, middle-class 'do-gooders' and the aspiring working class; hippies, ethnic minority groups and gays. Such a wide-ranging hit list is indicative of the extent of their anger and suggested that skinheads as a

Skinhead style and nationalist sentiment.

group felt alienated and besieged. They had a sense of belonging to a community that was, from their perspective, becoming fragmented and in decline. Their feelings of marginalization led to feelings of frustration and aggression. The skinheads' concern over territory, the marking and regulation of their neighbourhood by their presence and their graffiti, also pointed to a constant need to defend what was theirs – to say this part of the city/estate/street is our space, 'we rule here'. This assertion of authority in certain localities also brought into sharp focus the skinheads' feelings of dispossession and dislocation at a more general level, which could be interpreted as 'we rule here 'cos we don't rule anywhere else'.

So far, the portrait emerging is that skinheads hated everything and everybody. Was there anything that they did enjoy? Clarke's account suggests that the skinheads enjoyed the rituals of football and fighting. Within these spheres of activity, skinheads could display a style of masculine prowess premised upon being physically tough and being together. Clarke describes the skinheads' uncompromising stance in the face of violence and the highly prized feelings of group loyalty which made it important to support your mates when trouble erupted. 'Paki-bashing' and 'queer-bashing' provided an arena for the values of the skinhead group to be displayed and consolidated. Clarke suggests that these practices could be understood as defensive reactions to the breakdown of cultural homogeneity and traditional forms of masculinity. Here, ethnic minority groups and gays became scapegoats for the skinheads' sense of loss and feelings of powerlessness in the face of social change. Many of the themes discussed by Cohen and Clarke are developed in the following reading.

READING

Read Reading A by Anoop Nayak, ' "Pale Warriors": skinhead culture and the embodiment of white masculinities'. As you do so, make some notes on the following questions:

1   What reasons does the author give for the emergence of the subculture?

2   What are the defining features of the subculture? It may be helpful to include details of how the participants look, behave and feel.

3   As far as you can tell, what source material and research methods does the author draw upon to develop his analysis?

COMMENT

Nayak's study of skinheads in the Kempton Dene area of Birmingham, UK points to different ways of understanding skinhead style. Nayak's study is an illustration of the ways in which youth subcultures develop and change over time. The skinheads of Kempton Dene had features in common with skinheads of earlier periods, but there were also significant differences. Nayak points to the variations in haircut, clothes and musical influences to indicate the diversity and fluidity within the subculture. Furthermore, Nayak makes visible an account of white ethnicity that has not been central to earlier studies. Seeing skinheads through the lens of white ethnicity highlights the many points of engagement between black and white cultures and reveals the contradictions inherent in skinhead identity.

Nayak suggests that, although ethnicity remains a much studied aspect of black minority groups, little is known about the ethnicity of white youth and the way that racism may feature in their lives. In the light of this omission, his study explores the process whereby explicitly racist young men evoke whiteness within their suburban neighbourhoods in relation to their two obsessions – being authentic and being British.

Contemporary research on skinhead youth indicates that skinhead style can be appropriated and interpreted in different ways. In the context of 1980s Britain, anti-racist activists sought to challenge and invert the stereotypical image of the skinhead by appropriating the skinhead look. The most notable rebranding of the skinhead image can be found in the band The Redskins. As members of the Socialist Workers Party and the Anti-Nazi League, the band took up the skinhead look to promote anti-racism through grassroots political activism and popular social movements such as Rock Against Racism. Rock Against Racism was spearheaded by rock bands through gigs, rallies and mass demonstrations, and achieved success and widespread support as an energetic campaign to promote racial equality and celebrate diversity.

A further reworking of the skinhead look can be seen in a study referred to by Nayak, Murray Healy's (1997) analysis of working-class gay men in Europe and the USA. Healy documents the ways in which his respondents adopted the signature skinhead haircut and mode of dress to assert their working-class homosexual masculinity. The gay skinheads in Healy's study were keen to demonstrate that being gay did not necessarily involve a compromise with white class-coded masculinity and its associations with strength and resilience. The gay skinheads sought to distance themselves from middle-class homosexuals, who all too frequently adopted an effeminate, camp style that could be regarded as embodying the stereotype of the limp-wristed queen. The gay skinheads, however, unlike their predecessors in Clarke's study, did not espouse racist views and were not associated with racial violence. Looking at the skinheads over a period of time, from the 1960s to the 1990s, it is important to note that youth culture is dynamic; it evolves and develops in different ways and sometimes the meanings associated with being a skinhead can be dramatically changed by young people themselves.

3.2 Ducktails

Katie Mooney's (1998) study of the ducktail subculture in South Africa further illustrates diversity and the importance of context in the relationship between the youth cultures and wider society.

Mooney describes the ducktail subculture, a group of white males with a distinct style and attitude that emerged within the context of socio-economic change in late 1940s/early 1950s South Africa. The term 'ducktail' was used to describe the hairstyle favoured by the group, where all the hair is swept back with Brylcreem and moulded into a point at the back, reminiscent of a duck's tail (usually referred to as a DA – duck's arse). There are many parallels with the skinhead subculture observed and studied by Clarke, Cohen and Nayak. Like the skinheads, the ducktails were experiencing the effects of widespread change in their country and their locality. Like the skinheads, the activities of ducktail groups could be seen as antisocial: presenting a challenge to mainstream society, deliberately flouting Apartheid laws by selling alcohol to black South Africans and contesting the commonly held notions of appropriate behaviour shared by white middle-class South Africans. However, in other ways the ducktails were decidedly conformist: Mooney suggests that the subculture shared, and elaborated on, the cultural prejudices of mainstream white South Africa in relation to issues of racism and homophobia. In this respect, the skinheads and the ducktails differ and the differences can be seen to reflect the norms and values operating within each society, with ducktails sharing the racism to be found in the wider society in contrast to the skinheads' challenge to the liberal tolerance of the mainstream.

Mooney's study of the ducktail subculture is historical; she uses historical methods and sources such as newspaper reports from the period and oral history – interviews with individuals about their memories of the period – to construct a richly evocative account of this subcultural group in post-war South Africa (see Box 3).

Box 3 Ducktails, flick-knives and pugnacity

As a subculture they were hedonistic, convivial, rebellious, apolitical and had little respect for the law, education or work. Generally, the Ducktails were involved in both social and 'anti-social' activities. Their social activities were propelled by their pursuit of pleasure and entertainment. They frequented the cinema, bioscope-cafes, roadhouses, sessions, dance halls, billiard rooms, bars, public parks and experimented with dagga (marijuana) and alchohol. Some of the Ducktails – mostly the male members – were involved in quasi-criminal and criminal activities such as those reported by flat dwellers in Mooi Street, Johannesburg to a journalist from The Star. According to one female resident:

> The menace to the public of young men roaming the city streets by night and by day, selling liquor to natives, smoking dagga, and accosting and assaulting passers-by, had become completely out of hand. These young men were the White tsotsis of Johannesburg, the products of broken homes, the sons of mothers who thought only of having a good time. They were hardly out of school before they became members of liquor and dagga gangs operating in the heart of the city.

Another female flat dweller stated that, 'Words cannot describe the things which go on in and around Plein Street. Liquor is sold to Natives almost openly by long-haired, smartly dressed youths.' …

There were different levels of belonging in the subculture, which took diffuse and distilled forms and which could at times become conflated. For some, the Ducktail era was characterised by knuckle-dusters and bicycle chains, quiffs and Brylcreem, bioscopes and sessions, confrontations with the police and petty crime, whilst for others it represented weekend jolls, rock'n'roll and jiving, 'stovepipe' trousers and 'fifty-yard' petticoats. For the majority of Ducktails it was a fashion movement, a fad similar to the Zoot Suits, Hippies, Beatniks, the Mods and Rockers, Skinheads, Punks and the present day 'Ravers'. The latter group of Ducktails did not present a real danger to 'conventional' society and engaged predominantly with the stylistic elements of the subculture. The former group ignited very real concerns and fears in public opinion due to their aggressive and violent behaviour, which was attached to the subculture as a whole. Numerous social groups can therefore be identified within the subculture as a broader phenomenon. These can be divided into the more organised quasi-criminal gang and the more loosely based 'group of friends'.

(Mooney, 1998)

3.3 Rastafarians

The Rastafarians were a religious group that emerged in Jamaica in the 1930s, and found a following among black youth in the UK in the 1970s. The ways in which Rastafarianism was appropriated by young people is the focus of the following reading.

Rastas from JA to UK.

READING

Read the extract from *Subculture: the meaning of style* (Reading B), and then answer the following questions:

1   What reasons does the author give for the emergence of the subculture?

2   What are the defining features of the subculture?

3   As far as you can tell, what source material and research methods does the author draw upon to develop his analysis?

COMMENT

Hebdige suggests that Rastafarianism emerged as a way of making sense of the experience of being poor and black in Jamaica and, later, in Great Britain. Rastafarianism provided explanations that appealed to the young, particularly young males. Hebdige begins by discussing the importance of reggae music to black people in Jamaica and Great Britain. He points to the significance of the language, Jamaican oral culture, particular interpretations of the Bible and the use of percussion instruments as key features in the development of a musical form and a subcultural style. Hebdige suggests that reggae tells the story of a dispossessed people who were taken from Africa to Jamaica as slaves and subsequently made the journey from Jamaica to the UK as migrants. Central to this story is the place of Africa as a spiritual home and a potent symbol of loss, desire and hope.

Hebdige describes the ways in which Rastafarians combined elements of Jamaican culture with the Bible to create new meanings which articulated black experience in direct ways. Rastafarianism offered a different way of understanding the experience of material disadvantage and subordination faced by young, working-class blacks in Jamaica and Britain. Whereas their parents may have looked upon Britain as the mother country which promised economic salvation and security, Rastas (Rastafarians) looked to Africa as the homeland, the land where they would be free from oppression and servitude. This led Rastas to drop out of contemporary society, to regard Jamaica and Britain as Babylon – fallen places which offered them nothing and to which they didn't belong. Hebdige suggests that it was reggae music, available at underground record stores and social venues, that transported the Rasta message from Jamaica to Britain.

In both Jamaica and Britain, Rastas achieved a subcultural status defined by a particular belief system and marked by a visible style of dress and adornment. Rasta style was characterized by wearing hair plaited into dreadlocks, clothes and accessories in red, green and gold – the colours of the Ethiopian flag, and the use of marijuana. The style became synonymous with the times. Young, working-class blacks in Britain in the 1970s experienced alienation as a commonplace part of everyday life. In the context of bad housing, unemployment and police harassment, being a Rasta can be seen as an act of faith and a form of social protest.

Hebdige develops his analysis through a carefully crafted account of the details of Rastafarian culture in Jamaica and Britain. These details are drawn from a study of the cultural forms in both societies – including music, language, religion and dress – and the status these forms acquire in the subculture and the wider society. There is no evidence that Hebdige actually spoke with Rastas in either place and we can therefore assume that he did not engage in ethnographic research.

SECTION 3 SUMMARY

- Youth cultures exist in relation to the context of the societies in which they take shape.
- Subcultures may be a response to changing social and economic relations.
- Subcultural activity may be understood as an attempt to resolve some of the contradictions faced by young people in particular social and economic circumstances.
- Members of a subculture may celebrate certain aspects of their lives and identities such as ethnicity and class consciousness.
- Youth cultures change and develop over time.
- Studying youth cultures involves the use of different research methods, including participant observation, interviews and semiotic and textual analysis.

4 WHAT ABOUT GIRLS?

Looking at subcultural groups such as skinheads, ducktails and Rastafarians provides us with striking accounts of the differences between subcultures and their dominant cultures, as well as giving a glimpse into the lifestyle and outlook of young people who participate in subcultures. The subcultures we have looked at so far have been populated mainly by young men, although, as Nayak and Nilan point out, many subcultural groups do include female participants. Women researching in the field of youth challenged the masculine bias that was assumed in many studies of youth subcultures and asked the question: what about girls and subcultures? Joyce Canaan (1991), in an influential critique, asked, 'Is "doing nothing" just boys' play?' In other words, do girls have a presence in youth cultures and, if so, why are they absent from so many accounts? The following extract considers the status of girls in relation to youth cultures and provides a valuable insight into young people's cultural worlds from a gendered perspective.

Allow about
20–25 minutes

A C T I V I T Y 2   Girls' involvement with subcultures

Read the extract by Angela McRobbie and Jenny Garber (1975) below. Make a note of the main points and then answer the following two questions:

1   Consider some of the ways in which girls were overlooked or marginalized by youth subcultures.

2   What do we learn about young people and gender relations during this period?

Girls and subcultures

Though girls participated in the general rise in the disposable income available to youth in the 1950s, girls' wages were not as high as those of boys. Patterns of spending were also structured in a different direction. Girls' magazines emphasised a particularly feminine mode of consumption and the working-class girl, though actively participating in the world of work, remained more focused on home and marriage than her male counterpart. Teddy-boy culture was an escape from the claustrophobia of the family, into the street and the 'caff'. While many girls might adopt an appropriate way of dressing, complementary to the teds, they would be much less likely to spend the same amount of time hanging about on the streets. Girls had to be careful not to 'get into trouble' and excessive loitering on street corners might be taken as a sexual invitation to the boys. The double standard was probably more rigidly maintained in the 1950s than in any other time since then. The difficulty in obtaining effective contraception, the few opportunities to spend time unsupervised with members of the opposite sex, the financial dependency of the working-class woman on her husband, meant that a good reputation mattered above everything else. As countless novels of the moment record, neighbourhoods flourished on rumours and gossip and girls who spent too much time on the street were assumed to be promiscuous.

At the same time the expanding leisure industries were directing their attention to *both* boys and girls. Girls were as much the subject of attention as their male peers when it came to pin-up pictures, records and magazines. Girls could use these items and activities in a different context from those in which boys used them. Cosmetics of course were to be worn outside the home, at work and on the street, as well as in the dance-hall. But the rituals of trying on clothes, and experimenting with hair-styles and make-up were home-based activities. It might be suggested that girls' culture of the time operated within the vicinity of the home, or the friends' home. There was room for a great deal of the new teenage consumer culture within the confines of the girls' bedrooms. Teenage girls did participate in the new public sphere afforded by the growth of the leisure industries, but they could also consume at home, upstairs in their bedrooms.

(McRobbie and Garber, 1975, pp. 114–15)

COMMENT

McRobbie and Garber draw attention to the ways in which girls have been overlooked or misrepresented in studies of youth subculture. They argue that gender is, like social class, a structural inequality that materially effects the life chances and experiences of individuals. It is from this perspective that they discuss the role of girls in youth subcultural settings. A starting point for McRobbie and Garber is the social space that girls occupy in society generally. They speculate that the absence of girls in subcultures may be because girls are more centrally involved in the private, domestic sphere of home and family life rather than the public world of the street, where most subcultural activities seem to occur. Looking at girls in subcultures therefore shifts the focus from oppositional forms to a consideration of modes of conformity. There are dangers for girls in hanging around on the streets. Beyond the obvious danger of physical assault, girls' presence on the street could be associated with sexual promiscuity and so carry the ensuing risk of a damaged reputation.

Unlike the extracts we have looked at from Clarke and Hebdige, McRobbie and Garber discuss the significance of mass culture in the lives of young people, and particularly the ways in which boys and girls were targeted by companies as potential buyers of their products. For girls, new patterns of teenage consumption engaged them in more home-based activities: experimenting in changes of clothes, hairstyles and make-up, often in the confined space of the bedroom. Chapter 7 takes up this theme by looking at contemporary girlhood and the significance of the bedroom as a feminized space for relaxation and identity production.

Elsewhere in their study, McRobbie and Garber profile and discuss three images of girls as participants in subcultures: the motorbike girl, the mod girl and the hippy girl. These three images illustrate the range of ways in which girls may have had a presence in subcultures and the overwhelming tendency to associate girls with issues of sexuality.

New feminine subjectivities?

Mod girls.

Hippy girls.

In fact, young women are frequently defined in terms of their sexuality; their physical attractiveness, sexual availability and reproductive capacities become tropes for the general appraisal of girls as individuals and as a social group. The authors conclude that it is important to look at the ways in which young women interact among themselves to form distinctive cultures of their own. Engagements with teenage magazines and participation in 'teenybopper' culture are some of the ways in which young women create and structure their own cultural worlds.

But what about girls today? How has the experience of being a girl changed since the mid-1970s when McRobbie and Garber were writing? Contemporary research on girlhood indicates that there are different ways of being a girl and that femininity is no longer so rigidly defined. In fact it may be helpful to suggest that there are now *femininities* – multiple ways of living and identifying as female.

Anita Harris (2001) suggests that the lives and experiences of young women today can be understood in relation to two competing discourses – *girlpower* and *girls at risk*:

- The girlpower discourse has gained currency in recent popular culture through bands such as the Spice Girls. Girlpower suggests to young women that they can get what they want and do what they want. In this respect, girlpower exists as a seemingly new version of femininity that can be seen as an assertive and individualized expression of power.
- Girls at risk, on the other hand, articulates a set of moral and social concerns in relation to young women, such as: pregnancy and sexually transmitted disease; drug taking; involvement in crime, particularly young women's participation in gangs and violent crime.

In this context, Harris suggests that young women are active in shaping their own identities in new and interesting subcultural spaces. Harris argues that the Internet has become an important site for girls to express themselves as individuals and, through dialogue with other girls, develop a collective identity and attitude. Since electronic communication allows for the reformulation of various sorts of cultural activity, it becomes clear that youth cultures do not necessarily need to be face to face or local. The proliferation of electronic magazines, written by and for girls, points to a level of energy and an agency that are active in redefining feminine identities and also provides a commentary on contemporary girlhood. Significantly, the activities that Harris documents (see Box 4) play an important part in reshaping and redefining subcultures and subcultural space.

One example of young women challenging conventional representations of girlhood through their own publications is the girlzine comic *Naughty Bits* created by Roberta Gregory. In the cartoon on page 249, Roberta Gregory explains how she created the character Bitchy Bitch as a protest against patriarchal culture and pornography.

Box 4 The grrrl/gURL zine culture

The grrrlzine culture is made up of a loose global network of young women who self-publish newsletters, magazines and websites for and about young women. The word 'zine' comes from 'fanzine', itself derived from 'magazine': a kind of personalised newsletter and forum for 'rants' originating in punk and anarchist circles as alternative media and a platform for the voice of the 'ordinary' person. The origins of the zine culture can be found in subcultural communities organised around a critique of government, big business (and now multinationals), and their foundations in capitalism and its ideologies of liberal democracy and consumer citizenship. Grrrlzines, as an entirely separate category from punk fanzines, first appeared in the early 1990s. At this time, as a grassroots movement of young punk feminism developed, the word 'girl' became 'grrrl', to denote a snarling, angry young woman who was no longer prepared to be 'nice'. 'Grrrl' was then combined with 'zine', and thus appeared productions by, for and about young women who were interested in underground and alternative feminist and punk politics. During the mid 1990s, urged on by the original 'geekgirls' such as Rosie X, who proclaimed that 'grrrls need modems!', young women began to produce electronic zines and webpages on the internet. These young women often became known as 'gURLs', as a play on the word 'girl' combined with the cyberterm 'url' (Uniform Resource Locator) …

The zines … provide critical social commentary, they do not advertise commercial products or attempt to make a profit from sales, and their content is characterised by information sharing, editorials or rants, music/book/art reviews, art and creative writing around issues relevant to young women … This zine network is one that exists for the most part outside of dominant culture, functioning on a counter-capitalist economy and on the margins of what is recognised as political activism. It occupies this site purposefully, creating a space where young women can communicate and organise together outside surveillance, silencing and appropriation …

The e-zine *Grrrowl* advocates 'creative unemployment', saying 'to be creatively unemployed means to spend yr time and energy on (developing) yr interests, community and yr skills'. It recommends 'do-it-yourself everything! Yr educating yrself/learning new things on your own terms and according to what you consider to be important (which can be heaps different from what mainstream society considers important). This goes towards giving you back some sort of control in a society where much has been decided for us.'

Further, young women identify the ways the power and risk discourses work together to define girlhood, to connect resistance with danger, and to encourage girls to seek protection. For example, Sarah presents in her zine *Cavity* a collage with a piece of text at the centre that reads 'I am sure you are delighted to be here, entering into what is likely to be one of the most exciting and interesting times of your life.' Newspaper clippings about AIDS, rape, pregnancy, police numbers, Christianity; as well as voting requirements and other instructions for young people surround the text. The pixilated image all of these cuttings are presented on is a young woman with her middle finger raised.

(Harris, 2001, pp. 11–20)

Naughty Bits, 1991. Roberta Gregory explains the creation of Bitchy Bitch.

Roberta Gregory explains the creation of Bitchy Bitch in *Naughty Bits*, 1991.

SECTION 4 SUMMARY

- Early studies of subcultures focused on the participation of young men more than young women.

- Girls have traditionally been associated with the domestic sphere of the home rather than public spaces such as the street and the city centre.

- The subcultural activities of girls can be seen in terms of conformity to and rejection of the gender roles available to them.

- The Internet has redefined subcultures in ways that have been productive for girls and young women.

- Through subcultural activity girls may provide a social commentary on girlhood, gender relations and feminine identities.

5 THE CASE OF PUNK

In this section, we will focus on the cultural world of punk as a case study that illustrates the relationship between youth cultures and their place in the wider society. We will consider some of the defining features of punk as a movement and the way the subculture may change in different parts of the world. Punk may be familiar to some of you as a musical form and a visual style. Punk bands such as the Sex Pistols and The Clash emerged in the UK in the late 1970s/early 1980s and became renowned for their iconoclastic, energetic and dissonant sound, widely regarded as an audible assault on conventional pop harmonies and romantic themes.

Punks as a subcultural group displayed a style and an attitude that aroused a great deal of controversy in the wider culture and especially in the media, where responses to punk assumed the status of 'moral panic' (S. Cohen, 1972), a widely promoted belief that standards and values were in decline and that youth in particular was out of control. Punk style was commonly regarded as transgressive and deliberately shocking. Torn clothes, body piercing, Mohican haircuts, brightly dyed hair, the use of chains and safety pins became powerful symbols of punk style, drawing purposefully on notions of bondage and enslavement. At the same time, punks used the Nazi symbol of the swastika to decorate clothes and accessories. When asked about the use of the swastika, a punk in one study is reported to have said, 'We wear it because we love to be hated' (quoted in Frith, 1980). By the mid-1980s, however, postcards of punks were being sold to tourists as souvenirs of London as a vibrant, happening place to be. This indicates that the shock value of punk was short lived and that subcultures can be assimilated into mainstream society, often through commercial practices which treat aspects of subcultural style as products to be marketed and sold. In the following readings, Iain Chambers (1986) looks at some key features of punk subculture and the different ways in which these can be interpreted and understood. The reading by Andy Medhurst (1999), by contrast, takes an autobiographical approach to recall and reflect on some features of the punk movement.

The Sex Pistols play live.

READING

Read the extracts from:

1   *Popular Culture: the metropolitan experience* (Reading C by Iain Chambers);

2   'What did I get? Punk, memory and autobiography' (Reading D by Andy Medhurst).

Based on the insights you have gleaned from these readings and the understanding of youth cultures that you have developed throughout this chapter, write a retrospective review of the punk era that could be included in:

• the music press

or

• the notes that accompany a punk CD.

You may find it helpful to comment on punk style – clothes, music and attitude – as a way of expressing what punk represented.

COMMENT

Chambers' description of punk culture emphasizes the oppositional aspects of punk. He suggests that the punk movement drew upon examples from the musical underground of the 1960s and 1970s to provide a further demonstration of the links between sounds, sex and shock. In doing so, punk produced an eclectic style that bespoke a sense of crisis. Chambers suggests that punks constructed an 'iconography of disrespect', visibly displayed in the wearing of plastic bin-liners, torn clothing and urban rubbish. Chambers, like many other commentators, points out that punk is do-it-yourself pop music, made by the participants within the subculture, rather than professional musicians with an image makeover, a recording contract and a marketing team. Finally, Chambers argues that punk marks a turning point in popular culture, characterized by fusion and the blurring of boundaries.

Medhurst's (1999) writing on punk uses personal memory as a way of exploring some key features of the punk movement. As a teenager living in England in the 1970s, punk had an indelible impact upon his life. In a moment of reflection, he says that he has never quite recovered from 1977. But why? Well, punk for Medhurst extended beyond the music and the style to become a whole attitude or way of life that he refers to as a 'structure of feeling'. Medhurst's 'flashbulb memories' of the period can be seen as condensed moments through which he shapes his identity in relation to those around him.

Other writers have also commented on the unsettling aspects of punk and have cast around for explanations. Dave Laing's (1985) writing on punk focuses on musical form and particularly the effects on the listener. He suggests that punk studiously avoids the musicality of the recorded voice and the aesthetic pleasures associated with listening to music. He submits that punk music deliberately uses the declamatory mode of address where shouting is favoured over the confidential style of love songs and ballads. Local accents are preferred in contrast to the American accents of mainstream rock and forms of pornography and obscenity are freely drawn upon to disrupt and shock the listener. Punk music is uncomfortable by intention.

Simon Frith (1980) explores the difference between the phenomenon of punk and the meanings that have been attached to it by journalists and political activists. Basing his observations on punk subculture in the UK, Frith suggests that socialists embraced punk as a representation of working-class youth consciousness. Frith's analysis discusses whether punk can be read as an expression of real experience or a more artful construction of experience. Frith hints at the ways in which subcultures may be assimilated by other groups and ultimately incorporated into mainstream ways of looking at the world. In other words, subcultures are diverse and dynamic structures and cannot be clearly fixed in any way. Furthermore, subcultures may be found in different global locations, where they have fused aspects of the original subculture with features from the new cultural context. In the 1980s and 1990s, a variety of punk movements could be found outside the UK, in Europe, North America and Australia, as well some non-Western locations. The internet also created the opportunity for a virtual and global punk movement, usually referred to as cyberpunk.

Alan O'Connor's (2000) study describes a meeting of anarcho-punks in Mexico. As a Canadian, O' Connor is struck by the differences between anarcho-punk gatherings in Mexico and those in North America. While sharing membership of the same subculture, enjoying the same music and having similar value systems, it is clear that subcultural groups take on different characteristics in different parts of the world. In Mexico, anarcho-punks organize themselves into collectives which prioritize political activism over musical interests. Topics for discussion at the meeting were politically orientated and were identified by the whole group. Sub-groups called *mesas* then discussed the topics until a consensus was reached and a public statement was prepared and put in writing. This way of organizing, O'Connor suggests, drew upon forms of political activism in Mexican society more generally and was not a familiar practice to anarcho-punks who had travelled from other places. Anarcho-punk gatherings in North America worked in ways that were less centralized and tended to form caucus groups based around issues of identity politics: gender, sexuality and ethnicity. Two other differences O'Connor points to concern matters of regulation and competition. O'Connor describes the strict criteria that regulated attendance at the meeting and indicates that this is particular to the Mexican context, as is the rivalry between Mexican anarcho-punk groups. O'Connor's insights, based on participant observation, indicate that anarcho-punks in Mexico have an increased sense of collective consciousness that they prioritize over forms of individualism.

SECTION 5 SUMMARY

- However shocking a subculture may be, it can subsequently be assimilated into mainstream society.
- The internet creates the opportunity for virtual and global subcultural movements.
- Subcultural groups take on different characteristics in different parts of the world.

6 CONCLUSION

In this final section, you will be asked to consider ways of evaluating the concept of youth culture. We will also consider how the concept of subculture may shape our understanding of youth as a social group.

Allow about 20–25 minutes

A C T I V I T Y 3   Young people as a distinct cultural group

Divide a piece of paper into two columns. Drawing on the work you have done in this chapter, jot down in one column what you consider to be some of the strengths of seeing young people as a distinct cultural group. In the other column, suggest some of the limitations of this way of looking. Do any key themes or points emerge?

COMMENT

You may have identified the following:

Strengths of the youth cultures approach:

1   Youth cultures make young people visible and provide an insight into the position of young people in society and their perspectives.

2   Ethnographic accounts such as Nayak (Reading A) give voice to youth and offer ways of making sense of their experiences.

3   Accounts such as Hebdige (Reading B) acknowledge the importance of the cultural and offer ways of reading cultural artefacts.

Limitations of the youth cultures approach:

1   Youth cultures are not necessarily full time; they overlap with other spheres of young people's lives such as family, work and college.

2   There is a tendency to focus on the deviant and the spectacular, which overlooks large groups of young people who conform or who do not stand out.

3   Interpretations of young people's activity tends to be read as a form of protest or resistance rather than other forms of self-expression such as play or leisure.

Sarah Thornton (1997) points out that, in the process of portraying social groups, researchers inevitably construct them and bring them into being. This process of construction through observation and analysis could apply to all the youth cultures we have studied in this chapter. Subcultures such as the skinheads, Rastas and punks are given shape and substance not least because they are labelled, objectified and analyzed through the media and the research process.

What can we say about youth, then, by looking from the perspective of youth cultural formations? Andy Bennett (1999) has pointed out that participants in subcultures tend to be defined by their subcultural identity rather than by other identities that may shape their lives, such as being a member of a family, having a relationship or being a student. The Slipknot fans and ravers discussed at the beginning of the chapter are unlikely to spend all their time pursuing despair or getting drugged up. The self-pitying low and the ecstasy high may be intense but short-lived moments in the lives of many young people. Christine Griffin (1993) points to other implications when she suggests that, in societies in the North, the category 'youth' is 'treated as a key indicator of the state of the nation itself' (p. 9). In other words, the values, behaviour and attitudes of young people can be read as a comment upon the society at present and can also be seen to hold the key to the nation's future. Viewed in these terms, youth as a social category always represents something bigger than itself.

REFERENCES

BENNETT, A. (1999) 'Subcultures or neo-tribes? Rethinking the relationship between youth, style and musical taste', *Sociology*, **33**(3), pp. 599–617.

CANAAN, J. (1991) 'Is "doing nothing" just boys' play? Integrating feminist and cultural studies perspectives on working-class masculinities' in FRANKLIN, S., LURY, C. and STACEY, J. (eds) *Off-Centre: feminism and cultural studies*, London, Routledge.

CHAMBERS, I. (1986) *Popular Culture: the metropolitan experience*, London, Methuen.

CLARKE, J. (1975) 'The skinheads and the magical recovery of community' in HALL, S. and JEFFERSON, T. (eds) *Resistance through Rituals: youth subcultures in postwar Britain*, London, Hutchinson.

COHEN, A.K. (1955) *Delinquent Boys: the culture of the gang*, New York, Free Press.

COHEN, P. (1972) *Subcultural Conflict and Working Class Community*, Working papers in Cultural Studies 2, University of Birmingham: Centre for Contemporary Cultural Studies.

COHEN, S. (1972) *Folk Devils and Moral Panics*, London, Paladin.

CONNELL, R.W. (1989) 'Cool guys, swots and wimps: the interplay of masculinity and education', *Oxford Review of Education*, **15**(3), pp. 291–303.

CORRIGAN, P. (1979) *Schooling the Smash Street Kids*, London, Macmillan.

FRITH, S. (1980) 'Formalism, realism and leisure, the case of punk', extracted from 'Music for pleasure', *Screen Education*, **34**, pp. 51–61.

GELDER, K. and THORNTON, S. (1997) *The Subcultures Reader*, London and New York, Routledge.

GRIFFIN, C. (1993) *Representations of Youth*, Cambridge, Polity.

HARI, J. (2002) 'Meet the teenagers' latest idols', *New Statesman*, 18 March, p. 20.

HARRIS, A. (2001) 'gURL scenes and grrrl zines: girlhood, power and risk under late modernity', unpublished paper, University of Monash, Australia.

HEALY, M. (1997) *Gay Skins: class, masculinity and queer appropriation*, London, Cassell.

HEBDIGE, D. (1979) *Subculture, the meaning of style*, London, Methuen.

LAING, D. (1985) *One Chord Wonders: power and meaning in punk rock*, Milton Keynes, Open University Press.

MCLAREN, M. (2002) 'We meant it, ma'am', *The Observer*, 19 May.

MCROBBIE, A. and GARBER, J. (1975) 'Girls and subcultures' in GELDER, K. and THORNTON, S. (eds) *The Subcultures Reader*, London and New York, Routledge.

MEDHURST, A. (1999) 'What did I get? Punk, memory and autobiography' in SABIN, R. (ed.) *Punk Rock: So What? The Cultural Legacy of Punk*, London, Routledge.

MOONEY, K. (1998) 'Ducktails, flick-knives and pugnacity: subcultural and hegemonic masculinities in South Africa, 1948–1960', *Journal of Southern African Studies*, **24**(4).

NILAN, P. (1992) 'Kazzies, DBTs and tryhards: categorisations of style in adolescent girls' talk', *British Journal of Sociology of Education*, **13**(2), pp. 201–14.

O' CONNOR, A. (2000) 'An anarcho-punk gathering in the context of globalisation', paper presented at Crossroads in Cultural Studies conference, Birmingham, UK, June.

O'SULLIVAN, T., HARTLEY, J., SAUNDERS, D., MONTGOMERY, M. and FISKE, J. (1994) *Key Concepts in Communications and Cultural Studies*, London, Routledge.

POLLARD, A. (1984) 'Goodies, jokers and gangs' in HAMMERSLEY, M. and WOODS, P. (eds) *Life in School: the sociology of pupil culture*, Milton Keynes, Open University Press.

REDHEAD, S. (ed.) (1993) *Rave Off: politics and deviance in contemporary youth culture*, Aldershot, Avebury.

THORNTON, S. (1997) 'Introduction to subcultures' in GELDER, K. and THORNTON, S. (eds) *The Subcultures Reader*, London, Routledge.

READING A

'Pale warriors': skinhead culture and the embodiment of white masculinities

Anoop Nayak

Introduction – hybrid histories

The skinhead movement in post-war Britain grew out of, and elaborated upon, a number of competing youth influences. As a symbol of working-class pride, the skinhead look came to epitomize certain aspects of labouring culture as witnessed in the early penchant for braces, denim and Doc Marten boots. Inspired by working-class mods, life on the football terraces and a hatred of 1960s hippy peace culture, skinheads have been seen to embody an exclusive white nationalism. But, as we shall see, contemporary skinhead subcultures are dynamic, strikingly diverse and even contradictory in terms of their formation and ritualized activities. At an international level, skinhead subcultures have been found to include feather-cut girls, young women, as well as working-class people from various ethnic backgrounds.

Indeed, the first wave of skinheads from the late 1960s sought to emulate and appropriate the signs, symbols and meanings familiar in the protest music of Jamaican rude boys. Throughout the 1970s, skinheads populated dancehalls, moving in rhythm to the music of soul, blue-beat, motown and reggae. By the 1980s, they continued to dance to ska and two-tone – the shaggy, hybrid offspring that had emerged from the cultural promiscuity of youthful black–white interaction. Moreover, this multi-ethnic mixing of cultural styles was embodied in the clothing and mannerisms of skinhead youth. As Dick Hebdige explains, the cropped hair, boots, turn-ups and trilby hats formed part of a wider 'dialectical interplay of black and white languages' (1979, p. 57). This has led Kobena Mercer to compare skinhead style to a 'photographic negative' in which white youth adopts and adapts the meanings of blackness to enact a 'post-imperial mode of mimicry' (1994, p. 123). Paradoxically, while the popular representation of skinhead youth is synonymous with white racism, the indications are that behind the dazzling dance of the paleface may lurk the smudged shadow outline of black history.

Recognizably skinhead style has changed over time and place, taking on new meanings and inflections appropriate to the lived context and situation. This semiotic struggle for the sign was evident during the 1980s when the skinhead look was appropriated both by ultra-right youth and supporters of the Socialist Worker's Party Anti-Nazi League. Indeed, anti-racist bands such as The Redskins and organizations like SHARP (Skinheads Against Racial Prejudice) reveal the political fragmentation and variation within skinhead youth cultures. At a global level, the 'butch' image has also become popularized by queer subcultures, in a figurative transgression that now 'short circuits accepted beliefs about real masculinity' (Healy, 1997, p. 5). The stylized appropriation of the look by a new metropolitan gay scene represents a symbolic recoding of white masculinity that at once transgresses and resituates the meaning of skinheadism. Diasporic movement and settlement has also led to the scattering of youth cultures, as witnessed in Moore's (1994) study of Perth skinheads. Here, members were seen to continue to construct a 'traditional' sense of English ethnicity in the context of urban, multicultural Western Australia, through rituals of football, fighting and drinking. Moreover, where skinhead youth was once representative of the neighbourhood 'gang', new media technologies have given rise to 'virtual youth communities' and enabled meetings to occur that cross time and space, nations and continents. At the same time, there has been a worldwide branding of skinheadism through the marketing of clothes, records, books, nostalgia and accessories. Within the global marketplace, affluent youth consumers can now fashion a particular 'lifestyle' identity by purchasing subcultural styles over the counter. But as the ethnography will show, globalization and youth consumption have yet to render the meaning of place redundant.

Placing youth

Despite the enormous economic, political and cultural transformations that have shaped skinhead style over the years, place and neighbourhood continue to have marked significance in young lives. Recent work has shown how in 'new', global times locality and place-bound identities are still an important influence shaping the actions of young people (Skelton and Valentine, 1998). For example, the Kempton Dene Skins reside in a working-class estate situated on the outskirts of Birmingham, Britain's second largest city. In contrast to the region's principal city, Kempton Dene is an ostensibly white neighbourhood and has relatively few material resources compared with the affluent suburbs that surround the estate. The ethnography illustrates how adolescent males deploy the shaven-headed look in a performance of local 'hardness'.

DARREN:	That's what everyone has down the Dene: a skinhead. Don't they?
ROBBIE:	It's the trademark. [...]
[INTERVIEWER:]	What's it a trademark for?
ROBBIE:	Don't mess with the Dene.
DARREN:	Don't mess with the skinheads!
ROBBIE: [chanting]	Skiiiiin – 'eads!

The Skins continue to position their identities not only against the multicultural inner-city of Birmingham (which they perceive as 'black') but also in opposition to the white middle-class suburban districts nearby. For these young men, the haircut can be read as a cultural register for 'hard times' that reveals a certain naked vulnerability: the bald truth of a bleak future. Instead of playing down the image of Kempton Dene as a dodgy 'no-go' area, the Skins choose to celebrate this popular representation, turning it into a source of local pride. When asked if they liked living on the estate the responses were unequivocal.

ROBBIE:	Yeah, I love it. Got a name, that's what I like.
[INTERVIEWER:]	What kinda name?

DARREN: Born on the Dene, and I'll live on the Dene all my life.

ROBBIE: Ruff 'n' tuff. That's what we are. We stick together.

By adopting similar haircuts, dress codes and wider subcultural practices the Kempton Dene Skins could magically evoke a sense of community based on shared values and experiences (Clarke, 1975). This imaginative re-working commemorates masculine loyalty ('We stick together'), working-class conformity (the 'trademark' skinhead) and local toughness ('Don't mess with the Dene'). The Skins portray themselves as 'pale warriors', romantic defenders of an ever retreating English way of life now felt to be threatened by immigrants, outsiders and bourgeois gentrification. The pale warrior stance was further in evidence during conversations concerning immigration and employment. Here, the Skins discuss the plight of two local Asian shopkeepers who have set up trade in the area.

DANIEL: It's our country, not theirs.

LEONARD: Yeah, they don't belong in our country.

DANIEL: Fuck 'em off. They've got all the jobs. Like me and Mark could be working now but fucking two pakis have jumped in our place haven' they?

This sense of ownership over nationhood ('our country') and the labour market ('our place') shows how a 'rights for whites' discourse could be utilized and enacted at the local level. The Kempton Dene Skins used racist language, graffiti and violence to further produce their neighbourhood as a white place. They asserted that parents and elder family members were also prejudiced against the prospect of immigrant families moving into the neighbourhood and changing their 'way of life'. For the skinheads, the streets, shops and surrounding houses were also seen through a racial cartography. As Robbie revealed, 'The English fight for their territory … That's why we want them out of our country.' The perpetual harassment of Asian shopkeepers on the estate and the occasional rituals of 'paki-bashing' were violent reminders of how the local area could be constructed as a white space in which minority ethnic groups did not belong.

Contradictory cultural worlds: race, sexuality and gender

Despite this blanket expression of white hostility, the practices of the Kempton Dene Skins were highly contradictory with regard to the politics of race and ethnicity. Where early skinheads favoured a 'braces-'n'-bovver-boots' appearance, the Kempton Dene Skins reworked black cultural style in an altogether different manner. Participants frequently wore loose checked shirts, training shoes, baggy jeans and hooded anoraks; apparel that was familiar to many black youths in the city of Birmingham. Although the Skins enjoyed smoking marijuana, listening to black music and occasionally using inner-city language (e.g. 'wicked'), they were prone to 'bleach' these black cultural roots through white chauvinism. Where former skinhead cultures looked to reggae, blue-beat and ska for inspiration, the Kempton Dene Skins looked to the equally contradictory influence of rave, ragga and hip-hop. This suggests that skinhead style has developed, while continuing to be in dialogue with and against black culture. The loose and fragile identifications made by the Skins with elements of black culture provided for a partial and contingent acceptance of certain forms of blackness and rejection of other styles.

ROBBIE: Blacks ain't as bad as pakis.

MARK: We smoke their draw.

ROBBIE: I'd rather hang around with a black than a paki.

LEONARD: Pakis smell.

Here, Asian youth are constructed as misshapen others in the incomplete jigsaw of multi-ethnic dialogue. In contrast, the Skins had established friendships with Calvin and Leonard, who each had a black father and a white mother. By modifying their behaviour with the Skins, these young men managed to forge a significant, though precarious, relationship with the subculture. As Calvin remarked, 'When I first come round here I used to dress like the blacks do, and when I hang around with them lot I just [copied] their clothes dress.' By 'whitening' their identities in the presence of the Skins, Calvin and Leonard could deflect some aspects of racism from their lives. This in part was also a strategy of survival. 'I've mixed in with half of the crowd that are NF [National Front supporters],' recalled Calvin, 'And they know I'm alright … It's like if I didn't mix in with them they'd give me 'assel.'

If ethnicity was an issue that was subject to group- and self-regulation, then gender was also an arena in which whiteness was carefully governed through the techniques of verbal and physical abuse.

CALVIN: If a white bloke sees a white girl with a black guy they might get jealous.

ROBBIE: No, they say, 'Oh look at that dirty bitch with a black man.'

MARK: That's what I'd say if I saw a white girl with a black man, I'd call her a bitch.

[INTERVIEWER:] What about a white bloke with a black girl?

ROBBIE: Batter 'em.

Although on the surface the Skins were violently condemnatory towards the idea of mixed relationships, their discussions of sexuality were tinged with a high degree of ambiguity. Daniel had been expelled from school for paki-bashing and held pronounced views on mixed relationships. However, Calvin reminded the group that Daniel had once professed sexual desire towards the black pop artists Tina Turner and Janet Jackson. This comment was met with much jeering from the group and acute embarrassment from Daniel, who was now unable to square the circle of blatant contradiction. At this point, the group rounded on him and Robbie emphatically denounced Daniel as a 'nigger-lover'. Such illustrations reveal how the performance of whiteness through skinhead style is always cross-cut by the circulating currents of contradiction. These ambiguities can be traced in the black cultural roots of skinhead style, including music, language, dress and marijuana use. In the case of the Kempton Dene Skins, the discussions disclose how the dark zones of race and sexuality were tightly interlaced with fear and desire (Fanon, 1952). Here, it was quite possible for young people to draw upon the codes of black culture but still maintain a more general hostility towards black people. At the same time, this explicit hatred could be underscored by token black–white friendships or a covert admiration for street-based black masculinities or black female sexual icons. These contradictions reveal that the potential of cultural hybridity to break down youth boundaries may be rudely curtailed by racist activity.

Concluding remarks

In these 'new times' of global change, labour insecurity and gender restructuring, skinhead culture may have international appeal for particular isolated white youth. The resurgence of Fascist skinheads in Germany who oppose North African and Turkish *Gastarbeiter* (temporary guest-workers) is testimony to the revival of nationalism in a period when the power of nation states is felt to be receding. At the same time, however, the effects of globalization can be seen on even this most stalwart of British youth cultures. Steeped in the vibrant gloss of the black diaspora, before being hung out to dry on newly mown English lawns throughout the country, skinhead culture has always proffered a thoroughly inauthentic mode of whiteness. The transnational geographies of skinhead style vividly illustrate how the culture is emblematic of what Dick Hebdige describes as an oblique 'phantom history of race relations' (1979, p. 45). In the contemporary urban metropolis, the skinhead look remains a sign in perpetual motion, unstable and discursively replayed through multiple signifiers that fail to truly settle the question of whether this is a celebration of gay, straight, black, white, national or international identities. Unsettling the dominant meanings ascribed to skinhead culture offers at least one way for understanding youth cultures at different scales and in different places within what is a rapidly changing world.

References

CLARKE, J. (1975) 'The skinheads and the magical recovery of community' in HALL, S. and JEFFERSON, T. (eds), *Resistance through Rituals, youth subcultures in postwar Britain*, London, Hutchinson.

FANON, F. (1952) *Black Skins, White Masks*, London, Pluto.

HEALY, M. (1997) *Gay Skins: class, masculinity and queer appropriation*, London, Cassell.

HEBDIGE, D. (1979) *Subculture, the meaning of style*, London, Routledge.

MERCER, K. (1994) *Welcome to the Jungle: new positions in black cultural studies*, London, Routledge.

MOORE, D. (1994) *The Lads in Action: social processes in an urban youth subculture*, Aldershot, Ashgate.

SKELTON, T. and VALENTINE, G. (1998) *Cool Places: geographies of youth cultures*, London, Routledge.

Source

This reading was specially commissioned for this chapter.

Subculture: the meaning of style

Dick Hebdige

Back to Africa

Reggae draws on a quite specific experience (the experience of black people in Jamaica and Great Britain – a whole generation of young Black Britons have formed reggae bands in the last few years, e.g. the Cimarons, Steel Pulse, Matumbi, Black Slate, Aswaad). It is cast in a unique style, in a language of its own – Jamaican patois, that shadow-form, 'stolen' from the Master and mysteriously inflected, 'decomposed' and reassembled in the passage from Africa to the West Indies. It moves to more ponderous and moody rhythms. It 'rocks steady' around a bass-line which is both more prominent and more austere. Its rhetoric is more densely constructed, and less diverse in origin; emanating in large part from two related sources – a distinctively Jamaican oral culture and an equally distinctive appropriation of the Bible. There are strong elements of Jamaican pentecostal, of 'possession by the Word', and the call and response pattern which binds the preacher to his congregation, is reproduced in reggae. Reggae addresses a community in transit through a series of retrospective frames (the Rastafarian movement, the Back to Africa theme) which reverse the historical sequence of migrations (Africa–Jamaica–Great Britain). It is the living record of a people's journey – of the passage from slavery to servitude – and that journey can be mapped along the lines of reggae's unique structure.

Africa finds an echo inside reggae in its distinctive percussion. The voice of Africa in the West Indies has traditionally been identified with insurrection and silenced wherever possible (see Hall, 1975). In particular, the preservation of African traditions, like drumming, has in the past been construed by the authorities (the Church, the colonial and even some 'post-colonial' governments) as being intrinsically subversive, posing a symbolic threat to law and order. These outlawed traditions were not only considered anti-social and unchristian, they were positively, triumphantly pagan. They suggested unspeakable alien rites, they made possible illicit and rancorous allegiances which smacked of future discord. They hinted at that darkest of rebellions: a celebration of Negritude. They restored 'deported Africa', that 'drifting continent' to a privileged place within the black mythology. And the very existence of that mythology was enough to inspire an immense dread in the hearts of some white slave owners.

Africa thus came to represent for blacks in the Caribbean forbidden territory, a Lost World, a History abandoned to the contradictory Western myths of childhood innocence and man's inherent evil. It became a massive Out of Bounds on the other side of slavery. But beyond this continent of negatives there lay a place where all the utopian and anti-European values available to the dispossessed black could begin to congregate. And paradoxically it was from the Bible – the civilizing agent *par excellence* – that alternative values and dreams of a better life were drawn. It was in Rastafarianism that these two symbolic clusters (Black

Africa and the White man's Bible) so ostensibly antithetical, were most effectively integrated. To understand how such a heretical convergence was possible, and how the meta-message in the Christian faith (submission to the Master) was so dramatically transcended, one must first understand how that faith was mediated to the Jamaican black.

The Bible is a central determining force in both reggae music and popular West Indian consciousness in general. In the past, the scriptures had been used by the colonial authorities to inculcate Western values and to introduce the African to European notions of culture, repression, the soul, etc. It was under their sacred auspices that civilization itself was to be achieved: that Western culture was to fulfil its divinely ordained mission of conquest. Underpinned by the persistent dualism of Biblical rhetoric ('Black Satan' and 'the snow-white Lamb of God') slavery could flourish with a relatively clear conscience, transforming the 'savage' into an industrious servant, interpolating order and the godly virtues between the dispossessed African and his mutinous 'nature' …

The Rastafarian solution

It [the Bible] is the supremely ambiguous means through which the black community can most readily make sense of its subordinate position within an alien society.

The Rastafarians believe that the accession of Haille Selassie to the throne of Ethiopia in 1930 represented the fulfilment of Biblical and secular prophecies concerning the imminent downfall of 'Babylon' (i.e. the white colonial powers) and the deliverance of the black races.

It is apt that such a tradition of passionate heterodoxy, having generated so many 'contained' readings of the impoverished Jamaican's material condition should eventually produce the Rastafarian solution: the appropriation which removes the dark kernel from its European shell, which finds an 'Africa' marooned on the pages of the Bible. For Rastafarianism is a reading which threatens to explode the sacred Text itself, to challenge the very Word of the Father.

The profound subversion of the white man's Religion which places God in Ethiopia and the black 'sufferer' in Babylon has proved singularly appealing to working-class youth in both the ghettos of Kingston and the West Indian communities of Great Britain. This appeal requires little explanation. Clothed in dreadlocks and 'righteous ire' the Rastaman effects a spectacular resolution of the material contradictions which oppress and define the West Indian community. He deciphers 'sufferation', that key term in the expressive vocabulary of ghetto culture, naming its historical causes (colonisation, economic exploitation) and promising deliverance through exodus to 'Africa'. He is the living refutation of Babylon (contemporary capitalist society), refusing to deny his stolen history. By a perverse and wilful transformation he turns poverty and exile into 'signs of grandeur', tokens of his own esteem, tickets which will take him home to Africa and Zion when Babylon is overthrown. Most importantly, he traces out his 'roots' in red, green and gold, dissolving the gulf of centuries which separates the West Indian community from its past, and from a positive evaluation of its blackness …

The colours of the Ethiopian flag emblazoned on items as various as badges, cardigans, shirts, sandals, tams (woollen hats), walking sticks ('rods of correction').

Reggae and Rastafarianism

Even in the *ska* records of the early 60s, underneath the 'rudeness' and the light, choppy metre, there was a thread of Rastafarianism (Don Drummond, Reco, etc.) which became increasingly noticeable as the decade wore on until the Rasta contingent within reggae began, more or less exclusively, to determine the direction the music was to take. Reggae began to slow down to an almost African metabolism. The lyrics became more self-consciously Jamaican, more dimly enunciated and overgrown until they disappeared altogether in the 'dub', to be replaced by 'talk-over'. The 'dread', the ganja, the Messianic feel of this 'heavy' reggae, its blood and fire rhetoric, its troubled rhythms can all be attributed to the Rasta influence. And it was largely through reggae, played at local 'sound-systems' (i.e. discotheques frequented by black working-class youth) and available only through an underground network of small retailers, that the Rastafarian ethos, the 'dreadlocks' and 'ethnicity' were communicated to members of the West Indian community in Great Britain.

For the unemployed black youth, 'heavy dub' and 'rockers' provided an alternative sound-track, infinitely preferable to the muzak which filled the vast new shopping precincts where he spent his days 'doing nothing', subjected to the random tyrannies of 'sus'. But of course the original religious meanings of Rastafarianism suffered adjustment in the transition.

Somewhere between Trenchtown and Ladbroke Grove, the cult of Rastafari had become a 'style': an expressive combination of 'locks', of khaki camouflage and 'weed' which proclaimed unequivocally the alienation felt by many young black Britons. Alienation could scarcely be avoided: it was built into the lives of young working-class West Indians in the form of bad housing, unemployment and police harassment. As early as 1969, it had been estimated that white youngsters from equivalent backgrounds were approximately five times more likely to find skilled work (*Observer,* 14 July 1968). In addition, throughout the 60s, relations with the police had been deteriorating steadily. The Mangrove trial of 1969 marked the beginning of a long series of bitter confrontations between the black community and the authorities (the Carib trial, the Oval trial, the 1976 Carnival) which led to a progressive polarization.

It was during this period of growing disaffection and joblessness, at a time when conflict between black youths and the police was being openly acknowledged in the press, that imported reggae music began to deal directly with problems of race and class, and to resurrect the African heritage. Reggae, and the forms which had preceded it, had always alluded to these problems obliquely. Oppositional values had been mediated through a range of rebel archetypes: the 'rude boy', the gunfighter, the trickster, etc. – which remained firmly tied to the *particular* and tended to celebrate the *individual* status of revolt.

With dub and heavy reggae, this rebellion was given a much wider currency: it was generalized and theorized. Thus, the rude boy hero immortalized in ska and rocksteady – the lone delinquent pitched hopelessly against an implacable authority – was supplanted as the central focus of identity by the Rastafarian who broke the Law in more profound and subtle ways.

References

HALL, S. (1975) 'Africa is alive and well and living in the diaspora', unpublished paper given at UNESCO conference.

Source

HEBDIGE, D. (1979) *Subculture: the meaning of style*, London, Methuen.

READING C

Popular Culture: the metropolitan experience

Iain Chambers

Out of chaos

When in 1966 the Rolling Stones, by then the favourite targets of moral outrage, presented themselves in drag to promote the single 'Have You Seen Your Mother, Baby, Standing in the Shadow?', a glittering, androgynous future was staked out for male pop music. This mixing of sounds, sexual codes and deliberate shock, further distilled through the dark aesthetics of the New York group and Andy Warhol associates, The Velvet Underground, eventually became the *leit-motif* for the musical mannerisms of David Bowie. Bowie's transitory egos – whether they came from Mars or Weimar Germany – were the dandified heroes of a camp subversion. Through his testing of tastes and playing with the stylized signs of sex, Bowie rapidly ran through a repertoire that the rest of the decade spent exploring.

Relating sex to subversion and signs to shock was, of course, the twilight zone privileged by punk, ergo the nomenclature: The Sex Pistols, The Clash, The Damned, Johnny Rotten, Sid Vicious. In 1976, against a background in which the stylistic connections between music, youth and fashion had long been established and accepted, punk managed to produce a self-conscious style of crisis. The 'dumbest' face of subcultures proved to be the vehicle of some rather intellectual activity. Revivalist Teddy boys physically assaulted punks for 'being too clever'.

With punk, the traditional closure of subcultural style was subverted as it became the object of facetious quotations, irreverent cut-ups and ironic poses. Punks ransacked post-war subcultures for fashions and signs to re-cycle and re-live. In a blasphemous remixing of revered subcultural memories the sartorial signs of Teddy boy, mod and skinhead simultaneously hung in patchwork array from the same skinny shoulders, the same physical clothes-hanger, the same sign carrier. The punks constructed an iconography of disrespect, pillaging the subcultural past and attiring themselves in urban rubbish: bin-liner skirts, empty sweet packets pinned on ripped and torn clothing. Here we discover 'statement dressing', a 'shocking' punctuation of the public narratives of the everyday.

Clothes as 'our weapons, our challenges, our visible insults' (Carter, 1982): a sartorial parody of the social and economic crisis of the late '70s.

Punk emerged as an angry noise in the centre of white pop music. It began in London clubs, quickly spread to the provinces, and soon afterwards reappeared inside the record industry. The music was short, sharp and loud: lyrics shouted in an exaggerated naive style supported (or, more frequently, overwhelmed) by a barrage of frantic guitars and brutal drumming. It was a rude blast directed against the pretentious dominion of rock music.

It was do-it-yourself pop, music from below, your own sound, 'white roots'.

But the 'roots' in this case were ambiguous. For some they represented a mythical 'authenticity', the base line for political and group identities. This is The Clash, Rock Against Racism , and punk as 'white reggae' (Johnny Rotten). Later, this would also lead to the hard punk exit of skinhead fundamentalism and a refusal to betray the 'street sounds' of '76. For others, the 'roots', the icons of authenticity, represented ironic quotations of a lost innocence. Inside the circuits of contemporary representation – the press, television, the record industry – they were signs that served to disrupt the status quo; signs designed to provoke.

Punk marked a turning point in British youth styles. The self-conscious constructions – the deliberate choice of imagery guaranteed to shock: the swastika, the mutilation of the body by safety pins, its imprisonment in chains and dog collars – turned the attention of subsequent youth culture to the actual mechanisms of representation: the codes themselves.

This has turned out to be as true for music as for clothes. The musical chaos that punk proposed forced a stark reappraisal of pop's own sounds. The simple distinction between 'mainstream' and margin, between avant-garde and popular, between music and 'noise' were confused. The singular history of pop, seen as a set of successive waves – rock'n'roll, beat, progressive rock – was set aside and replaced by multiple histories. Crossover and synthesize becomes the choice: black rhythms and heavy metal, funk and punk, jazz and beat.

The resulting collage produces a frame in which diverse musical styles co-exist and combine – rockabilly and '60s soul, acoustic music and programmed drum machines, 'roots' reggae and computerized keyboards; where different rhythms are drawn from the global drum; where voices are retrieved from the past and remixed for the present (i.e. Keith LeBlanc and Malcolm X's 'No Sell Out'). The mainstream – the records that are chosen for publicity and promotion, that make money – remains, but, and now in the 1980s, it is flanked on several sides by an increasingly cosmopolitan repertoire in which the sounds of Africa and America, of New York and London, of the old and the new, not only co-exist, but quote and recall one another.

References

CARTER, A. (1982) *Nothing Sacred*, London, Virago.

Source

CHAMBERS, I. (1986), *Popular Culture: the metropolitan experience*, Methuen, London.

READING D

What did I get? Punk, memory and autobiography

Andy Medhurst

A not-quite-punk looks back

My involvement was simply that of an enthralled consumer – buying the records, reading the magazines, seeing the groups – yet being outside the subcultural elite didn't diminish the intensity of my attachment. As Gary Clarke has pointed out in an invaluable corrective to the more sweeping claims of subcultural studies, most young people never plunge entirely into subcultures but 'draw on particular elements of subcultural style and create their own meanings and uses of them' (1990, p. 92). The 'meanings and uses' I found in punk music were immense and irreversible, whatever the shortcomings of my wardrobe, however much of a fellow traveller I must have seemed, and may still seem now, to punk purists. I may not have had the bondage trousers (and even if I'd wanted them, the compulsory amphetamine slenderness of the time made them a dubious proposition for those of us whose waists demand an Extra Large) but that didn't stop punk seizing, shaking and rearranging my sense of self and the world I lived in.

Punk erupted into my life in the autumn of 1977. I knew about it before then from the music press and the radio, I even had a few of the records (the Adverts' 'Gary Gilmore's Eyes' was one of my favourite singles that summer and I'd been playing Patti Smith's *Horses* album obsessively all year), but I'd never felt the urgency of its call to arms, even when glancing up from my tea to watch the now-legendary Bill Grundy interview with the Sex Pistols, even though my council estate was only a mile or two from the one where Mark P. hatched the fanzine *Sniffin' Glue*. The decisive break came when I went away to university, a change in circumstances which offered a radical opportunity for self-reinvention. The new me, surrounded by new friends, involved in new activities, inhabiting a new landscape, demanded a new soundtrack – and punk, with its passionate commitment to the intensity of immediacy, was there for the taking. 1977 was a fantastic year to be 18, and I gorged myself silly on its riches. Swathes of my existing record collection had to be disavowed, of course, but other parts of it were suddenly reinvigorated under punk's new rubrics of credibility. I'd been right all along to like Bowie and hate Yes, I'd been presciently hip in buying *Horses* when I did, it was OK to have three Van Der Graaf Generator albums because Johnny Rotten said he liked their singer, Peter Hammill.

My first year as a student unfolded to a soundtrack of what now seems like an impossible profusion of wonderful records – the rallying cry of the first Clash album, the shimmering pure-pop poise of the Buzzcocks' 'What Do I Get?', the raw jolt of X-Ray Spex's 'The Day The World Turned Day-Glo' (on orange vinyl!), the fathomless caverns of Wreckless Eric's 'Whole Wide World', the sly perversities of Wire, Pere Ubu's cross-pollination of Beefheartian angularity and nameless dread, the knowing kitsch of Generation X's 'Ready Steady Go', the comedy and pain of Ian Dury's

'New Boots and Panties', Patti Smith raging and howling against the limits of gender and desire and the body, the skanked-up malevolence of Elvis Costello's 'Watching The Detectives', the crystalline splendours of Television's 'Marquee Moon', and towering over them all, totemic and definitive, *Never Mind the Bollocks*. Not all those records were classically 'punk', some sat better under the vaguer umbrella of 'New Wave', but to me then they all made sense together, united despite surface differences by their shared rhetoric of nowness and newness, and, perhaps more tellingly, by their shared rejection of the staleness and sterility of most previous musical styles. Provided a record sounded like it had been made by people who wanted to kill Pink Floyd and the Eagles, and had received the all-important sanction of my weekly bible the *NME*, it could be welcomed into the punk fold. The meanings of the music were still in flux, not yet fixed into manageable categories by the classificatory sobriety of history. Back then, in the middle of it all, everything felt intoxicatingly up for grabs.

The most vivid images people tend to have of their own pasts are not calm, measured narratives but sudden snapshots and erratic fragments, what psychologists working in this area call 'flashbulb memories' (Conway, 1990, pp. 61–88), which may help to explain why there are three moments from that year which burn brighter for me than any other. Firstly, the Students Union decided to occupy an administration building in protest at some injustice which I can (significantly?) no longer remember. Once we were on the seventh floor, the windows were thrown open, huge speakers rigged up and 'Anarchy In The UK' boomed out across the campus. Looking back, this seems touchingly naive, especially given the somewhat piquant fact that I now teach at the same university and attend committee meetings in those very rooms, and even at the time it felt a little self-conscious, but the wanton theatricality of the gesture, its strenuous attempt to marry our local dissatisfaction to a broader cultural dissent, makes it iconographically unforgettable.

The second flashbulb is seeing the Tom Robinson Band play in the Union building and joining the communal singing of 'Glad To Be Gay'. Most of the other students probably sang out of mild liberal rebelliousness, but I was a gay teenager on the brink of coming out and it meant more to me than I care to disclose. In terms of subsequent generic codification, few songs sound less 'punk' than 'Glad To Be Gay' (if anything, it's a folky protest song), but I had no doubts then or now that such a song would never have been so widely known without the cultural climate punk had made possible. When the band's live EP containing 'Glad To Be Gay' was released some months later, the back cover stated (with a punkish typography that spurned capital letters) 'recorded live nov/dec '77 at high wycombe town hall, sussex university, & the lyceum london'. Which tracks came from which venues wasn't specified, but High Wycombe and London stood no chance: in my mind the recording of 'Glad To Be Gay' was the one with me on it – me and a few hundred others. Coming out, after all, is primarily a process of affirmation, and what better way to be affirmed as a late 70s gay man than to take part in the recording of that song?

Both those flashbulbs are concerned, revealingly and influentially, with the relationship between music and politics, a linkage which for me has been punk's most lasting legacy. My third flashbulb, the most vivid memory of all, centres on subcultural inconsistencies and Caroline the campus punk. Caroline and her boyfriend Nigel (and non-British readers should note that those two names, particularly in tandem, connote a background of considerable class privilege) were the highest-profile punks at Sussex. Festooned in Westwood threads, twin visions in mohair sweaters and leather trousers, hair-dyed electric blue or bilious green, they would parade around striking the requisite poses. I can see her now, pulling him around the campus supermarket on a dog lead, and I can also hear her, with those giveaway Kensington vowels she usually took care to conceal, complaining in our hall of residence kitchen because I was playing loud music while she was trying to write an essay. Not just any loud music either – I was playing my tape of *Never Mind the Bollocks*. It's this image more than any other that makes me suspicious of retrospectively romanticised accounts of the purported coherence of youth subcultures. There we were, me (side-parting and flares) and my mate Steve (collar-length hair and rugby shirt) enjoying 'God Save the Queen' and 'Bodies', getting yelled at by a head-to-toe punk to turn down the Pistols. I had already grasped, from my own juggling act of loving the music and its cultural implications but declining to sign up to full subcultural involvement, the key point that being *into* punk didn't necessarily entail being *a* punk, but here, gift-wrapped with ribbons of irony, was proof of a related realisation: that dressing up in a subculture's trappings can be the most superficial of engagements with its deeper possibilities of meaning. Or, as I think I would have put it at the time, being a punk didn't stop you being a prat.

The seduction of nostalgia

According to Christopher Lasch, 'the victim of nostalgia … is worse than a reactionary, he is an incurable sentimentalist. Afraid of the future, he is also afraid to face the truth about the past' (quoted in Lowenthal, 1989, p. 20). This is a chastening rebuke, especially for someone who has enjoyed writing the previous paragraphs as much as I have, and it has a particular force when the object of such nostalgia is a discourse as rabidly unsentimental as punk. A central thread in punk's semiotic and ideological repertoires was its scorched-earth, year-zero attitude to tradition and the past ('No Elvis, Beatles or Rolling Stones in 1977, crowed the Clash; 'No future in England's dreaming', warned the Sex Pistols; 'Smash it up', suggested the (ever-helpful) Damned; 'Jesus died for somebody's sins but not mine', snarled Patti Smith), whereas nostalgia often springs from an attempt to seek consolation and security in times gone by. Getting nostalgic about punk is worse than a contradiction in terms, it's a kind of betrayal, trading in punk's forensic nihilism for a rose-coloured cosiness. Yet the situation is more complex. Of course my account of the punk era is saturated in nostalgia (anyone my age who isn't nostalgic about being 18 didn't deserve to be 18 in the first place), but nostalgia only takes hold out of 'some sense that the present is deficient' (Shaw and Chase, 1989, p. 3). When I look at the way many of the most successful British groups of the current moment, whether shrewd tunesmiths like Oasis or cretinous reactionaries like Kula Shaker and Ocean Colour Scene, court acclaim on the basis of their ability to look only backwards, or when I read a review in a music magazine that smugly begins 'Weren't the punk years tyrannical and horrid?' (Prior, 1997, p. 116) – and, to compound the offence, the review in question is a celebration of Supertramp, a paradigmatically loathsome outfit who occupied a deservedly high place in punk's demonology – the deficiencies of the present make nostalgia feel like an irresistible temptation.

It would be wrong to suggest, however, that my nostalgia for the late 70s is so all-encompassing that my tastes have remained stuck there. In fact I listen to punk so rarely now that the retrospective trawl I made through my collection for the purpose of researching this chapter was the first time I'd heard some of those records for years. It was exciting and reassuring to discover how fantastic many of them still sounded, but they're not going to resume a central place in my musical environment, since what gave them such a revolutionary impact on first release – their discordancy and disrespect, the seditious fury of their unforgiving confrontationalism – still seems largely and impressively intact, and that sits uneasily with the listening habits I have today. Punk as a visual sign may have been co-opted over the years into wider consumerist frameworks, but that late 70s noise still strikes me as very resistant to assimilation. Radio stations that specialise in playing past hits tend to agree with me, treating punk as a pariah genre, excising it from pop history. It still sounds like such a hell of a racket – a fact which delights the old fan in me enormously while simultaneously ensuring that I'll choose other sorts of sound to accompany daily domestic life. X-Ray Spex's 'Oh Bondage! Up Yours!' was never designed to be background music, and it still refuses, with commendably magnificent stroppiness, to occupy that role.

So if my nostalgia for punk doesn't take the form of wanting all music to be strapped to a late 70s template, in what sense is it nostalgic at all? Another flashbulb memory may be useful here. In the summer of 1978 I had a vacation job in a public library acquisitions department (which shows you exactly how much of 'a punk' I wasn't) and was chatting about favourite records to a fellow worker. She listened while I outlined my punk canon, considered it patiently, then smiled and said 'But you couldn't really call it music, could you?'. At the time I was outraged, but now I think she had a point, albeit not the point she thought she had. Punk was never just 'music' – if it was then I could only satiate my nostalgia by ploughing through those old singles. Music was the focus, the entry point, but punk went broader and deeper, offering a set of rules and a structure of feeling applicable way beyond the confines of sound. When, for example, anti-punk types sneered at my records by saying 'they can't play their instruments' they were quite right, in the sense that Emerson, Lake and Palmer were more instrumentally dextrous than X-Ray Spex, but those criteria meant nothing in the heat of the punk moment. The standard response of punk rhetoric to the charge of instrumental incompetence was 'it doesn't matter', a response which gratifyingly infuriated ELP fans and their ilk on two levels. First, it was a deliberate slap in the face for established pop aesthetics, declaring generational independence through a carnivalesque inversion of musical value, to the extent where not-being-able-to-play became a part of punk's holy writ – the punk-ness of anything could be determined by its not-being-able-to-play-ness. Second, and more importantly, 'it doesn't matter' established that the medium was secondary to the message, that popular culture could and indeed should be a vehicle for social and cultural intervention. Music, in other words, was political –

no, more than that, it was a form of politics itself, a politics that concretely engaged with contemporary issues.

That, above all, is the seed that punk planted deepest within me, leaving me with a set of expectations that form the core of my nostalgia. It's not a matter of wanting every record released now to sound like the Clash or the Adverts – far from it, since to do so, and this is a crucial point woefully misunderstood by groups who try to recreate and re-inhabit that early punk sound, would be profoundly un-punk, since punk was about the here and now, and now is no longer 1977 – but there will always be a part of me that requires new music to sound contemporary, to be political, to have something to say about the world around it. In that sense the Pet Shop Boys, Stereolab and Pizzicato Five are immeasurably more 'punk' than any set of retro-pogo punk revivalists.

References

CLARKE, G. (1990) 'Defending ski-jumpers: a critique of theories of youth subcultures' in Frith, S. and Goodwin, A. (eds) *On Record: rock, pop and the written word*, London, Routledge.

CONWAY, M.A. (1990) *Autobiographical Memory: an introduction*, Milton Keynes, Open University Press.

LOWENTHAL, D. (1989) 'Nostalgia tells it like it wasn't' in SHAW, C. and CHASE, M. (1989) *The Imagined Past: history and nostalgia*, Manchester, Manchester University Press.

PRIOR, C. (1997) 'Review of reissued Supertramp albums', *Mojo*, **43**, p. 116.

SHAW, C. and CHASE, M. (1989) 'The dimensions of nostalgia' in *The Imagined Past: history and nostalgia*, Manchester, Manchester University Press.

Source

MEDHURST, A. (1999) 'What did I get? Punk, memory and autobiography' in SABIN, R. (ed.) *Punk Rock: So What? The Cultural Legacy of Punk*, London and New York, Routledge.

Chapter 7

Consumption and creativity

Mary Jane Kehily

CONTENTS

When you have studied this chapter, you should be able to:

1   Explore the concept of consumption and the ways in which practices of consumption play a part in children's lives.

2   Develop ways of understanding issues of consumption and their relationship to children's agency and creativity.

3   Understand some of the different ways in which children are positioned as consumers of cultural products.

4   Use this understanding and insight to study examples of children as active, creative and critical consumers.

5   Develop an awareness of the ways in which issues of consumption and creativity have practical consequences for children's lives, experiences and identities.

6   Critically evaluate the relationship between consumption and creativity through an examination of children's engagement with cultural products.

1 INTRODUCTION

In the contemporary Western world children and young people are surrounded by commercial products that are made and marketed especially for them. A stroll through any shopping centre reveals a seemingly endless range of products: children's clothes, children's food, children's furniture, as well as conventional products designed for children's play and leisure such as books, toys and games. Developments in new technology have further increased the range of products available to children. Items such as CDs, videos, computer games and mobile phones play a part in many children's lives and day-to-day experiences.

In earlier chapters of this book you were introduced to children in different parts of the world and you reflected on the cultural resources that are available to them – in language, in peer groups and in media forms such as television. In this chapter you are invited to explore children's cultural worlds a little further. As the title indicates, the chapter is organized around two key themes – consumption and creativity.

First, we raise questions about commercial products and practices, questions such as: how are children positioned as consumers and in what ways do they engage in patterns of consumption? Second, we look at the theme of creativity and, particularly, children's agency and the ways it may be expressed in relation to issues of consumption. The chapter suggests that children exercise agency in their interactions with cultural resources and this gives rise to forms of creativity that shape and structure children's lives and experiences.

The chapter explores the commercial world that surrounds contemporary childhoods and the ways in which children interact with the world of commercial goods and products. In particular, we look at children and young people's engagement with popular music, magazines and new technologies. How and why do these commodities become part of children's lives? The chapter proposes that the concept of consumption is associated with mass production in industrialized and post-industrial societies. Consumption, however, is not only a Western phenomenon. Consumerism has had an impact on societies across the globe. While preparing this book we interviewed children in the US, Bangladesh and South Africa. In these diverse locations, children viewed forms of consumption as part of their daily lives. Within an international context, children are positioned as consumers and *engage with* the world of consumption in a variety of ways. Finally, the chapter argues that the sphere of consumption is an important site for the exercise of agency and creativity.

Girls go shopping.

2 CONSUMING CULTURE CREATIVELY

2.1 Defining consumption and creativity

In their original usage the terms 'consumer' and 'consumption' had negative associations with destruction and waste. From the fourteenth to the seventeenth centuries consumption meant to 'destroy, to use up, to waste, to exhaust' (Williams 1976, p. 69). With the growth of capitalism and industrialization in Western societies during the nineteenth century, the words took on an economic meaning. Consumption came to be understood as the opposite of production – the end point in a process that involved turning raw materials into products to be marketed and sold. In the twentieth century this use of the term spread with the economic boom that followed the Second World War, a period that made mass-produced goods widely available. Consumption is now commonly understood to mean the purchase and use of manufactured goods, though aspects of the earlier meanings still persist. Production and consumption can be seen as social processes that involve individuals in making, using and remaking the resources they have available to them.

More recently, the use of the terms 'consumer' and 'consumption' has expanded to embrace cultural as well as material products. Tim O'Sullivan *et al.* (1994) offer the following definition:

> The act or fact of using up the products or yield of any industry in support of any process.

> Production and consumption are terms borrowed from political economy, and they are now widely used … to describe the parties to and the transactions of communication. Thus meanings, media output, texts, and so on are said to be produced and consumed. Media professionals are seen as industrial producers while audiences or readers are seen as the consumers of meaning.

> The industrial metaphor is useful and suggestive as far as it goes, but there is a danger of taking it too literally. This is especially the case with consumption, which as a concept implies the using up of a finished product by an individual. Meanings and communication, however, are not consumed as finished products. The consumption of messages, therefore, is simultaneously an act of production of meanings.

> (O'Sullivan *et al.*, 1994, p. 244)

In this definition notions of production and consumption have been applied to the world of culture, cultural products and communication. O'Sullivan and his colleagues suggest that we are all consumers of meanings and messages that saturate our everyday cultural worlds. Furthermore, as consumers of messages, we also *create* and produce meanings by interpreting them in ways that make sense to us as individuals. In this chapter we will work with this contemporary understanding of consumption as part of a cultural process involving activity and agency.

The agency of children in relation to the world of cultural products, marketing and the media provides us with a way of understanding *creativity*. The consumption of cultural products is an active process through which children make sense of the world around them and define themselves and their place within it. The interrelationship between consumption and issues of identity is a central theme that we will return to throughout this chapter. The next section provides an illustrative example of the exercise of agency and creativity in the consumption of cultural products.

2.2 Agency and creativity

In Roddy Doyle's novel *Paddy Clarke Ha Ha Ha* (1993), the narrator is a ten-year-old boy growing up in Dublin, Ireland, in the late 1960s. Doyle recreates Paddy's childhood world in ways that illustrate his engagement with the cultural resources he has available to him. In the extract in Activity 1, Paddy describes a visit to the local library with his father.

Allow about 20 minutes

A C T I V I T Y I   Engaging with cultural resources

Read through the following passage from *Paddy Clarke Ha Ha Ha*. As you read:

1   Note the cultural products Paddy comes into contact with and the ways in which he integrates them into his own experiences.

2   Think about the ways in which Paddy's reading can be described as creative.

Extract from *Paddy Clarke Ha Ha Ha*

I could take two books. He looked at the covers.

– The American Indians.

He took the tag and slipped it into my library card. He was always doing that as well. He looked at the other one.

– Daniel Boone, Hero. Good man.

I read in the car. I could do it and not get sick if I didn't look up. Daniel Boone was one of the greatest of American pioneers. But, like many other pioneers, he was not much of a hand at writing. He carved something on a tree after he'd killed a bear.

– D. Boone killa bar on this tree 1773.

His writing was far worse than mine, than Sinbad's even. I'd never have spelled Bear wrong. And anyway as well, what was a grown-up doing writing stuff on trees?

[...]

There was a picture of him and he looked like a spa. He was stopping an Indian from getting his wife and his son with a hatchet. The Indian had spiky hair and he was wearing pink curtains around his middle and nothing else. He was looking up at Daniel Boone like he'd just got a terrible fright. Daniel Boone was holding his wrist and he had his other arm in a lock. The Indian didn't even come up to Daniel Boone's shoulders. Daniel Boone was dressed in a green jacket with a white collar and stringy bits hanging off the sleeves. He had a fur hat with a red bobbin. He looked like one of the women in the cake shop in Raheny. His dog was barking. His wife looked like she was annoyed about the noise they were making. Her dress had come off her shoulders and her hair was black and went down to her bum. The dog had a collar with a name tag on it. In the middle of the wilderness. I didn't like the Daniel Boone on the television either. He was too nice.

[...]

I liked the Indians. I liked their weapons. I made an Apache flop-head club. It was a marble, a gullier, in a sock, and I nailed it to a stick. I stuck a feather in the sock. It whirred when I spun it and the feather fell out. I hit the wall with it and a bit chipped off. I should have thrown away the other sock. My ma gave out when she found the one I didn't use, by itself.

– It can't have gone far, *she said*. – Look under your bed.

I went upstairs and I looked under the bed even though I knew that the sock wasn't there and my ma hadn't followed me up. I was by myself and I got down and looked. I climbed in under. I found a soldier. A German World War One one with a spiky helmet.

I read William. I read all of them. There were thirty-four of them. I owned eight of them. The others were in the library. William The Pirate was the best. I say! *gasped William*. I've never seen such a clever dog. I say! *he gasped*, he's splendid. Hi, Toby! Toby! Come here, old chap!

Toby was nothing loth. He was a jolly, friendly little dog. He ran up to William and played with him and growled at him and pretended to bite him and rolled over and over.

– Can I've a dog for my birthday?

– No.

– Christmas?

– No.

– Both together?

– No.

– Christmas and my birthday?

– You want me to hit you, is that it?

– No.

I asked my ma. She said the same. But when I said two Christmases and birthdays she said, – I'll see.

That was good enough.

William's gang was the Outlaws; him, Ginger, Douglas and Henry. It was Ginger's turn to push the pram and he seized it with a new vigour.

– Vigour, *I said*.

– Vigour!

– Vigour vigour vigour!

For a day we called ourselves the Vigour Tribe. We got one of Sinbad's markers and did big Vs on our chests, for Vigour. It was cold. The marker tickled. Big black Vs. From our diddies to our tummy buttons.

– Vigour!

Kevin threw the cap of Sinbad's marker down a shore, an old one on Barrytown Road with goo at the bottom. We went into Tootsie's shop and showed her our chests.

– One two three –

– Vigour!

(Doyle, 1993, pp. 56–8)

COMMENT

It is important to point out here that Paddy is the fictional creation of an adult who is drawing upon some familiar childhood experiences to write a novel from the perspective of a child. In this extract we gain an insight into Paddy's world through his engagement with cultural products that are clearly important to him – the two library books he has chosen. In the first book, on the Wild West, Paddy can be seen to identify more with the Indians than with Daniel Boone, hero and American pioneer. Paddy relates the words and pictures of his chosen book to the present and makes sense of it by placing the characters and images within his environment. So, for example, Daniel Boone looks like a woman from the local cake shop; the obvious hero of the text for adults, including Paddy's father, is not Paddy's hero at all. Rather, it is the Indians that capture Paddy's imagination and act as a trigger for the creation of a self-made Apache club.

Paddy's discussion of the William books, a popular series by Richmal Crompton written between 1922 and 1970, gives us further insight into his cultural world. Paddy is aware that the books form a series that can be read, collected and hierarchically ranked. His own collection amounts to eight books. These books provide Paddy with the inspiration for another passion – the desire to own a dog. Despite the class-cultural differences between William's middle-class world and Paddy's working-class environment, Paddy identifies with William as a boy in search of adventure. In a comic re-creation of the Outlaw's gang, Paddy and his friends create the 'Vigour Tribe'.

Doyle's account of Paddy's reading of library books and his subsequent play activities illustrates some key themes in relation to consumption and creativity. Children consume products in an active rather than a passive manner; their practices of consumption interact with aspects of their identity and with their context and everyday experiences. Representations such as the Wild West are read and interpreted in particular locales that may produce new meanings and new ways of seeing.

Anne Haas Dyson suggests that children imagine possibilities for themselves by appropriating heroes from other people's stories. In *Writing Superheroes* (1997) she argues that this form of appropriation may be drawn from cultural products such as music and computer games as well as from written texts, and can be seen as one of the ways in which individuals make sense of the world and attempt to create coherence out of chaos. Dyson suggests that superhero stories allow children to experience a sense of control and to feel powerful in an environment where they often have little power or control.

A boy in search of adventure: William with dog Toby.

"I SAY!" GASPED WILLIAM, "I'VE NEVER SEEN SUCH A CLEVER DOG!"

As consumers, children play a part in economic relations. However, through the practices of consumption they may, as Dyson suggests, produce meanings for themselves. Children use products as *resources* to define themselves, invest products with meaning and also use them to establish hierarchies of power and status. Section 3 considers the economic relationship between products marketed specifically for children and practices of consumption among children themselves.

SUMMARY OF SECTION 2

- Consumption is commonly understood to mean the purchase and use of manufactured products, including cultural products such as music, advertisements, films, TV programmes, magazines and computer games.

- Children engage with the cultural products available to them and use them in creative and sometimes unpredictable ways.

- Appropriating cultural products is one of the ways in which children and young people make sense of the world and their place within it.

3 CHILDREN AS CONSUMERS

In economic terms, children and young people are an important and influential consumer group. In most countries of the North the notion of the 'teenager' as a distinct life-cycle phase has been coupled with the emergence of a 'youth market'. With the rise in manufacturing industries and the mass production of goods after the Second World War, young people came to be seen in marketing terms as a specific group with a disposable income. The 'teenager' became identifiable as part of a generation with a distinct style expressed in the conspicuous consumption of records, clothes and leisure activities. More recently, attention has been drawn to the 'child market' and the commercial practices associated with the under twelve age group. Market researchers document the social trends that impact upon children and young people as consumers and their findings directly influence manufacturers and advertisers.

An example of these practices at work is the recent coinage of the term 'tweenage', or 'tweens', to refer to older children/young teenagers between the ages of nine and thirteen. Market researchers Datamonitor indicate that the spending power of tweens in the UK is rising faster than that of any other group. That tweens are big spenders is reflected in the way that large stores such as Boots and Woolworths have ranges of products such as cosmetics, CDs and magazines specifically targeted at them. Datamonitor, however, assert that the spending power of tweens extends beyond these everyday commodities to include more expensive purchases such as cosmetic surgery, laptop computers, hand-held computers and mobile phones. The importance of children and young people as consumers increases dramatically if account is taken of the influence that children can have on their parents' spending. The skilful wearing down of parental resistance is referred to colloquially as 'pester power'.

From the point of view of manufacturers and advertisers, children and teenagers are seen in the following terms:

- as a primary market in their own right;
- an influential market given their influence on parental household purchase;
- a market for the future of all nations;
- a particular demographic segment;
- a specific life-style segment according to the same criteria as their parents.

(Gunter and Furnham, 1998, p. 3)

Manufacturers and marketing and advertising agencies have devised strategies to tap into the lucrative child and youth markets. Typically, these organizations will be concerned to establish the size of the market in any one location, how much money this group have to spend and what they are likely to spend their money on. In 1979 the marketing agency Mintel estimated that there were ten million children in the UK with a combined spending power of around 600 million pounds per annum. A survey carried out in 2000 by the food production company Walls reported that children in the UK had an average of £6.09 per week to spend. In the USA in 1997 it was estimated that the country's 28 million teenagers spend approximately $57 billion of their own money and further influenced a substantial proportion of their parents' expenditure (Gunter and Furnham, 1998). Gunter and Furnham allude to the significance of 'pester power' by pointing out that children and young people are 'used to deciding what stereo is best, what car is "cool", what vacation to go on' (1998, p. 5). Some of these points are developed in Reading A.

READING

Read Reading A, which is an extract from *Consuming Children* by Jane Kenway and Elizabeth Bullen. The reading is extracted from an Australian study of children and their relationship to issues of consumption. The research reviews some of the ways in which children are constructed as consumers and explores some of the implications this may have for developing an understanding of childhood and youth. The reading elaborates on some of the points already made in this chapter.

As you read, make a note of the main points, then complete the following tasks:

1   The Reading draws on the work of Kline (1993) and Seiter (1995). Using two columns, make a note of the main points of their arguments.

2   What are the differences between the two approaches in terms of the way in which children are positioned?

3   Kenway and Bullen indicate that children are constructed as consumers by advertisers and marketing agencies. Make some notes on the strategies that may be used for this purpose and whether you consider them to be effective in their own terms.

COMMENT

Kenway and Bullen suggest that consumerism produces a particular version of the child. They use studies by Kline and Seiter to point to some of the different ways in which these issues can be understood. Kline's study can be seen as a top-down analysis of the power of production. Kline stresses the ways in which practices of consumption can shape the lives of adults and children in direct and powerful ways, cumulating in what he characterizes as the commodification of family life. Seiter acknowledges the power of the media to create markets. However, she also points to the potentially positive aspects of production and marketing, particularly in relation to gender issues. Seiter's approach sees children and young people as active rather than passive in the face of elaborate and pervasive marketing strategies.

Here we have two opposing views of the child as part of an economic system where consumption is seen to have a structuring presence in children's lives and experiences. From Kline's perspective the child, and indeed the family, is saturated by consumer culture, engulfed by it like a tidal wave sweeping over a surfer. Seiter, on the other hand, sees children's relationship with the commercial world as more interactive. She suggests that the effects of this relationship are diverse, producing fragmentation

Taking children's desires seriously: Fimbles (top left), Rapunzel Barbie (top right), Micropets (bottom left) and Bratz (bottom right).

that can be potentially empowering for children. These two views – of the child as passive recipient or as active agent – can be seen as part of the ways in which the meaning of childhood is struggled over.

Kenway and Bullen suggest that the allure of children's commercial culture for children themselves lies in the fact that the commercial world pays attention to play, pleasure and desire and seeks to understand these issues from the perspective of the child. They use the work of Hobson to discuss some strategies used by advertisers to encourage children to purchase particular products. Strategies such as the use of 'enduring themes', updating existing products and appealing to the 'now' factor play upon children's desires and aspirations as well as their passion for collecting and trading. Market research plays an important part in identifying potential markets through the use of 'profiling'. Profiling provides advertisers with an outline of what a particular group likes and how they can best be appealed to. Marketing agencies work with strong notions of age and gender as important factors in patterns and practices of consumption.

Contemporary approaches to the study of childhood involve developing an understanding of childhood as a diverse concept that is struggled over in different contexts and by people with different investments in what childhood is and what it should be. As in other parts of this book, we want to draw your attention to childhood as a multiple and fluid concept; there is no one perspective on childhood, rather there are many competing views.

3.1 Consumption and identity

MINNA: We like to listen to music, which is our favourite hobby, so we like to do that together and then we like to go shopping.

ELIZABETH: These are the [hair] clips that we've bought right now. These are really in fashion in Bangladesh right now…

MINNA: We both have the same taste in all things. We like the same kinds of bags and the same kinds of shoes and clothing even … We agree with each other's decisions always. Yeah. That's what the main thing is. She likes what I like, she dislikes what I dislike … We're just a photocopy of each other, that's what I think.

(Minna and Elizabeth, thirteen years old, Chittagong, Bangladesh, The Open University, 2003a)

Early research on consumer culture tended to cast the practices of consumption in a negative light. Studies from the 1950s and early 1960s pointed to the many ways in which consumption served the interests of manufacturers through processes whereby individuals become passive victims of consumer capital. This approach is reflected in the title of Vance Packard's influential book *The Hidden Persuaders* (1957). This study, like others of the time, characterized the expansion of mass production as a bad thing in itself; creating commodities which lack authenticity and meet 'false' needs. From this perspective, consumer needs can be understood as generated by marketing and advertising agencies which have ideological control over our lives. The emphasis on the power of production and the ideological hold over individuals places consumers in a passive position as the manipulated dupes of omnipotent and highly persuasive commercial forces.

By contrast, contemporary work on consumption tends to position consumers as active rather than passive and frequently focuses on the ways in which practices of consumption involve interaction, negotiation and issues of identity. It is interesting to note that in countries where consumption has been regulated and restricted, the ability to consume the products of modern Western capitalism may be seen as a new found freedom. The demise of communism in Eastern Europe, for example, has been marked by the opening up of new markets for Western goods in contexts where the ability to consume has been viewed as a form of liberation in itself.

A very early study of practices of consumption, first published in 1899, explored the world of the *nouveau riche* in late nineteenth-century America (Veblen, 1970). Veblen's analysis suggests that this group bought products to impress others and were more concerned with issues of taste, display and status than with function or use-value. Ideas of taste have been further explored in more recent work by the sociologist Pierre Bourdieu (1984), who suggests that identities are produced through practices of 'distinction'. Bourdieu argues that culture is concerned with the processes of identification and differentiation that allow individuals to distinguish themselves. Is this also the case for children and young people? Minna and Elizabeth, quoted above, identify with each other and consolidate their friendship by shopping together and developing a taste for the same music, clothes and fashion accessories.

Through the practices of consumption, individuals and groups exercise cultural capital, express taste and articulate a sense of identity. Bourdieu uses the concept of *habitus* to capture a sense of the cultural environment that is structured in terms of taste and distinction, learned in childhood and applied in later life. Section 4 focuses on children and young people's engagement with practices of consumption in three different fields: comics and magazines, pop music and new technology. In each field children and young people consume products and create meanings in relation to these products. As such, the practices of consumption involve children in participation within a *habitus* wherein they organize themselves and others into a classificatory system marked by identification with some and difference from others.

SUMMARY OF SECTION 3

- Children and young people constitute an important and influential consumer group.
- Manufacturers, marketing and advertising agencies devise strategies to tap into the lucrative child and youth markets.
- Consumerism produces different versions of the child – as passive recipient or as active agent.
- There has been a move away from seeing consumer culture in negative terms and towards seeing the practices of consumption as affirming and life-enhancing.
- Through the practices of consumption, individuals and groups exercise cultural capital, express taste and produce a sense of identity.

4 THE 'CHILD MARKET'

4.1 Comics and magazines

The comic book and magazine industry aimed at children and young people is a relatively recent example of cultural production which is usually located in Western societies from the middle of the twentieth century. Trina Robbins (1999) describes the development of the comic book industry in the USA in the following way:

> By 1941, the fledgling comic-book industry had been booming since 1938, when two teenage boys from Cleveland, Jerry Siegal and Joe Shuster, created *Superman*. Kids and adults had been reading comic strips in their daily and Sunday papers since the beginning of the century, but there was a distinct advantage to getting your comic story complete, between two covers. In those days, before television, comics provided a less expensive alternative to movies – they only cost a dime! – and they were disposable. You could roll up your comic book and stash it in your back pocket; better yet, you could conceal it in your loose-leaf notebook and read it beneath your desk during math class. But comic books, inundated with caped and costumed superheroes, served as entertainment for boys. Little existed in the way of comics aimed at girls.
>
> (Robbins, 1999, p. 8)

As Robbins points out, the early days of comic book production, which created some of the classic Marvel superheroes such as *Superman* and *Spiderman*, were associated with a male readership. Roddy Doyle's Paddy Clarke provided us with a fictional illustration of the ways in which characters from books may feature in the imaginative play of young boys (see Activity 1). Today, however, boys like Paddy are more likely to come into contact with their superheroes through film and television. While comics are still undoubtedly popular among many boys, it is girls who are more likely to be avid consumers of comic books and magazines. Publications aimed at boys and adolescent males tend to focus on hobbies and interest groups, such as football and computers, while those aimed at girls cover a general range of themes and issues that appeal to a broad female readership. We will explore some of the reasons for this gender difference below.

Comic books and magazines are a popular, mass-produced and publicly shared media form which address children and young people in particular ways. They can be seen as a cultural resource that children and young people can 'talk with' and 'think with'. In my own ethnographic study of teen magazines in the UK (Kehily, 2002), I observed and spoke with boys and girls aged between thirteen and sixteen in two different schools in a large, diverse and ethnically mixed urban area. All of the young women I spoke with, and some of the young men, were regular readers of magazines aimed at an adolescent female market. Many of the young women were aware that the magazines played a part in a developmental process that was guided by age and gender:

SOPHIE: I think that *More!* is for older girls really. Like the younger ones [*comics and mags*] where you've got, you've got ponies and stuff.

NAOMI: And pictures of kittens.

SOPHIE: Yeah, there's *Girltalk* and *Chatterbox* and you go up and you get *Shout* and then you get *Sugar* and *Bliss* and then it's like *Just Seventeen*, *Nineteen* and it's *More!* and then *Woman's Own* and stuff like that. So you get the range.

(KEHILY, 2002, p. 104)

The 'going up' that Sophie refers to is part of the gendered experience of moving from girlhood to adolescence and into womanhood, where particular magazines may be seen as cultural markers in the developmental process.

A selection of teen magazines.

Angela McRobbie has commented on the ways in which *Jackie* magazine of the 1970s introduced girls to adolescence by mapping out the personal terrain, 'outlining its landmarks and characteristics in detail and stressing the problematic features as well as fun' (1991, p. 83). McRobbie's analysis of *Jackie* argues that the different features of the magazine were involved in reproducing a culture of femininity that cohered around the concept of romance. From this perspective, *Jackie* can be seen as preparatory literature for a feminine rather that a feminist career. The search for a 'fella', the privileging of true love and the emphasis upon repetitive beauty routines can be read and understood as an induction into the future world of marriage and domestic labour.

Martin Barker's (1989) study of comics and magazines suggests a way of looking at girls' magazines that questions the feminist assumption that *Jackie* is 'bad for girls'. Barker's analysis points out that a knowledge of the production history of magazines can contribute to our understanding of the ways in which magazines can be seen as specific cultural products, produced within a context of technical constraints and compromises that change over time. Factors relating to the physical production of the magazine, such as machinery, financial resources, artistic input and marketing, have a bearing on notions of 'reproduction'; seeing *Jackie* as an ideological purveyor of femininity overlooks many other factors which make the magazine what it is. Barker's reading of *Jackie* postulates that the magazine has an agenda based on 'living out an unwritten contract with its readers' (Barker, 1989, p. 165).

> The 'contract' involves an agreement that a text will talk to us in ways we recognise. It will enter into a dialogue with us. And that dialogue, with its dependable elements and form, will relate to some aspects of our lives in our society.
>
> (Barker cited in Kehily, 2002, p. 105)

Barker points out that the contractual understanding between magazine and implied reader is reliant on social context. He emphasizes the interactive engagement of the reader with the magazine, where both parties are involved in a conversation premised upon shared social experiences and expectations.

My discussions with young men and young women referred to above indicated that gender plays a key role in shaping the attitudes and practices with which young people read magazines (Kehily, 2002). Many young women that I interviewed spoke of magazine reading as a regular *collective* practice among friends that they used as a springboard for discussions about parents, boyfriends and friendships. Many of the discussions were concerned to establish a moral consensus whereby the friendship group 'drew the line' between acceptable and unacceptable behaviour. By contrast, the reading of magazines did not appear to occupy a similar social space among male peer groups. In a group discussion with boys, the discussion about the absence of magazines for adolescent males appears to generate feelings of emasculation and suspicion:

MJK [*interviewer*]:	Do you wish there was a boys' magazine?
BLAKE:	Nah, you'd get called a sissy wouldn't you? (*all laugh*)
CHRISTOPHER:	Well there are some like *Loaded* and *GQ* and *Maxim* as well with things like football, sex and clothes and –
BLAKE:	You're an expert you are! (*all laugh*)
MJK:	If there were a magazine like that for your age group – what about that?
ANDREW:	Yeah, I wouldn't mind buying a magazine like that sometimes but I wouldn't, like the girls do, buy it every week, that's just too – I wouldn't like that. I'd only buy it when there was something in it like an article or something. You know, sometimes like when you get into a situation and you don't know what you're doing it would help then if there was a magazine to tell you what to do then.

(KEHILY, 2002, pp. 107–8)

The responses of the boys indicate that their reading of magazines is more of an individual than a collective activity as it is for the girls. Reading magazines could be regarded as 'sissy', and the shared laughter of the boys suggests that there is group recognition and surveillance relating to gender-appropriate behaviour for young males. Christopher's awareness of magazines, his 'expertise', may be hazardous to the presentation of a socially recognized male identity. Andrew's comments specifically see magazines as a manual or reference book to be consulted as and when necessary in order to solve particular individual problems. His expressed distaste for regular readership 'like the girls do' suggests that he may be afraid of being tainted by femininity.

Allow about 20 minutes

ACTIVITY 2   Reading comics and magazines

Prompted by your reading of this section of the chapter, think about the comics and magazines that played a part in your childhood/youth and complete the following tasks:

1   Make a list of some of the comics and magazines you came into contact with during your childhood and teenage years, either as a regular consumer or a casual reader.

2   Select two or three comics/magazines that you recall as being particularly influential for you and make a note of your favourite features, what you remember about them and why you liked them.

3   In what ways do you think your readership of comics and magazines played a part in developing your identity – your sense of self – who you were/are and how you think about yourself?

COMMENT

The comics and magazines you read during childhood and adolescence will of course depend upon where and when you grew up, as well as factors such as your gender, socio-economic position and the hobbies and interests you developed as a child. In my response to this activity I identified *Bunty* magazine as a text that has particular memories for me. *Bunty* was aimed at girls in the nine to twelve age range. Two stories stick in my mind. First, there was 'The Four Marys', the on-going tale of boarding school japes and girls' friendship that solved moral dilemmas by the score. Sharing the girls' first name, I could easily project myself into being a member of the gang, the fifth Mary, running amok in the dorm, making and breaking friends before finally doing the right thing. The only difficulty that I never bothered to address was the fact that I was highly unlikely to go to public school. The jolly romps of the girls were far removed from the mixture of rote learning and religion that passed for education at the Catholic primary school I attended.

The other *Bunty* story I really enjoyed – though I can't now recall the name of it – was about a girl whose parents had died suddenly in an accident (there were a lot of orphans in *Bunty*) and she was left to bring up her younger brothers and sisters. The poor girl was a paragon of virtue and selflessness who, somewhat unbelievably, managed to convince adults that she was up to the job and that the children should not be taken into care. Then there was the back page of *Bunty* with the cut-out model and the dazzling array of clothes with little tabs to fit around her. Sheer joy!

Moving into adolescence I was keen to leave girlhood behind and became an avid reader of *Jackie*. It was very much as McRobbie describes, an exercise in conventional femininity that I embraced with relish. Looking back, I see *Bunty* as a compelling articulation of my girlhood concerns to be 'good', caring and to put other people before yourself. *Jackie*, on the other hand, licensed a shameless style of individualism for me. It was okay to be preoccupied with boys and romance, pop stars and the wearing of fashionable clothes and make-up. I can trace my interest in retail flirtation and compulsive clothes shopping to this period. Being a good girl no longer involved the pursuit of selfless acts, but rather could be reconstituted as being feminine in particular ways; looking good without looking like a tart and engaging in romance without having sex.

Finally, if I'm thinking about my relationship to magazines, I feel duty bound to confess the guilty pleasure I take in adult readership: leafing through *Hello* magazine at the hairdressers, enjoying the gossip and the glossy photographs of Hollywood stars, I know that as a good feminist I shouldn't even be looking at. In the midst of these contradictory feelings there's my desire to research magazines for girls. Could this be a way of turning a guilty pleasure into a legitimate academic interest? Or maybe I'm not a good girl at all.

What can these recollections tell us about consumption and creativity? First, they illustrate Barker's (1989) point: reading comics and magazines is an interactive activity. We integrate what we read into the texture of our daily lives and make points of connection between the reading material and our own experiences. This activity may involve overlooking aspects of our lives that do not fit so readily into the spaces between the lived, the text and the imagined. Second, living, reading and imagining have implications for our identity. In Western societies gender becomes an important way of defining yourself in relation to others and in opposition to others. Finally, the ways in which children and young people create meanings through reading comics and magazines cannot be fully anticipated. While certain gendered themes may be common, the responses of individuals will always be contextual and contingent – they may even be contradictory.

A feature from Bunty: 1960s.

Another feature from Bunty: 1960s.

4.2 Pop music

Music plays an important part in the lives of many children and young people. We have already learned that listening to music is Minna and Elizabeth's favourite hobby (see Section 3.1). Children and young people may be involved in many different aspects of musical activity, as producers of music and as consumers, regulators and meaning makers. You will recall from Chapter 6 the ways in which music plays a key feature in the activities of sub-cultural groups such as punks, skinheads and Rastas. Music has long been associated with the teenage years, and particularly with the conspicuous consumption of popular music and forms of fandom. However, younger children, too, cite music as an important part of their everyday experience. Twelve-year-old Terina, living in Oakland, California, told us:

> I'm Terina and my whole world evolves around music … I can't imagine a life without music, I guess it's been a part of me for so long.

(The Open University, 2003b)

Children in Cape Town, South Africa, express a similar sentiment. Thirteen-year-old Nonhlanhla says that music is 'the centre of us'. Jazz, Quito and hip-hop bring Nonhlanhla and her friends together, providing a way of relaxing and having fun. Terina and Nonhlanhla place music at the centre of their lives and define themselves in relation to it. Terina buys and enjoys a range of popular music, from the Spice Girls to R & B and hip-hop. Terina also writes lyrics, sets them to music and performs her own songs as a way of expressing her feelings. It is commonplace to draw a distinction between being a fan of the Spice Girls and writing music for yourself. The former is seen as an act of consumption, whereas writing and performing songs is seen as a creative act of production. It is interesting to note, therefore, that Terina does not draw a distinction between the two when she speaks about her relationship to music. For Terina, listening to music and writing music are both forms of self expression that make her feel good and allow her to define herself in relation to her musical tastes and preferences.

Being a fan is usually regarded as less important, less significant and secondary to participating in the cultural form at first hand. Henry Jenkins characterizes fandom in the following way:

> One of its earliest uses was in reference to women theatre-goers, 'Matinee Girls', who male critics claimed had come to admire the actors rather than the plays … If the term 'fan' was originally evoked in a somewhat playful fashion and was often used sympathetically by sports writers, it never fully escaped its earlier connotations of religious and political zealotry, false beliefs, orgiastic excess, possession and madness, connotations that seem to be at the heart of many of the representations of fans in contemporary discourse.
>
> […]
>
> To speak as a fan is to accept what has been labelled a subordinate position within the cultural hierarchy, to accept an identity constantly belittled or criticised by institutional authorities. Yet it is also to speak from a position of collective identity, to forge an alliance with a

community of others in defence of tastes which, as a result, cannot be read as totally aberrant or idiosyncratic. Indeed, one of the most often heard comments from new fans is their surprise in discovering how many people share their fascination … their pleasure in discovering that they are not 'alone'.

(Jenkins, 1992, p. 507)

Here, Jenkins indicates that fandom cannot be viewed entirely in negative terms. Being a fan gives individuals a cultural reference point and a feeling of affiliation with others that produces a collective identity. The next reading explores the idea of being a fan further through a study of the Beatlemania phenomenon of the 1960s in the UK and the USA.

READING

Read Reading B, which is an extract from 'Beatlemania: a sexually defiant consumer culture?' by Barbara Ehrenreich, Elizabeth Hess and Gloria Jacobs, then answer the following questions:

1   In what ways do the authors argue that Beatlemania is 'revolutionary'? How convincing do you find this argument?

2   What links between consuming music, creativity and issues of identity do Ehrenreich *et al.* outline?

Beatlemania.

COMMENT

Ehrenreich *et al.* suggest that Beatlemania was remarkable as the first mass outburst of the 1960s to feature women. The mob-like behaviour of Beatles' fans, they argue, was in itself a form of protest against the sexually repressive climate of the period and the stifling authoritarianism of the adult world. Being a Beatles' fan involved an assertion of sexuality that was in marked contrast to the experiences of young women in school and the domestic sphere, where the emphasis was upon propriety and vigilance in order to maintain a 'good girl' reputation.

Ehrenreich and her colleagues also consider the pleasures and enduring appeal of fandom for young girls. They suggest that pop stars can appeal to the fantasy lives of girls by providing them with romance without the possibility of a relationship or the monotony of marriage. Being a fan, they argue, is based on activity that is positive, affirming and overwhelmingly creative; in its heyday the screams of abandonment and adulation expressed by Beatles', fans swamped the music to the point where the fans rather than the band became the focus of the show. Finally, it is of course the fan base that makes a band successful; by consuming their music and identifying with their image, fans turn musicians into stars.

Next, we explore issues of consumption and creativity a little further by looking at the role of new technologies in children's culture.

4.3 New technologies

Developments in new technology have brought about many changes that have had an impact upon the lives of children and the experiences of childhood. Children and young people participate in practices associated with CDs, digital television, DVDs, videos, computer games, the internet and mobile phones. In an Australian-based study of children and their relationship with computer culture, Green *et al.* (1998) argue that children born in the West in the 1990s are immersed in a world of electronic images and virtual reality, a world which they term 'techno-culture'. They suggest that techno-culture exists as a naturalized part of these children's lives: 'it is simply part of, and inextricable from, their lifeworld more generally – both as a context and a resource for their living and learning, their being and their becoming' (Green *et al.*, 1998, p. 23). Other researchers suggest that children now spend more time in electronic environments that they do in school or talking with friends or parents (Sheff, 1993, p. 7).

Should we be concerned about these changes? And how do children make sense of these experiences? Green *et al.* introduce a set of contemporary concerns in the following way:

> Two hundred years ago, children were not expected to live very long, and so much childhood education in the affluent middle-class home concentrated on teaching them to endure pain and prepare for an early death ... As we enter the twenty-first century, things have not changed much for most of the children in the world. Affluent children, however, are expected to live long and almost pain-free lives, and their home education therefore concentrates on teaching them about ways to fill

their time. Yet in many living rooms, playrooms and bedrooms around Australia, these children are still experiencing an early death. They are losing their lives and dying over and over again – not in reality, of course, and not with any physical pain to endure. Rather, these are electronic deaths, occurring vicariously, on the screens of their Nintendo machines.

As the children of the wealthy (white) First World become increasingly affluent, the emergence of a mass-market computer and video game culture is a marked and increasingly significant feature of contemporary everyday life. So significant, that reference is often made to 'aliens', 'New Kids' and 'the Nintendo generation' to describe and evoke a new generation of children.

(Green *et al.*, 1998, p. 19)

Here, the concern with new technologies is expressed in ironic terms in relation to themes of violence, early death and the production of an alien species of children hooked on playing video games. Children's relationship to new technologies, and particularly video games, is frequently described as a form of addiction – compelling, compulsive and dangerous at the same time.

Other studies point to the ways in which issues of gender feature in the video game industry, and particularly the emphasis on a dominant and aggressive form of masculinity. In their analysis of video-game culture, Alloway and Gilbert (1998) assert that the games and the magazines work together to 'align masculinity with power, with aggression, with victory and winning, with superiority and strength – and, of course, with violent action. They offer positions for young male game players that promise success as masculine subjects' (Alloway and Gilbert, 1998, p. 97). Alloway and Gilbert point to the under-representation of girls as game figures and as players and the derogatory ways in which female figures are positioned and spoken about when they do appear. Viewed in more positive terms, however, children's engagement with new technology can also be seen as a site for the development of new skills and competencies that draw upon increasingly complex modes of creativity and agency.

What emerges from these studies is a portrait of children and young people as technologically sophisticated. They feel at home with a wide range of media forms and engage with them as an everyday part of their lives. It is common, for example, to find a product such as a book produced also as a film, video and computer game with a plethora of complementary merchandizing such as CDs, toys, stationery, T-shirts, bed linen and wallpaper. Children and young people move within and between these products with ease in practices that engage with forms of intertextuality. In Chapter 5 you were introduced to the term *intertextuality* as the practice whereby media texts refer to and draw upon other texts, often in ironic ways. The practices of intertextuality address readers or viewers as 'media literate' consumers by assuming that they have knowledge of a wide range of media forms. Intertextuality can also be understood as part of the cultural practices that children and young people participate in when they watch the film, play the game and buy the T-shirt.

Artists and writers working with popular cultural forms have utilized techniques of intertextuality to produce new genres such as Japanimation, or 'anime'. Anime is the name given to videos and computer games that draw upon Japanese comics to produce a new cultural form which combines sophisticated graphic artwork with high-tech animation techniques (see Box 1).

Box 1   An example of Japanese Anime

Ghost in the Shell: director Mamoru Oshii, based on the Manga by Masaune Shirow

In a world caught up in the grip of information overload, where artificial intelligence is more than the real thing and cyborg cops spend their lives surfing on the electronic sea of living data, only the Ghost – the indefinable element of human consciousness – exists to determine who is alive and who is purely a creation of the Net.

Major Motoko Kusanagi is an elite officer in Shell Squad, the Section 9 security force: a cybernetic agent so heavily modified that little more than her Ghost remains. Along with fellow cyborg Bateau and the mostly human Togusa, Kusanagi is set on the trail of a computer-criminal known as the Puppet Master, a datathief skilled enough to hack into the very minds of his victims. His human marionettes live out existences that are nothing more than computer-generated fantasy, unwittingly committing their master's crimes while the Ghost-hacker hides in the darkness.

(Source: promotional material, 1996, Manga Entertainment Ltd)

Anime has emerged from the Japanese comic tradition known as 'manga', a large industry in itself, where one or two artists share responsibility for the story line, character creation and artwork. Many anime titles were originally published as manga comics. Anime develops the comic book story lines into three-dimensional films and computer games, resulting in a distinctive style of 'cartoon' quite unlike the Western forms associated with this term. Anime developed into a $60 billion industry in less than a decade (Perez, 1997).

Anime films provide a contrast with Western cartoons in their explicit treatment of themes such as violence, eroticism, homosexuality, death and immorality, and the ways in which taboo subjects can also be woven into aspects of romance and comedy. *Ghost in the Shell*, for example, depicts a high-tech futuristic world that deals with some of the challenges posed by new technology, such as the idea of 'becoming someone else'. Through the fantasy of changing identities and ownership of self, the video explores the differences between original and fake; reality and fantasy; memory and simulated experience; body and machine. Further differences can be found in the narrative structure and character-oriented plot. Anime narratives have been compared to the novel form in the way they call on the audience to interact with each character, to 'sense their emotions and to penetrate and unravel the psychology' (Perez, 1997).

In Section 5 we look at some of the ways in which children and young people use cultural products to personalize spaces. In particular, we look at 'bedroom culture'.

SUMMARY OF SECTION 4

- Comic books and magazines provide children and young people with a cultural resource that enables them to develop frameworks for talking and thinking.
- Magazine readership and video-game culture are marked by gender difference, age and class-cultural location.
- Music exists as a form of self expression for children and young people in practices where they may not necessarily draw a distinction between consuming music and performing music.
- The experience of being a fan may be positive, liberating and pleasurable.
- Children feel at home with a range of media forms and engage with them in sophisticated ways as part of their everyday lives.

5 THE CREATION OF PERSONALIZED SPACE

Langman (1992) described the shopping mall as a space where adolescents hang out and create a sense of 'pseudo-community' away from the gaze of parents and teachers. In these temples of consumption products can be bought and admired or used to provide the backdrop for a range of other activities. Langman suggests that the shopping mall serves several functions for young people:

- for the display of clothes, make-up and image;
- as an escape from the regulation of home and school;
- for meeting sexual partners;
- for the establishment of hierarchies of 'cool' – young people with self-defined tastes and aspirations who rank themselves in relation to others.

These activities point to the ways in which young people personalize highly impersonal spaces in ways that suit their needs and desires.

Inside the home, children and young people often regard their bedroom as a space within the household that can be personalized. The concept of 'bedroom culture' was developed by McRobbie (1978). McRobbie suggested that whereas young men tended to congregate in the 'street' to have fun, young women were more likely to get together in each others' bedrooms. There they could enjoy a range of self-consciously girly activities such as experimenting with clothes, hair and make-up, talking about boys and playing pop music. Indeed, the image of the teenage girl standing in front of the bedroom mirror singing along to a contemporary hit while using a hairbrush as a microphone is one that has been much parodied in adverts and comedy routines.

Lincoln's ethnographic study of teenage girls in the UK illustrates many points of continuity for young women in 2001, though mobile phones and CD players are obvious points of difference from the young women in McRobbie's 1970s study:

> For teenage girls in the late '90s, the bedroom is often the only space within the home that is personal, personalized and intimate. It is a space over which teenagers are able to be private from parents and siblings alike, often displayed on the bedroom door with signs such as 'knock before entering!' It is a room in which unmediated activities such as sleeping, reading books and magazines, daydreaming and 'chilling out' take place. The bedroom also exists as one of the central 'meeting' places in a teenage girl's social life world. It is the space into which friends are invited to listen to music, chat (either to each other or on the mobile phone), smoke, drink alcohol, experiment with hair, make-up and clothes and get ready for a night out. The bedroom is a biographical space. The posters, flyers, photographs, framed pictures, books, magazines, CDs and so on catalogue a teenage girl's youth cultural interests, bringing together past and present experiences ...
>
> [...]
>
> Eve, a research participant, indicated in one interview the amount of time she spends in her bedroom when she said, 'I just go downstairs for food'.
>
> (Lincoln, 2001, pp. 6–8)

Lincoln stresses the importance of music to the girls in her study. She suggests that in addition to the posters of pop stars and the mixture of fantasy and chat that surrounds listening to pop music, girls may use music to say something about their feelings and their identities. Different styles of music could be used to set the tone for a night in or a night out and could be seen as a 'constant mediator of the "emotional tone" of bedroom culture' (Lincoln, 2001, p. 12). In her Australian study of the everyday experiences of ten teenage girls, Gerry Bloustien (1998) points to further links between the bedroom space, music and moments of self-expression. Adopting an innovative approach to ethnographic research, Bloustien asked the girls in her study to use video cameras to document their daily lives:

> It seemed to me, as I looked at the girls' footage, that music continually served as a cultural thread and an effective link, moving between the worlds that we would popularly designate as private and public. Although the participants sometimes videoed their [bed]rooms without verbal commentary, music was frequently played in the background to provide a particular ambience. In cases where it became a vitally significant component of the *mise-en-scène*, the music was chosen quite deliberately to match a particular mood or to tie in with a specific poster of a pop or rock-star. As in all drama or film, the music integrated the characterization and themes of the scene. At other times, if the participant was in front of the camera, talking about herself, she often

had some appropriate music playing softly – and sometimes not so softly – in the background. In those situations, the music was often selected, seemingly to underscore an aspect of her sense of group identity. So, for example, Grace deliberately selected music from the Violent Femmes, 'a kind of 90's folk punk', she explained to me. Mary, from Papua New Guinea, played reggae music while she was taking the imaginary 'visitor' on a video tour of her house. It appeared as though the girls were making the music another symbolic aspect of their sense of self along with the posters and other cultural icons in their rooms and their homes.

Even when the music was not being played, the importance of its wider status as essential commodity was present in record sleeves, CD covers, posters and T-shirts that frequently decorated the wall spaces ... it was not simply the obvious significance of fan-group membership that the music implied, but the wider meaning that such an icon emitted. For example, in the bedrooms of Janine and her Aboriginal friends were posters of Bob Marley and, sometimes, Aboriginal musicians. Mary also had photos of Bob Marley and many posters of Jamaican and African-American basketball stars. For these girls, obviously the skin colour of the stars and personalities on their wall posters was significant. What their choice implied was not simply their own fandom of these cultural groups but that such membership cohered with their immediate familial and community values and expectations. Their choices suggested an awareness of the constraints in their performed subjectivity and of their investments in their chosen positions.

(Bloustien, 1998, pp. 127–8)

In this example the personalized space of the bedroom and the use of music is drawn upon by the girls to express a sense of identity that demonstrates the interrelationship between gender and ethnicity.

Many children and young people are likely to have a computer in their bedroom, indicating that the personalized space can also be seen as a multimedia site or a 'techno-cultural' space (Green *et al.*, 1998). The idea of the bedroom as a personalized space for children begins early and can be actively constructed by parents, sometimes in ways that assume highly normative gender identities. This was clear from interviews with children and young people in Oakland, California, conducted in the preparation of this book. The bedrooms of siblings Karen and Brian had been decorated by their parents in ways that emphasized and celebrated gender differentiated childhoods. Karen's retreat into the tranquil land of pink and Brian's all-blue action zone can be seen as perfect examples of gender-under-construction (see Book 1, Chapter 5 for a full discussion of the ways in which childhood is gendered).

In the following activity we will look at some of the issues faced by Cathy and Sharon, Chinese-American sisters who share a bedroom in Oakland, USA.

Allow about 15 minutes

A C T I V I T Y 3   **The personalized space of the bedroom**

Read through the following transcript and study the picture, then complete these tasks:

1   Make a list of the commodities and personal memorabilia to be found in Cathy and Sharon's bedroom.

2   In what ways do Cathy and Sharon use their bedroom as a personalized space?

3   What difficulties do Cathy and Sharon encounter in sharing a bedroom?

4   How do Cathy and Sharon present themselves as different kinds of people?

At home with Cathy and Sharon.

SHARON: Something very important to me is our system [CD and tape player] for instance because it entertains me, the music and these posters 'cos it's nice and colourful and it's just nice 'cos they look nice, anyways, and CDs are very important to me because you know sometimes when you see the kind of music that you listen to it tells you it kind of tell you what kind of person you are …

CATHY: The most important thing to me in this room is it's clean, only if it's clean. I hate when I walk in here and it's really messy, and I step on things in the middle of the night because it's usually her [Sharon's] things on the floor … Well I can't really do a lot in this room I only do my homework. I eat in here and I sleep in here, that's the only three things I can really do. If you expect me to get silence in this room I can't because somebody likes to turn up the music and the CD at the same time and do her homework too. It's amazing. And I sleep in here and she watches *The Simpsons* at night, so I don't get really any sleep until 12 o'clock and yet I still have to get up at 6.30 in the morning, lucky me huh?

SHARON: Well maybe if she doesn't like me having all this noise she should sleep on the couch … I like listening to music and watching TV, sleeping and eating and sometimes doing my homework in here. Basically it's the music and TV.

CATHY: This is like a house to her, this, the room is to me, is like she thinks this is the house. She had Cheerios laying around, you know cereal, and she has everything laying around here.

SHARON: If I could I wanna put a refrigerator in here.

CATHY: Yeah in the bathroom and in the closets and then she doesn't have to leave this room.

INTERVIEWER: So how do you sort this out between you?

CATHY: We kind of separate the room in half but not really separate it but, if she starts getting dirty on my side of the room I will yell at her so bad …

SHARON: These *[demonstrating]* are my Chinese CDs which this one I listen to sometimes, well my mum picked it out, and there's old music in there but then sometimes they're interesting to me, and this one is a singer which I listened to when I was young so it brings back memories of the past, and this CD is from my sister's friend for my birthday and I listen to it now so I'm trying to get used to Chinese music again …

INTERVIEWER: What would you like up here *[on wall]* if you were given a choice?

CATHY AND SHARON: Pictures of Justin Timberlake all over the room, yeah.

CATHY: He's really cute. He's just, you know, I mean, not just because he's cute but you know he has a charity and he travels around a lot, he does a lot of charity work. I think that's really what I know about him that I really like and I can't judge him based on what colour he likes or what food he likes you know … I mean I don't expect to meet him or anything but, it's just someone you admire and they may inspire you or something. Unlike Sharon, she chooses a guy based on their look you know, she doesn't know anything about Nick Carter here, from the *Backstreet Boys* but, you know.

(From recordings made for The Open University, 2003c)

COMMENT

Cathy and Sharon articulate the pains and perils of sharing a bedroom with your sister. Their bedroom looks like many of the teenage bedrooms described in the studies you have been introduced to in this section. Cathy and Sharon mention posters of pop stars on the wall, a CD player and a TV, and their room also contained much of the paraphernalia associated with teenage girlhood – make-up, clothes and soft toys. Like the girls in Bloustien's (1998) study, the bedroom also reflects their cultural identity as Chinese-Americans and demonstrates the ways in which gender and ethnicity can be interwoven into a developing sense of self.

Cathy and Sharon both regard the bedroom as a space set aside from the rest of the house where they can relax, and be themselves. They also want the bedroom to reflect something of their own personality, their tastes and interests. The difficulties arise due to differences in their approach to the space and their developing sense of identity in relation to each other. Cathy complains that Sharon 'thinks the bedroom is the whole house'. Sharon would like the room to be her self-contained space and laments the fact that she has to venture into the rest of the house to use the fridge. Cathy, on the other hand, has a more functional approach to the use of the space and (she claims) a more developed sense of order and propriety.

In the interview the girls present themselves *as against* each other, defining who they are by setting up a series of polarities and differences. For example, we have the tidy one and the messy one, the quiet one and the noisy one, the one who stays up late and the one who goes to bed early. In a final exposition of difference, Cathy and Sharon tell us that they both like Justin Timberlake, teenage heart-throb, member of pop group N Sync and proverbial ex-boyfriend of pop star Britney Spears. However, Cathy tells us that Sharon is only attracted to boys who are physically attractive while she is interested in their personality. Defining yourself in terms of difference is a common in siblings who are close in age; even when their tastes and interests coincide, points of difference remain to set them apart.

SUMMARY OF SECTION 5

- Young people personalize spaces in ways that suit their needs and desires.
- For teenage girls in particular, the bedroom is a space in which they can express a sense of identity, including their gender and ethnicity.

6 CONCLUSION

In this chapter we looked at the concept of consumption and considered some of the ways consumption can be defined and analysed. We considered the role of consumption in the lives of children and young people and discussed the many ways in which their daily experiences are immersed in the commercial world of products, marketing and consumption.

In the past there has been a tendency to view the practices of consumption in negative terms, as a case of individuals being duped by the power of market capital. Contemporary studies in this field, however, start from the premise that consumption is part of everyday cultural life that can have positive as well as negative effects. We focused on the theme of creativity and suggested that children and young people do not consume products passively. Their relationship with commodities is located within cultural practices that can be productive in themselves.

Using the examples of comics and magazines, music and new technologies, we explored some of the ways in which children and young people consume and use a range of products. What emerges is a picture of sophisticated use and diverse practice. The energy and agency of children and young people in this area point to the creative ways in which the practices of consumption can be used to elaborate on issues of gender, ethnicity, identity and self-expression.

REFERENCES

ALLOWAY, N. and GILBERT, P. (1998) 'Video game culture: playing with masculinity, violence and pleasure' in HOWARD, S. (ed.) *Wired Up: young people and the electronic media*, London, UCL Press.

BARKER, M. (1989) *Comics, Ideology, Power and the Critics*, Manchester, Manchester University Press.

BLOUSTIEN, G. (1998) '"It's different to a mirror 'cos it talks to you": teenage girls, video cameras and identity' in HOWARD, S. (ed.) *Wired Up: young people and the electronic media*, London, UCL Press.

BOURDIEU, P. (1984) *Distinction: a social critique of the judgement of taste*, Cambridge, MA, Harvard University Press.

DOYLE, R. (1993) *Paddy Clarke Ha Ha Ha*, London, Vintage.

DYSON, A. H. (1997) *Writing Superheroes: contemporary childhood, popular culture and classroom literacy*, New York, Teachers College Press.

GREEN, B., REID, J. and BIGUM, C. (1998) 'Teaching the Nintendo generation? Children, computer culture and popular technologies' in HOWARD, S. (ed.) *Wired Up: young people and the electronic media*, London, UCL Press.

GUNTER, B. and FURNHAM, A. (1998) *Children as Consumers: a psychological analysis of the young people's market*, London, Routledge.

JENKINS, H. (1992) '*Textual poachers*' in GELDER, K. and THORNTON, S. (eds) *The Subcultures Reader*, London, Routledge.

KEHILY, M. J. (2002) *Sexuality, Gender and Schooling: shifting agendas in social learning*, London, Routledge.

KENWAY, J. and BULLEN, E. (2001) *Consuming Children: education–entertainment–advertising*, Buckingham, Open University Press.

KLINE, S. (1993) *Out of the Garden: toys, TV and children's culture in the age of marketing*, London, Verso.

LANGMAN, L. (1992) 'Neon cages: shopping for subjectivity' in SHIELDS, R. (ed.) *Lifestyle Shopping: the subject of consumption*, London, Routledge.

LINCOLN, S. (2001) 'Teenage girls' bedroom culture: codes versus zones', unpublished paper, Manchester Metropolitan University.

MACKAY, H. (ed.) *Consumption and Everyday Life*, London, Sage.

McROBBIE, A. (1978) 'Working class girls and the culture of femininity' in CENTRE FOR CONTEMPORARY CULTURAL STUDIES, *Women Take Issue*, London, Hutchinson.

McROBBIE, A. (1981) 'Just like a *Jackie* story' in McROBBIE, A. and McCABE, T. (eds) *Feminism for Girls: an adventure story*, London, Routledge & Kegan Paul.

McROBBIE, A. (1991) '*Jackie* magazine: romantic individualism and the teenage girl' in *Feminism and Youth Culture: from* Jackie *to* Just Seventeen, London, Macmillan.

O'SULLIVAN, T., HARTLEY, J., SAUNDERS, D., MONTGOMERY, M. and FISKE, J. (1994) *Key Concepts in Communications and Cultural Studies*, London, Routledge.

PACKARD, V. ([1957] 1970) *The Hidden Persuaders*, Harmondsworth, Penguin.

PEREZ, C. (1997) 'Japanimation: appropriating a pop-cultural phenomenon', http://link1.mcmaster.ca/~osamu/japanimation (accessed November 2002).

ROBBINS, T. (1999) *From Girls to Grrrlz: a history of comics from teens to zines*, San Francisco, Chronicle Books.

SEITER, E. (1995) *Sold Separately: children and parents in consumer culture*, New Brunswick, NJ, Rutgers University Press.

SHEFF, D. (1993) *Game Over: Nintendo's battle to dominate an industry*, London, Hodder and Stoughton.

STAINTON ROGERS, W. (2003) 'Gendered childhoods' in WOODHEAD, M. and MONTGOMERY, H. K. (eds) (2003) *Understanding Childhood: an interdisciplinary approach*, Chichester, John Wiley and Sons Ltd/The Open University (Book 1 of the Open University course U212 *Childhood*).

THE OPEN UNIVERSITY (2003a) U212 *Childhood*, Video 3, Band 4, 'Friendship', Milton Keynes, The Open University.

THE OPEN UNIVERSITY (2003b) U212 *Childhood*, Audio 6, Band 9, 'Children and music', Milton Keynes, The Open University.

THE OPEN UNIVERSITY (2003c) U212 *Childhood*, Video 3, Band 10, 'At home with Cathy and Sharon', Milton Keynes, The Open University.

VEBLEN, T. (1970) *The Theory of the Leisure Class: an economic study of institutions*, London, Allen & Unwin.

WILLIAMS, R. (1976) *Keywords*, London, Fontana.

READING A

Inventing the young consumer

Jane Kenway and Elizabeth Bullen

> In *Shopping with Mother* (1958) Susan and John, the young
> protagonists, experience the excitement of shopping. Leaving Tibby,
> the cat, and Mike, the dog, at home, the children visit, under the
> careful guidance of 'Mother', the grocer's shop for jam and sugar, the
> baker's for cakes, the fish shop, the butcher, the green-grocer's and,
> finally, the ironmonger to buy a hammer for Dad. After a couple of
> hours this odyssey is brought to an end and Susan, John and Mother
> return home to unpack the goods – an event which excites even the
> animals.
>
> (Humphery, 1998, p. 61)

Introduction

As the child learns to shop, it also learns to be a particular sort of child. The
child is a social construct. To the extent that they exist, histories of
childhood indicate that the 'nature' of childhood, the relationship of
children to each other and to adults, to the family, and to other social
institutions such as work and school, have changed across time and place.
In the so-called developed world, the last two centuries have seen
sweeping changes in conceptions of childhood and children's culture,
child-rearing practices, family life and adult/child relationships. The
purpose of this [Reading] is to consider some distinctive features of
evolving and contemporary childhood and youth. We will make the case
that any adequate understanding of childhood and youth must recognize
the specific role played by consumer–media culture in broader social and
cultural change. Such an understanding provides the basis for a more
nuanced view of the constructions of children's and youth cultures and
identities.
   […]
In order to assist us to develop an understanding of the history of
contemporary childhood we will employ in particular two major texts,
complemented by others. These are Stephen Kline's study *Out of the
Garden: Toys, TV and Children's Culture in the Age of Marketing* (1993)
and Ellen Seiter's *Sold Separately: Children and Parents in Consumer
Culture* (1995). We have chosen them because of their location within
debates in the fields of consumer and media studies. In very broad terms,
both are interested in the ways in which meaning is conferred by
advertising on media texts and other children's commodities … However,
each employs a different theoretical framework. Kline's emphasis is on the
production of meanings in the first instance, and so represents consumer
culture as an implacable force which has shaped history, society and
individual identities over the past two centuries. In contrast, Seiter focuses
on the ways in which meanings are consumed and remade by their
'readers' (another view of production some may say) …

Kline offers a historical account of the rise of the child's place in the framework of consumption – the evolution of markets for children and the emergence of the child consumer. He argues that consumption (shopping, toys, TV, music, clothing) is now a central part of the 'matrix of forces' that socialize young children. It is just as central to children's development as the family, school and community life. Indeed, he implies that consumption is now an integral, if not overarching, feature of all of them. Elsewhere Kline has written with others (Leiss *et al.*, 2000) on the evolution of the bond between media and advertising …

Seiter's work brings additional feminist perspectives. She stresses the need to understand the rise of consumerism in 'the context of larger social changes – in domestic work, in mothers' labor force participation, and in patterns of child rearing' (1995, p. 4). It is her view that childhood and parenthood 'are expressed through and mediated by television, advertising, and consumer goods' (p. 6). She foregrounds the need for greater awareness of the ways in which 'television organizes, distorts, and expresses gender and race difference' (p. 6). However, in contrast to Kline, who argues that children's play culture has been largely defined by marketing strategies, Seiter stresses the agency of the child consumer. Thus, together they present quite a comprehensive picture of the young (see also Buckingham, 1995).

[...]

It should be noted at this point that it is important not to fetishize children's commodities. Explaining what such fetishization means, Lee (1993, p. 15) draws attention to the 'grubby chrysalis of production' and to 'the mysterious economic dark side of social exploitation which is so effectively concealed in the dazzling glare of the market-place'. Without doubt, the consuming child of the West is the beneficiary of labouring children of such countries as Indonesia, China and Pakistan.

[...]

Kline singles out for particular attention TV advertising and TV situation comedy, as they came together in the notion of family-orientated programming and domestic consumption. He shows how many … family tension[s] …were enacted and, indeed, mapped on the screen as the family came to be seen and played out as a site of 'chronic confusion and misunderstanding' (Kline, 1993, p. 67). These tensions were articulated as possession and consumption, offering what Kline calls 'consumerist solutions to parenting problems'. Products could help to assuage such tensions; families could be unified through common brand loyalties …

Seiter argues that as a result of market segmentation children and parents came to be 'sold separately'. She points to the selling of children's toys to parents on the basis of their educational and happiness value and to the complicity of the print and later the image media in this process. In contrast, and more recently, TV has sold toys to children on the basis of their 'badge appeal' to peers (Seiter, 1995, p. 5). Indeed, child and youth markets have themselves become segmented. In the next section we consider the reasons for the segmentation of the child and youth markets and how they are segmented according to age and gender.

Further fracturing children

Children's commercial culture appeals so much to children because it takes children's play, pleasure and desire seriously. Clearly it helps to construct their play, pleasure and desire, but it also seeks to understand and tap into them. At worst, it involves the cynical exploitation which Jacobson and Mazur (1995, p. 26) identify when they quote advertising agency president, Nancy Shalek:

> Advertising at its best is making people feel that without their product, you're a loser. Kids are very sensitive to that. If you tell them to buy something, they are resistant. But if you tell them they'll be a dork if they don't, you've got their attention. You open up emotional vulnerabilities and it's very easy to do with kids because they're the most emotionally vulnerable.

At best, children's commercial culture offers the insights into children's culture of an increasingly reflexive industry.

Hobson (1999) outlines three main strategies which advertisers believe act as triggers for child consumers. She calls the first 'enduring themes', which include: control (getting one over on adults, feeling intellectually superior, mastering skills); aspirational values (wanting to be older); social acceptance (friendship and peer group acceptance); possession (ownership, collecting, privacy, secrecy); and good versus evil (from Brothers Grimm to *Star Wars)*. At the same time, children are responsive to innovation and change. The second and third strategies are contemporary relevance and the 'now' factor – the former an updated version of an existing product, the latter a product of its times. As an example of marketing which adapts to the times, Hobson describes the metamorphosis of the Sugar Puffs character from Cuddly Honey Monster to a rapping Sugar Puff Daddy. She makes the point that 'Throughout its evolution, the core values of approachability and being the child's (slightly older and therefore aspirational) friend have been retained while growing and developing in line with children's needs and motivations' (Hobson, 1999). Products which capture the 'now' factor are usually novelty-based and likely to enjoy a shorter lifespan. Collectibles like Tazos, Tamagotchis and Pokémon, and associations with current film or television characters are typical of this phenomenon in advertising.

Segmenting by age

… Products and advertising which appeal to one age group will fail with another. Knowledge of the target audience is fundamental and advertisers have looked to market research for guidelines about what appeals to children, and for profiles of each age group when developing marketing strategies. How, then, do the advertising and marketing industries construct the child consumer?

Between the ages of 4 and 6, children are drawn to fantasy and gender-targeted design: 'They are less concerned with what a product is than how it looks' (Hobson, 1999). Though they have little money of their own, their 'pester power' makes them an attractive market. Children aged between 7 and 9 years particularly enjoy collectibles and can be motivated by humour. They have developed reasoning and literacy skills, which means they are more likely to be persuaded by verbal information on packaging. Profiling 9- to-11-year-olds, the *Kids Marketing Report* found that children in this age range: 'like "funny"; they like "stars"; they like "catchy music"; they like sound effects, liveliness, they like "weird" and "gruesome" and they particularly enjoy ads with a twist at the end. Boys especially respond to "action"; girls are more likely to appreciate "mood"' (Steward, 1998).

Gender differentiation becomes even more marked in the 10 to 12 year age group, with boys favouring sporting brands and girls fashion. This group is highly subject to peer pressure. These young people want to earn peer acceptance as well as to differentiate themselves from others. Brand clothing can act as a prop which marks their position in their peer culture, earns external approval and confers status. According to Duff (1999), by age 9 or 10, three-quarters of children shop alone or with friends. They have progressed from buying lollies, snacks and drinks to magazines and music. By 10 to 12 years they are expected to be more in control of their parents and have their own money to spend.

According to Hobson (1999) 12 years is the cut-off point of childhood in marketing analysis. However … we need to consider what Handel (1999) calls the 'tween generation': 12- to 14-year-olds. Whereas brand functions as the currency which buys peer acceptance in the previous age group, brands are now valued for their iconic associations – sporting heroes, supermodels, actors and pop culture idols – and the identities which can be constructed as a result. 'Cool' is an object of desire which can be bought. 'Link marketing' is the advertising strategy.

Identity is also a big issue for this age group. Not only are they becoming increasingly interested in the opposite sex, they have become focused on creating their own sexual identity. They are also seeking to construct identities which distinguish them from their parents and mark their independence from the family. Between 12 and 14 is the age range when parents 'just don't understand', and the age when kids 'want to know what is taboo' but are only just starting to test boundaries (Handel, 1999). This age group has high aspirational values. They are eager to 'trade-up' age-wise but are also territorial: 'successful products are designed with them as the sole target' rather than seeking to simultaneously engage the adult consumer *(Kidscreen,* 2000). Their product repertoire includes computer games, clothes, fast food, music, drinks, snacks, magazines and personal care items. They have a greater say in large family purchases like computers, cars and holidays. Handel (1999) notes that the 12 to 14 age group is particularly open to sponsorship and 'cause-related' marketing because of 'their curiosity and morality'.

[...]

Segmenting by gender

[...]

Young girls were first recognized as a market segment worth specific targeting by the electronic media in the 1980s. Although girls make up more than half of the children's TV viewing demographic, they were reconceptualized as a 'niche' market, differentiated according to the conventional wisdom about gender difference. While boys' programming focused on action, things and conflict, girls' programming privileged relationships, beauty and harmony. As Seiter (1995) says, girls and boys came to be 'sold separately'. At this time, the market for girls' toys was seen to have much untapped potential. Market research led to the production of licensed toy characters around which toy-based video series for girls were developed. These did not require girls to cross over and identify with males, as was the dominant tendency. By centring on female characters and on the concerns and play of little girls, these programmes offered an attractive fantasy space …

However, Seiter goes on to say that 'Something was gained and lost when marketers and video producers began exploiting little girls as a separate market' (1995, pp. 157–8). On the one hand, their culture was ghettoized by boys and despised by many adults (particularly male cultural theorists). On the other hand, it freed girls from the ambiguity and psyche-splitting involved in identification with the male characters of the dominant available forms. It offered them, instead, a utopian 'playful world of love and friendship' and 'magical physical abilities' (Seiter, 1995, p. 170) – not a bad choice in the commercial culture of femininity, according to Seiter. We now see similar patterns of gender segmentation emerging in the interactive games industry.

References

BUCKINGHAM, D. (1995) 'The commercialisation of childhood?: the place of the market in children's media culture', *Changing English*, **2**(2), pp. 17–40.

DUFF, R. (1999) 'Children are discerning customers', *Kids Marketing Report*, 30 June.
www.mad.co.uk.KMR/print/stories/1999/06/30/0029.asp (accessed 1 February 2000).

HANDEL, K. (1999) 'The Lineker effect: using icons to reach the tween generation', *Kids Marketing Report*, 2 May.
www.mad.co.uk/KMR/print/stories/1999/05/02/0041.asp (accessed 1 February 2000).

HOBSON, J. (1999) 'Tapping into a child's visual world reveals way forward for packaging', *Kids Marketing Report*, 27 January.
www.mad.co.uk/KMR/print/stories/1999/01/27/0034.asp (accessed 1 February 2000).

HUMPHERY, K. (1998) *Shelf Life: Supermarkets and the Changing Cultures of Consumption*, Melbourne, Cambridge University Press.

JACOBSON, M. F. and MANZUR, L. A. (1995) *Marketing Madness: A Survival Guide for a Consumer Society*, Boulder, CO, Westview Press.

KIDSCREEN (1996) 'Special report: NATPE – girls' shows a new attraction, but boys still set the trends', *Kidscreen*, January.
www.kidscreen.com/articles/ks16837.asp (accessed 5 June 2000).

KIDSCREEN (2000) 'The *Kidscreen* strategy challenge', *Kidscreen*, January.
www.kidscreen.com/articles/ks27665.asp (accessed 1 February 2000).

KLEIN, S. (1993) *Out of the Garden: Toys, TV and Children's Culture in the Age of Marketing*, London, Verso.

LEE, M. J. (1993) *Consumer Culture Reborn: The Cultural Politics of Consumption*, London, Routledge.

LEISS, W., KLINE, S. and JHALLY, S. (2000) 'The bonding of media and advertising' in LEE, M. J. (ed.) *The Consumer Society Reader*, Malden, MA, Blackwell.

SEITER, E. (1995) *Sold Separately: Children and Parents in Consumer Culture*, New Brunswick, NJ, Rutgers University Press.

STEWARD, J. (1998) 'Kids and advertising: kids clued up on the purpose of ads', *Kids Marketing Report*, December. www.mad.co.uk/KMR/print/stories/1998/12/01/0020.asp (accessed 1 February 2000).

Source

KENWAY, J. and BULLEN, E. (2001) *Consuming Children: education–entertainment–advertising*, Buckingham, Open University Press.

READING B

Beatlemania: a sexually defiant consumer subculture?

Barbara Ehrenreich, Elizabeth Hess and Gloria Jacobs

The news footage shows police lines straining against crowds of hundreds of young women. The police look grim; the girls' faces are twisted with desperation or, in some cases, shining with what seems to be an inner light. The air is dusty from a thousand running and scuffling feet. There are shouted orders to disperse, answered by a rising volume of chants and wild shrieks. The young women surge forth; the police line breaks…

Looking at the photos or watching the news clips today, anyone would guess that this was the 1960s – a demonstration – or maybe the early 1970s – the beginning of the women's liberation movement. Until you look closer and see that the girls are not wearing 1960s-issue jeans and T-shirts but Bermuda shorts, high-necked, preppie blouses, and dishevelled but unmistakably bouffant hairdos. This is not 1968 but 1964, and the girls are chanting, as they surge against the police line. 'I love Ringo.'

Yet, if it was not the 'movement,' or a clear-cut protest of any kind, Beatlemania was the first mass outburst of the 1960s to feature women – in this case girls, who would not reach full adulthood until the 1960s and the emergence of a genuinely political movement for women's liberation. The screaming ten- to fourteen-year-old fans of 1964 did not riot *for* anything, except the chance to remain in the proximity of their idols and hence to remain screaming. But they did have plenty to riot against, or at least to overcome through the act of rioting. In a highly sexualized society (one sociologist found that the number of explicitly sexual references in the mass media had doubled between 1950 and 1960), teen and preteen girls were expected to be not only 'good' and 'pure' but to be the enforcers of purity within their teen society – drawing the line for overeager boys and ostracising girls who failed in this responsibility. To abandon control – to scream, faint, dash about in mobs – was, in form if not in conscious intent, to protest the sexual repressiveness, the rigid double standard of female teen culture. It was the first and most dramatic uprising of *women's* sexual revolution.

Beatlemania, in most accounts, stands isolated in history as a mere craze – quirky and hard to explain. There had been hysteria over male stars before, but nothing on this scale. In its peak years – 1964 and 1965 – Beatlemania struck with the force, if not the conviction, of a social movement. It began in England with a report that fans had mobbed the popular but not yet immortal group after a concert at the London Palladium on 13 October, 1963. Whether there was in fact a mob or merely a scuffle involving no more than eight girls is not clear, but the report acted as a call to mayhem. Eleven days later a huge and excited crowd of girls greeted the Beatles (returning from a Swedish tour) at Heathrow Airport. In early November, 400 Carlisle girls fought the police for four hours while trying to get tickets for a Beatles concert; nine people were hospitalized after the crowd surged forward and broke through shop windows. In London and Birmingham the police could not guarantee the Beatles safe escort through the hordes of fans. In Dublin the police chief judged that the Beatles' first visit was 'all right until the mania degenerated into barbarism' (*New York Times Magazine* 1 December 1963). And on the eve of the group's first US tour, *Life* reported, 'A Beatle who ventures out unguarded into the streets runs the very real peril of being dismembered or crushed to death by his fans' (*Life* 31 January 1964).

[…]

Part of the appeal of the male star – whether it was James Dean or Elvis Presley or Paul McCartney – was that you would *never* marry him; the romance would never end in the tedium of marriage. Many girls expressed their adulation in conventional, monogamous terms, for example, picking their favorite Beatle and writing him a serious letter of proposal, or carrying placards saying 'John, Divorce Cynthia.' But it was inconceivable that any fan would actually marry a Beatle or sleep with him (sexually active 'groupies' were still a few years off) or even hold his hand. Adulation of the male star was a way to express sexual yearnings that would normally be pressed into the service of popularity or simply repressed. The star could be loved noninstrumentally, for his own sake, and with complete abandon. Publicly to advertise this hopeless love was to protest the calculated, pragmatic sexual repression of teenage life.

The economics of mass hysteria

[…]

Marketing strategies that recognized the importance of teens as precocious consumers also recognized the importance of heightening their self-awareness of themselves *as teens*. Girls especially became aware of themselves as occupying a world of fashion of their own – not just bigger children's clothes or slimmer women's clothes. You were not a big girl nor a junior woman, but a 'teen,' and in that notion lay the germs of an oppositional identity. Defined by its own products and advertising, slogans, teenhood became more than a prelude to adulthood; it was a status to be proud of – emotionally and sexually complete unto itself.

Rock 'n' roll was the most potent commodity to enter the teen consumer subculture. Rock was originally a black musical form with no particular age identification, and it took white performers like Buddy Holly and Elvis Presley to make rock 'n' roll accessible to young white kids with generous allowances to spend. On the white side of the deeply segregated music market, rock became a distinctly teenage product. Its 'jungle beat' was disconcerting or hateful to white adults; its lyrics celebrated the special teen world of fashion ('Blue Suede Shoes'), feeling (Teenager in Love'), and passive opposition ('Don't know nothin' 'bout his-to-r-y'). By the late 1950s, rock 'n' roll was the organizing principle and premier theme of teen consumer culture: you watched the Dick Clark show not only to hear the hits but to see what the kids were wearing; you collected not only the top singles but the novelty items that advertised the stars; you cultivated the looks and personality that would make you a 'teen angel.' And if you were still too young for all this, in the late 1950s you yearned to grow up to be – not a woman and a housewife, but a teenager.

Rock 'n' roll made mass hysteria almost inevitable: It announced and ratified teen sexuality and then amplified teen sexual frustration almost beyond endurance … Hysteria was critical to the marketing of the Beatles. First there were the reports of near riots in England. Then came a calculated publicity tease … five million posters and stickers announcing 'The Beatles Are Coming' were distributed nation-wide. Disc jockeys were blitzed with promo material and Beatle interview tapes (with blank spaces for the DJ to fill in the questions, as if it were a real interview) and enlisted in a mass 'countdown' to the day of the Beatles' arrival in the United States. As Beatle chronicler Nicholas Schaffner reports:

> Come break of 'Beatle Day', the quartet had taken over even the disc-jockey patter that punctuated their hit songs. From WMCA and WINS through W-A-Beatle-C, it was 'thirty Beatle degrees', 'eight-thirty Beatle time'… [and] 'four hours and fifty minutes to go'.

> (Schaffner, 1977, p. 91)

By the time the Beatles materialized, on 'The Ed Sullivan Show' in February 1964, the anticipation was unbearable. A woman who was a [14]-year-old in Duluth at the time told us, 'Looking back, it seems so commercial to me, and so degrading that millions of us would just scream on cue for those four guys the media dangled out in front of us. But at the time it was something intensely personal for me and, I guess, a million other girls. The Beatles seemed to be speaking directly to us and, in a funny way, *for us.*'

By the time the Beatles hit America, teens and preteens had already learned to look to their unique consumer subculture for meaning and validation. If this was manipulation – and no culture so strenuously and shamelessly exploits its children as consumers – it was also subversion. *Bad* kids became juvenile delinquents, smoked reefers, or got pregnant. Good kids embraced the paraphernalia, the lore, and the disciplined fandom of rock 'n' roll. (Of course, bad kids did their thing to a rock beat too: the first movie to use a rock 'n' roll soundtrack was *Blackboard Jungle,* in 1955, cementing the suspected link between 'jungle rhythms' and teen rebellion.) For girls, fandom offered a way not only to sublimate romantic and sexual yearnings but to carve out subversive versions of heterosexuality. Not just anyone could be hyped as a suitable object for hysteria: It *mattered* that Elvis was a grown-up greaser, and that the Beatles let their hair-grow over their ears …

[W]hen the Beatles arrived at crew-cut, precounterculture America, their long hair attracted more commentary than their music. Boy fans rushed to buy Beatle wigs and cartoons showing well-known male figures decked with Beatle hair were a source of great merriment. *Playboy,* in an interview, grilled the Beatles on the subject of homosexuality, which it was only natural for gender-locked adults to suspect. As Paul McCartney later observed:

> There they were in America, all getting house-trained for adulthood with their indisputable principle of life: short hair equals men; long hair equals women. Well, we got rid of that small convention for them. And a few others too.

> (quoted in Schaffner, 1977, p. 17)

What did it mean that American girls would go for these sexually suspect young men, and in numbers far greater than an unambiguous stud like Elvis could command? Dr Joyce Brothers thought the Beatles' appeal rested on the girls' innocence:

> The Beatles display a few mannerisms which almost seem a shade on the feminine side, such as the tossing of their long manes of hair…

> These are exactly the mannerisms which very young female fans (in the 10-to-14 age group) appear to go wildest over.

> (quoted in Schaffner, 1977, p. 16)

The reason? 'Very young "women" are still a little frightened of the idea of sex. Therefore they feel safer worshipping idols who don't seem too masculine, or too much the "he man".'

What Brothers and most adult commentators couldn't imagine was that the Beatles' androgyny was itself sexy. 'The idea of sex' as intercourse, with the possibility of pregnancy or a ruined reputation, was indeed frightening. But the Beatles construed sex more generously and playfully, lifting it out of the rigid scenario of mid-century American gender roles, and it was this that made them wildly sexy. Or to put it the other way around, the appeal lay in the vision of sexuality that the Beatles held out to a generation of American girls: they seemed to offer sexuality that was guileless, ebullient, and fun – like the Beatles themselves and everything they did (or were shown doing in their films *Help* and *A Hard Day's Night*). Theirs was a vision of sexuality freed from the shadow of gender inequality because the group mocked the gender distinctions that bifurcated the American landscape into 'his' and 'hers'. To Americans who believed fervently that sexuality hinged on *la différence,* the Beatlemaniacs said, No, blur the lines and expand the possibilities.

At the same time, the attraction of the Beatles bypassed sex and went straight to the issue of power. Our informant from Orlando, Maine, said of her Beatlemanic phase:

> I didn't feel sexual, as I would now define that. It felt more about wanting freedom. I didn't want to grow up and be a wife and it seemed to me that the Beatles had the kind of freedom I wanted: No rules, they could spend two days lying in bed; they ran around on

> motorbikes, ate from room service … I didn't want to sleep with Paul McCartney, I was too young. But I wanted to be like them, something larger than life.

Another woman, who was thirteen when the Beatles arrived in her home city of Los Angeles and was working for the telephone company in Denver city when we interviewed her, said:

> Now that I've thought about it, I think I identified with them, rather than as an object of them. I mean I liked their independence and sexuality and wanted those things for myself … Girls didn't get to be that way when I was a teenager – we got to be the limp, passive object of some guy's fleeting sexual interest. We were so stifled, and they made us meek, giggly creatures think, oh, if only *I* could act that way, and be strong, sexy, and doing what you want.

If girls could not be, or ever hope to be, superstars and madcap adventurers themselves, they could at least idolize the men who were.

There was the more immediate satisfaction of knowing, subconsciously, that the Beatles were who they were because girls like oneself had made them that. As with Elvis, fans knew of the Beatles' lowly origins and knew they had risen from working-class obscurity to world fame on the acoustical power of thousands of shrieking fans. Adulation created stars, and stardom, in turn, justified adulation. Questioned about their hysteria, some girls answered simply, 'Because they're the Beatles.' That is, because they're who I happen to like. And the louder you screamed, the less likely anyone would forget the power of the fans. When the screams drowned out the music, as they invariably did, then it was the fans, and not the band, who were the show.

Among male rock stars, the faintly androgynous affect of the Beatles was quickly eclipsed by the frank bisexuality of performers like Alice Cooper and David Bowie, and then the more outrageous antimasculinity of 1980s stars Boy George and Michael Jackson. The latter provoked screams again and mobs, this time of interracial crowds of girls, going down in age to eight and nine, but never on the convulsive scale of Beatlemania. By the 1980s, female singers like Grace Jones and Annie Lennox were denying gender too, and the loyalty and masochism once requisite for female lyrics gave way to new songs of cynicism, aggression, exultation. But between the vicarious pleasure of Beatlemania and Cyndi Lauper's forthright assertion in 1984 that 'girls just want to have fun', there would be an enormous change in the sexual possibilities open to women and girls – a change large enough to qualify as a 'revolution'.

References

SCHAFFNER, N. (1977) *The Beatles Forever*, New York, McGraw-Hill.

Source

EHRENREICH, B., HESS, E. and JACOBS, G. (1992) 'Beatlemania: a sexually defiant consumer culture?' in Gelder, K. and Thornton, S. (eds) *The Subcultures Reader*, London, Routledge, pp. 523–36.

ACKNOWLEDGEMENTS

Grateful acknowledgement is made to the following sources for permission to reproduce material within this book:

Chapter 1

Text

pp. 11–12: Wheelwright, J. 'Ghosts of a childhood past', *The Guardian,* 25 October, 2000. By permission of the author; *p. 25:* Grugeon, E. (1998) 'Children's oral culture: a transitional experience', in Maclure *et al.* (eds.) *Oracy Matters,* Open University Press; *Reading A:* Opie, I. 'Monday 4 June 1979', *The People in the Playground,* Oxford University Press. © 1993 Iona Opie; *Reading B:* Hewitt, R. ' "Box-out" and "taxing" ', in Johnson, S. and Meinhof, U. H. (1997) *Language and Masculinity,* Blackwell Publishing.

Illustrations

p. 1: copyright © 1996 PhotoDisc, Inc.; *pp. 4 and 6:* Martin Woodhead; *p. 9:* Mary Jane Kehily; *p. 19 (bottom):* Father Damian Webb O.S.B. © Ampleforth Abbey Trustees: *pp. 20 and 21 (top):* Kunsthistorisches Museum, Vienna/ Bridgeman Art Library; *p. 21 (bottom):* Bill Brandt/Getty Images; *p. 22:* Brian Mitchell/Photofusion; *p. 23:* John Birdsall Photography; *p. 29:* Christopher Walker; *p. 35 (left):* David Brown; *p. 35 (right):* © The Board of Trustees of the Victoria and Albert Museum; *p. 36 (left):* © Mary Evans Picture Library; *p. 36 (right):* Museum of Childhood, Edinburgh; *p. 38:* Mary Evans Picture Library.

Chapter 2

Text

Reading: reprinted by permission of HarperCollins Publishers © Lorna Sage, 2000.

Illustrations

pp. 47 and 55: Martin Woodhead; *p. 58:* William Corsaro; *p. 59:* Martin Woodhead; *p. 64:* Crispin Hughes/Photofusion; *p. 66:* Christopher Walker; *p. 71:* Pinto G. *et al.,* 'Similarity of friends in three countries: a study of children's drawings', *International Journal of Behavioral Development,* 1997, **20**(3), The International Society for the Study of Behavioral Development; *p. 73:* Martin Woodhead; *p. 80:* Paul Baldesare/Photofusion.

Chapter 3

Text

Reading A: Hoffman, E. (1989) *Lost in Translation: life in a new language,* Mandarin Paperbacks; *Reading B:* Davies, B. (1989) 'Becoming male or female' from *Frogs and Snails and Feminist Tales: preschool children and gender,* Allen and Unwin.

Illustrations

p. 89: Mike Levers/The Open University; p.92: Gloria Upchurch; p. 96: John Birdsall Photography; p. 101: Crispin Hughes/Photofusion; pp. 102 and 103: Martin Woodhead; p. 105: www.shoutpictures.com; p. 107: Janet Maybin; p. 108: © Paul Lowe/Magnum Photos; p. 109: Sally and Richard Greenhill; p. 111: Paul Doyle/Photofusion; p. 112: John Birdsall Photography; p. 117: Robert Brook/Photofusion.

Chapter 4

Illustrations

p. 133: Mike Levers/The Open University; p. 139: Bodleian Library; p. 140: The British Library; p. 144: Mary Evans Picture Library/Shirley Evans Collection; p.145: Illustration from *The Secret Garden* by Frances Hodgson Burnett, illustrated by Robin Lawrie (Puffin, 1994) illustrations copyright © Robin Lawrie, 1994; pp. 147 and 148: Mary Evans Picture Library; p. 157: Travers, P. L. (1962) *Mary Poppins in the Park*, illustrated by Mary Shepard, reprinted by permission of HarperCollins Publishers Ltd, © P. L. Travers 1962; p. 158: Mike Levers/The Open University; p.159: Cole, B. (1992) *Princess Smartypants*, HarperCollins Publishers Ltd, © 1986 Babette Cole; p. 163: Munsch, R. (1980) *The Paper Bag Princess*, illustrated by Michael Martchenko, Annick Press; p. 165 (top): from *Where The Wild Things Are* by Maurice Sendak, published by Bodley Head. Reprinted by permission of The Random House Group Ltd and Curtis Brown Ltd; p. 165 (bottom): McEwan, I. (1985) *Rose Blanche*, illustrated by Roberto Innocenti, The Random House Group/Editions 24 Heures; p. 166: illustration from *Black and White* by David Macaulay. Copyright © by David Macaulay, reprinted by permission of Houghton Mifflin Company. All rights reserved; p. 173: Bodleian Library; pp. 178–181: images reproduced from *The Story of the Falling Star* as told by Elsie Jones and courtesy of the Western Heritage Group and Aboriginal Studies Press, AIATSIS, Canberra, Australia.

Chapter 5

Text

Reading A: from *No Sense of Place* by Joshua Meyrowitz, copyright © 1985 by Joshua Meyrowitz. Used by permission of Oxford University Press, Inc.; *Reading B:* Wagg, S. ' "One I made earlier": media, popular culture and the politics of childhood', in Strinati, D. and Wagg, S. *Come on Down?*, Routledge 1992; *Reading C:* reprinted by permission of Sage Publications Ltd. from Davies, H. *et al.* 'In the worst possible taste: children, television and cultural taste', *European Journal of Cultural Studies*, Vol. 3 (1) January 2000. © Sage Publications Ltd., 2000.

Illustrations

p. 183: Mike Levers/The Open University; p. 186: The Ronald Grant Archive; p. 188: Ute Klaphake/Photofusion; p. 194: MX2; p. 195: Gamepod; p. 200: Mike Levers/The Open University; p. 201 (left): Teletubbies characters and logo © and TM 1996 Ragdoll Ltd. Licensed by BBC Worldwide Ltd; p. 201 (right): BBC; p. 205: © Nickelodeon; p. 207: The Ronald Grant Archive; p210: © Nintendo.

Chapter 6

Text

Reading B: Hebdige, D. (1979) *Subculture: the meaning of style*, Chapter 3, pp. 30–33, Taylor & Francis Books Ltd, copyright © Dick Hebdige; *Reading C:* Chambers, I. (1986) *Popular Culture: the metropolitan experience*, Part 3, Chapter 9, Taylor & Francis Books Ltd, copyright © Iain Chambers; *Reading D:* Medhurst, A. (1999) extract from *Punk Rock: So what? The cultural legacy of punk*, Roger Sabin (ed.), London and New York, Routledge (Routledge is an imprint of Taylor & Francis Books Ltd). Copyright in selection and editorial materials, Roger Sabin; copyright © in this extract Andy Medhurst.

Illustrations

p. 230: PhotoDisc/Getty Images; *p. 231:* David Redfern/Redferns; *p. 232:* Jess Hurd/Report Digital; *p. 234:* Hayley Madden/Redferns; *p. 238:* John Harris/Report Digital; *p. 242 (left):* Lennox Smillie/Camera Press Ltd; *p. 242 (right):* Roshini Kempadoo/Format Photographers; *p. 246 (top left):* Photodisc/Getty Images; *p. 246 (top right):* Leon Morris/Camera Press Ltd; *p. 246 (bottom):* Michael Ochs Archive/Redferns; *p. 249:* Roberta Gregory; *p. 250:* Dennis Morris/Camera Press Ltd.

Chapter 7

Text

pp. 275–277: extract from *Paddy Clark Ha Ha Ha* by Roddy Doyle, published by Martin Secker & Warburg. Reprinted by permission of The Random House Group Ltd. Copyright © 1993 by Roddy Doyle, by permission of Viking Penguin, a division of Penguin Putnam Inc.; *Reading A:* Kenway, J. and Bullen, E. (2001) *Consuming Children: education–entertainment–advertising*, Open University Press; *Reading B:* Ehrenreich, B., Hess, E. and Jacobs, G. (1992) 'Beatlemania: a sexually defiant consumer culture?', in Lewis, L. A. (ed.) *The Adoring Audience*, Routledge.

Illustrations

p. 271: Gloria Upchurch; *p. 278 (left and right):* *William – The Pirate* by Richmal Crompton, illustrated by Thomas Henry, 1932, published by George Newnes Ltd; *p. 281 (top left):* © BBC; *p. 281 (top right):* Press Association; *p. 281 (bottom left):* Copyright © Universal Pictorial Press; *p. 281 (bottom right):* Press Association; *p. 285:* Mike Levers/The Open University; *pp. 289 and 290:* D. C. Thomson & Co Ltd; *p. 292:* Chuck Boyd/Redferns; *p.299:* Rachel Burr.

Cover and title page photographs

top: John Birdsall Photography; *centre:* Ulrike Preuss/Photofusion; *bottom:* Tomi/PhotoDisc/Getty Images.

Every effort has been made to contact copyright holders. If any have been inadvertently overlooked the publishers will be pleased to make the necessary arrangements at the first opportunity.

INDEX

J

Jackie magazine 286, 288
Jackson, Michael 313
Jacobs, Gloria *see* Ehrenreich, Barbara, Hess, Elizabeth and Jacobs, Gloria
Jamaica, and Rastafarians 242, 243, 261, 262
James, Allison x
  on friendships 51, 81
    and gender 72–3, 79, 80
    stages of 61
Japanese Anime 295
Jenkins, Henry 291–2
Jones, Elsie, and *The Story of the Falling Star* 176, 177–9, 181, 182
Jones, Grace 313
Jordan, Ellen 32
Junk (Burgess) 159

K

Katz, J. 189
Kehily, Mary Jane x, 9, 38, 74, 75
Kennedy, P. 109
Kenway, Jane and Bullen, Elizabeth, *Consuming Children* 280–2, 304–9
Kinder, Marsha 200
King, Ross 219, 221
Kingsley, Charles, *The Water Babies* 146–9
!Kung people in Southern Africa, and friendship 68, 69, 83
Klause, Annette Curtis, *Blood and Chocolate* 160
Klein, Melanie 7
Kline, S. 36–7, 280, 304, 305
Korea, teenagers and the internet 113–14
Krappmann, L. 65

L

La Gaipa, J. J. 54, 55, 57, 61
Labov, W. 101
Lady: My Life as a Bitch (Burgess) 160
Laing, Dave 251
Lam, Wan Shun Eva 117–18
Langman, L. 296
language
  accents 91, 95
  choices 91–4
  code switching 93, 94, 97
  as a cultural resource 91
  dialect 91, 93, 94, 112
  mediated voices 107–18
    diary writing x, xii, 107–8
    on the internet 107, 110, 113–18
    mobile phones 107, 110–13, 118, 127–30
    telephone talk 108–10
  relationships and identity in conversation 91, 98–107, 119

    duetting and mirroring 102–3
    and gender 104–5, 124–6
    and school 105–6
    and story telling 101
  styles 90, 94–6, 97
  and talk between friends 57–62, 90
    girls 73–4, 90
  translation into a new language 96–7, 121–3
language xi–xii, 89–131
Larkin, Philip 15
Lauper, Cyndi 313
learning, play and 6–7, 39
Lee, M. J. 305
Lennox, Annie 313
Lincoln, S. 297
literature *see* children's literature
Little Red Riding Hood 152–3, 170–5
  and the Brothers Grimm 174
  initial oral version 153, 170–2
  more recent retellings 174–5
  Perrault's version 172–4
Locke, John 141
  Some Thoughts Concerning Education 137–8
longitudinal studies
  of friendships 81–2
  of young people's transitions to adulthood 127–30

M

Macauley, David, *Black and White* 166, 167
McCartney, Paul 312
MacKeith, Stephen 29
McLaren, M. 234
McRobbie, Angela
  and 'bedroom culture' 296
  and Garber, Jennie, on girls' involvement with subcultures 244–7
  on *Jackie* magazine 286, 288
magazines *see* comics and magazines
Mallett, Timmy 219
market research, and children as consumers 279–80, 282, 308
market segmentation 305–8
  by age 306–7
  by gender 307–8
marketing
  and children as consumers 272, 280–2
  cross-media 200, 209
  niche marketing of children 196, 199
  subcultural styles 250
Mary Poppins 157, 160
masculinities
  and boys' friendships 80
  and boys' talk about soap operas 206
  and magazines for adolescent boys 286–7
  play and the construction of 32–3, 44–6
  and Pokémon 210